Oscar

Wilde's

Last

Stand

Also by Philip Hoare

Serious Pleasures: The Life of Stephen Tennant

Noël Coward: A Biography

*The purple boards and silver blocking on the binding of this book
were chosen to imitate those found in the first edition of Oscar Wilde's* Salomé,
as stipulated by Wilde himself.

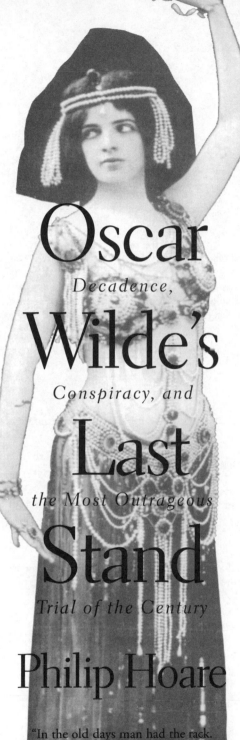

Oscar

Decadence,

Wilde's

Conspiracy, and

Last

the Most Outrageous

Stand

Trial of the Century

Philip Hoare

"In the old days man had the rack.
Now they have the Press."
—Oscar Wilde
The Soul of Man Under Socialism

ARCADE PUBLISHING ‖ NEW YORK

In memory of Peter

FIRST NORTH AMERICAN EDITION 1998

Library of Congress Cataloging-in-Publication Data

Hoare, Philip
    Oscar Wilde's last stand : decadence, conspiracy, and the most outrageous trial of the century / by Philip Hoare. —1st North American ed.
      p.   cm.
    Includes bibliographical references and index.
    ISBN 1-55970-423-3
    1. Billing, Noel Pemberton, 1880–1948—Trials, litigation, etc. 2. Trials (Libel)—England—London. 3. Allan, Maud. 4. Wilde, Oscar, 1854–1900. Salomé. I. Title
    KD373.B54H63 1998
    345.41'0256—dc21   97–52311

Published in the United States by Arcade Publishing, Inc., New York
Distributed by Little, Brown and Company

Picture credits

Plate page 5 above: collection of Peter Burton; 7, 8 above and below left, James Gardiner; above and below right, Terence Pepper; 11, 13, 18: British Library; 19 above, 20 (both), 24 (both): British Film Institute. Other illustrations are from private collections.

10 9 8 7 6 5 4 3 2 1

Designed by Ray Davies

BP

PRINTED IN THE UNITED STATES OF AMERICA

Contents

Plates between pages 90 and 91

Acknowledgements

It was in Paul Fussell's ground-breaking cultural study, *The Great War and Modern Memory*, which I read when working on a biography of Stephen Tennant, that I first heard of the Billing trial. Tennant conducted a traumatic post-war affair with Siegfried Sassoon, who reappeared in Pat Barker's *Regeneration* trilogy; as did an evocative recreation of the atmosphere around the Billing affair. In the meantime, the trial resurfaced in my research on Noel Coward's early life; reading original copies of the *Imperialist* and the *Vigilante* was a chilling experience, yet more so as the political complexion of Billing's campaign became clear. Discovering Michael Kettle's account in *Salome's Last Veil* (another coincidence; I had already decided on my title) led me to other, wider conclusions. This book owes much to Dr Kettle, Felix Cherniavsky, and the other historians and biographers on whose work I have drawn.

I am also indebted to Hugo Vickers for his usual clear-eyed and practical assistance. Mark Ashurst, Michael Bracewell, Peter Goddard, Clare Goddard, Robert Holden, Christina Larcombe-Moore and Neil Tennant provided encouragement and intellectual vision. Many others contributed material and ideas, among them: Elaine Burrows, Peter Burton, Jane Bywaters, Roger Cazalet, Terry Charman, Karl Chatfield-Moore, James Chatfield-Moore, Michael Cockerell, Bryan Connon, Betty Eastman, Claire Eastman, Stephen Fry, James Gardiner, Katherine Goonetillake, Alix Holden, Michael Holden, Clyde Jeavons, Adam Low, Stephen Moore, Theresa Moore, Peter Parker, Terence Pepper, Jane Preston, Kenneth Rose, Patricia Thompson, Paul Walter, John Waters, and Simon Watney. Vivienne Westwood supplied sartorial inspiration.

I should also like to thank the following institutions: the British Library Department of Manuscripts and Newspaper Library; Associated Newspapers; the Imperial War Museum; Royal Victoria Park, Netley; the British Film Institute; the *Southern Daily Echo*; Johannesburg Art Gallery; Somerset House; the Guildhall Library; the Barbican Library; and the Theatre Museum.

Lastly, I must thank my agent, the redoubtable Gillon Aitken; Robin Baird-Smith, my elegant, patient publisher; and all the staff at Duckworth who made this book possible.

Philip Hoare, Shoreditch, 1997

Introduction

They may be yellow and crumbling, but pages of the January 1918 edition of the *Imperialist* newspaper still make startling reading. 'There exists in the Cabinet Noir of a certain German Prince a book compiled by the Secret Service from reports of German agents who have infested this country for the past 20 years', it reports. 'In the beginning of the book is a precis of general instructions regarding the propagation of evils which all decent men thought had perished in Sodom and Lesbia. The blasphemous compilers even speak of the Groves and High Places mentioned in the Bible ... There are the names of 47,000 English men and women ... Privy Councillors, wives of Cabinet Ministers, even Cabinet Ministers themselves, diplomats, poets, bankers, editors, newspaper proprietors, and members of His Majesty's Household ... prevented from putting their full strength into the war by corruption and blackmail and fear of exposure.' No English man would be naturally guilty of such offences: it required the filthy Hun to lead him on. Naval dockyards and engine rooms were infiltrated, and 'the stamina of British sailors was undermined ... Even to loiter in the streets was not immune ... agents of the Kaiser were stationed at such places as Marble Arch and Hyde Park Corner ... Wives of men in supreme position were entangled. In Lesbian ecstasy the most sacred secrets of State were betrayed. The sexual peculiarities of members of the peerage were used as a leverage to open fruitful fields for espionage.'

The publisher of the *Imperialist* was Noel Pemberton Billing, thirty-seven-year-old Independent member of parliament for East Hertfordshire. A man of notable prejudices, he had been indicted for libel on at least two previous occasions, as well as being often censured for unparliamentary language and the odd prosecution for 'driving at excessive speed'. His politics were unerringly jingoistic: he called for internment of all enemy aliens, as well as punitive bombing of German cities; he called the scorn of his Parliamentary opponents 'the laughter of fools'. But Billing's latest campaign was a tour-de-force of prejudice, encompassing his manifold obsessions in one almighty conspiracy theory. At its centre was the allegation that the 47,000 were ruled by the still extant cult of Oscar Wilde, a foreign decadence corrupting the cultural and political elite. Billing's claims struck deep into the sensibilities of wartime Britain and its leaders, sensitive to criticism of the way the war was being fought. His allegations played on deep-seated ideas of nationalism, xenophobia, homophobia and anti-semitism which remain with us today.

The past is always changing; history never stays the same. It is constantly revising itself, and when it does, we realise how much things have changed, and how little. Even at the end of the twentieth century, the First World War is still only a generation or two away. The poignant songs I learnt as a child – 'It's a Long Way to Tipperary', 'Pack Up Your Troubles', 'The Roses of Picardy' – were sung to my mother by her father, who served in the war; my great-uncle was gassed on the Somme and suffered shellshock; a slow death for him, sometime in the 1920s. No family went untouched by the war, and for this reason, the modern memory of the catastrophe remains vivid. How could something so horrific have happened to a civilised world, so recently? It is part of the reason for the current interest in the period; so too is the fact that its unprecedented horrors set the tone for a century of violence. And yet our conception of the First World War is ironically romanticised by that horror, seen through grainy black-and-white film, the unremitting mud, blood and carnage replayed in slow-motion; patriotic scenes of union jacks on railway stations, women with white feathers, khaki troops singing as they march to war, heroically wounded when and if they return. It is difficult to imagine that any other life went on beyond the central, consuming fact of Armageddon.

Popular history has a habit of typecasting itself. Our century has been neatly divided by the watershed of its wars, conveniently defining and separating social and historical change. Yet there is a danger in the facile division of decades: the Jazz Age Twenties, the Austerity Forties, the Permissive Sixties; history becomes compartmentalised, an instrument of nostalgia. This book was partly motivated by an awareness of the manipulation of the history of the early part of this century: the notion that the gay Edwardian era was extinguished by the cataclysm of war, against which the hedonism of the 1920s was a reaction. This is a generalisation of a much more fluid period of history. As a century's dust settles, it now seems that the hedonism of the 1920s began during, or even before, the war; or indeed, may have only been a rerun, an aftershock, of the decadent Nineties. Conversely, in decadence can be detected the pre-shock of modernism.

As we drift through our own fin de siècle, as yet unsure of its historical significance, the notion of decadence retains a peculiarly modern relevance. The very word resonates: decade, decayed, decadence. It conjures up silent movie orgies or transvestite cabarets; excess and abuse; drugs, drink, and sex. A twentieth-century conception of decadence which, as this book tries to show, was largely formed during the First World War, in turn fed by nineteenth-century fin de siècle culture, and the overwhelming influence of one man. Oscar Wilde was, and is, a potent icon: to some, a sinner whose sins could not be named (writing this book on the hundreth anniversary of Wilde's imprisonment, I discovered that my mother, born just after the First World War, had never been entirely sure of the nature of Oscar's disgrace); to others, a representation of the civilisation which was destroyed by the war. And just as that war is near us, so is Wilde. His physical memory has only just left us. Given happier circumstances, Oscar could easily have lived into the 1920s. What would he have made of the war? We cannot know; but this book is about what the war made of him. A man before his time – he started the twentieth century ten years before the year 1900 – Wilde exemplified the coming age: the cult of the personality, the new, incestuous ties between the media and culture. He addressed pressing questions of social change in a superficially facile manner. His reward for his prescience and his lampooning of straight society was heterosexual revenge: ignominy, prison, exile and death. But the Billing trial proved that Wilde's spirit lived on, dangerously. It also proved that the casualities of war were not only the bloodied bodies of a generation of young men, but also the notions of truth, justice and toleration. These qualities are at a premium when a nation is threatened.

As with Wilde's story twenty years before, the drama of the Billing affair would be played out in what was still the world's capital. London's Edwardian boom had reconceived the city as a modern metropolis: the neoclassical solid stone of buildings such as the Admiralty Arch trumpeted the self-importance of the state, monuments to Empire mimicked by Selfridges' department store and other West End temples to Mammon. But the virile imperial facade hid other lives. From the bachelors' redbrick mansion blocks of Kensington to the genteel wedding-cake stucco terraces of Mayfair; from the artists' studios of the King's Road to the gas-lit bolt-holes of Soho's cafés and theatres; society went about its business of pleasure in sheltered places of entertainment and refuge and conspiracy; at night, glowing caves of security or abandon. Down darker, less frequented streets were upstairs rooms or subterranean cellars where more adventurous pleasures were pursued. Men and women of rank and importance could be found in such places, where their very presence was a threat to their careers and positions in a hierarchical society; precarious positions, as Wilde's fate had shown. One minute Oscar had been the toast of the town: publicly safe in connubial bliss in his family house in Tite Street, privately debauched in any number of hotel suites; the next, he was the greatest evil abroad, and was duly sent there. Now, in the depths of war crisis, new rumours of Wildean perversion emerged. No wonder, then, that in such places in the early summer of 1918, the small talk in certain circles had become more than a little disquieting.

Thanks to Billing and the 'yellow press', it was a subject not restricted to the cognoscenti. Gossip was everywhere, in the streets and shops and pubs of Georgian London. But it was most intense in the haunts of the hedonists who could afford pleasure, and often paid for it; in the private dining rooms of the rich; and the musty hush of Pall Mall gentlemen's clubs. It was whispered behind bevelled glass screens in wood-panelled restaurants and eavesdropped by young waiters – themselves objects of the lusts of those under suspicion. Blackmail was in the air; it had been since 1895. The illicitness of desire contributed to the excitement; it also marked the contrast between public and private life; and London was a city of contrasts. In 1918, it was also a city of danger. A new force was at work, determined to expose those nocturnal sinners to the cold puritan light of day. Its centrifugal power threatened to throw society apart in the process.

A sense of breakpoint was in the air, between a still largely Victorian era, and the modern age to come. It was an atmosphere manifest in the political sphere: not only that of a four-year war which was going disastrously wrong, but a foreign policy which imperilled the existence of the Empire itself, parts of which were 'sold' to America in return for their support in the war. It was an ironic price to pay: Britain had to sell its Empire to save it. (In the same way, British culture became increasingly prey to its transatlantic counterpart). The war had been a fight for honour, but after the Somme, there was a gradual realisation that it did not represent any advance in human progress; that mechanised killing had put paid to the idea of good succeeding evil. Such a realisation set the tone for the troubled twentieth century. For Wilde – a Utopian socialist – faith in progress and the betterment of humanity was destroyed by his ignominious trial; for his heirs, such progressive optimism was challenged by the carnage of the First World War. Indeed, Wilde and Billing, both visionaries, also shared a belief in socialism, in their own idiosyncratic ways. For both the socialist and sexual reformers, and the puritan moralists and radical right alike, the war threatened values: honour, Empire, the advance of civilisation and the greater good. As players in this drama, the actors in the Billing drama stood as symbols of the fight. In the belligerent atmosphere of the times, it was a classic clash of opposites: of good versus evil, of heterosexual and homosexual, of masculine and feminine, of the safe and the dangerous, of what was seen as morally right or morally wrong. In 1918, the war that was raging on the Western Front had its counterpart at home: an equally serious, equally vicious fight for the control of Britain's future.

1

The Cult of Wilde

In the days before the war there was growing in London, beyond any sort of question, that passion for excitement and for the latest novelty which is always the familiar beginning of a corrupt society ... If one of the consequences of the Billing case is to give new value to the ancient virtues ... then there may be some compensation after all for the work of a scandalous week.

The Times, 5 June 1918

The moral condition of the country was worrying. That much was clear to the respectable middle-class woman in her fur wrap and picture hat as she hurried along the Strand. Above the hoardings plastered with advertisements for the latest Olympia exhibition, the new six-hour boat to France, and the sensational Miss Maud Allan's Salome dance at the Pavilion, rose the facade of the British Medical Association. Adorned with Mr Epstein's stridently modern nude statues, their nether regions alarmingly explicit, this was not a sight for a decent lady. Modern London had become a strange place. Up in Regent Street young men wearing tight suits and nail varnish were sipping creme de menthe in the Café Royal, while down a dark cul-de-sac lurked a new and devilish sort of place where Futurists cavorted: a 'night club' profanely named 'The Cave of the Golden Calf'. Vague rumours had reached her that nowadays, the backstreets harboured all manner of such places, attended by members of the social elite. Such intimations confirmed all the suspicions of her class. At the root of these evils lay the name of Oscar Wilde, still unspoken in polite households. He may have been dead for more than a decade, but Wilde's decadence endured.

To the tabloid-reading middle class, for whom morality was paramount, the country needed saving, and the puritans and patriots of 1914 looked to the war to purge the country of this foreign influence. As Stephen McKenna's 1917 best-seller, *Sonia*, would remind them, pre-war Britain

... was a matter for considerable searching of heart. A spirit of unrest and lawlessness, a neurotic state not to be disassociated from the hectic, long-drawn Carnival that ... may be traced from the summer of the Coronation [1911]. It is too early to probe the cause or say how far the staggering ostentation of the wealthy fomented the sullen disaffection of the poor. It is as yet impossible to weigh the merits in any one of the hysterical controversies of the times ...

The first decades of the new century were an uncertain time. The violent struggle for Irish Home Rule, trade union disputes and the clamour of the Suffragette movement all threatened the 'ostensibly law-abiding country'. Many agreed with McKenna that the cause might be the sudden boom after ten years' post-Boer War depression:

The new money was spent in so much riotous living, and from end to end there settled on the country a mood of fretful, crapulous irritation. 'An unpopular law? Disregard it!' That seemed the rule of life with a people that had no object but successive pleasure and excitement and was fast becoming a law unto itself.

This was a new, modern world of aviation, wireless, automobiles and tabloid newspapers. Technology was reinventing society and the way people lived; soon it would revolutionise the way they died. In 1912 – the year of Epstein's BMA facade, of Roger Fry's Post-Impressionism show, of Madame Strindberg's Futurist cabaret club – the sinking of the *Titanic* was a vivid reminder of the speed of progress, and the dangers of placing too much faith in it. While some, like the aesthetic demagogue Marinetti and his Futurist rhetoric, celebrated the machine age, others felt more unsure. Much of the frenzy and apparent dissipation of the young century derived from the inconstancy of modern life and a new-born fear of the technological future. The world was no longer the stable place of the stolid nineteenth century, and no one could be sure of anything any more, not even the rich. The Edwardian era had seen the increasing visibility of the aristocracy, its wealth and privilege on display in the Season, spending the money that the generations of the Industrial Age had earned. It was, however, a last flowering. By 1914, they were rapidly losing their power. Lloyd George, as Chancellor of the Liberal government, had campaigned against the power of the House of Lords, and the so-called 'Peers versus People' election of 1910 returned a mandate for the Liberals' reforms. Ironically, it was the Liberal establishment, led by H.H. Asquith, which Billing would accuse of decadence.

Political Liberalism was symptomatic of a general liberality; socially and culturally, a libertine spirit reigned in the houses of the rich and fashionable. 'Night by night, during the summers of 1913 and '14, the entertainments grew in number and magnificence,' wrote Osbert Sitwell. 'One band in a house was no longer enough, there must be two, three even. Electric fans whirled on the top of enormous blocks of ice, buried in banks of hydrangeas ... Never had there been such displays of flowers ... lolling roses and malmaisons, of gilded, musical-comedy baskets of carnations and sweet-peas ... huge bunches of orchids, bowls of gardenias and flat trays of stephanotis lent ... an air of exoticism ... mounds of peaches, figs, nectarines and strawberries at all seasons, [were] brought from their steamy tents of glass. Champagne bottles stood stacked on the sideboards ... And to the rich, the show was free.' Their London was enclosed in extravagance; sheltered from reality by the glass verandahs of Park Lane mansions, the pink-and-gold Ritz foyer, the marble cavern of the Royal Automobile Club swimming baths. Opulent Edwardian interiors reflected the overblown age, self-secure in its imperial evocation. While pessimists murmured that the 'historic calm' was too good to last and rumours of war were discussed in the salons of the rich or sung in the music halls, a degree of disbelieving fantasy or devil-may-care hedonism reigned. Morality was the preserve – literally – of the middle classes; those at either end of the social scale were not obsessed with the moral glue that gave a new class its sense of cohesion. The rich could afford to flaunt old conventions, and seemed to be dancing on the edge of doom. Even the slang of the time – 'Isn't it killing' – had an inbuilt and not entirely unconscious irony. The *Titanic* may have been a portent of disaster; but the dance went on.

Its backdrop was provided by modern art: Walter Sickert's dark chiaroscuro paintings with their vague sense of evil; the perfervid sick colours of Leon Bakst's designs for the Russian Ballet; Nijinsky's narcissistic sexuality, falling onanistically to the floor in the closing scene of *L'Après-midi d'un faune*. Fashions, entertainments, manners still followed the decadent cue of the Nineties, a search for neurotic sensation. A foreign, European spirit invaded London. Roger Fry's Second Post-Impressionism show at the Grafton Galleries in 1912 had caused consternation, with its modern art from the Continent likened to that of lunatics. The new -isms espoused by rebellious young artists – Cubism, Orphism, Vorticism – were intimidatingly different, while the lavish gestures of the Russian Ballet heralded another escape from the Victorian century. The influence of Diaghilev – almost impossible to exaggerate – was at its height at the beginning of 1914. Harold Acton wrote: 'The great galas of colour organised by Diaghileff were being imitated even in private entertainments: fancy-dress balls and tableaux vivants became sumptuous and spectacular to a degree unrealised since ... "Persian" balls ... Venetian, Egyptian and Russian balls, with pierrots and black dominoes ... In some cases, as for the Marchesa Casati, Bakst himself designed the costumes.' Fabulously beautiful, attenuated, white-faced and kohl-eyed, Casati was a Beardsley illustration come to life, the visual embodiment and extremity of decadence, surrounded by 'albino blackbirds, mauve monkeys, a leopard, a boa constrictor, and, among Englishmen, Lord Berners ...'.

The Marchesa would have been at home in the newly-decorated rooms of Lady Drogheda, commissioned from the Omega apostate Wyndham Lewis.

Silver-foil ceilings and matt black velvet walls were bordered by a Vorticist frieze; blue glass witch-balls stood on columns in the centre of the room; all bathed in the unnatural glow of yellow alabaster lamps. The effect was cultish and pagan, a room set for a seance; its tenant, like many society ladies of the time, dabbled in the occult. Guests invited to view the rooms in February 1914 included Mrs Keppel, Baroness d'Erlanger, Lady Ponsonby, Jacob Epstein, Sir Ernest Cassel, Augustus John, and Wyndham Lewis himself, subject of whispered rumours about his relationship with their hostess. The rebel artist, with his centre-parted hair, dark eyes and cigarette stuck in the corner of his mouth, shared with Lady Drogheda a passion for technology, aviation, speed and sensation. The spirit of modernity was upon their age; for Wyndham Lewis, identifier of 'the enemy within' whose art protest magazine, *Blast*, appeared that summer, war was 'anticipated in the militant mood of the avant-garde'. In July 1914, he declared his own hostilities: 'Kill John Bull with Art.'

For socialite bohemians such as Diana Manners, famously beautiful daughter of the Duke of Rutland, and her aristocratic friends this rebellious modernity was a clarion call. Their generation were the daughters and sons of Empire, end products of a century's history. Anthony Powell's classification of the 'third generation type' applies as much to them as to its subject, Ronald Firbank, last in 'that trio of descending individuals in which the grandfather makes the money, the son consolidates the social position, the grandson practises the arts (or sometimes merely patronises them) in some "decadent" manner, thus expressing the still-existent, yet by now failing and feverish energy that suddenly, unexpectedly, welled up in the race.' They were also, crucially, the heirs of Oscar Wilde, modern icon and exemplar for their age. Diana Manners' account of her 'Corrupt Coterie' is consciously Wildean, flagrantly toying with convention. 'There was among us a reverberation of the Yellow Book and Aubrey Beardsley, Ernest Dowson, Baudelaire and Max Beerbohm. Swinburne often got recited. Our pride was to be unafraid of words, unshocked by drink and unashamed of "decadence" and gambling – Unlike-Other-People, I'm afraid.'

The spirit of Wilde seemed invested in this society; to outsiders, it was tainted with it. Members of Asquith's Liberal society had been, and continued to be, associated with Wilde, the avant-garde, and the foreign. They spoke French, holidayed in Venice and had German friends – as a de Meyer photograph of Diana in a fancy dress group with Kuhlmann, the Counseller to the German Embassy firmly at its centre, confirms. The social elite of 1914 mixed with the likes of Kuhlman and rich German Jews like Sir Edgar Speyer and his American musician wife. The Asquiths were specifically pro-German, as were their friends: the Bavarian-educated Lord Haldane, Asquith's best friend and Foreign Secretary, had in 1912 visited Berlin in an abortive attempt to defuse antipathy between the two countries. Yet the sons of this group, Diana's young beaux, were among the first to die in the dirt of the trenches: the Tennants, the Charterises, the Grenfells, doomed members of the Corrupt Coterie. Serving officers such as Raymond Asquith (the Prime Minister's son, with whom Diana was hopelessly in love) and Duff Cooper (whom she would eventually marry) were often the first over the top: 'Our generation becomes history rather than growing up', wrote Cooper. These golden youth were exemplars of Aryan Britishness (many, like Diana, were unconsciously anti-semitic, or, in the case of the Grenfell brothers, actively so). Their male role models were the pre-war dandies: Raffles, Sherlock Holmes, Anthony Hope's 'charmingly bored young men', A.E. Housman's 'handsome young men in uniform', and the smart-talking wits of Saki's epicene stories. These young men looked forward to an abbreviated future: ' ... I really think that large numbers of people don't want to die ...' wrote Rupert Brooke, 'which is odd ... I've never been quite so happy in my life'. Where the decadents of the 1890s had celebrated romantic death, their modern inheritors faced the reality. The mauve opium poppy of Chelsea became the blood-red corn poppy of Flanders.

*

With the outbreak of war in August 1914, life turned upside-down. Diana Manners became a V.A.D. at Guy's Hospital. It was a schizophrenic life: dealing by day in death and disease, while at night, 'I would fly out of the ward ... Five minutes would see me painted and powdered and dressed (as I hoped) to kill, and into the arms of friends or friend.' They held parties dubbed the 'Dances of Death'. War turned the make-believe decadence of the Corrupt Coterie into the real thing. 'The young were dancing a tarantella frenziedly to combat any pause that would let death conquer their morale ... Wine helped and there was wine in plenty ...' Parties 'became more frequent as leave became regular from the training centres and the trenches of France and the Middle East ...' It was, perhaps, the beginnings of youth culture: 'Parents were excluded. We dined at any time. The long waits for the last-comers were enlivened by exciting, unusual drinks such as vodka or absinthe. The menu was composed of far-fetched American delicacies – avocadoes, terrapin and soft-shell crabs. The table was purple with orchids.' It was a stark contrast to the ordinary lives around them; lives which had no access to American delicacies to assuage the pain of war and loss. 'The dancing, sometimes to two bands, negro and white (and once to the first Hawaiian), so that there might be no pause, started immediately before dinner.' Such nights presaged the dance-mad decade of the 1920s.

Their hedonism was not confined to private parties. In 1912, Madame

Strindberg, the sexually-liberated former wife of the playwright, decided to create an alternative to the Wildean Café Royal. Taking her cue from Marinetti's Futurist performance art rhetoric and the Kaberett Fledermaus of her native Vienna, she leased a draper's basement in Heddon Street, a cul-de-sac behind Regent Street, and created the Cave of the Golden Calf. This 'low-ceilinged nightclub, appropriately sunk under the pavement', was decorated by Spencer Gore in Russian Ballet-inspired murals, with contributions by Jacob Epstein and Wyndham Lewis; Eric Gill designed the club's motif, a phallic Golden Calf, symbol of biblical dissipation and idolatry. Here the cult of Wilde could continue to worship. The club's self-advertised aim was to be 'a place given up to gaiety', its art-subversive interiors 'brazenly expressive of the libertarian pleasure-principle ...' It was intentionally international and unEnglish, full of modern young artists and poets like Gaudier-Brzeska and Ezra Pound with their quiffed hair and razor-point sideboards, sipping anisette as they watched the Spanish dancers and fire-eaters. Osbert Sitwell witnessed bohemian artists drinking with Guards officers in a 'super-heated Vorticist garden of gesticulating figures, dancing and talking while the rhythm of the primitive forms of ragtime throbbed through the wide room'. 'Exotic gentlemen sang ballads,' noted another observer. 'A young actor with a beautiful voice recited Wilde's story of "The Happy Prince". Then a lank-haired, aquiline-featured youth with a Cockney accent strolled nonchalantly on to the stage and delivered a serio-comic homily on the Cave of the Golden Calf, its objects and reasons. He made very personal references to all the protagonists in this enterprise, not forgetting to remind his audience that Gore's uncle was a bishop.'

The Cave of the Golden Calf set the precedent for the modern night-club. 'London is in the midst of another new movement,' the *Sketch* announced in January 1914. 'It is evident she desires to keep later hours ... Hence the fact that there have risen three Supper Clubs ... the Four Hundred, Murray's, and the Lotus ... At all the clubs of course, members may sup as they please.' And more than just sup: 'A very bad fellow, Jack Mays, is the proprietor of "Murray's Club" in Beak Street – quite an amusing place,' wrote one Captain Ernest Schiff to Sir John Simon. 'But for vice or money or both he induces girls to smoke opium in some foul place. He is an American, and does a good deal of harm.'

It was a startling new environment. First to strike a visitor was the raucous music: strident jerking jazz, faster than anything that had gone before; it was the sound of speed. Yet more striking were the dancers: thin young women, diaphanous short skirts showing their legs, their heads crowned with iridescent feathers twitching in time to the music. To those used to Strauss waltzes, these 'flappers' seemed to be suffering from some new nervous disorder. This was dancing from the hip – as one visiting French diplomat remarked, never had the *derrière* been so prominent on the dancefloor. Girls made up in public, their encardined lips pursed in contemptuous social flagrancy, sipping newly-invented cocktails and smoking Turkish cigarettes held in languid hands, ostentatiously modern against a Futurist backdrop. The smoky, feverish, frenetic atmosphere was as unlike the genteel debutante balls of Mayfair as the mechanised war of the Western Front was removed from the cavalry charges of nineteenth-century stage-set battles.

That sexual roles and expectations were changing was evinced in the fashions of the time; people had begun to look recognisably modern as strict gender codes began to blur. Men wore lounge suits and soft collars, while women's mannish tailored suits with ties, shorter skirts and masculine hats were severe and practical, announcing fierce determination rather than acquiescent femininity. One member of the Corrupt Coterie epitomised the new woman more than any other. Nancy Cunard, wayward daughter of the socially-addicted Maud Cunard (wife of the shipping magnate), rebelled violently and publicly against her mother. When staying with the Asquiths, Nancy had joined in a Coterie game: who would they like most like to walk in the door? Nancy said, in her high voice, 'Lady Cunard dead.' Determined not to be defined as a debutante and mere marriage-fodder, she worked with the Sitwells on their modernistic journal, *Wheels*, and led a wild life in London. She and her friend Iris Tree were the truly bad girls to Diana Manners' Marie Antoinette naughtiness; renting a studio room in Fitzroy Place, the heart of Bohemian Fitzrovia, which Diana described as 'squalid'. Nancy wore men's clothes – an evening waistcoat, her father's top hat – and was pursued by Alvaro 'Chile' Guevara, the artist, drug addict, and bisexual, while being engaged to 'Bim' Tennant. In 1915, she married, unexpectedly, a respectable army officer named Sydney Fairbairn. At the wedding party, she snatched the gold flower wreath from her head and threw it on the floor, a prescient gesture to the next decade in which Nancy would become famous for her promiscuity, drinking and drug-taking.

As the war progressed, the mere fact of high society appeared decadent, especially in a world which was changing so quickly. The war introduced Britain to the notion of the state-organised society. The all-encompassing Defence of the Realm Act, passed by Parliament on 8 August 1914 and added to on successive occasions, restricted the liberty of British civilians in many ways, some still with us, such as the licensing laws, designed to keep munitions workers sober. DORA, as it was unaffectionately known, also installed newspaper censorship, enabling the government to quash anything 'calculated to jeopardise the success of the operations of any of His Majesty's forces or to assist the enemy'. Passports were introduced; for the first time, an individual's movements were to be controlled.

Conscription, forced labour and other punitive measures soon followed. Britain was becoming a society not of individuals, but of units.

These measures most affected the lower orders, but soon the upper classes were feeling the changes: for them, as much as for the tenants of their estates, society would never be the same again. Reverence for the old went out with the new; the young were breaking the barriers of social class and re-establishing new demarcations of age. The *Manchester Guardian* commented on 'War Matches': 'Duke's daughters are marrying social nobodies and finding it a delightful innovation, and bewildered parents have given up all attempts to control their children's matrimonial careers.' As the war reduced the supply of eligible young men, there was a scramble for partners. Cynthia Asquith, daughter-in-law of the Prime Minister, attended a dance in Mayfair at which Society mothers were throwing their daughters at the Prince of Wales. 'Irene's ... "dash for the throne" we called it', wrote Cynthia, who told her hostess she did not dance, as her husband was at the front. Such rectitude was not observed by others, she noted, as she perched on a sofa like Jane Austen, watching the evening's proceedings. 'I do hate the teasing catastrophic music thrummed out by those leering Negroes, and I can't believe the stuttering, furtive, modern dances can be as much fun as our valses ... Certainly they aren't as becoming ... Just before leaving at 12.30, saw the Prince of Wales dancing round with Mrs Dudley-Ward, a pretty little fluff ... He is a dapper little fellow – too small – but really a pretty face ... I have never seen a man talk so fluently while dancing. He obviously means to have fun.'

As did the rest of young London. Despite DORA's strictures, night-clubs continued to grow, especially as the American imports of jazz and ragtime took hold. One of DORA's proscriptions in 1915 was to order clubs to close at 10.30 pm – a ruling dubbed 'the beauty sleep order'. But as with any such regulation, prohibition merely sent the culture underground. By the end of the year it was estimated that there were 150 night-clubs in Soho alone. New regulations were constantly being applied, to the distress of their habitués. 'And after the Grafton – the ban on Ciro's!' lamented a 1917 issue of the *Tatler* in a breathless, slangy text that pre-empts the coming decade, '... no khakied lad or cherub in gold and blue may now sup anywhere after 10 pm. Of course the result would have been a t'rific increase of home shows – all the hostesses rushing in quick with little dances (and daughters) and lots of nice things to drink, to try and make up for that gorgeous dancing floor, and noisy niggers and top-hole ched, and free-and-easy ladies in Orange Street. But with the risk of being pilloried in Printing-House Square, it's hardly good enough.'

*

War stilled history. Everything, every resource and energy, was funnelled into its pursuit. Young lives were frozen as war overrode normal prospects. And yet, paradoxically, the war accelerated change. The role of women altered drastically, class barriers eroded, attitudes to age, race and culture changed. These effects, however, were less obvious than the fear of society for itself. For the first time, it seemed, war threatened civilisation as a whole (it was, after all, the Great War). But compared to the threat of decadence, it was the lesser of two evils. Edmund Gosse wrote, in his 1914 essay on 'War and Literature':

> War is the great scavenger of thought. It is the sovereign disinfectant, and its red stream of blood is the Condy's Fluid that cleans out the stagnant pools and clotted channels of the intellect ... We have awakened from an opium-dream of comfort, of ease, of that miserable poltroonery of the 'sheltered life'. Our wish for indulgence of every sort, our laxity of manners, our wretched sensitiveness to personal inconvenience, these are suddenly lifted before us in their true guise as the spectres of national decay; and we have risen from the lethargy of our dilletantism to lay them, before it is too late, by the flashing of the unsheathed sword.

It is ironic that that very 'disinfectant' created the conditions for the sort of hedonism which represents decadence at its height.

Among the moralists, there was a call for a new purity in culture, and a move against the 'degeneracy' of modern art. The avant-gardists were inevitably seen as decadent, merely for having concerns other than the pursuit of war, or for criticising it. Indeed, it is difficult even for the dispassionate to know where the avant-garde and the decadent part company. Both pursued extremes and their social behaviour – their recreation – reflected such extremism, as was evident to any visitor to the Cave of the Golden Calf. The right-wing *Morning Post* approved of signs of patriotism in such a figure as Sickert, in whose painting, 'The Soldiers of King Albert the Ready' it discerned his arousal 'from the gloomy analysis of unsavoury types to the representation of nobler specimens of humanity.' The ironic ambivalence of Sickert's work – painted from photographs – escaped the critics of the *Morning Post*. Others looked to the war to save Britain from decadence. In *A War Imagined*, Samuel Hynes quotes from a wartime lecture by the sculptor W.R. Colton:

> ... It was high time that war should come with its purifying fire ... A wave of diseased degeneracy had submerged Philosophy, Music, Literature, and Art to such a depth that, looking forward, I venture to prophesy that future centuries will gaze back with pity upon this period of mistaken morbidness.
>
> We find, perhaps, in the German philosophers and musicians the first crystallised expression of this viciousness, but unfortunately we, with all other nations of Europe, cannot pretend that we are exempt. The morbid invention of the artistic

mind is seen everywhere. We have Oscar Wilde, Aubrey Beardsley, and others. The futurists, the cubists, the whole school of decadent novelists.

The war would cut out the rotten core of culture, gone sour with the evil of Wilde. It would sweep away the Nineties decadents and the Edwardian hedonists. Rupert Brooke extolled English purity in his most famous poem – 'Stands the Church clock at ten to three?/ And is there honey still for tea?', itself inspired by the worldly decadence of Berlin, where he wrote it. Brooke rejected the city's forced bohemia and young women in black satin carrying scarlet tulips; 'Modernist Berlin was the contrary that generated this classic example of fetishing the English past', writes Paul Delaney. Meanwhile, another doomed young poet was facing a similar transition. In 1914, Wilfred Owen was a long-haired, boyish-faced English teacher in France, under the influence of the poet, pacifist and anarchist, Laurent Tailhade, decadent 'ornament of the Paris salons'. Instead of enlisting, he stayed in France, experimenting with poetry in Tailhade's style: Wildean verse on opium poppies, blood, sacrifice and sin, dreams and veiled sexual allusion. When he did return to England briefly in May the following year, it was not as a soldier, but as a sales representative for a scent manufacturer.

Having enlisted in 1916, his aesthetic hair cropped and his body made fit by military training, Owen was sent to France the following year. He returned to England months later, shellshocked. He was initially sent to the Royal Victoria Hospital at Netley, the largest military hospital in Europe, boasting the first purpose-built military psychiatric wing where victims of 'war neurosis' were filmed as part of the therapeutic process, their ataxic walks and nervous tics resembling nothing so much as the frenetic dances of modern ragtime. Posted to another hospital, Craiglockhart, Owen stopped in London, calling at the Royal Academy, and taking tea at the Shamrock Rooms, 'perhaps the most eminently respectable and secluded in Town. There was the usual deaf old lady and her Companion holding forth upon the new curate. I happen to know that a few stories higher in the same building is an Opium Den. I have not investigated. But I know. That's London.'

At Craiglockhart, Owen introduced himself to Siegfried Sassoon, whom he found sat up in bed, bright sunlight falling on his purple dressing gown (Owen himself used a padded kimono). Lean-limbed with a delicately masculine face – he resembled nothing so much as an aristocratic antelope – Sassoon, scion of a famously wealthy Jewish banking family, had never needed to earn his living, a daunting provenance for someone as 'perceptibly provincial' as Owen. But the war had begun to change social structure and expectation; sudden death on the Western Front meant that middle-class upstarts like Owen could become officers, and the sense of change allowed him to describe his hero in admiring yet ever-so-slightly ironic tones as 'very tall and stately, with a fine firm chisel'd (how's that?) head ...'. At Craiglockhart, and under Sassoon's influence, Owen began to write the poems which would ensure his immortality, fusing his vague Uranian sensibilities and Decadent nightmares with the horrific reality of trench warfare; the aesthete's heartfelt reaction to the antithesis of beauty that war represented.

When Owen left Craiglockhart, Sassoon handed his disciple an envelope. Inside was a ten shilling note, Robert Ross's address, and a message: 'Why shouldn't you enjoy your leave? Don't mention this again or I'll be very angry.' Over lunch with Ross at the Reform Club, both Arnold Bennett and H.G. Wells came over to the table. But it was Ross who would make the greatest mark on the young poet. Ross's aestheticism was announced by his large turquoise blue scarab ring and jade-green cigarette holder, and underlined by his reputation as Wilde's devoted friend and literary executor. By associating with Ross, Owen was allying himself with the cult of Oscar Wilde: hero, mentor and martyr to an entire culture.

*

By the time of the First World War, thirteen years after his death and nearly twenty years after his disgrace, Wilde was a mythic figure: to some, a demon; to others, a saint. It is a reputation which Wilde himself purposefully established and encouraged. As the first cultural figure of the modern era to invent himself through the new media, he believed his own publicity (albeit filtered through his very modern use of irony). That much is evident from his prison tract, *De Profundis*, a text which would both directly and indirectly contribute to the sensational Billing trial of 1918. 'I was a man who stood in symbolic relations to the art and culture of my age ... I felt it myself, and made others feel it ... I awoke the imagination of my century so that it created myth and legend around me.' Such was Wilde's own view of himself: it was a legend taken and promoted with ceaseless energy by Robbie Ross, both in Wilde's lifetime, and beyond.

Grandson of the Governor General of Canada, Robbie Ross had come to England when his father died, and was at an Oxford crammer studying for Cambridge when Wilde met him in 1886; Ross, then aged seventeen, had recently been beaten for reading Wilde's poems. In Richard Ellman's account, 'What must have astonished Wilde was that Ross, so young and yet so knowing, was determined to seduce him.' Oscar 'acceded, perhaps out of curiosity or caprice. He was not attracted to anal coition, so Ross presumably introduced him to the oral and intercrural sex he later practised. First as lover then as friend,

Ross was to keep a permanent place in Wilde's life.' Rupert Croft-Cooke, friend of Lord Alfred Douglas, portrays Ross as 'an amusing little queen when Wilde met him ... a small kittenish creature born in Canada but brought up in London by his widowed mother.' Ross boasted to Douglas that he was 'the first boy Oscar ever had'; it was rumoured that they had met in a public lavatory.

Talented, erudite and loyal, Ross worked at the friendship, flattering Wilde's ego with generous and shrewd praise. He had also befriended Aubrey Beardsley, and attempted to keep the peace between his two talented friends, persuading Wilde to allow Beardsley to illustrate his play *Salome*, and then pacifying the situation when the artist lampooned the author. He also introduced Wilde to William More Adey, Reggie Turner and Arthur Clifton, to Croft-Cooke, 'all young queers with enough money to be idle and give themselves up to admiration for Wilde. Ross was the most single-minded in this exhibitionistic devotion, and, until Wilde met Lord Alfred Douglas, the most successful.' Jealousy was the most potent source of the enmity between Ross and Douglas. Among Ross's other characteristics was a formidable tenacity and a sharp waspish wit. He would need both assets in the fight to come.

After Wilde's death, Ross refused, like his hero, to behave 'normally'; his homosexuality was well-known, especially to the authorities. His indiscretion laid the way open for the Billing trial and its disastrous consequences. In more ways than one it was a rerun of Wilde's trials: Ross presuming on his high-ranking friends to protect him from his own flagrant behaviour, just as Wilde had relied, fatally, on his own celebrity to protect him. To circumspect homosexuals, Wilde had been guilty of a transgression of an immutable rule; that of discretion. It is an accusation which would not have hurt Oscar deeply – had he survived to hear it. He died in improverished exile in Paris as the century turned – 'I am dying beyond my means' – but his memory – and the battle between his friends – lived on.

*

In late middle-age, Lord Alfred Douglas, Wilde's Bosie, retained the looks of a ravaged beautiful boy. His thick silky blond hair was barely touched with grey, his figure was slender, his skin pale and delicate with a tendency to 'flush rosily like a boy's. He dressed simply, with a liking for heavy boots rather than shoes and a habit of wearing battered hats.' But the physical portrait betrays a certain neuroticism. His voice was 'delightful when he laughed but shrill when he was angry'; and Douglas was often angry. To Croft-Cooke, who met him in 1922, 'he looked like a hurt boy. The eyes were brilliantly expressive, often merry but sometimes pained and resentful. The features which in boyhood were so delicately modelled had grown pronounced, the nose formidable, the corners of the mouth turning down petulantly.'

In the years after the Wilde trials, Douglas had sought domesticity, marrying Olive Custance in 1902, with whom he had a son, Raymond. Bosie's cousin and childhood friend, Pamela Tennant, and her husband Edward (Margot Asquith's brother) had offered the Douglases a house on their land at Wilsford in Wiltshire. Here Douglas enjoyed a rural existence, fishing the river Avon which ran through the quiet downland valley. But when Edward Tennant bought the literary weekly, *The Academy* in 1907, Pamela invited Douglas to become its editor. Robbie Ross, a regular contributor to the magazine, had already suggested the post to the still-friendly Douglas, who professed himself to be bored with life. Edward Tennant did not suspect that Douglas would use the magazine as a means by which to attack not only his own politics (Tennant became Liberal MP for Salisbury, while Douglas was a dyed-in-the-wool Tory) but the policies and politics of Tennant's brother-in-law, H.H. Asquith, whom the Tennants helped finance in his progress to becoming Prime Minister the following year.

Douglas moved back to London, and set about campaigning. His right-hand man at *The Academy* was T.H. Crosland, a laddish and scruffy product of a Leeds suburb who looked as though he slept in his clothes; when Douglas took him to the Café Royal, he would have to do Crosland's tie for him. Douglas and Crosland were aware of a renaissance in Wilde's reputation. In the difficult years since Oscar's disgrace, his name had been kept alive by the faithful. Now, with Richard Strauss's acclaimed opera based on *Salome*, and Ross's social acceptance by the Asquiths, there was 'a new sense of sexual liberation in literature and the arts, and ... the reinstatement of Oscar Wilde as a cultural figure'. Ross's articles in *The Academy* did not mention Wilde, but they evoked his spirit in discursions on such subjects as anti-semitism and xenophobia, pertinent in the light of recent anti-immigration laws. Reviewing an exhibition of Jewish art at the Whitechapel Art Gallery, Ross noted: 'One of the greatest bores on earth is the Anti-Semite, and for him, at least, the show should be a liberal instruction. He will be disappointed to find no examples of those peculiar knives used in the ritual murders of young boys ...'. Elsewhere he wrote, 'English criticism brings out a sort of unrepealed Aliens Act from the recesses of its hollow mind ...'.

To the right-wing Crosland, with his instinctive distaste for all things decadent and homosexual, Ross was anathema. He told Douglas that he had heard that Ross was 'an unsavoury person' and ought not to be writing for the magazine; Pamela Tennant apparently agreed, and told Douglas so. As a married man drawn towards Roman Catholicism, Bosie had 'conceived a distaste (which later became ... a loathing) for his own homosexual past and those associated with it'. He attempted to drop Ross quietly. But Ross would not go quietly. The affair began to escalate when Douglas wrote in his accustomed intemperate manner – his father's legacy – telling Ross: 'I no longer care to associate with persons like yourself who are engaged in the active performance and propaganda of every kind of wickedness, from Socialism to Sodomy.' On 1 December 1908 a public dinner was given in Ross's honour at the Ritz, to celebrate the solvency of the Wilde estate and the publication of Oscar's *Collected Works*. H.G.Wells, Sir William Rothenstein and Somerset Maugham numbered among the two hundred guests, whose celebrity irked Douglas greatly.

For the next five years, the spat between Ross and Douglas was a social skirmish for the upper hand. In 1913, it became open warfare. Arthur Ransome had published a biography of Wilde, written with Ross's help. Douglas, annoyed by the way he had been portrayed in it, took out a libel action against the book. Ross had recently resigned as art critic on the *Morning Post*, partly because his views on such subjects as Futurist art conflicted with those held by its reactionary new editor, H.A. Gwynne. He had however taken up a new job as Valuer of Pictures and Drawings for the Inland Revenue, as well as London director of the Johannesburg Art Gallery. Douglas and Crosland were infuriated by the public nature of such appointments, and the Ransome case allowed them to intensify their vendetta against Ross.

The case was tried by the perhaps inaptly named Justice Darling (Max Beerbohm told Reggie Turner of a 'bogus telegram' which had been read out at the Chelsea Arts Club, 'from Mr. Justice Darling, "Regret dare not venture out. Much worried by letter from Lord A. Douglas beginning 'My dear Darling.' " ') The judge made no secret of his dislike for the action and for Wilde, and seemed openly prejudiced against Douglas, directing all of his 'frequent and crushing' interventions against him. Douglas faced a formidable array of barristers, including F.E. Smith, later Lord Birkenhead. Through Ross, the unpublished section of *De Profundis*, Wilde's open letter to Bosie, was produced, although it was supposed to be kept secret, at the British Library, until 1960. It destroyed Douglas's case, being clear evidence of his homosexual relationship with Wilde. Douglas felt posthumously betrayed by Wilde when he heard the new portions of *De Profundis*, and the trial had the effect of turning Douglas violently against Ross and Wilde – just as his father had turned on Wilde.

Douglas would have been better advised not to have brought this action; as F.E. Smith noted, 'With regard to Oscar Wilde, years have passed since his fall, and men are beginning to think of the artist rather than the man's life. Now this legacy of infamy has been resurrected – unnecessarily resurrected – again.' Such would be the effect of the Billing trial, too. It was a difficult time for Douglas: his wife left him, and he was allowed only limited access to his son; he subsequently moved back to live with his mother at 19 Royal Avenue, Chelsea. Bosie was beaten down. Ross, victorious, went off to Moscow to see the first Russian production of Wilde's *Salome* by the Moscow Art Theatre, unaware that that play would soon see his downfall, too.

Douglas determined to turn the tables on Ross. He was 'the High Priest of all the sodomites in London', Douglas declared, '... held up to the world as the faithful friend of Wilde (out of the exploitation of whose cult he had made a fortune), the noble disinterested friend, the pure, the holy person, in contrast to the wicked and depraved Alfred Douglas who had "ruined" Oscar Wilde and "deserted" him. Flesh and blood couldn't stand it, and I swore the day after the Ransome trial that I would never rest till I had publicly exposed Ross in his true colours.' A publisher gave Douglas the opportunity to set the matter straight in print, along with a £500 advance. Bosie was in no position to write a book of 80,000 words, and Crosland offered to do the job in return for half the proceeds. But they reckoned without having to seek permission from Ross to quote from *De Profundis*. He obtained an injunction against them, and the book – *Oscar Wilde and Myself* – would not be published until 4 August 1914 – the day war was declared.

Douglas's announcement that he was about to publish his memoirs created an impossible situation for Ross, obliging him to resign as London director of the Johannesburg Art Gallery. Returning his salary to Lady Phillips, who had founded the gallery, Ross wrote, 'My name being associated with what seems likely to become perpetually recurring scandal would eventually do the Gallery harm. So far, I am glad to think, no harm has been done, except that the stress and anxiety of eight months made it physically impossible for me to give that attention to the affairs of the Gallery which was required ...' The illness which would eventually kill him was a result of the pressure. And with the news that even in South Africa interviews with Douglas were appearing in the press, announcing the 'contents of his "Memoirs" ', Ross knew that further trouble was in store.

*

In January 1914, Douglas encouraged Crosland to write a deliberately libellous letter to Ross, accusing him of 'villainy' and 'foulness' and demanding he resign his executorship of the Wilde estate, having created for Wilde 'a literary and general reputation which is to a great extent a fraudulent one'. Ross ignored it, so Crosland wrote again. 'A letter nailing you down has been sent by Lord Alfred Douglas to the following persons: Mr Justice Darling, Mr Justice Astbury, the Recorder of London, the Prime Minister, the Public Prosecutor, Mr Basil

Thompson (Scotland Yard), Mr Gwynne (*Morning Post*), Mr John Lane, Sir George Lewis, and the Master of St Paul's School.' The exact contents of Douglas's letter are not known, but it did contain such Douglasean phrases as 'an unspeakable skunk', a 'filthy bugger', a 'notorious Sodomite', and 'habitual debaucher and corrupter of young boys right down to the present day', and a 'blackmailer'. The letters were not sent until Crosland and Douglas had evidence to substantiate their claims.

At the trial of Charles Garratt, a boy arrested for importuning, Christopher Millard had volunteered to speak for the prisoner. Millard, Wilde's bibliographer, had already served a prison sentence for gross indecency with a nineteen-year-old boy in Oxford. He had pleaded with Ross to help, and Robbie risked himself in giving it; Millard had since become his secretary. Crosland and Douglas assumed that the boy Garratt had been sexually involved with Ross, and went to see him in prison. Garratt, seeing a potential opening, said he did know Ross, but would give no more details until he came out of prison.

For the moment, Ross seemed secure. The Asquiths were firmly behind him; he stayed at their country house, the Wharf, and Margot professed herself dismayed by the way the police and Scotland Yard were treating Ross; she determined 'to have it out' with Charles Mathews, the Director of Public Prosecutions. But Ross was so apprehensive of Douglas's behaviour that, as he told Edmund Gosse, he had resorted to keeping a firearm. Gosse sought Lord Haldane's advice. As Lord Chancellor (and Asquith's close friend), Haldane – who had visited Wilde in prison – made it clear that, 'while he could not promise that any protective measures would be taken officially on my behalf ... he promised to do all he could for me in his personal capacity ...' Ross's solicitors issued various writs, and Crosland was arrested on a charge of having conspired, with Douglas, to accuse Ross of 'having committed certain acts with one Charles Garratt'. With Sir George Lewis – Wilde's lawyer and friend – acting both for Ross and for his father-in-law, Douglas saw little hope of winning. He escaped to Boulogne, and stayed out of the country and out of reach.

Ill-advisedly, Ross did not withdraw his libel charge against Douglas. When war was declared, Bosie returned to England, intending to join the army; in a brazen act reminiscent of Wilde's contemptuous attitude towards the law, he also informed the police exactly when he would be arriving. He was duly arrested on a charge of criminal libel and spent five nights in Brixton Prison. The row was now spilling out onto society's marble floors. At a party given by the Tennants (Edward was now ennobled as the first Baron Glenconner) at their palatial London house at Queen Anne's Gate, the Prime Minister, Asquith, was standing with the host and hostess, receiving guests; Marie Belloc Lowndes, sister of

Hilaire Belloc and family friend of Wilde's, was sitting with Robbie Ross near the door. Douglas made a loud entrance. Ross stood up, and the two men confronted each other. Douglas began to shout 'various violent terms of abuse'; witnesses heard him say, 'You have got to clear out of this: you are nothing but a bugger and a blackmailer'. Friends of Ross's rushed up to manoeuvre him into the next room, 'followed the while by the still shouting Lord Alfred Douglas'. Ross's friends got him behind a broad table, but Douglas lunged across, trying to get at him. It was an astonishing scene to be taking place in full view of London society. Douglas was pulled back, and Ross was ushered into the next room, 'leaving Lord Alfred shouting with rage at being baulked of his prey'. Lord Glenconner 'went from one lady to another', apologising to his guests. Douglas refused to leave until persuaded to do so by his mother, Pamela's aunt. Afterwards Marie Belloc Lowndes was asked to testify to the attack. 'Fortunately for me,' she wrote coyly, 'certain of the words which Lord Alfred had shouted were quite unknown to me.'

These two men who had loved Wilde now faced each other across the court room. The trial began on 19 November 1914 with the war in full swing. Despite the powers of DORA, 'the case could not be "kept out of the papers" altogether,' writes Croft-Cooke, 'but on the plea of patriotism, and to "conceal British decadence", a good deal was done and even *The Times* reported it scantily.' No details emerged of evidence almost as sensational as that heard at the Wilde trials. The court heard stories of Ross at a New Year's Eve party in 1911 'at which twenty or thirty men had danced together'. A soldier said he had confronted Ross at a bar in Copthall Avenue, Moorgate, over the disappearance of his sixteen-year-old brother from home. Another boy associated with Ross, named Smith, was a member of a dramatic society connected with a London parish; he admitted to 'painting and powdering his face'. Was this not usual for an actor? queried Ross's counsel, only to be told, 'Hardly, when they come to church.' The case went against Ross, and he abandoned it before the verdict could be reached, offering to pay Douglas's costs. Douglas accepted, but Ross had to resign the remainder of his posts and retire from public life.

Still Douglas continued to hound Ross. He thought it outrageous that Ross should be a regular visitor to Downing Street, and wrote to Asquith in January 1915, demanding he renounce Ross as a disreputable character. In response, Edmund Gosse prepared a testimonial for Ross, published in newspapers on 29 March 1915 and signed by three hundred supporters, including the Asquiths, confirming Ross as a respected 'man of letters' – as well as presenting him with a 'purse' which Ross requested be used to set up a scholarship for boys at London University. Douglas noted that signatories included Bernard Shaw, More Adney, the Earl of Plymouth, William Rothenstein, Philip Morrell MP, Lady Ottoline

Morrell, H.G. Wells, Sir George Lewis, Lady Lewis '(née Marie Hirsch of Mannheim)', he added pointedly, the publishers Methuen and Heinemann, and the Bishop of Birmingham.* It is not difficult to understand why the testimonial enraged Douglas; it was a public witness to his enemy's social position. Rather than convince Douglas to drop his vendetta, it had the more predictable effect of enraging him. He wrote again to Asquith, and then to the King, urging the latter to take action against his Prime Minister.

Douglas's campaign continued in a series of privately published poetic tirades. In April 1915, his satiric sonnet, 'All's Well With England', appeared, followed in May by 'To A Certain Judge':

> Blackness descends on England like a pall,
> And in this obscene night, borne down and stoned,
> Calling on God, lies Virtue. Brazen-toned
> Through the shamed land rings out this trumpet call:
> 'Injustice shall be done though Heaven should fall.'
> In the high places lo! they sit enthroned,
> Lust unashamed and Filthiness condoned
> And crowned and comforted. Thou whited wall!

The fact that the blackness of war had that month claimed Wilde's elder son – Cyril Holland, killed at the battle of Neuve-Chapelle on 9 May 1915 – did nothing to abate Douglas's spleen. His pièce de résistance appeared in January 1916. *The Rossiad* was at once Douglas's response to Ross's testimonial, and to Wilde's *De Profundis*, which had been used against him in court, as well as being a narrative of the recent history of his country, which he considered to be threatened by decadence. The poem, which would appear in four editions to certain public acclaim, dwelt on the current miasma which allowed men like Ross to stay in the country:

> But times have changed, the country's rife
> With people of progressive views,
> Nor are they 'mostly German Jews',
> As some fool said not long ago,
> We've seen them, and we ought to know.
> True, Germany (like classic Rome
> In its decline) is now the home
> To which all cultured spirits soar

* Russell Wakefield, Bishop of Birmingham, a widower with four sons and 'a pillar of the Established Church', became president of the Cinema Commission of Inquiry, set up by the National Council of Public Morals, in 1917. Marie Stopes, the campaigner for sexual emancipation, represented the Society of Authors on the commission, and later told Douglas that she was the subject of the Bishop's amorous advances: 'The Bishop was so devoted to me, he implored me to marry him and said he would give up being a Bishop if I would only promise. But of course he was far too old for me ...'

1. The Cult of Wilde

In spite of this unhappy war,
And you would doubtless find a 'pal' in
Our dear friend Haldane's friend, Herr Ballin,*
But that is neither here nor there,
London's the place. How they would stare,
Those fellow-citizens of Lot's,
At some of our compatriots
Who've done their best to build again
Those grand old Cities of the Plain.
For London in the cultured sin
Can give points even to Berlin.

Running dyspeptically through his rage at the establishment figures ranged behind Ross, Douglas concluded his epic poem with exhortation against 'The foe without, the foe within':

This Island once the bourne of saints
Where Vice now reigns, and Virtue faints
And cries in vain to outraged lawn,
While cynic 'Justice' twists the cause
To the fee'd side. Go, now the knees,
And make thy prayers thy argosies
Across the sea of Doubt and Pride
To the old Faith thou hast denied;
Make, ere the Furies sound thy fate,
Thine agony articulate;
Raise up the best, hack down the worst,
Tear from thy heart the thing accurst.
Two foes thou hast, one there one here,
One far, one intimately near,
Two filthy fogs blot out thy light:
The German, and the Sodomite.

The final section – which so impressed one Catholic cleric of the 'old Faith' that he wrote a unabashed panegyric to the poet – was a full-blooded and dramatic patriotic call to arms, employing biblical imagery of Apocalypse, threatening Britain with the visitation of all manner of obscenity, precipitated by the state condoning of Ross: known pervert and supporter of perversion. The basest fears were played upon; most potently in time of war (and with greatest contemporary resonance), evoking the 'enemy within', with all its concomitant perils of what would be called the Fifth Column in the next war; an inexorable conflation of perversity, decadence, foreignness and the threat of the other.

Crucially, Asquith was no longer in Downing Street after 1916; Ross had lost his protection. Ailing, weary, and well aware of his vulnerablity, Ross knew it

___

* German Jewish businessman and politician, his dialogue with Sir Ernest Cassel led to the Haldane Mission of 1912, intended to end the naval race between Britain and Germany.

would only be a matter of time before Douglas launched his next attack. He did not know, but may have suspected, that in the prejudiced climate of wartime, this would involve all society in a display of English justice and prejudice; a final nail in Oscar Wilde's coffin.

*

In 1914 Ross had moved to a first-floor flat at 40 Half Moon Street, an elegant street opening onto Piccadilly and Green Park. Ross's was an aesthete's lair: in a flagrant gesture against war economies, he had recently had his rooms redecorated in dull gold, reflecting their inhabitant's 'intense love of comfort and luxury' and 'natural inborn laziness ...'. Ross kept open house into the early hours for his friends, most of whom were, in the parlance of the time, 'so'; the proximity of the cruising-grounds of Piccadilly and the park being an extra attraction. Here, in his gilded room, Ross entertained Wilfred Owen. A long table was laid with Turkish delight, biscuits, brandy and cigarettes; the host, in his black silk skull cap, presided over his guests' discussions. It wasn't until the early hours that Owen left Half Moon Street, in buoyant mood: 'I and my work are a success.' More personally, the meeting with Ross and his friends did much to open Owen up to his own sexuality; soon after, he admitted to his cousin, Leslie Gunston, that there was a secret 'key' to his poems.

Back with his regiment in Scarborough, in the turret room of his cliff-top hotel, Owen read *De Profundis* and Sherard's biography of Wilde; his poems also took on a new Wildean manner. He returned to London in January 1918 for Robert Graves' wedding at St James's, Piccadilly, where he was introduced to C.K. Scott Moncrieff, the Scottish poet and later translator of Proust, recently wounded on the Western Front; he still walked with a limp. He was also an Edwardian Uranian boy-lover, author of *Evensong and Morewesong*, a 'bravely obscene story of adolescent fellation', and had come directly from a police court, where he had been giving evidence at the trial of his sometime lover, Christopher Millard (about to receive his second jail sentence for sexual indecency). Owen was being drawn yet further into the Wildean circle at a dangerous time. These people were specific targets for Billing's attack, already being drawn up in the offices of the *Imperialist*. When Scott Moncrieff's closest friend, Philip Bainbrigge (an owlish schoolmaster who shared his Uranian tastes) told Owen in a Scarborough oyster bar that 'the whole of civilisation is extremely liable to collapse', it was a comment not only on the overwhelming German advance of that spring, but also a presentiment for his kind.

2

That Awful Persecution

He failed to summon up any enthusiasm whatever over the current war, protesting that for his part he had always found the Germans 'most polite'. In fact 'that awful persecution' was the phrase which it was most often his wont to use in alluding in after years to the first World War.

Osbert Sitwell, Introduction to Ronald Firbank, *Five Novels*

Ronald Firbank's camp epithet for the war could equally well have been applied both to the Billing affair and to his personal situation. With the outbreak of war, Firbank found wartime London a 'hurried, harried city' where he felt alien; 'the gloom and tension increased each month', and eventually he fled to Oxford, to make his forays into the capital from its spired safety. Boredom forced him to write the first of his convoluted, decadent novels full of ambivalently-sexed characters and implied debauchery – surely one of the more ironic products of the period; Osbert Sitwell remarked that Firbank was 'in the best, least boring, sense a "war writer" '. For his kind, 1914-18 was not a propitious time, as Robbie Ross's experience indicated. The brief sway of those whom Cyril Connolly called the avengers of Wilde's death on the bourgeoisie – Diaghilev, Proust, Cocteau and Gide – was, in England at least, replaced by the moralists' reign. The world changed from a liberal society which, if not condoning aberrant sexual behaviour, at least appeared to tolerate it, to a world which blamed its ills on such practitioners and associated them with the enemy.

Wilde's legacy was strongly felt by those growing up in his shadow. When Beverley Nichols's father discovered that his son had a copy of *The Picture of Dorian Gray*, he reacted violently. 'You pretty little bastard', he shouted, 'you pretty little boy'. Nichols senior – whose apoplexy rivalled the Marquess of Queensberry's – enunciated the word 'pretty' 'in a shrill parody of a homosexual voice' as he slapped his son in the face, spat on the book and tore the pages with his teeth. 'Oscar Wilde! To think that my son ...' Beverley protested he did not know what Wilde had done. ' "What did he do? Oh, my son, my son!" – and he collapsed on the bed and burst into tears.' The following morning, Beverley was given a piece of paper on which were written the words, *Illum crimen horribile quod non nominandum est*, which he translated as 'The horrible crime which is not to be named'.

In 1917 Nichols was conscripted, working in the Intelligence department of the War Office in Whitehall. His unit decided he should be sent to such places as the Café Royal – just up the road – 'to act as a sort of agent provocateur to lure pacifist activists into trying to entice them to their cause'. Such methods of entrapment – ironically similar to the German practices described in the Black Book – were not unusual techniques for intelligence and policing authorities then (and after). Nichols's mission had yet a more ironic outcome, 'for the constant presence of this baby-faced officer in the Bohemian surroundings of the Café Royal attracted the attention of plain-clothes police, whose suspicions of him could only have been fuelled by his fairly obvious sex life'.

The Café Royal still retained the decadent allure it had enjoyed in Wilde's time, and soon Nichols was consorting with Ronald Firbank, Augustus John, Osbert Sitwell and Jacob Epstein. Alvaro 'Chile' Guevara picked him up there, and the impressively muscled sometime boxer took Nichols to his studio for 'prodigious drinking bouts, violent sex and violent rows' in between which Guevara painted a full-length portrait of Nichols in uniform, described by Firbank as 'charged with exquisite menace'. Meanwhile, the police searched Nichols's rooms in Bryanston Street, apparently looking for evidence of his taking drugs, 'presumably because others in the Café Royal set did so, passing round cocaine quite openly. Such evidence would have added dramatically to the dossier they were compiling about him.' Nichols's landlady was questioned about his male visitors, and whether they stayed the night. The investigation proved only an association with 'undesirable people'. The army was informed, and Nichols was sent away to Cambridge as instructor to the Office Cadet Battalion, where his superior officer, Colonel Craddock, called him into his office. 'People were saying he was a sod because he behaved like one, and he added, somewhat curiously, "Sodomy is more prevalent than you may imagine, dear boy".'

This was certainly the fear of the authorities, a fear which the Billing affair exploited. The need to control the urban population had been felt since the nineteenth-century campaigns 'to make urban life respectable and to police public spaces and gatherings in cities and towns so as to inhibit social interaction'. With the advent of war, a direct correlation was made between such social aberrations and the nation's struggle. There was a 'home-front war against sex, and especially what one might call dissenting sex – that is, homosexuality'. And to many minds, homosexuality was subversion, so associated with Germany that the two had almost become synonymous. Lord Alfred Douglas quoted with approval a paragraph by Austin Harrison from a Sunday paper:

2. That Awful Persecution

When we hear of German brutality in Belgium, of their employment of chlorine, of the Lusitania and the bombardment of open towns, there should be no surprise. For years the Germans have cultivated a wholesome brutality as part of the military training, and latterly this brutality has found vent in sexual perversion. Such things do not make men gentle, humane or noble.

Douglas added, 'Here is something for Mr. Harrison and all other parties concerned to remember: It is just as important to civilisation that Literary England should be cleansed of sex-mongers and pedlars of the perverse, as that Flanders should be cleared of Germans.'

Douglas's assertions chimed with a general English suspicion about German culture. *The Rossiad* had referred to the 'cultured sin' of Berlin, a city which had long celebrated Prussian pomp and might, yet was also a focus for homosexuals drawn by its permissive nightlife. Its image of military masculinity became, inevitably, a sexual image of potency and romance (realised in the American artist William Hartley's Cubist tributes to his German soldier boyfriend), and, therefore, decadence. The city's reputation went before it, and was used by its enemies to undermine its power. As the war progressed, so did the British tendency to portray the Germans as sexual perverts. Casting aspersions on the masculinity of one's foes was an age-old military tactic, from the Romans to the Zulus, but no less effective for that. In John Buchan's *Greenmantle*, published in October 1916, the villain is a 'huge, brutal' German officer, Ulric von Stumm, whose private quarters are decorated with statues and velvety grey carpet, and where the scent of burning oils hangs in the air.

> At first you would have said it was a woman's drawing room. But it wasn't. I soon saw the difference. There had never been a woman's hand in that place. It was the room of a man who had a fashion for frippery, who had a perverted taste for soft delicate things. It was the compliment to his bluff brutality. I began to see the queer other side to my host, that evil side which gossip had spoken of as not unknown in the German army. The room seemed a horribly unwholesome place, and I was more than ever afraid of Stumm.

In such foreboding, menacing terms (which imply the worst fate an Englishman could suffer – Teutonic rape), Buchan evokes a popular fear – mixed with fascination – of German decadence which would last through the Weimar period and into the Third Reich; the scene is but a step away from Ernst Roëhm's orgiastic Brownshirts and Goering's predilection for phallic furniture and sexual excess. The fear that such practices might be taken up by their own men encouraged the British army to proscribe homosexuality with vigour:

It is a misdemeanour punishable with two years' imprisonment for any male person, either in public or private, to commit or be a party to the commission of any act of gross indecency with another male person, or to procure or to attempt to procure the commission by any male person of such an act; and it is also a misdemeanour to do any grossly indecent act in a public place in the presence of more persons than one, or to publicly expose the person, or exhibit any disgusting object.

The minimum sentence, if convicted of sodomy, was ten years; the maximum was life, and officers found guilty of either offence would be cashiered before being sentenced. Records show that from 1914-19, 22 officers and 270 ORs were court-martialled for indecency. Raymond Asquith acted as legal counsel to one defendant in August 1916. An officer in the Grenadier Guards (as was Asquith), the defendant was the sixth generation of his family to hold a commission in the regiment, and was the son of an officer who had been killed in action earlier in the war. He was accused on five charges of 'homosexualism'. Asquith told his wife he thought the case 'quite hopeless'. Most of the witnesses were

> fearful liars and in other respects tarred with much the same brush as the accused … One of the 2 principal ones was a queer fellow in the Irish Guards … a tiresome officious puritanical creature full of the missionary and detective spirit and apparently with a bee in his bonnet about the corruption and decadence of the English upper classes and particularly of Etonians.
>
> The other was a nephew of Robert Ross [a connexion enough to raise anyone's suspicions], lately a scholar at Eton, who aroused everyone's suspicions by knowing Latin and Greek [at the Billing trial, the judge made a point of not knowing any Greek, and disparaged those who did] and constantly reading Henry James's novels. He was not ill-looking but with an absurdly cushioned figure and a rather hysterical temperament more like a girl than a boy. He was the accomplice who turned King's evidence.

'Two ideas were at work, in Asquith's account, that would defeat his case' writes Samuel Hynes; 'the notion that the English upper classes were corrupt, and the notion that public-school boys were effeminate aesthetes. Both relate to the idea of English decadence as a cause of the war, which had first appeared in the war's early months, and had been a commonplace of English war talk since then. The war was to have been the Condy's Fluid that would cleanse society of its decadence; but here, two years later, and with the war's greatest battle in progress, that cleansing had not occurred. Instead, the infection had burst out here, where one might least expect it, in the officer-class that was charged with directing the war, and in the most elite of regiments.'

2. That Awful Persecution

The Guards regiments represented the apogee of aristocratic military narcissism; it was the Brigade of Guards in which Osbert Sitwell felt most comfortable as a newly-enlisted officer, describing in almost fetishistic detail, the fitting of his tunic of scarlet Melton cloth, the all-important 'smoothness of shoulders and waist', and accoutrements requiring 'esoteric' perfection. Stationed in London, the regiments were open to the capital's temptations: Sitwell received his cultural education whilst barracked at St James's, running up huge bills with ticket agencies as he attended the ballet, theatre and opera. For some Londoners, the Guards represented an attainable masculinity – their other ranks were notorious for their sexual availability, 'a bit of scarlet'. One relic of the Nineties, Charles Dalmon, told the writer Michael Davidson: 'My dear, my ambition is to be crushed to death between the thighs of a guardsman!'

London's sexual subculture had always existed, but in wartime, a hedonisitic spirit of *carpe diem* combined with the throwing together of large numbers of young men to bring many into contact with worlds they would never otherwise have experienced. The capital had escaped the moralising campaigns, leaving it with the reputation of 'the nation's pleasure ground'. The theatre was the nexus of this culture of pleasure, and was also peculiarly open to outside influences; from the new syncopation from across the Atlantic to the avant-garde from Europe, their influence was often felt first in the world of the theatre. Here Londoners first heard American slang such as 'kid' and 'okay', and saw dances like the Apache, the Tango and the Bunny Hug, unprecedented in their body contact. It was also a liberating arena for women. The stage was one of the few places where they could pursue and succeed in independent careers, and stars like Gaby Deslys, Phyllis Monkman, Beatrice Lillie and Teddie Gerrard led fast lives in modern revues; many, like Gerrard, also worked their way through a string of lovers, male and female. The theatre's mixing of class and sexuality, and its susceptibility to the suspiciously new, combined to produce a threat to the moral status quo. The old social demarcations had gone.

For Captain Leo Charlton of the Royal Flying Corps, 'it was so ridiculously easy, during the war, to hob-nob with women, and men too for that matter, whose names and faces were continually advertised in the dreary photographic pages of society weeklies'. Charlton, an aristocratic Catholic homosexual, was representative of a subculture within the armed forces. His London home boasted an indoor swimming pool where he would entertain 'young officers of the Flying Corps in whom he was interested' and 'one or two of the West Indian boys, his gymnastic pupils ... It cannot be claimed that the scenes which were enacted late at night were uniformly decorous. Much licence was allowed, especially to those who had just come from, or were immediately returning to, the agony of life at the war.' A similar figure was Major-General Edward Bailey

'Splash' Ashmore, a comrade of Charlton's in overall command of London's air defence, famous for his 'musical parties' as Noel Coward recalled, perhaps with a little subtexual innuendo – 'musical' being another euphemism for homosexual.

*

Eighty years later, evidence of wartime 'decadent' behaviour is not easy to find; not least because of the authorities' efforts to control public opinion and maintain a moral status quo. Court and newspaper reports occasionally give a glimpse of another world beyond the bland, necessary patriotism of Britain at war: a deserter arrested in South London, found hiding under the bed of a female impersonator; 'bohemian' parties in Chelsea; a dragoon arrested on Salisbury Plain wearing female dress; chorus girls and streetwalkers found in possession of cocaine. But such hard facts give only brief glimpses of secret lives, and for one documentor and analyst of exotic social and sexual behaviour, Dr Magnus Hirschfeld, an enlightening picture of the wartime subculture could only come from the frank testimony of those who took part in it.

Hirschfeld, a Jewish physician with literary interests, was part of a German movement to recognise the natural state of homosexuality as a biological theory. He followed in the footsteps of Richard von Krafft-Ebing, who pioneered the idea that homosexuality was not an illness but a sexual variation, and Karl Heinrich Ulrichs, who coined the term 'urning' for the 'third sex'. Hirschfeld founded the Scientific Humanitarian Committee (SHC), pledged to the abolition of Paragraph 175, the German law which punished homosexuals. His campaign coincided with the emerging 'New Age' sensibility, and alternative movements in Germany: he connected lesbianism with the women's movement, and sexual emancipation with naturism. In 1904 he wrote *Berlins Drittes Geschlecht* ('Berlin's Third Sex'), in which he detailed the underworld of drag balls and homosexual tearooms such as the Café Dorian Gray. Hirschfeld had continued with his pioneering research work during the war, and subsequently conducted a survey of sexual life during the period, advertising for material in 'leading newspapers of every land'. The result was *The Sexual History of the World War*. First published in English by the Panurge Press, New York in 1934, its chapter subtitles alone promise lurid sensation: 'Mad Lust for Pleasure'; 'Night Life Excesses'; 'Extra Marital Affairs Increase'; 'Sexual Crimes': 'Sexual Aggressiveness of Women'; 'Nudist Dens and Naked Parties'; 'Societies of Drug Addicts'; 'Women's Slave Club'.

Hirschfeld addresses the notion of a society thrown into licentiousness. Sexual liaisons proliferated everywhere in the abandoned atmosphere of war:

for instance illegitimate births rose by thirty per cent in Britain during wartime. Where eligible males were lacking, young boys became the objects of older women's affections; prisoners-of-war and 'even unattractive men suddenly found themselves successful and desired by women'; Hirschfeld's book has perhaps the first account of female rape of men. He also deals with the phenomenon of lesbianism: 'We may assume that the sexual hunger of soldiers' wives very frequently led to pseudo-homosexual actions', although he did not ascribe the increasing assumption of masculine garb by women – boots to the knee, shorter skirts and hats like military caps – as evidence of Sapphism, rather as an expression of their greater assertiveness.

Hirschfeld's portrait of sexual excess in wartime cities is supported by contemporary press accounts. With London nearer to the front lines than it was to many of its provincial cities, the capital acted as one huge war camp, with an attendant 'camp-follower outlook. The bushes of Hyde Park – and the Marlborough Street Police Court Register – bore witness to that.' The *Weekly Dispatch* noted that

> Men and women who led sober lives in 1914 have abandoned themselves in many cases to orgies which are incredible. But a few weeks ago at a great London music hall two women arrived in a Rolls-Royce car, sent for the commissionaire, and said they would like to entertain a couple of guardsmen if such were in the house. They gave the man a sovereign. The soldiers were brought in, entertained afterwards to a champagne supper, and remained with the women until morning. The incident is characteristic of what is being done every day in the West End. The air is electric with this current of abnormal sexuality.

In the burgeoning London nightlife, the Cave of the Golden Calf had set a precedent, inspiring such clubs as Elsa Lanchester's Cave of Harmony in Seven Dials, which opened in 1917 and would remain famous throughout the late teens and early Twenties as a refuge for the theatrical, the bohemian and the homosexual. In London, Hirschfeld recorded, there were 'orgiastic outgrowths ... night life in secret clubs and amusement places ...' The authorities tried to exert some influence. 'A number of secret clubs were shut down by the police and in the wardrobes of these establishments there were found not only the elegant coats and wraps of the ladies and gentlemen, but also the rest of their costume for all clothing had come to be regarded as a hindrance to their social intercourse.' Hirschfeld's informant – presumably a participant – noted, 'The guests, of whom there were usually between thirty and fifty, women predominantly, were all recognised, and in the catalogue of names, there could be found some of the most distinguished ones in English society.'

Such nudist clubs may have had overtones of the German naturist movement;

31

not so other haunts. 'Certain secret clubs had the reputation of being play-grounds of narcotic addicts, and many women were among the devotees ... These places were all remarkably alike. At the centre of the festivities there would usually be some famous dancer whose erotic dances would lend the requisite sensual atmosphere ...' Moral campaigners would not have been surprised to find that the patrons and owners were the war profiteers whom they so hated, 'manufacturers and traders who had come to wealth by the fortunes of war and the crowd of ne'er-do-wells who clustered around the infamous profi-teers. The "artistic" dance in the nude by one or more dancers – in one particular case it was announced to the guests as the "dance of crime and of vice" and acted out before the guests by a dancer who had grown famous in this speciality and her partner – was sometimes just a program number and something to set the mood; but in other cases it was an end in itself and was participated in by all the guests.' It was a scene worthy of Weimar Berlin. 'These gay parties did not always remain concealed, for occasionally a participant would reveal these orgies and the matter would come to the attention of the police who would one day raid the given temple of love and disrupt the festivities.'

For those with reputations at risk, there were less public venues. With the erosion of class barriers, upper-class social gatherings were no longer restricted to formal dances in Mayfair ballrooms. 'Men and women of the higher ranks of society crowded most eagerly to the studio parties held by artists at that time at which Bohemians and their models carried on in the most animal fashion ... For the rich bourgeois, who were interested in such scenes of nakedness and lust as were here enacted, these parties lacked the material wealth and splendour to which they were accustomed but to compensate for that the anomal [sic] vitality was higher.' To the 'normal' world, such scenes were fascinatingly depraved. The voyeurism and excitable horror of the English middle classes is crucial in these accounts. Not only German, but European culture as a whole was held to blame. Moralists looked askance at the avant-garde antics of the Russian Ballet, the Cubists and the Vorticists. The shock of the new, the advancing guard of the modernists from the Continent, threatened Britishness. Even supposedly un-biased sources such as *Chambers Twentieth Century Dictionary* adopted a disapproving Europhobic tone: 'Decadence: 'n. state of decay; a term for a school in modern French literature not distinguished for vigour or originality.'

The subtitles of two of Hirschfeld's chapters – 'Homosexuality and Transves-titism' and 'Sensuality in the Trenches' – would have been enough to vindicate any moralist's concern about wartime debauchery among fighting men: 'Mastur-bation a Necessary Evil'; 'Plaster Phalli Found in the Trenches'; 'Anal Eroticism of Soldiers'; 'Sodomy'; 'Instances of Bestiality'. Hirschfeld noted the 'extremely common notion that there were two homosexuals to every hundred men', a percentage which he would rapidly revise upwards. 'The outbreak of war produced the remarkable phenomenon that an unusual number of homosexuals streamed into the army and voluntarily joined the ranks. In this group there were a large number whom public opinion on the subject of homoerotic love in Germany and the fear of Paragraph 175 had driven from their homeland before the war.' Yet 'homosexual soldiers were very brave warriors ... [and] homosexual officers were especially noted for their kindly treatment of the men entrusted to them'. It was a phenomenon borne out by the experience and practice of officers such as Sassoon and Owen. Hirschfeld did not regard homosexuality as immoral, and much of his work sought to establish the humanity of those with desires other than the norm. In doing so, he uncovered some sad stories of suffering. There was a surprising apparent enthusiasm for the war among homosexuals, some of whom went to war in the hope 'that a bullet might put an end to their life which they regard as being a complete failure from their point of view of the present conditions and notions. Driven by this feeling, many an urning officer exposed himself to the thickest rain of bombs and the most deadly attacks. Only recently a flier whom I had congratulated on his distinctions replied that in truth, his disregard of death was nothing more than disgust with life.' Such fatalism accords with a certain death cult aspect of decadence, reflected in the work of such poets as Owen, Sassoon, and Brooke. To die outside a rejecting society, but with men one loved, seemed a fitting end in a time of apocalypse.

Hirschfeld found that the issue of homosexuality in the armed services was most acute in England and Germany. In his homeland homosexual officers had been blackmailed because of Paragraph 175, and expelled from the army. The French were much more tolerant, and 'the native population of the occupied districts in northern France looked with sympathetic understanding upon such friendships among German soldiers. In many cases such friends could meet at certain French homes.' One specific report came from an officer, the youngest in his battalion. 'Despite my very respectable size I was known as Baby. One day there came an ensign from the cadets corps, Count L, with whom I immediately fell in love ... He returned my love entirely for he, a blond, blue-eyed fresh youth of eighteen, was also an urning. Soon we became inseparable friends and the major and other older officers rejoiced at the splendid relationship which had grown up between superior and subordinate, for Karl had been placed in our company and had been more or less entrusted to my hands ...' It is a hearts-and-flowers picture of love among the soldiers, Germanic in its sentimentality. 'So Karl and I lived together, went into service together, etc. When we didn't go out of an evening, we dismissed the servants and sat for a long time arm in arm, in close embrace, saying many tender and lovely things to each other, spinning golden [dreams] for the future and building beautiful castles in the air ... We also engaged in sexual activity, but only rarely and in a thoroughly fine, aesthetic, but never punishable form.' Then came the inevitable day that they were discovered in bed together by a lieutenant. Karl was sent to the front, where he died a week later. Hirschfeld's informant was court martialled, and discharged from service, on account of his 'neuropathic condition'.

Most surprising of all Hirschfeld's anecdotes are tales of transvestism in the trenches. They may have marched to war to ragtime tunes, but few troops could have suspected that among their ranks were men with ballgowns packed in their kitbags. One soldier felt so uncomfortable in his army uniform that as soon as he got home on leave, he changed clothes with his sister. She looked 'very masculine and very much like him', and wanted to go into the army herself. The siblings were persuaded not to swap roles completely by their doctor – evidently a broad-minded man – who warned them of the punitive consequences.

Yet more remarkable was a case of two transvestites, a twenty-four-year-old salesman and a twenty-six-year-old singer who were arrested while strolling down the street, dressed in women's clothes. The salesman said he had enlisted 'to find death. After seven months during which time I strove desperately to bear the fearful burdens of war, I found a number of men with like inclinations and even had the opportunity to go strolling with a lieutenant, both of us wearing female garb. In addition we arranged several dances at which we danced as women. For years I have endeavoured to suppress the desire to wear female clothes but latterly it has become absolutely impossible for me to inhibit this inclination.' The singer said that he had taken onto the battlefield an entire female wardrobe 'in order to be a human being at least for a moment'. He appeared in costume to sing at a local casino, and danced with fellow officers: 'One evening he danced with a group of paymasters without any of them realising that he was not a woman.' It is surely one of the more bizarre images to emerge from the war to end all wars, yet not as uncommon as might be supposed. When the more lurid popular newspapers in England mentioned men in women's clothing 'nigger-dancing' at Chelsea parties, the 'blame' was laid on the frontline custom of soldiers donning dresses for troop shows.

Whatever the real percentage of homosexuals or transvestites there may have been on active service, the phenomenon was one which was newly identified. The American historian George Chauncey notes that 'Until World War I, the societies [for social concern] did not identify homosexuality as a social problem so threatening that it merited more than incidental attention.' The generally burgeoning homosexual subculture in Western cities is an identifiable characteristic of the period. That the war brought into focus the 'threat' of homosexuality is explained by a number of factors: the legacy of the Wilde trials and attendant cultural notions of decadence; the social reform movements in Germany which were advocating homosexuality; and the mass bringing together of men in all-male environments during the war. The fact that these also mixed all classes is crucially important, especially as regards the officer-private relationship, an established homosexual pattern of cross-class relationships.

Chauncey would add the general notion of 'urban degeneracy' to this list; his remarks about wartime America hold equally true for Britain. 'World War I was a watershed in the history of the urban moral reform movement and in the role of homosexuality in reform discourse. The war embodied reformers' darkest fears and their greatest hopes, for it threatened the very foundations of the nation's moral order – the family, smalltown stability, the racial and gender hierarchy – even as it offered the reformers an unprecedented opportunity to implement their vision.' Mass troop movements through major cities and ports created conditions in which any sort of sexual behaviour was opportunistic: Chauncey describes the attempts of various welfare and moralist societies to control such behaviour in wartime New York. 'As the war progressed, the societies were astonished to detect "an apparent increase in male perversion". Agents report seeing "perverts" approaching soldiers and sailors on the streets, in theaters, and in hotel lobbies, meeting them in bars, and taking them to assignation hotels. They saw suspicious-looking civilians inviting servicemen to join them in saloons and hotel bars ... Agents had noticed fairies fraternising with sailors for years, but it was at the beginning of the war that they witnessed the spectacle of "sex mad" sailors near the Brooklyn Navy Yard "walking arm in arm and on one dark street ... a sailor and a man kissing each other ... an exhibition of mail [*sic*] perversion showing itself in the absence of girls". At the moment of their triumph, the social-purity forces were confronted with mounting evidence that the war somehow unleashed the most appalling of urban vices.'

The same sort of behaviour was becoming all too obvious in England. During the war, ports such as Plymouth, Southampton and Portsmouth were venues for homosexual soliciting in the streets. So socially unacceptable did the morally outraged find this behaviour that they could not accept that it was a British phenomenon. It had to be the product of German infamy: hence the scenes of dockyard entrapment that were directly alluded to and recycled in Mr Billing's Black Book.

*

Just as sex and drugs remain the mark of modern dissipation, so they were eighty years ago. Narcotics had been identified as a public menace in the United States by 1914, with international conferences on the subject. Britain, however, declined to legislate against abuse, and drugs such as opium, heroin and cocaine continued to be available over chemists' counters. To the British, the notion of the drug addict had been a foreign one. The war changed all that. The influx of foreigners into London, especially American troops, brought cocaine and heroin into the night life of the West End, and along with the other scares of the time – white slavery, spy scandals and a particular obsession with Oriental organised crime – combined to make both the public and the authorities sensitive to such indications of moral turpitude.

Certain members of high society were already acquainted with the pleasures of drug abuse. In June 1915, Diana Manners had broken her leg whilst walking drunkenly on Brighton beach with Duff Cooper. 'Morphia dulled the agony and, taken in company, helped create a festive atmosphere', notes her biographer Philip Ziegler. Diana found the narcotic an amenable escape. She later described to Raymond Asquith how she and his wife Katherine had lain

> in ecstatic stillness through too short a night, drugged in very deed by my hand with morphia. O, the grave difficulty of the actual injection, the sterilising in the dark and silence and the conflict of my hand and wish when it came to piercing our flesh. It was a grand night, and strange to feel so utterly self-sufficient – more like a Chinaman, or God before he made the world or his son and was content with, or callous to, the chaos.

Wartime use of narcotics for medicinal purposes, and their consequent overproduction by the pharmaceutical industry, had made drugs much more widely available, and the problem of abuse was increasing. By 1915, Quex, the *Evening Standard*'s columnist, was calling for a similar drug prohibition to the United States':

> I see that other people are turning their attention to the growing craze for opium smoking, to which I referred last week. West End Bohemia is hearing some dark stories of what is going on. But still more prevalent is the use of that exciting drug cocaine. It is so easy to take – just sniffed up the nose; and no one seems to know why the girls who suffer from this body and soul racking habit find the drug so easy to obtain.
>
> In the ladies' cloakroom of a certain establishment two bucketfuls of thrown-away small circular cardboard boxes were discovered by the cleaners the other day – discarded cocaine boxes.

The drug was said to have been introduced by Canadian troops, being readily available in their country. By 1916, the cocaine scare was firmly in the British headlines: 'The Cocaine Curse – Evil Habit Spread By Night Clubs', reported the *Evening News*. 'Social workers, mental experts and police officers all bear testimony to the ravages of the drug habit among young women especially of the leisured class that regards itself as Bohemian.' It hinted at a widespread net of dealers selling 'snow', used by weary soldiers to enliven themselves, or by nightclub flappers to stay the course through the night. It was the perfect social drug. Unlike morphine, cocaine did not require a hypodermic, and was easy to take in situ, snorted from the knuckles or off nail files; chewing gum masked the teeth-grinding side-effect, and afterwards, alcohol calmed the sleep-depriving frenzy. The *Umpire* had yet more sensational reports of 'hop joints' popularised by Americans and Canadians, where 'needle dancers' could be found. 'Vicious Drug Powder – Cocaine Driving Hundreds Mad – Women and Aliens Prey on Soldiers'; London was 'In Grip Of The Drug Craze' at 'Secret "Coke" Parties of "Snow Snifters" '. The police bore witness to the phenomenon, associating it with thieves, sodomites, 'retailers of Malthusian appliances [i.e. contraceptives], quack medicines and that class of offensive literature'.

The result was that the all-encompassing powers of DORA were once again brought into play. From 28 July 1916, Regulation 40b forbade, for the first time, possession of opium or cocaine by other than authorised persons. In June 1918, it was announced in *The Times* that soldiers would henceforth require a doctor's prescription to obtain twelve named drugs: 'barbitone, benzamine lactate, benzamine hydrochloride, chloral hydrate, coca, cocaine, codeine, diamorphine, Indian hemp, opium, morphine, and sulphonal and its homologues, and any salts, preparations, derivatives, or admixtures prepared from or with any these drugs.'

Throughout the war, officers were routinely sent narcotics through the post by loved ones. Many pilots – with their pitifully short life expectancy – used morphine, and other members of the armed forces became addicts after morphine treatment for wounds; as those going into action were issued with glass phials of liquid morphine in doses large enough to help mortally wounded men to die, there was a plentiful supply at the Front. Back in Blighty, they had to resort to pushers. New efforts were made by the authorities to deal with the problem of drug use, as the police surveillance at the Café Royal and their raid on Beverley Nichols's flat indicate. Indeed, in 1918, the same year as Billing pursued his moral campaign, an equally sensational case came to trial. The fate of Billie Carleton, a popular young actress, filled the papers with tales of high society decadence. It is telling that the venue of her demise was the Savoy, where evidence of Wilde's disgrace had been collected.

*

Billie Carleton had risen from illegitimacy via the chorus line to theatrical celebrity. At twenty-two, she was a friend of Beatrice Lillie and Gertrude

Lawrence, and a prime example of the nightclub flapper. Like her fellow actress, Meggie Albanesi (who died of a botched abortion), Billie Carleton epitomised the fast and loose-living girl of the time. In 1915 she had been introduced to opium either by Jack Mays, the American who ran Murray's nightclub, or by Captain Ernest Schiff, a man-about-town with a suspiciously German surname and a Teutonic habit of filing his fingernails to a point. She had also fallen in with Reginald de Veulle, a cross-dressing women's fashion designer who had picked up a coke habit in New York. Soon Billie was smoking opium acquired from Chinese suppliers in Limehouse, or from Lionel Belcher, a handsome young actor with a heavy heroin dependency.

Billie and her friends attended a fancy dress ball at the Albert Hall – de Veulle in a tight-fitting Harlequin outfit, complete with ruff – and danced energetically until the small hours, assisted by cocaine which Billie carried in a silver box. A few hours later, she was found dead in her flat at the Savoy. The newspapers made much of Miss Carleton's associations with de Veulle and his wife, as the inquest court heard how 'disgusting orgies took place extending from Saturday night until early in the Sunday afternoon' at 16 Dover Street. Here Billie stayed with the de Veulles for a fortnight, during which 'the high priestess of unholy rites' Ada Ping You (Scottish wife of their Chinese dealer) would arrive at weekends to cook for the opium parties. 'After dinner the party adjourned, at about 10 o'clock, to the drawing room of the flat, and provided themselves with cushions and pillows, placed these on the floor, and sat themselves in a circle. The men divested themselves of their clothing and got into pyjamas, and the women into chiffon nightdresses. In that manner they seemed to prepare themselves for the orgy ... Miss Carleton arrived later at the flat from the theatre, and she, after disrobing, took her place in this circle of degenerates.' At the centre sat Mrs Ping You, preparing the pipes which would keep the party 'in a comatose state until about 3 o'clock on the following afternoon, Sunday'.

De Veulle was accused of manslaughter, and the prosecution brought evidence of his bad character, including descriptions of a drag party he had attended in Maidenhead with one Donald Kimfull (later to metamorphose into the legendary 'Dean' of Dean's Bar in Tangier). He was sentenced to six months' imprisonment. The newspaper-reading public found such descriptions of vice during wartime horribly thrilling, and the tabloid headlines and photographs of the depraved protagonists confirmed their suspicions about a decadent society. The fact that Billie probably died, as Marek Kohn convincingly asserts, of a barbiturate overdose (taken to calm her cocaine hangover) was not important; the moral welfare of the nation was. *The Times* called for more effective means of controlling an epidemic of drug abuse thrown up by the war, and informed its readers that research in India 'proved' that addicts died within three months.

It recommended public education: 'The clergy could help materially here, for there is no doubt that it is in the darker walks of life that this drug is most likely to be encountered in the first instance.' The *Daily Express* sent off its 'special correspondent' to investigate this drug subculture, and he came back with a lurid picture of decadence. At a dope party in a Piccadilly flat decorated with 'sensual-coloured carpets, curtains and hangings, low-shaded purple lights and [an] uncanny atmosphere of lassitude', the host 'lisped like a woman, had a nervous, jerky motion of the hands, and reeked overpoweringly of perfume'. A guest's hand was 'limp and clammy to the touch', with 'dull, heavy eyes, a languorous manner, and a silent, almost cat-like gait'.

Popular culture reflected such concerns about morality. In her diary, Cynthia Asquith records having seen two sensational new productions in the theatre in 1918: *Damaged Goods*, a drama about a man who discovers his fiancée is not a virgin; and 'London's greatest thrill', *The Knife*, 'a really good flesh-creeper with very clever acting by Kyrlie Bellew in the part of the drugged girl'. Within twelve months, at least three plays with drug themes were running in the West End: *Dope* by Frank Price; *Drug Fiends* by Owen Jones; and *The Girl Who Took Drugs* (aka *Soiled*) by Aimée Grattan-Clyndes. In 1919 D.W. Griffith's film *Broken Blossoms* threw Lillian Gish into a Limehouse opium den; David Garnett's novel, *Dope-Darling*, appeared; and Noel Coward, then a budding eighteen-year-old dramatist, wrote an untitled play: 'Doping is quite a hobby among society women in Paris', comments one dinner guest, to which another replies, 'I knew a girl who used to drug a lot. Her descriptions of the sensation were most interesting.' Coward, who was to draw on Billie Carleton's fate for his post-war drug play, *The Vortex*, spent Armistice Night driving in a Rolls-Royce with the opium-addicted bisexual aristocrat, Antonio Gandarillas. His great female friends of the time, Beatrice Lillie and Gertrude Lawrence, Carleton's co-stars, also mixed aristocrats (Lillie married one) with drug addicts; people who were now, in the wake of DORA's Regulation 40b, criminals, and would remain so for the rest of the century. Forty years later, when she was dining with pop stars in Cheyne Walk, Lady Diana Cooper announced, with a perceptible degree of ennui, that in her day, post-prandial cocaine was served in salt cellars.

3

The Self-Appointed Task

Billing: ... You said in this letter that the best men in the best society, members of the smartest clubs, members of Parliament, Peers, were all sodomites?
Douglas: I believed it and knew it as a fact when I wrote it; and it is a great deal truer now than then, because it has advanced tremendously.

Billing trial, 1 June 1918

In early 1918 an atmosphere of desperation seemed to rule. Despite its dreadful new technologies, total war was getting nowhere: neither poison gas, Zeppelin raids, nor armoured tanks could grind either side into submission. After three years of inconclusive, bloody fighting, dissent was growing, and such incidents as Sassoon's war protest, mutinies on the Western Front, and widespread strikes in Britain gave the government cause for concern in their determination to pursue the conflict to its bitter end. Was the population about to rise in revolt against their rulers, as they had done in Russia? Civilian England, suffering from war sickness, seemed a society in flux, its former stability gone. Instead, it was a country inhabited by shifting masses of men marching to Armageddon; a million munitions girls whose faces were turned yellow and whose fertility was endangered by their work; and mourning mothers and wives who in their grief turned to Spiritualism and the occult rather than the Christian church. The threatening shapes of deadly Zeppelins, looming death over London and other cities, merely added to the rising sense of hysteria barely contained beneath even the calmest streets. There was overt rebellion among sections of the politically-aware population, from London's Bloomsberries to the socialist-inclined working-class cadres of the Midlands, Scotland and the North. Even the Metropolitan Police went on strike that summer. The stalemate of the war augured ill for a political defeat of these tendencies. Instead, the government used the unprecedented powers of DORA to keep public opposition under control.

After the disastrous Passchendaele offensive, it seemed the Allies were about to lose the war. Generals feared it would drag on through 1919 into 1920, even with American assistance. After the Russian Revolution, Berlin's military strength had been reinforced by fifty-two battalions released from the east. They launched a massive attack, pushing the British towards the coast. In near-panic, the War Cabinet considered pulling out altogether, and evacuating the army back to England. Back in Blighty, the reverberations of what Sassoon called '... that huge thunderstorm/ Which blares and billows doom beyond the Channel' seemed tangible; the whole country seemed to be suffering shell shock at one remove. Under such strain, the national mentality was ready for an exposé of some sort. If the might of the German Army could not be defeated, then softer targets would be attacked. The first to be found were the literal enemy within: the German aliens who continued to live openly in Britain, especially in London. Ever since the anti-immigration laws of 1905, such minorities had found life in the capital difficult, and wartime pressure on them came as nothing new. But the moralists did not stop there. They rummaged about in the 'German mentality' for evidence of the decadence of that nation, and found it in the works of Krafft-Ebing and the other 'homosexualists'.

The notion of a perverse foreign conspiracy was encouraged by recent political history. In 1908, the Eulenburg scandal had rocked Germany, involving Kaiser Wilhelm and his intimate friends, 'known to their enemies as the Knights of the Round Table or the Camarilla' and hated 'not so much for their morals as for their pacifism and advocacy of friendship with France'. The parallels with the Billing trial – which would make similar allegations of a 'camarilla', secret peace negotiations and pro-German sympathies in high places – are probably not coincidental.

Prince Philip von Eulenburg, the Kaiser's 'bosom friend' since his youth, was concerned at the influence of the militarists on Wilhelm. He was also close to his fellow aide-de-camp, General Cuno von Moltke – they called each other 'Philip' and 'Tutu', and Moltke referred to Eulenburg as 'my soulmate, my old boy, and my one and only cuddly bear'. In October 1907 both were attacked by a right-wing journalist, Maximilian Harden, who called Eulenburg 'the leader of a sinister and effeminate camarilla'. The Kaiser, horrified by the allegations, dismissed his aides-de-camp. A series of court cases followed in which Magnus Hirschfeld, to his discredit, gave evidence as to Moltke's homosexual behaviour. 'The wretched Eulenburg was confronted with a boatman and a milkman, both now middle-aged, with whom he had had improper relations long ago in the 1880s ... The milkman, as it turned out, was under the impression that the word Camarilla ... was a technical term for a particular perversion.' Such terminological confusion would recur in the Billing trial. 'If the Prince swears he never did Kramilla,' he averred, 'then he's a perjured liar.' None of the evidence stuck, but Eulenburg's career was ruined. The Kaiser abandoned his old friends and was left with the militarists as his sole advisors. As a result, some historians conclude, the affair contributed to the outbreak of the war.

3. The Self-Appointed Task

Marcel Proust, who 'prided himself on his knowledge of all the prominent, undiscovered inverts of Europe', found details of the trial 'extremely comic', as did many of his compatriots, forgetting that 'Eulenburg was their friend, and that the existence of homosexuality is far from impairing the fighting qualities of an enemy nation' – a fact to which Hirschfeld's researches would attest. 'The unhappy Prince was nicknamed "Eulenbourge", Berlin became known as Sodom-on-Spree, and ... "Do you speak German?" was now among the most familiar graffiti in the public conveniences of Paris.' In Germany, the affair had a similar effect to that of the public disgrace of Wilde, producing a backlash against homosexuals, and encouraging notions of conspiracy. Unlike racism, anti-semitism and homophobia play on the fear of the superior, rather than the inferior. In Germany, the fact that both Harden and Hirschfeld were Jewish (and the latter homosexual) encouraged a conspiracy theory that there was a Jewish-homosexual plot to discredit the Kaiser and the upper classes. Indeed, after the war, the Kaiser claimed as much himself, as did German nationalists seeking to find a cause for their country's defeat.

Britain was to prove itself equally susceptible to such prejudice. War hysteria and the instability of society were fertile grounds for conspiracy theories, from rumours of Russian troops landing in Scotland, snow still on their boots, to rampant spy mania – the book *German Spies in London* sold 40,000 copies in its first week of publication in 1915. As the war brought foreigners from all ends of the Empire onto the streets of London, xenophobia increased, combining with drug and sex scandals to set the tone for a century of sexual and political exposés; from the sins of silent stars in Hollywood, through the McCarthy hearings, to the spy scandals of Burgess and Maclean. Since the nineteenth-century Austrian homosexual spy scandal of Colonel Redl, sexual perversion had played a large part in such affairs. Homosexuals in positions of influence were seen as weak-willed men susceptible to blackmail, evading disclosure because of the velvet underground, that apocryphal freemasonry who shared their 'terrible vice', as Goronwy Rees would write of Guy Burgess's treachery. (Rees's 1956 *Sunday People* exposé of his former friend shows that forty years after Billing, Britain was still obsessed with the same fears: 'Yet I must place the facts before you because they disclose a state of affairs that remains to this day a terrible danger to Britain's security.')

Such scandals were exposed and exploited by the new tabloids which had become positively overactive in wartime, billboards for the prejudices of such demagogues as Horatio Bottomley, the rabidly patriotic MP who published his own paper, *John Bull*, full of jingoism and tales of Hun atrocities. By 1918, Britain in late war crisis was ripe for a new demagogue, and Noel Pemberton Billing was more than a suitable candidate for the job. Building on his flamboyant reputation and the precedent set by Bottomley, he seized the opportunity to pursue political fame, and through a remarkable set of circumstances, coincidental and otherwise, made his mark on British history.

*

In an era of self-made men, no one was more aware of the importance of self-publicity than Billing. In May 1917, he published his autobiography, *'P.B.' The Story of His Life*. Issued by the Imperialist Press, it was paperback bound with a cover decorated in loud heroic, 'P.B.' in white on blue; price, one shilling net. A frontispiece portrayed the writer, dashingly photographed with his monocle firmly in place, a printed signature guaranteeing the authenticity of his story for his fans. A preface 'To My Readers' declared, 'my fighting principles, from my boxing days onwards, have always been to ignore defence and concentrate on attack'. The accompanying text did much to substantiate this claim.

The book is an account of a dyed-in-the-wool son of Empire, an ambitious and patriotic product of the Victorian middle class; to his supporters, a healthy breath of fresh air set to dispel the foetid miasma of decadence. Billing was born on 31 January 1881 in Finchley Road, Hampstead, the son of Charles Eardley Billing, an iron founder with works in London and Birmingham; his mother was Annie Amelia Claridge, of Coventry. Noel was the youngest of their children; one of his earliest memories was of being reprimanded by his mother for exaggeration. He was educated at a series of minor schools and colleges in London and France, from which he either absconded or was expelled. Having left Craven College, Highgate, he got a job in the City, but left after throwing ink at 'a peculiarly offensive German clerk'. He went off to sea on the *Bampshire*, bound for Delagoa Bay, South Africa, thence to Durban, taking odd jobs in Natal and having adventures in 'Zululand': 'There was a good deal of faction fighting and internal unrest among the niggers just then.' Having fought in the Anglo-Boer War, Billing returned to England 'obsessed with the idea of the Munitions of War'. 'I invented many and patented some', he wrote, 'more particularly a gun-carriage ... and various other items of military equipment and utility.' Billing's passion for invention was in accord with the age of technology, a dash to invent anything and everything; in that, he was a Futurist of his profession. He took a brief turn on the stage with George Conquest's touring company (a drama with the appropriately patriotic title, *Serving the Queen*), before becoming fascinated by the developing motor car industry. He returned to South Africa full of enthusiasm, publishing his first periodical, the *British South Africa Auto-car* – a bold step as there were as yet no motor cars in South Africa.

Billing also took to singing under the stage name of Noel Pemberton, playing in musical comedies in Kimberley, Cape Town and Johannesburg. He settled in Johannesburg, aged twenty-one, living a good life. He liked the city and South Africa, and distinguished himself one day by intervening in a street brawl – 'seeing a big bully dishing out injustice' – nearly losing his hand in the process, he claimed. But Britain beckoned and Billing returned to London, where he became manager of the Richmond Theatre and wrote his first play, *Memory*, unsuccessfully produced at Greenwich. He subsequently toured in *The Geisha* in the North and Midlands, before coming back to London and a flat in the Adelphi. It is notable that a man with such an extensive experience of the theatre should become a champion of homophobia; perhaps Billing's experiences in the profession led him to 'unsavoury' brushes with 'perverts'.

Billing's parents were then living at Hyde Park Mansions, and at dinner there with his sister in 1903, he met her friend, Lilian Maud Schweitzer, daughter of Theodore Henry Schweitzer of Swansea* and Sarah Louisa Montague of Edinburgh. With characteristic impulsiveness, he asked Lilian to marry him. She said no, but Billing was a persistent man. Within a fortnight, they were indeed married. Soon after, he resumed inventing, producing a machine for making and packing 'self-lighting' cigarettes, which he took a shop in Bond Street to sell. This dangerous-sounding innovation did not spark the West End, however, and the Billings moved to Hampstead, where Noel started the *Hampstead Social Review*. This too failed, so Billing sold up and moved to Crawley where he built himself a bungalow on a ten-acre site. He also made all the furniture, dug a well, built 'little brick dairies' and 'tried my hand at amateur farming' – Billing was never loath to try his hand at anything. In such projects, he rejoiced in the friendship of another man, as he recorded under the sub-heading, 'My Many Mates': 'I always worked with a mate, another boy who stuck loyally by me right through, even to the "owning up", which, as a point of honour, was always the immediate sequel to our escapades.'

It was now that Billing became interested in the exciting and romantic new science of aeronautics. He and his long-suffering wife moved to East Grinstead in 1904, where he built a glider and nearly killed himself when he jumped off the roof of his house on its inaugural flight. Undaunted by technical hitches he persevered, inventing a 'man-lifting glider' (as well as 'the Digit Typewriter' which could be worked with the index finger). With most of their valuables in pawnshops, Billing returned to the stage and a four-week tour with Mrs Patrick Campbell. But he kept the inventions coming: a petrol automatic gun; a

---

* Schweitzer was a cousin of Albert Schweitzer, the well known philosopher, theologian, missionary and musician whose zeal – and moral concerns – both contrasted and compared with Billing's.

cloth-measuring contraption; and a pencil which calculated 'as you write'. He also had ideas of setting up a 'State Service Club' equipped with his latest invention, the 'Proxy Phone'.

As soon as he had acquired enough capital, Billing returned to aviation. Building an aerodrome at South Fambridge, he began constructing aircraft and attracted the serious interest of other pioneers such as Howard Wright with a light monoplane which left the ground for sixty feet – the first British-made aeroplane to do so. But the business failed to take off in a similar manner, and another period of itinerancy followed: from expeditions to the Riviera to work a system at the Monte Carlo casinos, to property developing on the Sussex coast. But gradually Billing was being drawn to politics; his determination was such that he first trained as a barrister, enrolling as a student of the Middle Temple, and taking chambers at 3 Essex Court. He published his political ideas as *An Empire in Embryo*, proposing a 'national science' of 'Endowment by Increment', sickness benefit, accident insurance and a pension at fifty; such notions of 'imperial socialism' belonged to the radical right of British politics, with whom Billing was evidently already acquainted. The scheme was submitted to Austen Chamberlain and was covered in the press, but its author did little to benefit from such publicity. He was now living on bread and cocoa, 'which, remembering the effect cocoa is said to have on the liver, may account for my occasional attacks of passionate irritability today'. It was rather more likely that Billing owed his personality to pathological and psychological quirks rather than to the cocoa bean.

His one asset was a steam yacht, the *Violet*, bought in Southampton for fifty pounds, which he sailed to the Isle of Wight, intent on selling it. Billing's account of the trip is hilarious, *Boy's Own Paper* stuff (indeed, most of Billing's life reads like an Edwardian comic), 'with my wife steering, myself stoking and driving, and an adventurous young friend of my wife's as passenger, Miss Dorothy Dear'. Instead of crossing the Solent, they ended up on the other side of the Channel, off Le Havre. Eventually they moored in Cowes, where Billing sold his yacht for £275. The broker dealing with the trade was so impressed by Billing's intrepid adventures that he and Billing set up a ship-running business together on Southampton Water – which he financed.

It was Billing's most successful period: 'Oh, those buccaneer days!' But he was seldom content to sit still for long, and in 1912 Billing bet Frederick Handley Page, another aviation pioneer, that he could learn to fly and acquire his Royal Aero Club Aviator's Certificate within twenty-four hours. In the event, he did it between 5.45 am and breakfast at the Vickers School of Flying at Brooklands – and duly won £500. 'There was only one moment of anxiety during his first solo [flight]. That was when his aircraft suddenly dropped like a stone for a hundred and fifty feet. Billing's explanation of the error was simple. He had taken his hands off the controls to wave to his wife.'

In 1912, using the capital he had accrued from yacht-dealing and with an additional financial backer, Billing bought a disused coal wharf on wasteland close to the Floating Bridge ferry on the river Itchen at Southampton (he was living on a boat moored on the river). Billing intended to produce fast launches and marine aircraft, but became obsessed with the notion of flying over the sea, rather than through it: 'a boat that will fly, not an aeroplane that will float'. Hence his term 'Supermarine', a sort of Futurist antonym and a typically Billing invention, full of modernistic zeal and aplomb. Nor was this project as hopelessly quixotic as it may have seemed: 'Supermarine' would prefix the names of some of the most famous British aircraft of coming years. Billing's first flying-boat, the Supermarine P.B.1, was displayed at the Aero Show at Olympia in March 1914. Its proud designer posed next to his aircraft, in silk hat and frock coat, his elbow resting on its fish-shaped hull and his hand resting pensively on his chin.

Unfortunately, the craft refused to take off. Billing secured an Admiralty order for twelve biplanes – although not built to his designs, of which there were many; as aviation historians noted, 'a bewildering series of unorthodox project ideas poured from the fertile brain of Pemberton Billing'. Had it not been for Billing's eccentricity, short attention span and lack of application, his inventions may well have had proper success. However, Billing did secure an option from Germany for two P.B.7 flying-boats; he noted that trials held at 'aero shows' on Southampton Water were attended by 'alert Germans'.

In August 1914 Britain had just 100 aircraft; and only forty-three of them were serviceable. Government lack of interest in his work frustrated Billing greatly. 'It's a dangerous thing to criticise incompetence in Authority even to your acquaintances', Billing confided to his readers. 'Do you know that? I do! Don't make a hobby of it, it's a life's work!' However, Billing was in close contact with Murray Sueter, the chief of the Air Department of the Admiralty, who certainly patronised the works: a number of Billing's designs were given the governmental 'E' for experimental prefix. (Billing's air crusade would have brought him into contact with Leo Charlton and 'Splash' Ashmore, to whom Billing's designs for anti-Zeppelin aircraft must have been shown, and rejected. If Billing knew of either's predilections, he would surely have taken it as confirmation of his theories about homosexuals in high places.) By the outbreak of war, Billing had decided to build a single-seat fighting aeroplane, P.B.9; Supermarine's first landplane and the distant ancestor of the Spitfire.* The

---

* R.J. Mitchell, the designer of the Spitfire, joined the firm in 1916.

first aeroplane to be built in nine days, it was dubbed by Billing, with his usual exaggeration, the 'Seven Day Bus' (subsequent research has shown that Billing's claims to have drawn up the designs himself in a day are untrue). But behind such projects was political intent, as aviation historians note: 'It had now become obvious that Pemberton Billing used the exercise of designing and building a small aeroplane of this type to create a political lever capable of influencing the sensitive emotions of the British public during the confusions of a democracy going to war.'

Billing had resumed his pursuit of a parliamentary career. The Conservative Chief Whip, Lord Edward Talbot, evidently loath to entertain this maverick, showed little enthusiasm. Billing 'had long considered the Party system rotten' anyway, and when a vacancy arose at Mile End, he decided to finance his own fight. Using 4 Elm Court, Middle Temple as campaign headquarters, he adopted his slogan, 'in support of strong Air Policy' and paraded his aircraft round Mile End, aided in his plan to 'demolish the War Office aviation policy of the day' by his friend, C.G. Grey of *The Aeroplane* magazine. Despite his high profile campaign, Billing lost to a Coalition candidate. 'What a political education!' he wrote in 1917. 'The administration of the country appeared to me then – as it does now – as a sorry and sordid play, in which the politicians are the actors, the Pressmen are the dramatists, vested interests pack the house, and – the public pay the price!' It was an histrionic simile in which he would become complicit.

Vexed by the lack of official interest in his aircraft, Billing 'went off in a huff to do some service with the naval air arm', leaving his business at Woolston in charge of Hubert Scott-Paine, an ambitious young man with red hair, another of Billing's 'mates'. This part of Billing's career is rather mysterious. According to records, Billing served in the Royal Naval Air Service, 1914-16, and retired as Squadron Commander (a title which suited his swaggering mien). He was said to have organised the first bombing raid on Germany, at the huge Zeppelin base at Friedrichshafen; the Germans replied with a raid on Dover and the Thames at Christmas, 1914. However, his autobiography makes no mention of his service record, either for security reasons, or because of later criticism by government sources that he inflated his achievements in the service to political ends.

In February 1916, Billing fought the East Hertfordshire by-election as an Independent candidate. It was a case of David versus Goliath, he maintained, intimating that the powers-that-were wanted him excluded from Parliament, 'a certain London daily – notoriously under Government control ... had written four or five columns of inspired and virulent abuse of one ...'. Despite this, he won the election on 10 March. He gave up his interest in the Supermarine-Aviation Works, 'in accordance with my fixed principle that no Member of

Parliament should be involved in any business engaged in Government contracts, and profiting by the war – whether he puts "Limited" after his name or not.' The factory came under government control for the remainder of the war.

Billing took his Commons oath on 14 March 1916. 'My first sensation was almost exactly similiar to that I experienced when I first entered the rooms at Monte Carlo. The whole plan seemed so absolutely unreal ...' Billing's maiden speech on air power got good coverage in the press, and he moved to Hertford House in Hertford 'in fulfilment of the promise I had made to my constituents'. Billing's soapbox autobiography ends with characteristic exhortations under sub-headings in bold type: 'The Self-Appointed Task', 'Still Striving', 'The Root of Evil'. 'I shall struggle on with my self-appointed task,' he told his followers, 'spending my strength, my ability, my means, in the service of my country, and in the direction that, as I see it, appears most necessary. That's all!'

*

As a new and self-made politician, proudly independent of any party, Billing was able to take advantage of the uncertain politics of the time. Politicians in high and low office alike were taking the brunt of the criticism for the way the war was being fought. Asquith was particularly blamed by Commons backbenchers for the ill-conduct of the war; it was rumoured that he had been willing to accept the German offer of peace in the autumn of 1915. His colleagues' opposition brought about Asquith's downfall, and Lloyd George's coalition came to power on a ticket of 'Win-the-war' – at any price, it seemed – but did little to quell the misgivings of the backbenchers.

In his short career as an MP, Billing became known as the 'Member for Air'; he acknowledged the *double entendre*. He joined forces with Lord Montagu of Beaulieu and William Joynson-Hicks (later Lord Brentford) to agitate for a government inquiry into the flying services organisation, a campaign which brought about the Air Ministry in 1917, and subsequently, the birth of the RAF. His campaign was very popular with the public, and very unpopular with the government; Billing was exposing them to deserved criticism. In the Commons on 22 March 1916, Billing had remarked that British machines were referred to as 'Fokker fodder': 'I don't wish to touch a dramatic note this afternoon', said Billing – and went on to do so: 'If I did I would suggest that quite a number of our gallant officers in the Royal Flying Corps have been murdered rather than killed.' Such high-flown challenges were not only embarrassing; they required swift retaliatory action. The government selected their ace, F.W. Danchester (a member of the Government Advisory Committee on Aeronautics), not only to shoot down such claims, but also to prove Billing a liar. Under a punning newspaper sub-heading, 'Mr Billing As Inventor', Danchester enumerated six different occasions during Billing's election speeches in which he had made false claims; he had not designed a working aircraft to fight Zeppelins, nor did it take twelve months to persuade the Admiralty to build it.* 'On February 26 Mr Billing stated: "I have had 18 months of the war on two fronts"; to which the official reply was "Mr Billing was 12 months in the Royal Naval Air Service. He has only spent a short time abroad, and has never flown in any raid or in the face of the enemy".'

The mystery of Billing's war service was revealed; embarrassing facts for the all-action champion of the people. 'On March 3 Mr Billing said: "In throwing up my commission as a squadron commander I threw up a considerable income. Squadron commanders are well paid. I threw up that and a very great deal more, and I am going on if East Herts will not have me." ' The facts, said Danchester, were that Billing applied to resign his commission as flight lieutenant at the end of December 1915, 'on the grounds that he wished to devote his services to work more likely to prove of value to the country than the duties he was performing'. His resignation was accepted on 5 January 1916, as from 2 January, and he was given the rank of squadron commander as from 1 January. 'Therefore, he was – nominally only – squadron commander for one day, viz., from January 1 to 2, and was not actually appointed until after that day elapsed. Had he remained in the Service, it would have been with the rank of lieutenant, at the pay of £1 a day, which is considerably less than that of a member of Parliament.'

Billing refused to be deterred by such minor matters of fact. On 1 May 1916 the *Daily Mail* reported that 'Mr Pemberton Billing's air policy was approved by a meeting of almost 4,000 men and women at the Albert Hall on Saturday afternoon.' It was a popular venue for rousing right-wingers. 'Mr Arnold White presided, and the presence of such an audience on the Saturday half-holiday in beautiful weather was a remarkable demonstration of the discontent with the present air service. Mr Billing, who had an enthusiastic reception, declared that this country was only a third-class air-Power. Germany … not only beat the Allies at the front, but had machines enough to spare to carry the air war into their respective countries. He had heard that Germany had just launched her 100th Zeppelin … Each raid threw us into a state of confusion and muddled impotence … It was time to take the conduct of the war out of the hands of the politicians and place it in the hands of soldiers, sailors and statesmen.' To this end, Billing

---

* The P.B. 29E 'Zeppelin destroyer' – ironically equipped with Austro-Daimler engines – was a quadruplane designed in 1915; it crashed soon after its first flight. An improved version, the P.B.31E, known as the Supermarine NightHawk, was built soon after, and two were ordered by the Admiralty (although only one was actually built, and that after Supermarine Aviation Works Ltd had been taken over by Hubert Scott-Paine).

proposed an 'Imperial Council of Nine', a war council of military and political representatives drawn from the Empire as well as home, whose aim would be 'to secure for this country the same supremacy in the air as our forefathers had secured for it on the sea ... The nation that was supreme in the air would in future dictate to the world.'

Such prophetic words did not impress Billing's political superiors, who regarded him as a loose cannon. 'This man is dangerous,' said Lloyd George. 'He doesn't want anything.' From his home in Hertford, Billing ran his self-promoting broadsheet, the *Imperialist*, at a loss, making moralistic statements about the corrupting nature of advertising. In truth it was impossible to attract advertisers because his inflammatory articles were couched in such terms as to provoke libel suits – still an affordable occupation for a gentleman, as Lord Alfred Douglas's frequent clashes with Robert Ross show. Billing relied on friends in high places for financial and moral support; the press baron and Minister of Information, Lord Beaverbrook, being a notable benefactor.

Billing was a very visible, vocal politician, appealing to voters who saw a 'real man'; a man of action, no dry, stale politician with vested interests. His private life matched his cavalier profile. Billing was an archetypal playboy, 'fascinated by fast aircraft, fast speed-boats, fast cars and fast women – he was highly attractive to women'. He was certainly a handsome man: tall, thin and sleek with high cheekbones, long expressive hands and a nervous energy that was evidently magnetic. He drove a lemon yellow Rolls-Royce and dressed in 'unusual clothes' – a contemporary noted that he sported long pointed collars 'without the usual accompaniment of a necktie' – and generally wore the air of a political, and occasionally pugilistic maverick. On one occasion in July 1917, Billing made a slighting reference to army officers in the Commons. Colonel Archer-Shee mildly defended his fellow officers, but the combative Billing leapt to his feet. 'If the gallant Member wishes to be offensive to me personally, I hope he will repeat it outside so that I may be able to deal with it.' Later that evening, the police were forced to separate the two honourable members as they rolled about on the grass in New Palace Yard, punching each other. Billing was outraged at the interference. 'This is a private fight,' he told the officers. The following day he challenged Archer-Shee to twenty rounds in the boxing ring at the National Sports Club, the loser to pay one hundred guineas to the Red Cross. The colonel declined the offer.

Billing and his campaign may have appeared thoroughly upstanding and decently British, but beneath the almost cosy eccentricity of this quixotic crusader was a deeper, darker undercurrent; the political radicals from whom he took his ideas, and with whom he had become closely associated, were

51

certainly not mild eccentrics. In fact, they were busy inventing a virulent British strain of fascism.

*

During the war the extreme right wing of British politics was beginning to coalesce into a discrete group, product of the 'social tensions and ideas fostered by an age of modernisation and change'; they were the legacy of the Empire and the problems its world colonisation introduced. The immediate pre-war era had seen Liberal Britain challenged by radicalism: labour unrest, syndicalism, the Suffragette movement and the Ulster Volunteer Force. In opposition rose the 'Die-Hard' Unionists championed by the Duke of Northumberland; reactionary representatives of the landed gentry who believed in compulsory military service, social welfare, expanded military and naval strength, an end to 'alien' immigration, and armed resistance to Irish Home Rule. Tellingly, for present and future events, their attitude towards Germany was ambivalent. While they feared Germany's fast-growing military and industrial strength as a threat to the Empire, at the same time they admired its administrative efficiency, social welfare programme and state role in national development; they wanted Britain to go the same way. Indeed, Joseph Chamberlain, an influential figure on the radical right, proposed an Anglo-Saxon alliance of Britain, Germany and the United States in 1899, an idea resurrected by the British National Front in the 1980s.

In recent years Britain seemed to be losing its grip on world politics; the Die-Hards cited the fact that it took five times the number of British troops to suppress the Boer guerillas. They were afraid that Germany had superseded Britain in Europe, a notion which had been popularly stoked by literary fantasies such as George Chesney's *Battle of Dorking* (1871) and culminated in Saki's *When William Came* (1914) which imagined a German invasion and encouraged 'spy mania'. The anti-alien note set by the (largely unnecessary) immigration laws of 1905, was followed by the Marconi scandal of 1912 and overt anti-semitism in politics. Cecil Chesterton, brother of G.K. Chesterton, edited *Eye-Witness*, a 'gossip-sheet' which alleged that certain high-ranging figures in Asquith's cabinet – including the Postmaster-General, Herbert Samuel, the Liberal Chief Whip, Lloyd George and Rufus Isaacs – had bought Marconi shares at a time when Samuel was awarding the company a major government contract. The accused sued for libel in a ten-day, highly publicised trial. Chesterton was found guilty but fined only £100; the public were left with the impression that Jewish interests in the government were self-seeking.

Nationalism associated all too easily with anti-semitism. The huge leap in population growth of the nineteenth century, migrations and contacts with other racial groups, had led to theories of eugenics – subscribed to even by intellectual socialists such as H.G.Wells – which advocated drastic and racist measures to accomplish restriction. Others such as Baden-Powell and Kipling were concerned that western civilisation would dissolve if its white blood was thinned. Meanwhile vague anti-semitism developed into fully-fledged hatred, derived from specious and elaborate notions of Jewish conspiracy such as *The Protocols of the Elders of Zion*. Translated by V.E. Marsden, correspondent of the *Morning Post*, the book purported to prove the existence of an age-old Zionist plot to take over Europe; in fact, it was an invention of Tsarist secret police in Russia, a 'farrago of nonsense' given plausibility by the events of the First World War. Such notions thrived as eugenic purity was espoused by Chesterton and Hilaire Belloc in *Eye-Witness* (which achieved a circulation of 20,000, rivalling the largest-selling weekly, the *Spectator*). Their National League for Clean Government, founded in 1913, prompted the resignation of such influential Jewish businessmen as Ernest Cassel and Edgar Speyer. A strong Jewish identification with Liberalism further tainted Asquith in the eyes of the right.

During the war, the radical right sought victory without compromise; ironically, their *bête noire*, the left-wing Lloyd George, seemed the only man likely to achieve this. The Unionists backed Lloyd George's coalition government, but in the continuing stalemate of 1917-18, the right became restless, and campaigned for Lloyd George's removal. In 1917, when the Russian Revolution strengthened the Die-Hards' anxieties, two Tory MPs, Henry Page Croft and Sir Richard Cooper, founded the National Party with the backing of such aristocrats as Lord Beresford and Lord Montagu of Beaulieu. Page Croft became National Party member of Parliament for Christchurch, and noted that in a recent article in *The Times* entitled 'The Ferment of Revolution' 'it was suggested that there was a danger of the vast mass of the people becoming revolutionary in their ideas'. This he found an insult to the working classes.

The party had their headquarters at 22 King Street, St. James's; it was perhaps no coincidence that Horatio Bottomley lived at 26 King Street. Protesting against the coalition government, they advocated conscription up to fifty, closure of all German-owned businesses, internment of enemy aliens, conscription in Ireland and counter air raids against German towns. They also campaigned against the honours system and Lloyd George's use of patronage. This was very much Billing territory. He picked up on the literary, journalistic and political notions of the radical right: proposals for Jewish ghettoes and yellow star badges; anti-German and anti-alien strictures; moves against the sale of honours and internal corruption; and, crucially, took them to the masses.

In June 1917 Billing founded the Vigilante Society, its self-proclaimed aims 'the promotion of purity in public life, the upholding of political honour, and the fearless exposure of corruption in the conduct of all public offices ...'. No public servant should accept 'honour, title or dignity, or any office or place of profit'. Billing's campaign was fed by the able prejudices of notorious right-wing radicals. His co-founder in the Vigilante Society was National Party member Henry Hamilton Beamish. Born in 1874, the son of an admiral who was aide-de-camp to Queen Victoria, Beamish was typical of the protofascists with his military background and restless, adventurous life in the British Empire and colonies, where he experienced the practice of white supremacy. Like Billing, Beamish had served in the Anglo-Boer War, and subsequently with the Natal Regiment of South Africa Infantry. 'In South Africa he came to the conclusion that the Boer War had been fought for the benefit of Jewish gold and diamond financiers, who were exploiting British imperialism for their own international purposes. This, combined with the presence of Jewish revolutionaries in the Bolshevik uprising, and the alleged Jewish capitalist funding of the communists from Wall Street, convinced him that there was a plot to undermine civilisation and the British Empire.' Since the Marconi scandal, Beamish had seen the government as dominated by Jews, with Rufus Isaacs, Sir Alfred Mond and Edwin Montagu as Lloyd George's advisors; Britain was now ruled by a 'Jewalition' and Jews were responsible for a quarter of the war's casualties.

A fellow traveller in nascent fascism, and another founder of the Vigilante Society, was the elderly and sinister Dr J.H. Clarke. He was chief consulting physician to the Homeopathic Hospital, Bloomsbury, a profession at odds with his self-proclaimed mission to protect England from the Church of Rome. He also adhered to an unpleasant strain of scientific, Malthusian racism.

The Vigilantes' moral campaign was pursued in the pages of the *Imperialist*. Like Horatio Bottomley's *John Bull*, the newspaper was in effect a sounding-board for Billing's prejudices, with pages devoted to his actions and questions in Parliament. Elsewhere, there were 'Toasts of the Empire' eulogies to such figures as Rudyard Kipling and Henry Page Croft (who had recently become Deputy-Lieutenant of Hertford), and pieces with headlines such as 'Symbols of Shame', dwelling on

the 'flapper' scandal, one of the most grievous and piteous of the many social scandals of this tragic time. Do these thoughtless chits, little more than children, realise that the regimental badges they display so exultantly, are in many cases nothing less than symbols of shame, obtained in exchange for more or less dangerous familiarities? The whole thing is significant of the craving for excitement which has become a national disease, a national menace, largely fostered by the swagger restaurants where these foolish children, like their still more foolish – and wicked – elders, imagine that they are 'seeing life'. If all the smart restaurants were closed down, the 'flapper' trade would probably close down also, and the flappers, disdaining the more humble eating-houses they were wont to frequent, may even return to their homes, which they left to imperil, if not to sacrifice, their chastity. Though what sort of homes and what sort of mothers can these girls have? The answer would supply an explanation of, but no excuse for, our national decadence and degradation.

In wartime, even the notion of restaurants seemed decadent.

In October 1917 the Vigilantes put up their first election candidate, at East Islington: Alfred Baker, Town Clerk of Hertford and Treasurer of the Society of Vigilantes. Their campaign slogan ran:

> HINDER THE HUNS
> PARALYSE PROFITEERS
> PURIFY POLITICS
> WIN THE WAR

The election was held on 23 October 1917, 'On Friday night, while the Zeppelin raid was in progress, Mr Baker and Mr Pemberton-Billing drove round in the famous car, and addressed the crowds overflowing from the "Tube" exits; and tragic it was, every evening to see, as dusk drew on, poor women with babes in arms and tiny children clustering round them, lingering wistfully round the Tube entrances fearful of what the night might bring forth.' Baker lost; Smallwood the Coalition candidate was returned; and the *Imperialist* of 27 October offered a £500 reward 'to any person furnishing evidence to support a successful petition under "The Corrupt Practices Act" '.

The defeat encouraged more dramatic tactics. Billing was determined to expose the decadent spirit sapping Britain's strength, and to do so he sought the assistance of a man eminently suited to the task. Arnold White – editor of the *English Review* and accomplished nationalist – was then aged seventy, an 'international expert on anti-semitism' and instrumental in advising the Russian government on plans for a forced Jewish colony in Argentina. White believed that there was a secret force at work in the British government working against the national interest for a German victory. His ideas contributed greatly to the concept of the Billing Black Book campaign; indeed, his interest in the British navy may explain the particular details of shipyard entrapment in the Black Book, and betray his involvement in the affair.

The unrestrained titles of White's published works announce his preoccupations: *The Navy and Its Story*, *The Modern Jew*, *Efficiency and Empire*, *Is The Kaiser Insane?* and *The Hidden Hand*. The latter was particularly popular at the time, its lurid black cover and shocking red lettering a stern warning to all patriots. When Billing reprinted White's latest article, 'Efficiency and Vice' in the *Imperialist*, it provided the keynote of his campaign with its timely if irrational attack on German decadence. 'Of the vices of the Cities of the Plain, Palestine taught nothing to Potsdam', wrote White, expressing the firm belief that 'England will best Germany because Germany is wicked, and the English, if not salt of the earth, are "good" men'. Germany was in a state of moral degeneracy owing to the power of sexologists such as Otto Weininger – who had committed suicide – and Iwan Bloch. 'Weininger's theory is that women cannot love ... have made no ideal of man to correspond with the male conception of the Madonna ... The German conception of women is lower than that of the Zulus in Tschaaka's day', he summarised, conflating racism and xenophobia for readers whose knowledge of South Africa was defined by reports of the British victory in the Anglo-Boer War.* Bloch, the German Jewish sexologist and supporter of Hirschfeld, wanted the repeal of Paragraph 175 – which forbade homosexual activity – and estimated that 56,000 Berliners were homosexual.

'How does all this German garbage, which I am forced to quote, affect the course of the war?' asked White. He alleged that the London District Command employed intelligence officers to counteract 'the infection of Londoners, especially young soldiers, by the doctrine of the German homosexual'. White's evocation of family values and xenophobia chime uneasily with more recent politics: 'Men are willing to die for their homes, but if the conception of home life is replaced by the Kultur of Urnings, the spirit of the Anglo-Saxon world wilts and perishes.' It is also a rather cynical comment on how to fight (or lose) a war of attrition.

The intrepid officers of the London District Command were unfortunately hampered by the restrictions of common law. 'Londoner urnings have more in common with Teuton urnings than their own countrymen. Espionage is punished by death at the Tower of London, but there is a form of invasion which is as deadly as espionage: the systematic seduction of young British soldiers by the German urnings and their agents ... Failure to intern all Germans is due to the invisible hand that protects urnings of enemy race ...' Thus did White's theory of sexual subversion set the stage for the *Imperialist*'s far-reaching conspiracy. 'When the blond beast is an urning, he commands the urnings in other lands.' White evoked a potent image of an unnatural and inhuman being; a Nietzschean superman, perhaps: an ironic presentiment of the standfast vision of the fully-fledged fascists to come, and doubly ironic because of its homoerotic overtones. These German-sponsored agents of corruption were 'moles. They burrow. They plot ... Father, Mother and children are the microcosm of the little grey homes

---

*The Zulu emperor supposedly had abortions performed on his seraglio so that no heir would threaten his position.

that make the British Empire. The poison gas of the suicide [another uncomfortably prescient image], Weininger, and the champion of the urnings, Ivan Bloch [*sic*], reveal the nature, the geist, which seems not wholly uncongenial to some of our British Teutophiles.'

However, by publishing White's wild claims, and numerous libellous attacks on 'Teutophile' or German Jewish public figures (who refused to rise to the bait), Billing and his colleagues unfortunately also scuppered their primary source of finance. Put off by such ranting (and probably prompted by highly-placed targets of the paper), Beaverbrook withdrew his support from the *Imperialist* in January 1918 – to Billing's extreme annoyance. He was not a man to be treated thus, and soon was lambasting Beaverbrook – the hand that had fed him – in the privileged confines of the House, where he could say what he liked.

Billing had noted in his autobiography his need for a mate in his projects. It was fatal for this affair that a disaffected and mentally-disturbed young American stepped into this role. Harold Sherwood Spencer had just been invalided out of both the British Army and the British Secret Service; a sallow, hard-faced man with an overly well-clipped moustache, deep-set staring eyes and a vaguely neurotic air, he was labouring under a sense of injustice, having been badly treated by his superior officers and higher authorities who had refused to take seriously his claims of German conspiracy. He was thus spoiling for a fight when he was introduced to Billing by Beamish at a National Party meeting. At this meeting the story of the Black Book emerged – and from there, it was but a short step to the inflammatory pages of the *Imperialist*. An article in the edition of 26 January 1918, headlined the 'The Forty-Seven Thousand' announced:

> There exists in the Cabinet Noir of a certain German Prince a book compiled by the Secret Service from reports of German agents who have infested this country for the past 20 years, agents so vile and spreading such debauchery and such lasciviousness as only German minds can conceive and only German bodies execute.

The piece – written by Billing – alleged that 'there had been many persons who had been prevented from putting their full strength into the war by corruption and blackmail and fear of exposure; and that there were reasons for supposing that the Germans, with their usual efficiency, were making use of the most productive and the cheapest methods ... [T]he dossier ... was in course of preparation, and when it was ready the necessary steps to bring some of those people to justice would be taken ... More than 1,000 pages are filled with the names mentioned by German agents in their reports. There are the names of 47,000 English men and women', practitioners of vices 'all decent men thought had perished in Sodom and Lesbia'. 'The most sacred secrets of State' were threatened, and German agents 'under the guise of indecent liaisons' had obtained information about the British Fleet; 'the thought that 47,000 English men and women were held in enemy bondage through fear calls all clean spirits to mortal combat. All the horrors of shells and gas and pestilence introduced by the Germans in their open warfare would have but a fraction of the effect in exterminating the manhood of Britain as the plan by which they have already destroyed the first 47,000.'

It is a most catholic list. The names of Privy Councillors, wives of Cabinet Ministers, even Cabinet Ministers themselves, diplomats, poets, bankers, editors, newspaper proprietors, and members of His Majesty's Household. The officer who discovered this book while on special service briefly outlined for me its stupefying contents. In the beginning of the book is a precis of general instructions regarding the propagation of evils which all decent men thought had perished in Sodom and Lesbia. The blasphemous compilers even speak of the Groves and High Places mentioned in the Bible ... As an example of the thoroughness with which the German agents work, lists of public houses and bars were given which had been successfully demoralised. These could then be depended upon to spread vice with the help of only one fixed agent. To secure those whose social standing would suffer from frequenting public places, comfortable flats were taken and furnished in erotic manner. Paphian* photographs were distributed, while equivocal pamphlets were printed as the anonymous work of well-known writers.

Agents were specially enlisted in the navy, particularly in the engine rooms. These had their special instructions. Incestuous bars were established in Portsmouth and Chatham. In these meeting places the stamina of British sailors was undermined. More dangerous still, German agents, under the guise of indecent liaison, could obtain information as to the disposition of the Fleet. Even to loiter in the streets was not immune. Meretricious agents of the Kaiser were stationed at such places as Marble Arch and Hyde Park Corner. In this black book of sin details were given of the unnatural defloration of children who were drawn to the parks by the summer evening concerts ... Wives of men in supreme position were entangled. In Lesbian ecstasy the most sacred secrets of State were betrayed. The sexual peculiarities of members of the peerage were used as a leverage to open fruitful fields for espionage.

This extraordinary piece of journalism with its sensational sub-headings, 'Harlots on the Wall', 'Spreading Debauchery', 'Sodom and Lesbia', drew on deepseated fears and prejudices: the threat of the foreign and the sexually aberrant. It sought to burn its allegations into popular public imagination by employing the same sort of rhetoric used by White: 'The First 47,000' was a parody of Ian

---

* 'Paphian – *adj*. pertaining to Paphos in Cyprus, sacred to Aphrodite: lascivious. – *n.* a native of Paphos: a votary of Aphrodite: a whore.' *Chambers Twentieth Century Dictionary*.

Hay's *The First Hundred Thousand*, a patriotic and highly popular tribute to Kitchener's army published in 1915; a similarly popular title was *The First Seven Divisions*, which 'thrilled' Cynthia Asquith when she read it in April 1916. The notion of the Black Book also drew on the popular conception of Teutonic efficiency in matters of cataloguing, a predilection perhaps borne out by Krafft-Ebing, Magnus Hirschfeld, and, some time later, the National Socialist Party.

The outrageousness of the piece was not mere sensation for its own sake, however. Billing and Spencer deliberately invited a libel suit in order to publicise this peril to national stability, and draw out the enemies within. Yet the hoped-for writs did not appear. Although Spencer would claim they received many letters of support for their attack, the article was greeted with hilarity in the trenches in France, and copies sent to ministers and government departments received no reply. Obviously, stronger methods were required to worm out this decadent corruption.

On 9 February the *Imperialist* was reborn as the *Vigilante*. The change came when Billing was 'repeatedly urged by certain enthusiasts to alter the name of the paper so as to indicate, by its title alone, its connection with the movement for Purity in Public Life known as the "Vigilante" movement ... Not to be confounded,' added Billing, '... with the objects aimed at by the various "Vigilance" Societies which appear to be limited to the suppression of sexual vice.' The revamp gave the newspaper renewed impetus. With headings such as 'Scotland Yard Awake', the *Vigilante* turned bitterly on Beaverbrook, whose ancestry it questioned: 'Isaacs, Aitken or Beaverbrook', mused the new edition, noting that the Minister of Information's surname, Aitken, 'some people believe is derived from an original name of Isaacs. If this is true, he belongs to the same tribe as our Lord Chief Justice Ambassador, and the ruling and representing of Britain has become a close tribal affair.' The paper warned against an 'alien controlled Press'. But the *Vigilante*'s best chance of causing a nationwide uproar came the next day, 10 February, when the *Sunday Times* advertised a performance of Oscar Wilde's *Salome*. The celebrated dancer Maud Allan was to play the lead role, and the play would be produced by the *Sunday Times*'s own dramatic critic, the flamboyant and well-known man of theatre, Jack Grein.

Jack (Jacob) Thomas Grein was born in Amsterdam on 11 October 1862 (his mother was Jewish), and came to work in London in 1885; ten years later he was naturalised as an Englishman. Grein had begun his career as a businessman and diplomat in the City of London, but now combined such duties with those of playwright, manager, and critic. Inspired by Ibsen, and Antoine's *Théâtre Libre*, he had founded the Independent Theatre Club in 1891. 'The Ibsen movement became more mobile ...' wrote Max Beerbohm, chronicler of the era, 'when a very dynamic and fervent little Dutchman, J.T. Grein, who was not at all content with being "something in the City" and being also Consul for Bolivia, rushed in, founded the Independent Theatre and produced *Ghosts*.' Their version, translated by William Archer,* was hated by the critics – particularly by Clement Scott, Archer's rival, who famously condemned the play in the *Daily Telegraph* as 'a wretched deplorable loathsome history'. In 1892 the group produced the first Shaw play to be seen in London, *Widower's Houses*, and remained devoted to plays thought 'modern', 'psychological' or 'decadent', many of them German. Grein's links with Germany were strengthened when in 1900 he founded the German Theatre in London, to realise 'cherished dreams of tightening the bonds between nations by the interchange of dramatic art ... He contemplated with some surprise the extent of the German colony in London and the fact that they had not ere this, clamoured for what he instantly decided was a long-felt want.' Grein made various trips to Berlin, and in 1907 persuaded Beerbohm Tree to take his company on tour there, inspired by the Kaiser's comments 'referring to the drama as a mediator between nations'. Wilhelm awarded Grein the Order of the Red Eagle for his efforts.

If Billing was a derring-do Buchanite, an inexorably entrepreneurial product of the British Empire, then Grein was in contrast a cosmopolitan European of the modern age, a deep-dyed bohemian of progressive, socialist outlook. An ardent suffragist who dressed like a dandy, his whole demeanour would have shrieked decadence to Billing – not least because of his past. At Wilde's first trial in April 1895, Grein had represented (very badly, says Ellman) Alfred Taylor, who had procured young men for Wilde. Grein's inadequacy as a legal counsel may have been due to inexperience: there is no mention elsewhere of his having been trained or having been called to the Bar, although his wife notes that Grein used to visit the police courts every Saturday morning, and was 'as familiar in the Marlborough Street Police Court as in the theatres'; he regarded the courts 'as a valuable contribution to his profession of dramatic criticism'. The fact that he represented Taylor provided a connexion to the cult of Wilde which may well have been known and used by Billing, who would make insinuations about Grein's sexuality.

It is telling that there is no mention of the Wilde case in Grein's biography. Written by his wife (under her pen-name, Michael Orme†), it relied, like Billing's memoir, on heroic initials for its title: *J.T.: The Story of a Pioneer 1862-1935*. It depicts the handsome, moustachio'd Grein as a saviour of the theatre, and deals

---

* Scottish-born critic and pioneer of modern drama, Archer was first English translator of many Ibsen works. Wilde had sent him a presentation copy of the French edition of *Salome* in 1892, a possible reason for the Independent's production of the play.

† A stylistic affectation of the period, when many women, especially lesbians, took masculine pen-names. Alix Grein/Michael Orme (née Greeven) was herself an actress (she appeared in *Salome*), dramatist and later film critic. She died in 1944.

with the Billing episode brusquely. 'Permission to do the play [*Salome*] was granted by Robert Ross, Wilde's executor, and preparations [were] made for private performance as the Censor's ban on biblical subjects precluded public presentation ...' Grein had seen Max Reinhardt's production at the Neues Theater in Berlin, and was 'immensely impressed. He considered it, rightly or wrongly, a work of art, and from that opinion he never diverged.' Ross, who knew that Wilde had regarded *Salome* as his 'finest dramatic work', disapproved of Richard Strauss's opera, considering that it had 'lost much of its mystique'. He may have hoped for better things for a new production of *Salome*, although he must have known the difficulties that it would face. Ross 'saw no reason to refuse Grein's request ... but it was an act of extreme carelessness of Robbie's part'; if not flagrant foolhardiness. Wilde's play had ever been a potential timebomb; now, it threatened to detonate.

Public performances of *Salome* were banned by the Lord Chamberlain in 1892 because they would violate a two-hundred-year-old proscription on the depiction of Biblical characters on stage. The issue had been raised again in 1910, when the Lord Chamberlain once more refused a licence. Robbie Ross criticised the decision, and the controversy had occupied the letters column of *The Times*. Ross was annoyed that the public could see *Everyman*, a sixteenth-century morality play, or even witness 'a burlesque dance of the seven veils by Maud Allan', titillating audiences 'with her strange gyrations to erotic music'; yet Wilde's 'beautiful and reverential play' was forbidden. Now, in the puritan atmosphere of 1918, any new application for a licence would be additionally problematic: in reactionary wartime, any piece of art regarded as modernist, decadent or foreign – and Wilde's *Salome* appeared guilty on all three counts – would not be looked upon favourably. Ross's failed libel action against Douglas in 1914 meant that 'Wilde was in eclipse, not among normally intelligent people but with the philistine masses who were just then more than usually vocal'; precisely the people whom the Lord Chamberlain's office had to consider when *Salome* came before them in March 1918.

Newly released documents reveal the machinations behind the attempted production, private and public, of Wilde's play. They also indicate how Billing used to his own ends the apparent censorship of the play. The playscript was examined by the Lord Chamberlain's reader, George Street. Like other readers, he was a critic and writer himself, author of *The Autobiography of a Boy* and known to Wilde, who mentions him in *De Profundis*, remarking on the literary gossip brought to him in prison by Robbie Ross, 'that George Street was writing dramatic criticism for the *Daily Chronicle* ...'. Street likewise was well acquainted with Wilde's work: 'It is hardly necessary to give more than a brief account of this well-known Play before coming to the arguments for and against its being granted a licence', he wrote. However, Street's synopsis of the play gives an insight into what Wilde's contemporary professionals thought of the work. It also gives a rather less biased opinion of its moral impact: Street was no prude, and was quite prepared to allow art a certain rein; what reservations he had were the concerns of the normal mores of the period:

> It takes the simple story of the New Testament and adds to it a passion of Salome for John, who is called Jokanaan throughout and is described simply as 'The Prophet'. It is in effect a study of passion carried to a morbid and horrible degree expressed in the wealth of strange imagery dear to its author. To my mind there is little genuine poetry in it or other merit than the achievement of an effect of wierd [*sic*] horror: of that, however, there is no question. In an eerie atmosphere, full of impending doom, Salome makes love to Jokanaan and is contemptuously repulsed. Herod comes in with Herodias and his guests. After vague dialogue in which Herodias complains of the Prophet and rebukes Herod for his gazing upon Salome, Herod persuades Salome to dance with the vow to give her anything, to the half of his kingdom. She dances and asks for the head of Jokanaan. Herod offers her anything else but keeps his oath. The head of Jokanaan is brought on a charger. Salome apostrophises it and at the last is slain by the command of the horrified Herod.

It is clear that Street was not of a mind to follow his predecessors and ban the play.

> The original refusal of a Licence was based, I suppose, on the introduction of scriptural characters. That rule has been relaxed. It may be further objected that it has been relaxed (so far as Plays are concerned) only in the case of Plays with some religious motive. This Play, of course is neither religious nor irreligious: it simply takes a scriptural theme for a merely artistic effect. But it is to be observed that Jokanaan, or John, is treated with propriety by the author, everything said by him being full of dignity, and that the other characters are not important from a religious point of view.

It is remarkable to see how few objections the sensible Street had, considering the proscriptive nature of his office.

> A second objection is the lascivious language of Salome, especially likely to shock because of its object. But there is nothing indecent in it, in the ordinary sense of the term. A third objection is the horror of the end. But the Lord Chamberlain has decided that is not a sufficient objection in such plays as those of the Grand Guignol.* Personally I think the audience should not see the severed head: that could easily be managed and I should advise that condition be made.

---

* The French Théâtre du Grand Guignol, which originated in Paris, specialised in violent scenes of rape and murder, spectral apparitions and suicide. It had appeared in London in 1908, in a less extreme form, doubtless to appease the Lord Chamberlain.

3. The Self-Appointed Task

Street's main concern seemed to be that audiences should not be shocked by the realistic depiction of the Baptist's severed head. Indeed, when Phyllis Dare had pasticHed Maud Allan's *Vision of Salome* in 1908, using a group of little girls dressed up as Salomes, each toying with papier-mâché heads of the Baptist, the NSPCC objected strongly to the use of children in such horrific scenes. 'Apart from this balance of arguments', continued Street, 'there are positive arguments in favour of granting a licence, that the opera has been licensed [these words have been crossed out in the manuscript], that the Play itself has been played in most other countries, and that a dance was allowed which merely took the crudest part of it [Maud Allan's *Vision of Salome*]. I do not think that the more ignorant sort of audience is likely to be attracted.' He trusted in the discretion of an intellectual audience. 'In fine, while I am aware of the force of arguments against it, so far as I am concerned the Play is Recommended for Licence.' A note was appended: 'I quite agree with Street that the balance of argument is in favour of a Licence. Ernest A. Bendall.' However, a further note by the Lord Chamberlain, Lord Sandhurst, recommended that, as Strauss's opera based on Wilde's piece had been refused a licence, the play should go to the Advisory Board:

> In reporting to the then Lord Chamberlain Lord Althorp, Sir D[ouglas] Dawson wrote 'that in his opinion the Biblical allusions were harmless, but there were various lascivious and lecherous passages concerning the personality of St John with whom Salome had fallen in love having failed to attract him by advances, when she had succeeded in obtaining his head she continues her obscene advances to his dead lips, and the language used is so positively disgusting that were it even addressed to an ordinary individual it could not possibly be allowed to be spoken or sung on the London stage.
>
> All who took part in the discussion regretted extremely that Strauss' beautiful composition must perforce be banned, but the style of the libretto left them no alternative. So much for the German opera edition. *Salome* now comes up for licence in English.
>
> The scene of Salome with the head reads to me to merit almost – if not quite – the epithets applied to the German version.
>
> However I append this note with the Synopsis by the reader for the consideration of the Advisory Board.
>
> S[andhurst] 6/4/18

But the arguments over *Salome*'s licence would be superseded by events. Billing's antics would put a halt to rational debate; and indeed, call a halt to the remarkable career of a highly successful and extraordinary star who had become publicly identified with the image of the biblical temptress – Miss Maud Allan.

4

Salomania

Bedecked in beads and little else, her ample white flesh beckoning yet elusive, Maud Allan was a stage icon of Edwardian sexuality, a siren who exemplified the escapism of the age. Combining the innocent and the sexual – a powerful appeal to a culture which inherited the Victorian confusion of childhood and sexuality – she exuded the exotic air of Eastern Europe, or the deeper Orient, with all its abandoned allure. Her image was as much a self-creation as Billing's, but in her case its provenance was deliberately mysterious, as veiled as Salome's dance. Maud Allan had good reason to wrap her origins in myth.

She was, in fact, a Canadian, born Beulah Maud Durrant in Toronto in 1873. Maud's wildly inaccurate memoirs, *My Life and Dancing*, tell of prosperous doctor parents – her father was actually a cobbler from East Anglia – and of an Indian kidnap attempt on the six-year-old Maud when the family moved to San Francisco – the squaws were allegedly entranced by her red hair. Maud was certainly a striking child, and grew to be an attractive woman: she was long-limbed, almost gawky, but her far-apart eyes, red-gold hair and high cheekbones suited the fashion of the times. In the unconventional artistic atmosphere of San Francisco, Maud's vivid imagination flourished. She claimed two influences, one more credible than the other: that her feet had been set dancing when she trod in a nest of rattlesnakes; and that she was inspired when she saw Sarah Bernhardt play San Francisco. She also adored 'living pictures', the *tableaux vivants* craze which had swept across from the East Coast. But her first ambition was to be a concert pianist. By 1892, aged nineteen, she was a music teacher; and her brother, Theodore, was her closest friend.

Theo had left high school, determined to become a doctor. As charming as his sister, he was a good boy: a member of the National Guard, the model of an American youth. Both he and his sister were active Christians in the local Baptist church, where he was also a handyman – Theo was clever with his hands. He attended medical school, but in his early twenties suffered from a mysterious illness, later called 'brain fever' by the press. It left him unstable: 'As his mother was somewhat strange and his sister became *very* strange, Theo may have suffered from some unidentifiable family affliction', wrote Felix Cherniavsky, nephew of Maud's later lover. Indeed, in photographs, there is a vaguely unsettling look about Maud, a propensity for perverse behaviour in her wide-set eyes. It was a strange family. Maud's predilection for the macabre was matched by Theo's belief in omens and dreams, while their father was prone to odd fits of abstraction, and was involved in a strange episode when he was coerced into a scheme to make money in Pennsylvania, only to be robbed when staying with a family who were – so Theo's oddly worded statement to police alleged – 'found under the influence of some drug …'. But none of this was so strange or terrible as the events about to befall the family.

On Saturday 13 April 1895, the body of twenty-three-year-old Minnie Williams was found in a cupboard of Emmanuel Baptist Church, the Durrants' local church. She was naked, and had apparently been hacked to death. The police arrived, and on searching the church, found the body of twenty-one-year-old Blanche Lamont in the belfry. This too was naked, and had been laid out as if for medical examination. Circumstantial evidence linking Theodore Durrant – who knew both girls – to the crime led to his arrest the following day. According to the local paper, when Theo was shown newspaper reports of Minnie Williams' murder, 'the muscles around his mouth twitched and his face turned pale. Then he looked at [Detectives] Anthony and Palmer and said, "I am sorry only for my mother. How can she stand it?" ' Isabella Durrant would not be the only family member irrevocably changed by the fate of this good son. For Maud, who was yet closer to her brother, the affair 'radically altered her psyche'. The idea of a 'mad family' would be reflected in future accusations of genetic perversity that Maud would face; the notion is underlined by the fact that during Theo's trial, the local press was full of 'hints that she [Isabella] was perverse'.

The concept of perversity seemed to grip modern urban society. Life in close proximity demanded normality of one's neighbours. The fear of social misfits – foreign or semitic, sexually perverse (as in Wilde's case) or criminally perverse (as in Jack the Ripper's) – was encouraged by the new tabloid press which fed the modern witch hunt, the collective need to apportion blame. It was a syndrome which would reach its hysterical height in the Billing affair. In America as in Europe, it was feared that the decadence of the post-industrial city encouraged perversity. News of Theo's crime accorded with a general perception of San Francisco as debauched; a neighbouring local paper described the city as 'the hotbed of licentiousness and crime on this Coast'. Although Theo's female victims had not been sexually abused, the horrific nature of their wounds – one had had her breasts slashed – led the press to make obvious comparisons with London's Jack the Ripper, and play on the idea that a new Ripper might be at work. The *Los Angeles Times* reported:

> The prosecution had produced in evidence a large photograph of the dead girl. It was a ghastly thing, showing her in her casket, stripped, with the hideous wounds in her head, breasts and wrists in strong relief ... So ghastly was it that the lawyers, in showing it to the witnesses to identify it as the dead girl, only unrolled enough of it to show her face ... When the picture was unrolled on the table before them, [Theo Durrant] leaned forward and looked at it curiously ... It might have been the cover of a law book for all the impression it produced on the man who was there to answer for the infliction of those wounds.

The Cooper Medical College advanced the theory that Durrant was afflicted by '*psycho mania sexualis* ... A similar theory is accepted by the medical profession as the incentive of the Whitechapel murders. Sporadic cases are recorded of this condition in every country.' This diagnosis came straight from the pages of Richard von Krafft-Ebing's 1893 work, *Psychopathia Sexualis*, much discussed in medical circles at the time. As with the Ripper murders – thought to be the work of an American homosexual obsessed with gynaecology[*] – the serial murder of prostitutes was a vivid reflection of attitudes towards women, and society as a whole. Also lurking in the cultural background was *Dr Jekyll and Mr Hyde*, Stevenson's story of the beast within the inner city which was conflated with the Ripper legend (and drew subliminally on notions of homosexual panic). Were such murders an expression of a decadent city society, breeding sexual neuroses which could only have their outlet in violence? Reaction to Theo's crimes appears to have fixed on this notion: commenting on the case, Dr Dille of Central Methodist Episcopal Church noted 'the lowering of the moral tone of society growing out a weakening of religious restraints'.

It is significant that shortly before Theo's misfortune, Maud went to Berlin; although the city was a common destination for girls to be 'finished', she would later be accused of naturally gravitating towards such a centre of European decadence. In Berlin Maud found the cult of decadence at its height, and her experience of it would crucially shape her life and career. She learned to speak fluent German, and began to attract suitors, including one Ernst, with whom she presented a 'living picture' entitled *Lebensmude* – 'Tired of Life'. This world-weary pose was also evident in Maud's reaction when Ernst's sister guessed at

[*] Dr Francis Tomblety, who eluded capture by the embarrassed British police and appeared in the US, where he was widely reported as the suspect for the Ripper murders. Tomblety had carried on an affair in Britain with Hall Caine, the then best-selling author.

their affair: 'Ha! Ha! Life is short!' And when Maud found Ernst flirting with her best friend, May, she became, in her words, 'so blue that my whole demeanour change[d] and my face grew hot. Why am I so? He is nothing to me.' She was casting herself in the prime decadent role of *femme fatale*.

News from home was as bad as it could be: Theo had been found guilty and sentenced to death. Isabella Durrant announced she would attend her son's execution, and that 'instead of being the greatest criminal of the century, he is the greatest martyr', a characteristically perverse, if not schizophrenic familial response. From prison, Theo wrote to Maud with unsubstantiated claims of a family connexion with the Durrant baronetcy of Sotton, Norfolk, whose motto, *Labes pejor morte*, he translated as 'A Dishonouring Stain is Worse Than Death'. The end came only after four stays of execution and numerous appeals which raised Theo's hopes. The family employed all manner of press stunts to gain support: Maud wrote an extravagant plea for leniency to the Governor of San Francisco, and it was suggested to her that she should make phonographic recordings of 'a few tunes or a duet with your prof ... a pathetic song' to turn the hardened hearts of home. The Durrants used yet more modern technology to propagate their message. Theo invited the owner of an animatoscope, an early kind of film camera, to record him picking flowers in the prison garden, raising the blooms to sniff them delicately – presumably in an effort to convince viewers that he was a sensitive young man incapable of horrible murder. He also wrote an unpublished history of his case, and a bad novel, *Azon*, in which Maud appeared as the heroine; evidence of his close – to some, unhealthy – relationship with his sister.

In true melodramatic fashion, there was last-minute sensation when one of the jurors who had convicted Theo was accused of having reached his verdict on information received outside the courtroom. The *San Francisco Examiner* would not publish the 'alleged expressions used by Juror Smyth in characterizing Theo Durrant as a monster' as they were 'not intended for delicate ears and belong in the domain of the abnormal'. In the contempt hearings, three witnesses – all attorneys – testified that Smyth had said 'Durrant was a moral monster ... Smyth then repeated the disgusting gossip he had heard about the Durrant family'. This is probably the source of the allegations about Theo's supposed sexual molestation of his victims, and his incestuous relationship with his mother. After Maud's death, her lover, Leo Cherniavsky, admitted to burning some of Theo's letters to Isabella 'in which he clearly referred to his intimate relationship with his mother', as well as letters from Isabella which appeared to show that Maud had known of her brother's guilt all along, and had only maintained his innocence as a public facade.

Courtesy of a cruel anonymous sender, Maud read in Berlin the *Examiner*'s lurid account of her brother's last hours, surrounded by extraordinary behaviour to the end; the Durrants appear to have been infected by their own publicity value, and played up to their public profile, victims of an age in which publicity was already paramount. In the papers, Theo's father discussed the disposal of his son's body (local cemeteries and morticians refused to deal with it 'for fear of local outrage'); while Isabella was banned from joining the two hundred witnesses invited by Theo to witness his death, but went nonetheless. Determined to 'die like a Durrant', Theo stood with his head in the noose: 'Don't pull that rope, my boy,' he is supposed to have said, 'until I talk. Well, don't tighten it, then.' 'I have never seen such nerve,' said the hangman, 'and never expect to see anything like it.' Isabella had given him a locket containing Maud's picture; Theo's last words were, 'Now we are together again.' And so he swung. Afterwards, reported the press, Isabella became 'hysterically morbid; she publicly kissed her dead son's lips' – a macabre foreshadowing of her daughter's role as Salome. When the body was returned to the Durrant family home, Isabella spent hours talking to it, and later had recourse to the psychic services of mediums. All this served to further sensationalise the story, and burn it into American folk memory.

*

Back in Berlin, Maud was not living the life of an ordinary downhome daughter. In between attempts to break into the theatre, she was earning money illustrating Dr Penn's *Illustriertes Konversations-Lexicon der Frau*, in effect a sex manual for women, and an example of advanced German attitudes towards sexuality. She was also deep in an affair with the sculptor, Artur Bock. Isabella was aghast at this, the effective loss of her other child, so she sold Theo's possessions in order to finance a trip to Germany. She wrote to Maud before setting off: 'You have an opportunity that you must not overlook, for in it lies your whole future success. Your sorrow with your personality ought to give your playing a charm that cannot be taught. Now don't lose the opportunity to allow the public to judge what you can do.' These were prescient and extraordinary words: for a mother to convince her child to take advantage of family trauma in order to make a successful theatrical career seems more than a little odd. But it was an odd family: Isabella arrived in Berlin in summer 1899 and stayed for a year and a half; with her she brought an urn containing Theo's ashes.

Maud's affair with Bock would finish abruptly, but not before he had sculpted Maud as Salome. It was a fateful creation, heralding the beginning of Maud's identification with the biblical temptress. She began to dance with a shawl for the benefit of her piano tutor, the celebrated Ferruccio Busoni. Busoni introduced her to Marcel Remy, who would help her attain her creative vision, becoming her agent-manager and writing the music for the work that would make Maud famous throughout Europe: *The Vision of Salome*. It was, after all, the age of Trilby and Svengali.

Maud Allan did possess particular skills: she was an accomplished musician and a born actress, 'albeit untrained and of a melodramatic order ... particularly suited to mime, that most subtle art form'. She also designed and made her own costumes, and saw, with a modern eye, the effectiveness of clever lighting, a result of photography lessons with Artur Bock. He also taught her sculpture, and shaped the exotic poses she threw in her dance. To hone her art, Maud spent two years researching in libraries, consulting Grecian amphorae for inspiration. She also adopted the stage name (the 'Allan' came from her father, William Allan Durrant) which disassociated her from her family's shame. Finally, Maud Allan was ready for her grand debut, on Christmas Eve 1903 in the Theatre Hall of the Conservatory of Music, Vienna. Even more than Berlin, the Austrian capital was associated with the spirit of decadence. Themes of death and sexuality ran strong in the Expressionist art of Schiele, Kokoschka and Klimt, particularly in their stylised depiction of orgasmic women. Such sexuality was reflected in the work of another Viennese. Freud had published his *The Interpretation of Dreams*, and the story of Salome, with its associations of the avenging, castrating female and *vagina dentata*, was essential Freudian material; indeed, Maud Allan's art and life could almost have been one of the doctor's case histories.

Maud's career – predicated on notions of death and decadence, sex and sensuality – reflected changing attitudes which the coming cataclysm of war would intensify. Maud Allan and her type – Isadora Duncan, Mata Hari, Theda Bara – followed Bernhardt's cue as *femmes fatales*, delving in a bohemian dressing-up box and finding new roles to play. They challenged Victorian concepts of femininity, how women should behave and what their place in society should be. This scared men and thrilled women, and vice versa. While apparently pandering to male sexuality, they yet celebrated their own, and sought, consciously or not, to modernise the image of women. Thus liberated, free-thinking, modernistic, decadent Vienna was an obvious place for Maud's debut. Classically draped in virginal white or funereal black, she danced to Mendelssohn's *Spring Song*, Chopin's *Marche funèbre*, Schubert's *Ave Maria*, and Rubenstein's *Valse caprice*, and received excellent, if occasionally puzzled, re-views. Her strong imagination and recent history made her performance personal and expressive, although not, to some, original. Maud was much compared to her fellow San Franciscan, Isadora Duncan. Duncan, born in San Francisco in 1878, had established her classical style in Berlin, Moscow, Paris and London, and in 1906 set up a school in Berlin where her espousal of free love confirmed her bohemian reputation. When Diaghilev's Russian Ballet – which she had influenced – threatened to eclipse her popularity in Europe, she returned to America, and triumphant success. Although they met on a number of occasions, drew on similar influences and even looked the same, Duncan and Allan were certainly not friends: the comparisons annoyed both women, and stoked their public rivalry. Artistic posterity made Duncan the winner, yet when Doris Langley Moore saw Maud Allan perform in South Africa in 1911, she noted that Allan was then 'an exponent equal in renown to Isadora Duncan, or rather, more famous still in English-speaking countries'.

Isabella Durrant gave her daughter advice on how to deal with Isadora. 'Many people think she is going too far now', she wrote from San Francisco, 'and will be classed as a fanatic.' 'I wonder how Miss Duncan likes to have a rival, or did she know you were preparing to be her rival?' But unlike Isadora, Maud avoided publicity about her private life, as her mother acknowledged, writing of 'those who would go to see you for what you were' – that is, Theo Durrant's sister. Isabella advised her to maintain her image. She should not marry, nor proclaim free love, but project chastity: 'the ideal purity of your work is so much better portrayed by a virgin than by one who has been contaminated by men.' While Maud drew on her murderer brother for inspiration, she still must appear, like Salome, a virgin to do it; conversely, and perhaps perversely, Isabella argued that dancing was not fit for a married woman.

On 4 March 1905, Maud made her all-important Berlin debut. The *Berliner Tageblatt* considered her performance too derivative of Duncan's, yet thought Allan had 'greater musical talent, her movements are in better accord with the music, and she seems to have better control over her body'. Isabella's letters warned her daughter not to indulge too much in Berlin's nightlife – late nights and too much wine could induce a dissipated look. It was a city that did not sleep; how far Maud indulged in its plentiful nocturnal diversions is unknown. But both Berlin and Vienna certainly had their effects on her creative development. Suffused with the spirit of decadence, both from life in such Old World cities, and from her artistic, bohemian friends, Maud had begun to devise her *Vision of Salome*.

*

The story of Herod's daughter had preoccupied many writers and artists since the middle of the nineteenth century. Flaubert and Heine wrote about her, Max Klinger and Franz Stuck painted her, and perhaps most famously, the decadent artist Gustave Moreau produced his *Tattoed Salome*, shutting himself up in the apartment he had shared with his lately-dead mother, obsessively painting and repainting the subject. The results – dark, opulent and mysterious – convey the century's fascination with the teenage temptress. Indeed, it was a description of two of Moreau's paintings of Salome in J.K. Huysmans' fantastical novel of decadence, *À Rebours* ('Against Nature'), which gave Wilde the idea for his *Salome*.

Like Huysmans' book, Wilde's verse-drama is infused with decadent references, from allusions to green flowers (an echo of Oscar's green carnation, supposedly worn by Parisian homosexuals as a dress code) to the metaphorical moon hanging over the proceedings, a decadent perversion of the more normal poetic use of the sun. *Salome* is bathed in insipid reflected lunar light, prefiguring madness and doom for Herod (who is incestuously attracted to Salome), and driving his daughter to her unnatural passion. In the Billing trial, much would be made of the moon's effect on Salome, a cultural reference to vampires and, subconsciously perhaps, to menstruation and therefore misogyny. Wilde's fear of women and their seductive power – a result of his youthful contraction of syphilis from a prostitute – pervades *Salome*, as does a definable homoeroticism. Wilde's Jokanaan is a beautiful man, intensely attractive to Salome, and her purple-prose tributes to his beauty underline the homosexual subtext of the play (elsewhere a page confesses his love for a young Syrian officer, as does Herod).

Wilde's play was very much a work of his time, drawing on contemporary obsessions with the East, and notions of oriental cruelty (elsewhere exploited in the 'white slave traffic' scare). In a world torn between the pagan and the Christian, the play reflected current concerns of the heathen and the holy. Christ is about to come, announced by the Baptist, but God is an ambivalent presence; 'His ways are very dark', remarks a Jew. The atmosphere of the play is therefore both biblical and decadent – the meeting of the spiritual and sensual symbolised by Salome and Jokanaan. The critic Melissa Knox relates *Salome* to Wilde's childhood love for his sister Isola, who died of scarlet fever, aged nine, when Oscar was twelve. Knox interprets Wilde's relationship with his deceased sibling as strongly sexual (she cites poems written by Wilde about Isola's loss which compare her to a prostitute), a disruptive force on Wilde because of the intense emotions her life and death elicited. These are reflected in *Salome*, as is his relationship with Lord Alfred Douglas, whom Wilde had met ten months before writing it, and whose destructive behaviour Wilde feared would ruin him. And just as Wilde drew on the memory of his dead sister to write his play, so Maud Allan drew on the memory of her executed brother to perform it. The themes of incest and childhood sexuality which underlie Wilde's work reverberate in Maud's life and art.

The history of Wilde's *Salome* is inextricably bound up with his personal relationships: for Wilde, art and life intermingled, ultimately tragically. Having written his play in French, he asked Douglas to prepare a translation of it; partly a ruse to flatter, partly to keep Bosie occupied. But he did not like Douglas's translation of *Salome*, and allowed Beardsley to write another. This he also disliked, and so returned to Douglas's version with his own emendations. Although Wilde credited the play's translation to Douglas, Douglas 'never considered the published version as his work'. Plans were laid for the British production of *Salome* in 1892. It was to have starred 'the divine' Sarah Bernhardt – the epitome of belle époque sensuality – in a production designed by Charles Ricketts, another decadent aesthete. However, the public performance was 'interdicted' by the Lord Chamberlain, Lord Lathom.* Outraged at this philistine censorship of his art, Wilde defiantly published his play in February 1893, 'bound in "Tyrian purple" wrappers to go with Alfred Douglas's gilt hair. He liked to speak of the lettering as in "fading" or "tired" silver. "That tragic daughter of passion," Wilde wrote to a friend, "appeared on Thursday last, and is now dancing for the head of the British public." ' In the end, it was only on the Continent, in Paris – city of the green carnation – that Wilde's scandalous play could be performed. *Salome* was produced by the actor-manager Aurelien-François Lugné-Poë at the Théâtre de l'Oeuvre on 11 February 1896, while Wilde was in prison. The production revived Wilde's reputation, and did something to restore his spirits. When favourable reports appeared in the British press, Wilde noted that the prison officials changed their attitude towards him.

Wilde's reputation on the Continent was undiminished, and in 1904, the impresario and producer, Max Reinhardt, presented an innovative and daring version of Wilde's play which Maud and Marcel Remy saw in Berlin. Reinhardt's production also inspired Richard Strauss's opera, which appeared the following year to sensational effect; its swelling score and sense of impending violence seemed to make Wilde's drama more explicit. Strauss dedicated his opera to its financial patron, Sir Edgar Speyer, the influential Jewish businessman born in Germany but later resident in Britain (where he founded the Whitechapel Art Gallery), a fact which would help condemn *Salome* as a foreign work in the eyes of the British radical right. In 1907 the Lord Chamberlain banned it from London, only allowing a production four years later after modifications (Diana Cooper recalled that 'a dish of gravy' was substituted for the head of the Baptist). The opera was also banned in New York after objections by J. Pierpont Morgan and his daughter. In Berlin, the Kaiser would allow it only on condition that a twinkling star of Bethlehem be incorporated into the backcloth. It was however

---

* Whose son, Ned Lathom, conformed to Antony Powell's definition of the decadent son by spending the entire family fortune on the production of unlicensed plays, the lavish decoration of his country home (complete with crystal bannisters) and private trains sent to London to fetch his favourite scent.

Reinhardt's production of Wilde's original rather than Strauss's opera which inspired Maud's own version – a performance that was to fix her in the public imagination. By excerpting (some would say bastardising) her version of Salome from Wilde's work, Maud readily identified herself with a figure who, 'by the end of the century ... personified the decadence of an old society on the brink of radical reform or dissolution'. It was a significantly titillating act: as one who aspired to high society herself – or at least acceptance by it – Maud appeared as a modern-day Salome, dancing for the delectation of its endangered aristocracy.

*

Maud Allan returned to Vienna for the debut of *The Vision of Salome* in December 1906. On the same night, Ruth St. Denis, then appearing in her 'Dance of the Sense of Touch' (which 'sent the city ... into raptures') – and Mata Hari, the ultimate *femme fatale* – were performing in the city. Both dancers affected oriental costume and imagery like Maud; Mata Hari in particular wearing beaded breastplates very similar to Allan's. With such rivals, Maud's dance had to be sensational. 'It is as if a wildly jerking sensuality were driven into the slender body, as if it began to blossom and swell forth and glow through her skin ...' wrote a later reviewer witnessing her perform in Prague. His description vividly evokes Allan's dance and its overt sexuality, a Klimt come to life:

> In naked sensuality, her body calculating, she meets the eyes of Herod; the rhythm of her motion accelerates; she knows what she wants, and suddenly in its grisly horror the head of the prophet is handed her from the cistern. With the natural motions of the wild ash she dances Salome, the demivierge of the perverse instincts, gaze now focussed on the pale head in heated ecstasy. Wildly she revolves her head in jerking madness; her eyes and fingers groping in the cramps of love, they fantasise about unheard-of desires; shame seems to have vanished from her perspiring body; one draws back from the flame of this passion. Finally abrupt shock overcomes her, freezes her motion, forces her to lay aside the dead head and to be paralysed in the numb pose of nameless self-disgust ...

It was a scandalous act, and calculated to appear so; Maud's flimsy costume had to be amended when an anonymous princess who supported the Court Opera objected to the dancer's 'nudity'. This was all good publicity, as was a stunt organised when Maud performed in a lion's cage in Budapest, having been challenged to do so by Count Geza Zichy, 'scion of one of Hungary's most powerful families'. Maud appeared behind bars, but with cute little lion cubs instead of ferocious feline predators. Zichy paid up his wager – 10,000 marks, which Maud donated to a hospital – but determined to have his own back. Zichy had her dance a private performance of *The Vision of Salome* in the hall of a palace. One American newspaper got hold of the story:

> To Maud Allan, swaying like a passion flower in the last steps of the Seven veils, a giant negro brought upon a great salver Jokanaan. Her eyes half closed, the dancer raised by its dank hair the ghastly prize of Herodias' daughter. She leaned towards its lips. Gently the severed head touched her wrists, and there shot through her a terrible tremor, a shivering of the soul. Upon her white flesh were the stains, dark crimson clots. It was blood. Her body rigid as though carved in marble, the dancer slowly forced her eyes to the face she held aloft. It was the face of a man not long since dead. As one from whom life passes very quickly, she crumpled to the floor. From her hands dropped the head. It rolled upon her breast and fell beside her, leaving upon her white body a crimson trail. So was the dancer Maud Allan taught that it is not well to jest with a Noble of Hungary.

But the Count may not have been responsible for the macabre substitution; his wife was American and probably knew of Maud's family history: the trick was her revenge on the Count for his interest in the dancer, at the same time confronting Maud 'with the most intense of her private feelings'.

It was this private history that made Maud's performance passionate. When helping her devise her *Vision of Salome*, it was Marcel Remy's idea – although encouraged by Isabella, and evidently with Maud's complicity – for her to identify the Baptist's execution with that of her brother, 'and, more forcefully, [John's] decapitated head, whether papier mâché or invisible, with that of her brother ... Maud was giving vent to her fierce passions with the aid of her intensely vivid imagination.' The sense of the macabre was further reflected in Maud's dance to Chopin's requiem, shrouded in black chiffon like a mourning statue. Gothic in fantastic widow's weeds one moment, sexually predatory in bead armour the next, Maud's performances were the essence of decadence; yet more so for those who knew the source of her powerful stage presence.

Maud Allan capitalised on the decadent *Zeitgeist*: her 1907 Parisian debut was carefully scheduled to coincide with a performance of Strauss's *Salome*. Europe seemed filled with vampish women dancing out the Salome myth. Loie Fuller, whose dance troupe Maud joined to tour France, was a renowned Chicago-born dancer who had performed her own three-dance version of *Salome* in 1895 – an obvious influence on Allan. But Maud did not repay her mentor kindly. Although she acknowledged that Fuller, a lesbian known for her kindness towards young dancers, had done her a favour some years previously, she accused both Fuller and her lover, Gabrielle Bloch, of having swindled her. In her memoirs, Maud made insinuations about Fuller's sexuality and her relationship with Bloch. Ironically, Maud herself would become subject to similar accusations.

Maud was now beginning to make large amounts of money, and her fame and reputation spread through Europe. Her star status was confirmed at Marienbad in September 1907, when she was invited to perform privately for Edward VII – despite the reservations of his secretary, Sir Frederick Ponsonby, who wrote in his diary: 'I had been told that she dances more or less naked, and I was afraid the English press might get hold of this and make up some wild story.' His concerns were justified by the presence of the *Daily Mail*'s social editor, Charley Little, prevailed upon to play piano for the occasion. He was sworn to secrecy, but nonetheless, stories emerged about Maud being the king's latest mistress – stories she did little to deny.

The king's approval set the tone for her London debut. Maud arrived in February 1908, and took the capital by storm. Dance was not yet a respectable art form in Britain, and dancers were forced to work the music hall circuit for exposure. But in Maud's case – in which exposure was all – this had the effect of widening her audience and maximising her success. The young impresario, Alfred Butt, had the foresight to contract her for a two-week engagement at the Palace Theatre. Butt and Allan appear to have been intimate; he was certainly jealous of his 'discovery', and sought to have destroyed all copies of an illustrated pamphlet which had been distributed about London, advertising Maud's erotic charms:

> ... Miss Allan is such a delicious embodiment of lust that she might win forgiveness with the sins of her wonderful flesh. With her hot mouth parched for kisses the impeccable saint had refused to give her, she lures an invisible Herod to grant her fiendish prayer. In the very height of her furious exaltation at winning her request, the change comes. Before her rises the head she has danced for, and the lips that would not touch her in life she kisses again and again.

This dark-eyed temptress, her voluptuous flesh tantalisingly exposed, performed the nearest thing to pornography the 'respectable' public stage had seen.

Two days before her public debut appearance at the Palace Theatre, Maud gave a private matinee performance for an audience selected from the press, government and aristocracy. Her appearance was breathtaking. She wore nothing above her waist but breastplates of pearls and jewels held in place by a open mesh of gold and pearls. Around her hips hung more strings of pearls over a transparent black ninon skirt, its hem embroidered with gold and jewels. In this jangling, swaying costume, the dancer transfixed her audience: wide eyes hypnotic, serpentine arms and hips moving in mesmeric time to the swell of Remy's music. To present such a vision to such key members of the establishment – for their entertainment and their approval – was a clever ploy to gain support and precipitate publicity. It was a technique worthy of modern manipulators of public relations: establishing Maud Allan as the latest in theatrical fashion and giving her erotic performance an overlay of artistic respectability pre-empted criticism. If, as some said, Maud did work a sort of hypnosis over her audience, then this private gathering was duly entranced, and the resultant reviews lived up to expectation. The *Observer* called her 'a reincarnation of the most graceful and rhythmic forms of classic Greece', and 'in *The Vision of Salome* her writhing body enacts the whole voluptuousness of Eastern femininity'; despite her state of undress, *The Times* thought both dance and dancer 'absolutely free of offence'; while the *Labour Leader* wrote:

> One moment she is the vampire ... next she is the lynx. Always the fascination is animal-like and carnal ... Her slender and lissom body writhes in an ecstasy of fear, quivers at the exquisite touch of pain, laughs and sighs, shrinks and vaults, as swayed by passion ... She kisses the head and frenzy comes upon her. She is no longer human. She is a Maenad sister. Her hair should be dishevelled, her eyes bloodshot. The amazing crescendo ceases, she falls to the ground a huddled yet wondrously beautiful mass ... London has never seen such a graceful and artistic dancing. It is of a magical beauty. But the beauty is magic; and the magic is black and insidious.

Such was the hypnotic quality of her performance that some who saw her would afterwards swear that Maud had been naked as she danced.

Did she also mesmerise her audience into believing that they were witnessing high art? To Cherniavsky, 'only her intensely imaginative response to the scenario coupled with her commitment to artistic perfection disguised the fact that *The Vision*, sensational and extravagant, was an inferior product of *fin de siècle* decadence ... much of Maud's success was a fluke'. Her interpretation of the decadent spirit may have verged on the kitsch, but it did not prevent Maud from becoming an Edwardian sex symbol, a phenomenon of her day. Maud was taken up by high society in a way no comparable star of the music hall would be precisely because of the artistic pretensions of her performance. The classic and biblical references gave her a certain intellectual respectability, and made her art suitable for the drawing-rooms of the rich. But Maud's decadent appeal did not please everyone. The familiar outcry among self-appointed guardians of public decency was led in London by Archdeacon Sinclair, a campaigner for 'muscular Christianity'. The Archdeacon declared her use of the Baptist's head 'an unwise and unnecessary accessory'. Maud decided to go and see the cleric in person, at St Paul's Chapter House, using her charms like Salome to win him over. In June, Maud's intention to take *The Vision of Salome* to the provinces had other moralists up in arms. The Watch Committee barred her from Manchester, Bournemouth council didn't want her at the Winter Gardens, and in Cheltenham a deputation of local clergy protested loudly – until it was revealed that some of the town's senior Church leaders had already booked their seats for *The Vision of Salome* at the town hall.

But the first real attack came in Lord Alfred Douglas's magazine, *The Academy*. 'All We Like Sheep', a critique written by Christina Marshall (secretary to Ellen Terry and companion to her daughter, Edith Craig), under her masculine pseudonym, 'Christopher St John', pointed out that Maud's appearance was predated by Isadora Duncan's London debut nine years previously; and alleged that Maud was pretending the invention to be hers alone.* The press had blinded London: Miss Allan was not a 'genuine dancer' at all, and Marshall accused the Maud-smitten public of mass hysteria. 'She dances like a revivalist preacher and makes as many converts', wrote Marshall. 'It would be stupid not to admire the character which has brought about so great a success. But it would be just as stupid to mistake this American "grit" and "bluff" for beautiful art.'

Not for the last time in her life, Maud threatened a libel action; Douglas retracted and printed a vague apology. At a garden party that summer, Maud confronted Douglas, presuming him to have been the author of the *Academy* article, and delivered a 'gross insult' – presumably something to do with Bosie's murky past. Such an affront, although nothing new to the irascible aristocrat, was not to borne lightly. He replied, 'But your brother was a murderer!'† At which point, Maud struck him across the face with her fan. The incident would have serious reverberations in years to come.

Maud had thought herself safe in England from this family skeleton in the closet. In America, every report of Maud's European success mentioned the taint of her brother's crime, but London newspapers did not appear to consider it relevant, or were warned off by Maud's readiness to sue. When one magazine, *New Age*, published 'The Maud Allan Myth', another attempt to undermine Maud's kudos by alleging that she had bluffed London 'with a réchauffe of her past', Maud had a lawyer contest the claims, and extract another printed apology.

---

* Marshall was not quite impartial in her observations; her brother, Gordon Craig, fathered Isadora Duncan's first 'love child'. As Christopher St John, she lived with Edy Craig and Clare 'Tony' Attwood in a lesbian menage in Smallhythe, part of the literary and homosexual population of Romney Marsh which included E.F. Benson, Francis Yeats-Brown, author of *Bengal Lancer*, and, later, Radclyffe Hall and Una Troubridge.

† Lord Alfred Douglas probably knew of Maud's own murky past through his younger brother, Sholto (fourth son of the 9th Marquess), who had been in California when Theo came to trial, and whose adventures with an eighteen-year-old actress were reported alongside accounts of Theo's crime and trial.

4. Salomania

In contrast to Christina Marshall's antipathy, one contributor to Douglas's *The Academy* was very much an admirer of Miss Allan. Ronald Firbank was spellbound by Maud's *Vision*, and it inspired him to travel to Vienna and Berlin, which he accurately identified as the spiritual home and source of the cult of Salome. Berlin rewarded his expectations with a 'really exquisite' fancy dress ball; his description reads like one of his novels, with its scenes of exotically dressed and flamboyantly named figures striking decadent poses: 'So many interesting people were there, & the Russian dancer Napierkowskja did the most extraordinary dance with flowers between everybody on Eastern rugs lying on the floor! Granier was there in a yellow wig & hareems! De Max also, the Infanta Eulalia & one of the Spanish pretenders – the oddest mixture –'

Firbank was nothing less than an exemplar of his own fiction, a relic of Wildean decadence. When walking in London, habitually dressed in a tight-fitting lounge suit, a black bowler hat tilted back on his sleek head, his hands 'white and very well kept, the nails long and polished ... and stained a deep carmine' carrying gloves and cane, he would make a detour to avoid Covent Garden's 'massacre of flowers' and hold a handkerchief in front of his eyes when passing butchers' shops. Entering Cyril Beaumont's bookshop, he would declare, 'Have you anything in my line today, you know, something vague, something dreamy, something restful?' 'Even a study in the baroque such as Beardsley's *Venus and Tannhauser* he would term "restful" ', noted Beaumont. In 1910 he saw Strauss's *Salome* at Covent Garden, 'moralised and *sans* John the Baptist's head'. In his fervid imagination, Salome was a symbol of scandal 'and, in particular, of the Wilde scandal – whose repetition in his own life ... Firbank both dreaded and, Wilde-fashion, flirted with,' wrote Brigid Brophy. Salome retained her ability to scandalise, as the Billing case would prove. From 1909 to 1912, Firbank worked on what would become *The Artificial Princess*, then entitled 'Salome Or 'Tis A Pity That She Would'. Its preface acknowledged its source: 'It was about the time of the Maud Allen [*sic*] boom & the Straus [*sic*] cult (a little previous to the Russian Ballet) & the minds of young boys turned from their Greece towards the Palace Theatre, Vienna & Berlin.'

Maud Allan and her art appealed to a particular type of young man. The dramatist and critic Herbert Farjeon declared that 'in the band of her admirers, there was no more fervent Maud-Allanite than I'. He would rush from 'a late set of lawn tennis' to the Palace Theatre without changing his clothes, 'to stand in the crush at the back of the circle ...', a well-known cruising ground where crowds stood six deep. Her fans relished Maud's every move, both on and off stage. 'Whether it was all derived directly from old books, old pictures and old frescoes, as Miss Allan declared, or from Isadora Duncan, as the *cognoscenti* asserted, it was good enough for me. Possibly I was easy game, for those were the days when I would respond as though by reflex action to any suggestion of naiads and dryads and the now all-too-familiar pipes of Pan ... Pince-nez on nose and Edward Carpenter in hand, I would dabble barefoot in the dew, which can be extremely cold before breakfast, steeling myself valorously against the stubble to which the fair soles of the fortunate Maud Allan were, it seemed, so mercifully impervious.'*

Maud's appearances at the Palace continued to draw huge crowds, and she was now earning equally large sums: Alfred Butt reported 'she can sign her cheque for £25,000'. For her private recitals – of which she gave a large number – she charged £250; at the theatre, she broke box office records. At one performance no less than twenty members of Parliament were seen in the audience. She had become a modern star, her image reproduced *ad infinitum* on postcards for her adoring public. In the burgeoning Edwardian consumer society, Maud was a marketing dream: Maud Allan statuettes were sold in Bond Street, her classical sandals were worn by society ladies, and jewellers copied her costume jewellery with beaded necklaces and bosses worn as breastplates. Diana Manners was sent by her enthusiastic 'Soul' mother, the Duchess of Rutland, 'to watch and learn, in spite of the number finishing with "Salome's Dance" – considered scandalous, for she was all but naked and had St John's head on a plate and kissed his waxen mouth ... My mother was untrammelled by convention.' Lady Constance Stewart Richardson, 'a refreshingly deviant member of the British aristocracy', arrived at a house party in a replica of Maud's Salome costume, threw herself at the king's feet and asked for the head of Sir Ernest Cassel, his Jewish financial advisor and the wealthiest man in England. Maud's social ubiquity soon introduced her to Herbert and Margot Asquith, social and political leaders of London; her friendship with the unconventional and outspoken Mrs Asquith would involve both women in the drama to come.

*

Margot Tennant, as she had been before she married Henry Herbert Asquith in

---

* From the pantheism of the Neo-Pagans frolicking naked in the countryside, to the whimsy of Arthur Rackham, Pan and notions of classical rustic mythology were symbols of liberality, breaking away from Victorian fundamentalism. In 1919 a magazine entitled *Pan* was devoted to the new youth culture, self-admittedly 'a journal for saints and cynics'. During the war, the young Noel Coward ran round his aunt's garden in Cornwall pretending to be a faun, and wrote a novel (unpublished), entitled *Cherry Pan*, which invented a renegade daughter of the god. The imagery had an especial appeal for the Uranians. In his introduction to E.F. Benson's novel, *The Inheritors* (Millilivres, 1993), Peter Burton notes 'it is interesting to consider how much paganism and especially pantheism are a feature of the fiction written by late Victorian and Edwardian writers of clearly homosexual inclination', such classical allusions being 'encoded symbols for homosexuality and homosexual desires'. Burton cites short stories by Forster, Saki, and M.R. James, and 'The Piper at the Gates of Dawn' chapter in Kenneth Grahame's *The Wind in the Willows*.

1894, was known as the 'electric charge' of the aesthetic aristocrat 'Souls'. Fast-talking, audacious, and shocking, she was satirised by E.F. Benson as 'Dodo' in his best-selling novel of the same name. Dictatorial and socially demanding – at dinner she would rap the table and demand 'General Conversation' – Margot was well known for her *bon mots*, declaring that if she had been Christopher Columbus and had discovered America, she would have 'taken very good care not to tell anyone'. Her vaguely equine face lacked classic beauty (Cecil Beaton would pointedly photograph her from behind), but she was a glamorous hostess, and took advantage of her position to throw open 10 Downing Street to Society. That year, 1908, she invited Poiret to show his new collection of high-waisted, uncorseted and loose-flowing gowns at her house, which the press promptly renamed Gowning Street; neither the first nor the last time Margot was criticised for her flamboyant gestures. Poiret's clothes reflected the *Zeitgeist* as did the new classically-inspired dance, and Margot had a taste for both. She entertained the Souls with her risqué 'skirt dancing', invented in Chicago by Loie Fuller wearing a huge billowing silk skirt while dancing on a glass platform lit from below by multi-coloured electric lights. Margot was therefore a natural admirer of Maud's art. Quite publicly, the Asquiths adopted Maud for their own, and by seating Maud next to important political figures at Downing Street gatherings, they risked criticism for their patronage of an American dancer. H.H. Asquith's morals were already under suspicion after his relaxation of the licensing laws. To those who suspected a general air of hedonism behind the black door of No. 10, Maud Allan was new evidence of high society decadence.

Margot Asquith was probably a guest at the women-only Salome evening held in Mayfair that August. 'Each of the ladies proceeded to outvie her sisters in providing herself with a costume matching in all details the undress effect of Miss Allan's scanty costume', ran the faintly salacious report in the *New York Times*. 'The party passed off successfully and beyond the hostess' fondest expectations.' 'Salome' music was played by an orchestra – presumably male – segregated by a 'fortification of palms and flowers' from the loosely-clad ladies; although a violinist or two doubtless took a peek through the fronds. After dinner, 'some of the more graceful members of the party demonstrated that they had not only succeeded in matching Miss Allan's costume, but had learned some captivating steps in movements'. To the puritanical, it was but a short step from such refined entertainment to licentious decadence; and the vaguely lesbian tone would encourage rumours already at large. The Maud Allan phenomenon occasioned more copy in the *New York Times* the following week, when a 'veteran diplomat' wrote a piece on the alarming growth of bohemianism in England. He reported that Maud 'is not only accustomed to gyrate in a state of almost absolute nudity but that she had moreover inaugurated a fashion of dancing which has unfortunately found innumerable imitators on both sides of the Atlantic'. Edward VII was supposed to be introducing a programme of social reform to deal with such tendencies; while it was acceptable for the king to frequent risqué entertainments abroad, he sought to protect his family from 'any [who] by their reputation, their antecedents, their characters or their manners were calculated to offend'. As well as an example of Edwardian hypocrisy it was a veiled reference to Maud's past. The 'diplomat' stressed that the English gentleman should look after 'the sanctity of the fireside' and keep it 'inviolate from the invasion of people whose notions of decency and respectability are of a distinctly inferior, and sometimes even the lowest, order'.

*

In October 1908, Maud celebrated the 250th performance of the *Vision of Salome* at the Palace Theatre. To mark the occasion, her memoirs – which had already been serialised in the *Weekly Dispatch* – appeared in book form; *Punch* joked that they were to be published without a dust jacket. *My Life and Dancing* romanticised Maud's life, serving to further her star status. At the same time, a thirty-six page portfolio called *Maud Allan and Her Art* was produced, containing a tribute by Frank Harris (no better Edwardian roué than he to assess Miss Allan's charms; his essay reeks of a rake lasciviously examining a postcard of the star) and two sonnets by Aleister Crowley, the Great Beast of modern myth. As champion of the perverse, he too was a suitable appreciator of the art of the decadent. That Maud's art was respected by such a 'mystic' is a telling indication of her cultural significance. Maud herself was keen to mythologise her life and art, both through her fictitious memoirs, and her use of classical references; but beyond that, much of what she evoked in her dance related to ancient myths; and whether hackneyed or not, Maud's use of such myths reflected the age and its concerns. Indeed, the whole Billing affair resonates with arcane knowledge and atavistic themes which deepen its conspiratorial tone: from the comparison of Theo's crimes to those of Jack the Ripper (rumoured to be a Freemason); to the notion of the Black Book containing the names of the perverted, which, with its keeping-place as the 'cabinet of a German Prince', is redolent of the Masonic 'Blue Cabinet' of the Herrhunter, a voyeuristic contraption of Teutonic sexual rituals; while the book itself is an echo of the conspiratorial *Protocols of the Elders of Zion*.

These secrets from dark Central Europe formed new myths around Maud Allan and the Black Book. They drew on ancient folk tales which lurked beneath the apparently rational modern age, exploiting age-old fears. The Victorians had celebrated rationality and science as controlling conquerers of such beliefs; but their power remained, and they were now being rediscovered after an age of remorseless reason. Maud's success came at a time of New Age philosophy and a revival of the occult, in itself a concomitant of Victorian concerns over the role of women, who were polarised as either angels or harlots; as spiritualist mediums (and Maud's act resembled a medium's trance) women wielded a certain power. The notion of dualism was strong. In an essay on 'The Erotic Freemasonry of Count Nicholas von Zinzendorf', Tim O'Neill observes that 'throughout the history of Western occultism ... there has been a constant and intriguing tendency toward heterodox sexual suppression ... From the psychological and mystical viewpoints alike, it is clear that ascetism and libertinism are simply the two opposing poles in a larger archetypal constellation, based upon the experience of ecstasy.' Not only do these themes directly relate to the story of Salome, but real-life players appear to take up the roles allotted to them. Maud as the Prostitute; Billing as the Ascetic; the idea of sacrificial victims during a time of disaster, propitiates to the Gods. The characters polarise into ancient archetypes in a battle for souls. O'Neill continues: 'The legend of John the Baptist, holy man extraordinaire and his perversely and insistently erotic relationship with his seductive decapitator, Salome, is one of the most powerful examples in the Western Tradition, of this complex relationship between sadism, sexuality, asceticism and mysticism.'

Sexuality and mysticism combined powerfully in the age. Such interpretations give credence to the contention that Wilde was reading Krafft-Ebing while writing *Salome*. 'Exstasis, the freedom of the soul from what gnostics considered to be the prison of the flesh, can be sought through either pole of this complex and in certain rare instances, both ascetism and libertinism can operate together to produce extraordinary states of altered awareness. As ... Krafft-Ebing pointed out: "Religious and sexual states of excitement show, at the height of their development, a conformity in the quality and quantity of excitement; therefore, under suitable circumstances, [they] may be interchanged." '

Aleister Crowley's endorsement of Maud Allan is also germane from the perspective of the occult sects and subsects which eddy through the culture of the period. Crowley was involved in the Golden Dawn and the Theosophists (as was W.B.Yeats, whose social gamut encompassed both Crowley and the Asquiths). Both mystical movements also had links with the emerging British fascists through the German mystics of the Thule Society which, in 1919, helped form the Nazi party. Much of developing fascism in the early twentieth century – with which Billing and his cohorts would be intimately associated – drew on the concept of the 'underground of rejected knowledge'* running counter to

---

* '... useful as a concept,' writes Richard Thurlow on the subject of British fascism, 'precisely because by developing a focus for anti-establishment thought, it provided a relatively coherent framework for otherwise contradictory notions, such as atavism and modernity.'

established or conventional ideas. Members of the aristocracy with bohemian inclinations connected with such tendencies, playing host to Madame Blavatsky and her charlatan mediumship, or donning the robes of the Golden Dawn.

In the fin de siècle such pagan mysticism proliferated as a reaction to encroaching and irrevocable change, of the recent past (the effects of the industrial society) and the near future (its acceleration into the modern era). As an embodiment of decadence, Maud Allan tapped a potent source with her evocation of 'asceticism' (John the Baptist) versus 'libertinism' (Salome); the Christian ethic versus the pagan; east versus west. The coming battle with Billing would be couched in terms of a dualistic fight between good and evil. To the morally righteous, Maud represented an insidious evil: she was characterised as almost satanic, and her influence was such that five years after the first questions had been raised about her moral degeneracy, Canon Newbolt of St Paul's preached that 'the current evil is the indecent dance, suggestive of evil and destructive of modesty'. Like the Blond Beast, she was the potential destroyer of all that was good, of family life, and normalcy. One Watch Committee member declared, 'If people [want] to look at women they should look at their wives'. She became a Medusa figure, on whom merely to gaze would be to risk danger; or Lamia, the serpent witch about to wrap her coils around unsuspecting man; or the east European vampire (from which came the word 'vamp'), recently reinvented by Bram Stoker, ready to suck her victim's blood. As the vivid incarnation of European decadence, Maud was the object of vilification for the puritans and the religious, a scapegoat for the pervasive miasma of perversion derived from Victorian notions of the ill-effects of the speed of modern life, hereditary insanity and moral degeneracy. When it reported Canon Newbolt's speech, the *New York Times* said that his example 'should be followed in all the churches of England and the United States. We are drifting toward peril, and the peril must be checked.' Such words were not only prophetic, but indicate how the psyche of the Western world regarded its society as corrupt and decadent, requiring the purification of war to cleanse it of the Wildean tendency.

*

The moralists were right to be concerned at Maud's influence; from 1908 to 1909, she became a nationwide celebrity. On 22 May 1909 the *Daily Telegraph* noted 'a red-letter day in the history of Miss Allan'. It described how Alfred Butt had taken Maud to Birmingham on a midnight train from Euston, with a special supper car laid on especially for her. In Birmingham she performed *The Vision* at the Prince of Wales's Theatre and received no less than eight curtain calls, twenty bouquets, and a thousand fans at the stage door; hundreds more bought platform tickets to see her off at New Street Station. That evening, she returned to London and the Palace Theatre for her usual evening performance, and ended a long day dancing for the Earl and Countess of Dudley at Carlton House Terrace, at a party attended by the King and Queen.

Maud was everywhere in demand, giving extensive and not entirely truthful interviews to the press; she remained keen to obscure her origins, but her image was ubiquitous. On both sides of the Atlantic she was parodied by comedians, burlesqued in music halls, and mocked in mime: the female impersonator, Julian Eltinge, presented his own vision of Maud in New York, where, as in London, Berlin and Vienna, she became an icon for homosexuals. Olympia started a Salome Competition and received over two hundred applications; *The Referee* published a skit in which Maud was kidnapped from the House of Commons (a swipe at her popularity with politicians); and in 1910, E. Nesbit wrote a novel, *Salome and the Head*, in which the 'Salome dancer' has a character 'only a shade less repulsive than that of her greedy entourage, who gloat with her every night over the day's rich tributes of jewellery'. A parcel is delivered to the dancer's 'House of No Address'. It is soaking with blood, and when unwrapped, reveals a severed human head. It was inspired by Count Zichy's trick, the Count being in London at the time, and doubtless circulating the story, which Nesbit – herself an habituee of bohemian circles* – picked up as gossip.

Such gossip also inspired *Maudie*, an Edwardian pornographic fantasy in which the 'heroine' sates the sexual appetites of four lovers, and indulges in another orgy which begins with her photographing nude models in a studio. As Maud had learnt photography in Berlin with Artur Bock, this book too seemed to have been written with inside information. As with any star, and particularly with a female dancer given to exposing her flesh on the public stage, it was inevitable that stories of sexual debauchery should surround Maud. She certainly seems to have been sexually active. There is reason to believe that Maud conducted an affair with the Duke of Westminster, Bendor, and rumours of her liaison with the king still lingered: Maud would hint that she had been a member of his entourage on private visits to Paris. She was also supposed, during her success in London, to have had an abortion. But such intimations may have served to deflect yet deeper rumours about Maud's sexuality. She certainly had lesbian relationships in later life, and it is likely that these were no sudden Sapphic flowerings; her experiences in decadent Berlin and Vienna, with their openly homosexual societies, would have encouraged this side of her sexuality.

---

* One of her early lovers had been Richard Le Gallienne, the poet and writer supposed to have been a lover of Wilde's. Both his daughters had lesbian inclinations: Eva Le Gallienne, the actress and director, who had been infatuated with Eleonora Duse and was lover to Alla Nazimova, and Gwen Le Gallienne, who had an affair with Djuna Barnes.

Inevitably, Maud's friendship with Margot Asquith gave rise to speculation – which Billing would later turn to his advantage. Most importantly as regards the events of the Billing trial and its impact on the public consciousness, such gossip was rife at all levels of society. During the trial, Cynthia Asquith lunched with her old friend, Harold Baker, 'famous for his calculatedly discreet indiscretions'. He told Cynthia 'the Billing cesspool ... will do untold harm. He said the soil was well prepared for the evil seed and that rumours of what came to us as a fantastic shock had been rife in the mind of the public for years. Scandal – as to Maud Allan and Margot – had been started and widely diffused by the suffragettes. [Why suffragettes? Perhaps because they were generally seen as lesbians themselves, claiming such celebrities as Sapphic sisters-in-arms.] Once in a big shop, a showman, exhibiting a specimen of furniture and decoration, had said to Bertie Stopford, "This would make a nice little Lesbian bower for Mrs Asquith – wouldn't it?" '

Isabella Durrant had advised that a virginal appearance was necessary for the gravitas of Maud's art; but by attempting to project such an image, Maud invited the sexual speculation which comes with star status. The pornographic *Maudie* dancing naked at private orgies showed that she and Salome had become inseparable. Maud was trapped by her success; for her detractors and admirers alike, she became what she portrayed on stage: a vampish *femme fatale* of the first order. Such was the potency of her performance – drawn from life as it was – that it blurred the line between fantasy and reality.

Maud's insinuation into Society was confirmed when she persuaded Margot Asquith to rent for her the West Wing of Holford House in Regent's Park. It was one of London's grandest addresses, part of a hundred and fifty room palace, formerly George IV's residence. Its interior became a temple to the dancer: floor to ceiling practice mirrors, extravagant European furniture, lion- and leopard-skins; all suitable for the 'lesbian bower' which Maud and her benefactress were supposed to inhabit. At the centre of this theatrical set was a large sculpture of Maud by Epstein, an artist whose social commissions ensured a certain immortality – a quality which Maud Allan positively sought, but crucially would not achieve. Maud may have been fêted by Society, yet her true ambitions were not to be realised. For the next twenty years she would tour the world in search of artistic recognition, a futile quest, 'because she mistook her indisputable uniqueness for greatness'.

*

Maud looked for new lands to conquer. She went to Russia, but Moscow found Maud a pale imitation of its beloved Isadora. In January 1910, she sailed to New

York for her American debut. Again, this was not propitious. Carl Van Vechten, then dance critic for the *New York Times*, had seen her perform in Paris and London, and was overtly disgusted with 'Salomania' which he found an unsubtle debasement of the art of Duncan and Diaghilev. To the Americans, Maud's European success was a mystery. What was hailed as art in London and Vienna was in the USA considered obscene (especially from the sister of a murderer), and America refused to take Maud seriously. Maud replied by extolling herself and denigrating Isadora. She pointed out the respectability of her daywear, as opposed to Duncan's revealing chitons, worn offstage as well as on. But the ploy backfired. Maud's Carnegie Hall debut – from which she purposely excluded her *Vision of Salome* – was called 'monotonous' by *Variety*, and Van Vechten, in a cool review all the more notable for its ambiguity, said she had 'a picturesque quality which is all her own'. He observed, 'New York has seen so many dances of this sort by now that there were no exclamations of shocked surprise, no one fainted, and at the end they was very little definite applause.' However, by the time Maud, her companion-secretary Violet Carl Rosa, and her set (consisting mostly of heavy grey velvet curtains) had reached the West Coast, matters began to improve. In San Francisco, she delivered the best perform-ance of her career, and her hometown audience reacted accordingly, as if to make amends for the past. At the curtain, Maud declared histrionically, 'Take me to your hearts. I know you have, but oh! keep me there?' Unfortunately for Maud, they would not. From now on, her brilliance as a star would begin to fade.

Maud succumbed to performing *The Vision of Salome*; she hoped she would not have to rely on it much longer. She and a devoted admirer, William Leonard Courtney (then sixty-one-year-old theatre and literary editor of the *Daily Telegraph*, he had been an Oxford professor of philosophy until forced to resign when his homosexuality became public knowledge) worked on a new scenario, *Khamma*, with obvious Diaghilev overtones. Maud commissioned Debussy to compose the music; the composer accepted the commission for 'des raisons d'economie domestique' (his first instalment was 10,000 francs – about £400) but fell out with the 'detestable Maud Allan'. Maud never performed the work.

In November 1911, Maud left to tour South Africa, this time accompanied by her confidante, Alice Lonnon. In Johannesburg's Carlton Hotel she met the Cherniavsky Trio, Ukranian Jewish musician siblings, with the eldest of whom, the dashing twenty-three-year-old Leo Cherniavsky, she fell in love. They toured India, after calls for Maud to be banned from performing there; imperial values imagined that Maud's erotic dance would excite the 'rich native' to an unsafe degree, and an anonymous 'British Consul' observed that an Indian was used to paying his dancing girls, and would accord Maud's art little respect. It was excellent publicity, all entirely engineered by the Cherniavskys' devious manager. But by the time the tour reached Australia, Maud's relationship with Leo Cherniavsky had broken up, as had Maud and the Cherniavsky Trio. Maud's career was visibly declining. By February 1915, she was back in California, living with her parents in a seedy part of Hollywood, making a film, *The Rugmaker's Daughter*, featuring extracts from three of her dances, including *The Vision of Salome*. There is no record of it having survived. She took a new dance, a 'pantomimeopera' called *Nair the Slave*, to New York and Europe, but it was seen as a pale imitation of Diaghilev's *Scheherazade*, and reviews 'ranged from patronising to rude'.

When Maud arrived in London in the winter of 1917 to play a season at St Martin's Theatre with a solo pianist and a 'little symphony', it was in marked contrast to her glorious assault on the capital in 1908. She tried to pick up on old friendships; perhaps more for professional purposes than on grounds of real warmth. Yet her relationship with the Asquiths seemed genuine enough for Margot to continue to subsidise Maud's London residence. Had Billing known of this particular act of charity (and he may well have done, just as he may have known of the pornographic *Maudie*), his insinuations about the relationship between Maud and Margot would have been unstoppable.

5

The Forty-Seven Thousand

The tendency in Germany is to abolish civilisation as we know it, to substitute Sodom or Gomorrah for the new Jerusalem, and to infect clean nations with Hunnish erotomania.

Arnold White, 'Inefficiency and Vice'

Known until now as a dancer, Maud Allan was keen to move into legitimate theatre in order to revive her flagging career; when offered the lead role in *Salome*, she leapt at the chance. Jack Grein had seen her perform in her London heyday, and was an aficionado of modern dance. As a regular at the Cave of the Golden Calf, he had particularly enjoyed 'the Spanish dances of Señor Matthias ... Not for a long time has a male dancer, whose art is not academic but intuitive, roused so much enthusiasm among an audience, many of whom were *connoisseurs* and *gourmets* of choreographic art.' Maud was an obvious popular choice for *Salome*, and Alix Grein claimed that there was much support for the performance. 'The papers announced the production of *Salome* with no indication of surprise or perturbation,' she recalled. 'I find no fear for England's morals in the following quotation from *The Globe*, for instance: "Theatrical experiment can hardly be expected in the fourth year of the war, Mr J.T. Grein's private production ... will in itself save the year from the charge of artistic sterility." '

Others would not agree. Wartime public opinion had turned against Wilde, who represented everything the war was against. Ross's defeat in his 1914 libel suit against Douglas proved that, as did the 1916 publication of the notoriously pro-German Frank Harris's biography of Wilde; overseen by Robbie Ross, it was regarded as an attack on the country. In such a light, Grein's decision appears arrogant; as Rupert Croft-Cooke noted, 'Grein ... seems to have deliberately flouted popular opinion as from the beginning his Independent Theatre had been designed to do.' To produce such a play with such a history and with such a leading lady was a gesture of rebellious defiance much in the spirit of an habitué of the Cave of the Golden Calf, and, indeed, of the play's author. Apparently aware that the play was unlikely to receive the Lord Chamberlain's approval, Grein decided to produce the play for 'private performances'; although *Salome* was also sent to the Lord Chamberlain for possible public licence, by the time it was read by George Street, Billing's campaign had already endangered any such overt exhibition.

On 10 February, Marie Corelli – a founder member of the Vigilante movement, and a constant correspondent of Billing's – cut out the *Sunday Times* advert and sent it to Billing at the *Vigilante*, along with a letter:

> Mason Croft, Stratford-on-Avon, February 10, 1918
> PRIVATE
> Dear Mr Billing, – I think it would be well to secure a list of subscribers to this new upholding of the Wilde cult among the 47,000. Yours sincerely
> [signed] Marie Corelli. (Why private performances?)

Corelli was the best-selling novelist of the time, a bizarre character who lived in Stratford-on-Avon with her companion, Bertha Vyner (whom Stephen Tennant recalled as having a black moustache) and her own private gondola and gondolier imported from Venice. An inveterate newspaper correspondent and pursuer of moral causes (although she herself was probably a lesbian), she had more than one good reason for disliking Wilde and his associates. William Rothenstein told a story of Wilde in his prison cell being quizzed by one of the warders as to the relative merits of various writers. Having discussed Dickens, and John Strange Winter – whose sex, Wilde had to point out to his interlocutor, was female – talk turned to another popular author: ' "Excuse me, Sir, but Marie Corelli, would she be considered a great writer, Sir?" This was more than I could bear, continued Oscar, and putting my hand on his shoulder I said: "Now don't think I've anything against her *moral* character, but from the way she writes she *ought to be here*." "You say so, Sir, you say so," said the warden, surprised, but respectful.' Corelli had also been the butt of Robbie Ross's 'incautious humour. Indeed, on a cold winter afternoon in Davos in 1894, in his lecture to the Literary Society, he had been extremely rude about her ...' Her letter, therefore, had the whiff of revenge about it.

Billing was ill in bed when the letter arrived; it was opened by Harold Spencer, who saw in it 'the outline of a devilish plot'. Here was Grein – a foreigner – producing a decadent play by the perverted Wilde, starring a woman rumoured to be involved in a lesbian relationship with the Liberal leader's wife. With the Asquiths also entertaining the known homosexual and pro-German, Robert Ross, a perverse, treacherous circle joined up. Billing and Spencer's '47,000' campaign had been something of a damp squib; Marie Corelli's letter provided them with a much more powerful device.

In his hurry to put something in the paper, Spencer wondered how to phrase

Noel Pemberton Billing, MP, aged 37, in 1916

Cynthia Asquith *c.* 1918: an observer of
the scene

Diana Manners as 'Russia': the Corrupt
Coterie alternated wartime uniform with
fancy dress

Diana Manners and Nancy Cunard
at the races

Margot Asquith as an oriental snakecharmer
at the Londonderry Ball

Cabaret
Theatre
Club

The Cave
of the
Golden
Calf

9, Heddon Street
Regent Street
W.

Wyndham Lewis's brochure
design

A NIGHT IN THE CAVE OF THE GOLDEN CALF.

The *Daily Mirror*, 4 July 1912

AT THE CAVE OF THE GOLDEN CALF

Eric Gill's golden phallic idol for the Cave

Billie Carleton in a dress designed by
Reggie de Veulle

Bateman's impression of the 400 Club

Beverley Nichols, 1918

Ronald Firbank, London, 1917

Dorian Gray: Lord Alfred Douglas, with spaniel, around the time of the Billing trial

The Enemy Within: Robert Ross, with scarab ring, 1916

Aubrey Beardsley's original design for Wilde's *Salome*

J.T. Grein, theatrical pioneer and founder of the Independent Theatre

Maud Allan: a siren in 'Spring Song'

Gothic: in Chopin

Voluptuous: *The Vision of Salome*

Macabre: in Prague

Wistful: a portrait for her fans

Billing under instruction at Vickers Flying School, Brooklands, 1912

Mr and Mrs Pemberton Billing

Mosley before his time: Billing electioneering in the Mile End Road, 1916

THE LEAGUE OF PEACE
(With apologies to the "Truth" Cartoon).

Cartoon in the *Imperialist*, 22 December 1917

Advertisement for Billing's patent slip-wing flying-boat

Billing, air pioneer and MP, 1916

FOUR

Imperial Air Convention.

PEMBERTON BILLING, M.P.

WILL SPEAK ON

AIR POLICY.   THE CONDUCT OF THE WAR.
THE POLITICAL SITUATION.   THE "VIGILANTES."

AT

Two Mass Meetings

ON

SUNDAY, JULY 29th,

AT

Queen's Hall, Langham Place,
W.

At 3.30 p.m. (Doors open at 3).   MUSIC.

AND AT

Shoreditch Town Hall, Old St.,
E.C.

At 7.30 p.m. (Doors open at 7).   MUSIC.

(Chairman - The MAYOR of SHOREDITCH).

ADMISSION FREE.

Applications for Tickets, stating how many are required, and for which of the two
Meetings, and enclosing stamped addressed envelope, should be addressed to—

The Organising Secretary,
Imperial House, Hertford.

Printed by Simson & Co., Ltd., 4, Market Place, Hertford, for the Proprietor and Publisher, N. Pemberton-Billing, M.P., Imperial House, Hertford.

Advertisement in the *Imperialist*, 21 July 1917

'Send Up Your Own Airman': Billing canvasses an eighty-one-year-old farm labourer in Hertford, March 1916

'Sweet Charles of the Old Bailey' – caricature by 'Quiz'

THE ACCUSED

H.H. Asquith   Margot Asquith   Lord Haldane

THE WITNESSES

Left: Capt. Harold Spencer and wife; *inset:* Lt. Thomas Galbraith

Mrs Eileen Villiers-Stuart, with the Billings

Billing leaves the Old Bailey, triumphant: 4 June 1918

M.P. CHARGED WITH LIBEL.

THE DEFENCE OPENED.

DRAMATIC INCIDENTS IN COURT.

31 MAY 1918

REMARKABLE ALLEGATIONS.

The action against Mr. N⸺
Billing, M.P., relati⸺
Miss Maud A⸺

The Daily Mirror

FRENCH FALL BACK FIGHTING ON SOISSONS

CERTIFIED CIRCULATION LARGER THAN THAT OF ANY OTHER DAILY PICTURE PAPER

One Penny

THURSDAY, MAY 30, 1918.

HOW THE ENEMY FEARS ALLIES' LORDSHIP OF THE AIR

MR. PEMBERTON BILLING, M.P., CALLED TO ANSWER CRIMINAL LIBEL CHARGE AT THE OLD BAILEY.

Daily Mirror

"P. B." LIBEL CHARGE.

Mrs. Eleanor Villiers Stuart, first witness for the defence.

Mr. Justice Darling, who is presiding at the trial of Mr. Pemberton Billing.

Lord Alfred Douglas, who is to be called as one of the witnesses for the defence.

There were some dramatic scenes at the trial of Mr. Noel Pemberton Billing, M.P., yesterday, when witnesses for the defence were called.—(*Daily Mirror* photographs.)

Daily Mirror

IN THE NEWS TO-DAY.

Miss Teddie Gerard, the popular actress, who is to make a re-appearance today in "Tails Up," at the Comedy Theatre, London.

Mrs. Alfred Vanderbilt, whose engagement to marry Mr. Ray F. Baker, Director of the U.S.A. Mint, has just been announced to the public.

PEMBERTON BILLING TRIAL.

Captain Harold Sherwin Spencer (in mufti) and Lieutenant T. G. Galbraith leaving the Old Bailey after yesterday's hearing.

THE BILLING TRIAL.

EXTRAORDINARY SCENES AND SUGGESTIONS.

The trial was resumed yesterday at the Old Bailey of Mr. Noel Pemberton Billing, M.P., who is charged with publishing false and defamatory libels on Miss Maud Allan and Mr. J. T. Grein, and also with publishing an obscene libel.

The alleged libel on Miss Maud Allan was contained in a paragraph in a paper called the *Vigilante* on February 10 and stated that she was about to give private performances of the Independent Theatre.

There was a reference, in the indecent character, designed to foster immoral practices.

It was explained in the course of an issue of 47,000, which paragraph was also stated that the first 47,000 number called Imperialist so as to render them noted in the list social, financial and political life whose names and weaknesses have been compiled by German secret agents so as to render such persons easy victims of pressure under fear and threats of exposure.

THE BILLING TRIAL.

"NOT GUILTY."

CHEERS IN COURT.

The Billing case at the Old Bailey ended yesterday in a verdict of Not Guilty.

Noel Pemberton Billing, M.P., was charged with publishing libels concerning Miss Maud Allan the dancer, in regard to "Salome"; and also with publishing an obscene libel. His allegation was that a performance for the Independent Theatre, with which Mr. J. T. Grein is identified, was calculated to attract some of the "first 47,000." By this he contended that the Germans have evidence of misconduct by numbers of British people which enables them to blackmail persons in high positions here. He pleaded not guilty and also justification.

The jury's verdict of Not Guilty on the first charge above was also accepted in the other cases—alleged criminal libel of Mr. Grein and publication of an obscene libel. The whole case was thus disposed of.

Yesterday Mr. Hume-Williams, K.C., addressed the jury for the prosecution and Mr. Justice Darling summed up. There were several angry passages. Two of Mr. Billing's witnesses were ejected and five times the judge threatened if Mr. Billing again interrupted to have him removed from the dock to down below.

The jury took 1 hour 25 minutes to consider their verdict.

Marshalling support for the Vigilantes: still from propaganda film, summer 1918

Billing and Spencer campaigning in East Finsbury, July 1918

Badge-wearing fashion futurist: Billing in Vigilante propaganda film, 1918

The dynamic member for East Herts: Billing in his Torpedo car, propaganda film, 1918

Wilde's *Salome* realised for
cinema, complete with
Beardsleyesque decor:
Alla Nazimova, 1924

Reaching for lost fame:
Maud Allan after a tour
of Egypt, 1923

Fallen idol: Maud reclines at West Wing in 1938, aged 65

The Goering we never had: Billing in 1938, aged 67

Billing's futurist vision of 1950: stills from *High Treason*, 1928

his attack on Allan, Grein, and the putative perverted audience of *Salome*. He couldn't accuse Allan of sodomy, so he called the local village doctor, who furnished him with 'a certain anatomical term'. The result appeared in the 16 February edition of the *Vigilante*, in a boxed paragraph under a heading in bold black type:

THE CULT OF THE CLITORIS

To be a member of Maud Allan's private performances in Oscar Wilde's *Salome* one has to apply to a Miss Valetta, of 9, Duke Street, Adelphi, W.C. If Scotland Yard were to seize the list of these members I have no doubt they would secure the names of several of the first 47,000.

Never before had a newspaper used such a salacious headline (although the salacity was lost on most of its readers, few of whom knew the meaning of the term). Billing's friends warned him that this time he had gone too far – the heading was 'manifestly obscene' – and pointed out that he could be prosecuted by the Director of Public Prosecutions (Mathews), with the possible penalty of a heavy fine and penal servitude. But Billing and his mate were not to be deterred, and both in print and in Parliament Billing pursued his campaign. In the Commons on 12 February he referred to 'the mysterious influence which does exist in this country. We hear people asking all round, Why German banks are allowed to continue? Why Germans continue to be uninterned. Why do we find it so difficult to take a strong hand? Why, whenever we threaten Germany to-day in the matter of reprisals or anything else, the matter never actually comes to fruition? There are many in this country in high positions being blackmailed by the German Secret Service. One of these days I propose to bring proof in this House to bear on that question. There are men, and women, too, in high positions being blackmailed. It is a very terrible thing, after four years of war, that that can be possible.'

The public were perfectly ready to accept such a theory, and their reaction convinced Billing that he had struck a raw nerve. On 21 February in the Commons, Billing asked Sir George Cave, the Home Secretary, to prevent enemy aliens from using air raid shelters 'until all British women and children obtain shelter'; he wanted the police to prevent aliens leaving their homes for the shelters 'until a warning is given'. He also called for the continued use of poison gas (in France), after suggestions that the Germans, through neutral channels, were seeking to agree its abandonment by both sides (a telling contradiction of the popular conception of Hunnish cruelty). War hysteria was growing desperate. Set amid scares that poisoned confectionery was being dropped by enemy aircraft to kill British children (sparked off by the discovery in Hull of boiled sweets containing arsenic – subsequently found to be the result of contamination from the machine which produced them), Billing's attacks can be seen in context. As Rupert Croft-Cooke observed, 'there is a kind of story which gains currency especially in wartime. However far-fetched it may be it has some picturesque coincidence, some flashy detail, which appeals to the credulous ... There are always plenty of people to believe in dark mysteries in high places and to champion the brave man who dares to expose them. Horatio Bottomley made several fortunes out of this kind of credulity.'

*

On 23 February 1918 the *Vigilante* reported on an article in the tabloid *Sunday Referee*, whose columnist, 'Vanoc' (Arnold White's *nom-de-plume*), 'boldly takes up the subject of the 47,000 ... Let us carefully investigate the names in the list furnished by the Hun "urnings" which Mr Arnold White tells us is to be made public in the near future.' In the following issue Billing informed readers that 'Sir Algernon Methuen, the publisher of Oscar Wilde's works', 'whose real name was changed ... from Stedman by deed poll', was pro-Boer. 'As I happened at the time to be in South Africa myself, taking an active part in the anti-Boer movement, my ignorance of Sir Algernon's political activities then may be excused.' Other topics aired in Billing's paper during that spring included the allegation that 'Jew boys' were being smuggled to Ireland (where German-Fenian plots were suspected), and the damning fact that 'Jews speak German'. Readers were invited to send in instances of 'aliens' crimes, profiteering in all its branches ... parasites who live on the blood of fighting men'. The purity of British blood was paramount. In the 23 March issue there were warnings about venereal disease: 'The German through his efficient and clever agent, the Ashkenazim, has complete control of the White Slave Traffic. Germany has found that diseased women cause more casualties than bullets. Controlled by their Jew-agents, Germany maintains in Britain a self-supporting – even profit-making – army of prostitutes which put more men out of action than does their army of soldiers.' Following the lead of the Empire-raised radical right, it was a potent mixture of misogyny and sexual repression, a rearguard action in a modern world in which women were gaining increasing power.

Billing's Commons performances reached fever pitch; he was becoming more than an irritant in the government's side. On 28 February he asked Parliamentary questions about British prisoners of war being badly treated in the Westphalian mines where they were employed as 'slave labour ... beaten till their flesh is like pulp'. (Again, this must be set against a background of other similar stories, such as that of the British officer prisoner 'murdered' by his guard, left to burn to death in his cell when the castle in which he was kept caught fire.) In March, Billing floated tales of German spies in Bristol Channel ports. In April, he proposed a poll tax on aliens: 'What is the matter with taxing our enemies? The country is full of them.'

But Billing had gone far enough. He had enemies in high places: F.E. Smith, for one. Smith, then Attorney-General, had been appointed as head of the government press bureau at the start of the war, responsible for issuing war news as supplied by the War Office and the Admiralty, and for censoring war news the papers might obtain for themselves. He had long held a grudge against Billing (probably because Billing had made the usual sort of accusations about him), and wanted to see him brought to court, but as Attorney-General, he could not find a crime with which to charge this nuisance of a man. Conversely, he argued that a government prosecution would give Billing's allegations unwanted publicity, and recommended that the government should ignore the rantings of the *Vigilante*. 'No doubt at the back of F.E.'s mind there was the hope that if Billing continued to make his allegations, some upright citizen would eventually seek the redress of the civil law.' And so Jack Grein and Maud Allan stepped forward to take their allotted roles.

On 5 March, Jack Grein saw the 'Cult of the Clitoris' paragraph, and showed it to Maud Allan. They immediately consulted their solictors. As Grein's wife wrote, 'When the paragraph was brought to J.T.'s notice, his indignation and chivalry flamed high. He could not entertain the thought of inactivity where the honour of his leading lady and of their project were at stake. Redress was sought in action for libel.' Robbie Ross – who from personal experience and good judgement foresaw no happy outcome – tried to dissuade Grein from his course. But Maud Allan did not hesitate to resort to the processes of law in order to clear her name. She may well have recalled the Durrant family motto, as interpreted by Theo: 'A Dishonouring Stain Is Worse Than Death.' On 8 March, Allan and Grein appeared in Chambers before Mr Justice Salter for leave to start proceedings for both criminal and obscene libel against Billing on the strength of the title of the paragraph; they had been unable to get hold of a copy of the 26 January edition with the '47,000' article. Billing protested to Salter that he had only been told of the hearing late the previous night, and that his intention in publishing the offending paragraph was to stop the *Salome* performance taking place. The case was reheard on 12 March, when Billing put forward the Plea of Justification that as a medical term, 'clitoris' would only be known to the 'initiated', and was incapable of corrupting moral minds.

In the meantime, Grein had been invited by Robert Donald, Director of

Propaganda in Neutral Countries at the Ministry of Information, to organise tours of plays in Scandinavia and Holland, using 'typical English plays ... I consider that propaganda in this way will be most valuable ...' The tour should be self-supporting, but the Ministry would cover travelling costs. The timing of this invitation may have not been coincidental: Donald was also the editor of the *Daily Chronicle*, which supported Lloyd George and opposed Billing. Grein subsequently planned the tour, which was approved by Donald on 25 March. Grein wrote: 'I add once more my services as organiser are, under all circumstances, part payment of my debt of gratitude to the nation.' But Beaverbrook, as Minister of Information, was alarmed by the news of the case, and quickly issued a statement to the press: 'The Minister of Information says he has never authorised any scheme or granted any subsidy for the production of plays in neutral countries. Lord Beaverbrook does not know Mr Grein and has had no correspondence with him. Mr Grein is not employed by the Ministry.'

On 24 March, Allan and Grein's aptly named solicitors, Messrs Strong and Bolden, sent a clerk to the *Vigilante* offices to obtain the 26 January issue. Having discovered the meaning of Corelli's reference to the '47,000', they immediately issued a summons for defamatory libel. It was served on Billing, who said, 'I expected this ... I wonder why it was left so long. When is the hearing? I see it is on the 6th April, that is significant, as the Salome dance is to take place on Sunday the 7th.' Grein went ahead, and on 3 April announced in the *Morning Post* that *Salome* would be performed, for subscribers only, on 7 and 14 April at the Prince of Wales Theatre. Although George Street had recommended the play for licence on 28 March, the Lord Chamberlain, concerned by the publicity Billing's campaign was already receiving, objected to a Sunday performance. For the same reasons, André Charlot objected to his theatre being used, so on 6 April – the day of the libel hearing – Grein changed the venue to the Kennington Theatre, Tuesday 9 April. A circular was issued by the Independent Theatre Club, advertising 'J.T. Grein's Players' performance of *Salome* and Ibsen's *The Lady from the Sea*'. Of *Salome*, Grein wrote that there would be 'Two Private Performances For Members Only ... To the Public that cares for the Artistic Drama. I invite you to support two productions which, I am convinced, must further the cause of dramatic art in this country. I have persuaded Miss Allan to act under my banner, and to appear as Oscar Wilde's *Salome*. The cast will include Mr Ernest Milton, and will be chosen with the greatest care under the direction of Michael Orme [Alix Grein, his wife].'

Grein was defiantly flying the flag of modern, decadent art. 'If these performances are successful the scope of the Independent Theatre will be still further widened. Let me impress on you that the Independent Theatre makes no profits. I am a dramatic critic endeavouring to practise what I preach, and I receive no pecuniary reward either directly or indirectly, from the performances for which I am responsible. During the war the proceeds, after the expenses have been paid, will go to the Y.M.C.A. or the Red Cross. When peace comes again, they will be used solely for the furtherance of dramatic art in England.' The programme for the eventual performance announced that 'Miss May Haystack will recite "A Tribute to Britain" by J.T. Grein', a defensive and perhaps cynical play on patriotic spirits informing the audience that *Salome* was not an 'impure work'.

That was certainly not the impression readers of the national press would have gained. Editors – doutless encouraged by Billing – duly sent along their reporters to Bow Street Magistrates' Court on 6 April, where advance press provided a large crowd to see these noted or notorious figures do battle. *The World* described the scene: 'in a downpour of rain a queue some fifty yards long formed outside the Bow Street Police Court. The people composing it were mainly associated with the theatrical profession, and they were eager to hear exactly what it was that Miss Maud Allan and Mr Grein alleged against Pemberton-Billing whom they had summoned on a charge of criminal libel ...' It was a celebrity occasion, and the press revelled in it: theatre, politics, power, corruption and sex – just what their readers needed to take their minds off four years of war. 'Miss Allan, wearing a black fur cape with spangles on the bodice, sat with friends in the front row of seats usually reserved for witnesses. Mr Grein was at the solicitor's table, where Mr Billing had also seated himself.' The stage was set.

The libel was read out by the counsel for the prosecution, Mr Travers Humphreys, a rising legal star married to the daughter of a Belgian artist, who, like Jack Grein, also had a connexion to the Wilde trials. His father, C.O. Humphreys, was Ross's lawyer, recommended by Ross to represent Wilde in the libel suit against the Marquess of Queensberry; Humphreys senior displayed 'a combination of opportunism and naivete' by urging Wilde to prosecute. His son Travers had a similar taste for sensation. When Wilde lost his libel trial against Queensberry and his own prosecution was about to begin, Travers Humphreys was appointed to represent Wilde at the preliminary hearings at Bow Street. There, evidence was given of Wilde's involvement with various young men – supplied by Alfred Taylor, whom Jack Grein represented at Wilde's trial at the Old Bailey.

More than twenty years later, the same issues were to be tried in the same courts. At Bow Street, Maud Allan gave formal evidence, and was not cross-examined by Billing, who had declared that he would draw on his training as a barrister and conduct his own defence. For the moment, he concentrated his attack on Grein: 'Is it a fact that you have recently been appointed to some official position in connection with the propaganda of British drama in neutral countries?' Grein confirmed this. 'Will *Salome* be one of the repertory?' 'Yes, if we have sufficient money,' replied Grein. He also confirmed that he had founded the German Theatre in London, and that he held the Order of the German Eagle, Fourth Class, and the Order of the Prussian Crown.

With the libel discussed in open court for the first time in the national press, the *Vigilante's* accusations became public – as Billing and Spencer hoped they would. It is hard now to assess the effect that the publication of the paragraph referring to the German prince's 'cabinet noir' and its staggering contents must have had on 1918 society. For a public largely innocent of the finer points of sexual deviance and the sort of society scandal in which modern tabloids revel, the dramatic revelations had maximum impact: a famous dancer/actress, a well-known drama critic, a high profile MP, and the moral state of Britain; in those crisis-ridden days, the very future of the nation – no, the Empire – was at stake. The case would be defined by its press coverage. Comparisons with Mata Hari, the dancer who had also insinuated herself into high society, but had been shot as a German spy the previous year, were obvious as Maud Allan made her fur-swathed appearance in court; the notion that Maud may have been contracted as a German agent during her lengthy stay in their country was never far from the journalistic subtext. Mata Hari's career had paralleled Maud's, moving in a similar trajectory through European and British high society and the theatre; although Mata Hari's was definably the more risqué profile, her more or less naked performances for the likes of Natalie Barney's lesbian salon in Paris 'later used as potent evidence of her sexual depravity which indulged the espionage writers' voyeuristic fantasies'. The connexion between decadence and German espionage was strengthened in the minds of the public on both sides of the Atlantic by press reports of 'the Kaiser's "Vampire" Spies', as the *San Francisco Sunday Chronicle* announced in early 1918. America was subject to the same war hysteria as was Britain: in 1917, the morphine addict and German agent, Madame de Victorica had been charged with treason in the United States, while new Congress legislation was passed to control enemy aliens. The American-Canadian Maud Allan fell easily into this new concept of the spy-courtesan: another spy, Madame Storch, was compared to Theda Bara with her olive complexion, dark eyes and 'mass of heavy black hair from the Orient'.

Such powerful visions of corruption were perfect newspaper material. But reports of the proceedings at Bow Street hardly required the tabloid treatment to inflate the outrageous claims; in fact, many papers withheld certain details from their readers, so obscene were they. And all this was actually going on as the horrified readers perused their morning papers. It was crucial to the effect and momentum of the Billing case that the hearings at Bow Street took place simultaneously with the Independent Theatre's production of *Salome*; the timing meant that publicity was at its height. It also made life difficult for the company. 'The matinee was something of a nightmare,' wrote Grein's wife. 'For, with the trial in the offing, we had been sent from pillar to post.' The Kennington Theatre had disowned them, and the production switched to the Royal Court Theatre in Sloane Square. 'The scenery, designed for a much larger stage, was being lopped off and fitted with its reduced frame at the eleventh hour. The dress rehearsal was therefore a scramble and, indeed, never got further than Miss Allan's dance.' Meanwhile, the actor playing the Cappodocium disappeared, pleading 'military duties'.

Salome, along with Miss Haystack's recitation of Grein's 'tribute', was performed at the Royal Court at 3 pm on 12 April 1918. With the Billing case already receiving nationwide publicity, the performance was widely noted and extensively reviewed. G.E. Morrison's notice in the *Morning Post* conveniently appeared on 13 April (the paper was tacitly supporting Billing's campaign), as that Saturday morning, proceedings reopened at Bow Street. Such press coverage would jeopardise the impartiality of any jury. To Morrison, the play was,

... a bizarre melodrama of disease ... One may admit its atmosphere though it is an atmosphere people who are healthy and desire to remain so would do well to keep out of ... One is reminded of some richly jewelled watch that does not go ... At the same time, high praise is due ... to Miss Maud Allan for her excellent reproduction of the symptoms of Salome ...

Other reviewers found the play similarly distasteful. 'We cannot in the least share in the view that *Salome* is "not an impure work" '; wrote Bernard Weller in *The Stage*:

This view was very emphatically expressed by Mr J.T. Grein in his brief speech at the close of the Independent Theatre private performance on Friday afternoon. We think that, on the contrary, *Salome* is a very impure work. It is impure in its theme – the explicit carnal desire of the daughter of Herodias for Jokanaan the Prophet, otherwise John the Baptist. It is even more impure in its atmosphere, which is charged with a sickly voluptuousness. A decadent literary art would scarcely go farther than the gaudy harlotry of words in which *Salome* is set out. If there were anything of the tragic spirit behind it, if there were any psychology of character, the manner, while it could not be overlooked, might perhaps be borne with. But the late Oscar Wilde, though an adroit writer of showy, insincere comedies of modern society, had no perception of tragedy.

Evidently the reviewer had not read *The Picture of Dorian Gray*, *The Ballad of Reading Gaol* or *De Profundis*. He concluded that '*Salome* is little more than a mass of luscious verbiage, with the adjective doing most of the work ...' and considered Wilde's perfervid dialogue 'rouged and painted like a courtesan's face ... very repellant to a healthy taste'.

> This kind of stuff has no relationship to art. It is animalism, or worse; for animals have their decencies. As a study in decadent expression, and also from the personal point of view as a human document, *Salome* is interesting in the library, but it is not fitted for stage representation.

The critic did not rate Maud as an actress:

> In her acting as Salome she seemed to feel more than she could express, and her elocution was very faulty. To the suggestion that Salome is only a child influenced by the first stirrings of puberty, Miss Allan did not lend any support. Her Salome, on the contrary, suggested a passionate woman, and this reading is of course the only one consistent with the text.

Had *Salome* been available to a greater public, such notices would have guaranteed full houses. But Grein and Allan's show was a one-night stand, and that would not even provide enough seats for their supposed supporters among the '47,000'.

With the play performed, libel hearing preliminaries resumed at Bow Street. Billing continued to cross-examine Grein, trying to prove that *Salome* was an immoral work, and that the *Vigilante's* statements were justified. 'Are you of [the] opinion that this play is of a type calculated to raise the opinion of neutrals as to British morals and art?' asked Billing. 'It has already done so,' said Grein. This was greeted with laughter in the court room. Grein continued, perhaps a little disingenuously but with certain indignation, 'It is a healthy performance for healthy people.' Billing told the court that there was no libel. He concentrated on 'the presentation of a physical orgasm' in the play, which was 'calculated to attract moral perverts who ... seek sexual satisfaction in the watching of this exhibition by others'. Nevertheless, he was committed for trial at the Central Criminal Court, the Old Bailey, for obscene and defamatory libel, 'his own recognisance in £500 being accepted'. But Billing requested an adjournment, for a secret motive: he had suddenly become involved in a political plot in which his libel trial and the attendant publicity were used as a tool in a struggle for the machinations of war and peace, and, indeed, for control of the country itself.

The Trial

First soldier: What an uproar! Who are those wild beasts howling?
Second soldier: The Jews. They are always like that. They are disputing about their religion.
First soldier: Why do they dispute about their religion?
Second soldier: I cannot tell. They are always doing it. The Pharisees, for instance, say that there are angels, and the Sadducees declare that angels do not exist.
First soldier: I think it is ridiculous to dispute about such things.

Oscar Wilde, Salome, Scene 1

Billing's campaign had pervaded public consciousness and political life with insidious ease. Many feared its repercussions, for differing reasons; all sorts of interested parties, from low life to high office, hurriedly sought to cover their traces. The Ministry of Information and Lord Beaverbrook disclaimed all knowledge of Grein, and denied having supported him. The atmosphere of xenophobia and anti-semitism had already contaminated public life; anyone suspected of conflicting loyalties was forced to reassess their position. Lord Haldane, widely seen as pro-German, resigned from the coalition government; influential Jewish figures such as Sir Ernest Cassel and Sir Edgar Speyer withdrew (indeed, Speyer was later found guilty of continuing to trade with Germany and was struck off as Privy Councillor). Prince Louis of Battenberg had to resign his Admiralty post. Every level of society was affected, from German-Jewish businesses in the East End of London to the British Royal Family. But while the East End 'aliens' suffered abuse and internment, their royal counterparts were able to take pre-emptive action. *The Times* of 25 April announced under the heading, 'The House of Windsor', that the king had decided to adopt the name of the Royal Borough with which the Crown had long been associated.

Haldane, War Minister for the Liberal government from 1905 to 1912, and Lord Chancellor to Asquith from 1912 to 1915, was dismissed after Conservative objections to his declaration that Germany was his 'spiritual home', the philosophical context of which statement was undermined, for them, by the fact that Haldane spoke fluent German. Marie Belloc Lowndes, sister of Hilaire

Belloc, noted that Haldane was 'undoubtedly Asquith's most intimate man friend'; his Teutonophilic stance therefore reflected on Asquith: 'He [Asquith] always accepts and repeats without question, anything which is disparaging either to France or Italy. He has a slight bias towards Germany because of Margot and Elizabeth Bibesco's [his daughter] curious affection for anything German, an affection and admiration the more odd, because they really, one feels, know nothing about the country.' Margot's visits to German officer prisoners of war, bearing gifts, were widely criticised in the press. In Belloc Lowndes' opinion, the Asquiths' predilection for the country was due to domestic arrangements: 'One may almost say that both mother and daughter adore Germany because of the German governess who was so long with them, and who is supposed to have saved Elizabeth's life when she was terribly ill many years ago in Switzerland, and who stayed with them for a considerable time after the War started. In fact, as Lord Grey [the Foreign Secretary] told me himself, it fell to him to tell the woman that, under all the circumstances, it was not fitting that she should go on belonging to the household of the then Prime Minister of England.' Margot's influence over her husband, and her almost arrogant pro-German stance, were much to blame for the criticism the Asquiths received.

But beyond questions of personal affiliations, the power struggle of 1918 was the old conflict of military and political interests, a fight for control of the country's destiny in wartime. With ever more drastic news from the Western Front, foreign policy was in crisis. The generals of the War Office despaired of what they considered to be Lloyd George's amateur attempts to run the war, while Lloyd George thought that they had wasted thousands of lives at Passchendaele and was attempting to circumvent their control by working directly through the Supreme War Council, recently set up at Versailles. The generals responded by contacting the former *Times* military correspondent, the combative and colourful Lieutenant-Colonel Charles A'Court Repington.

*

Repington was an influential figure in wartime politics. Neither politican nor journalist nor aristocrat, he yet moved between all three worlds, pursuing his own particular agenda, and wielding a considerable amount of power in the process. His military career had been compromised by an affair with a married woman, and he had subsequently become a 'cunning and serpentine politician'; a 'distinct asset to *The Times*', not least because many of their wartime correspondents were employed by the British Secret Service: Repington had actually run its French section. H.G. Wells called him 'our one and only British Military Expert'. Cynthia Asquith described him as a 'powerful-looking man, with a very clever face – extraordinarily German-looking, I think.' Repington was part of a society where war appeared to be merely a social condition; when he published his war diary in 1920, its portrait of aristocracy carrying on regardless made him a social pariah among those whom he had previously called friends. A typical entry was that for 22 February 1917: 'Wrote all day till 5. Then to the Tribunal. A very late sitting, and we had many cases; several conscientious objectors, including Wyndham Albery [scion of the famous theatrical family], to whom we gave no exemption. Was fearfully late for dinner at the Ritz. We went to see a Revue and had a very pleasant evening.' Interspersed with an insider's narrative of the progress of the war are innumerable references to lunches with hostesses Lady Cunard and Lady Londonderry, dinners with the Churchills, the Montagus, Lady Juliet Duff and Edmund Gosse, and admiring, flirtatious friendships with celebrated actresses such as Maxine Elliot (one of Edward VII's mistresses) and Doris Keane. Another entry, for 9 May – as the Billing case was about to begin – noted a lunch at the Spanish Embassy with the Lyttons and the de Noailles: 'Lady Curzon produced a phial of amber and anointed our cigarettes with a drop of it. Could not get it out of my holder all afternoon. It is said to give visions and leave no one responsible for his or her actions. A dangerous drug. A discussion on ladies' boots, and whether toes should be pointed or square.'

To Osbert Sitwell, Repington's diary was 'a sort of *Catalogue Raisonné* or Doomsday Book for a Social Revolution', portraying 'very accurately the feeling of a time when ... people of all kinds and ages sought by means of pleasure to forget the war'. Sitwell cites an entry for 26 August 1916, recording a house-party given by George and Alice Keppel at their country house in the Chilterns. It was a 'gay party' consisting of the Keppels and their daughters Violet ('such a clever girl and so attractive') and Sonia; Harold Nicolson and Vita Sackville-West, Baroness Daisy de Brienen and Sitwell himself (who brought with him 'another young fellow in the Guards'). During the weekend Repington discussed the war with Mrs Keppel (whom he knew well) and Baroness de Brienen (whom he referred to as 'Miss Daisy'), with special reference to Holland. The collection of personalities at this gathering would prove accessories to the developing drama; most especially Alice Keppel, who, as perhaps the most glamorous former mistress of Edward VII, remained a cynosure of society. Robbie Ross, who met her at the Asquiths' country house, the Wharf, in May 1917, was charmed: she had 'no airs and graces and tells amusing stories'.

Repington's diary proves that he saw Mrs Keppel often during the period (although the published version of his otherwise detailed diaries makes no mention whatsoever of the Billing affair). After the weekend, Repington returned to London with Sitwell, his friend, and Nicolson. 'Instead of discussing soldiering, we talked of nothing but pictures, Palladio, and palaces ... The war

has brought a strange medley of capacities and incapacities into the war,'
commented Repington. (Such talk was 'more than mere idle gossiping about the
arts,' writes John Pearson, Sitwell biographer. 'Osbert, the Wildean aesthete, was
starting his own aesthete's revolt against the war and the society that bore the
guilt for making it. Art and the idea of artistic pleasure had become ... a bond
of union between those who were for "civilisation" and against the generals.')

Repington could draw on contacts in the highest military and political circles
to write articles which could shape public and private opinion about the war. He
had recently resigned from *The Times*, angered by what he saw as the conceal-
ment of the truth from the public by the Northcliffe press who were 'coddling
the War Cabinet'. Repington had protested at the suppression of his articles
about the shortage of men at the Front: 'I should deserve to be hanged as a Boche
agent if I remained with these imbeciles any longer.' He now intrigued with the
generals and Admiral Jellicoe, himself a disgruntled former First Sea Lord
dismissed from his post after arguing with Sir Eric Geddes. On 21 January
Repington became military correspondent for the *Morning Post*, whose anti-
semitic editor, H.A. Gwynne, was influential in supporting the nascent British
fascists. Repington sympathised with the radical right, as did many of the
military cadre ranged against Lloyd George.

From his new appointment, Repington would choreograph the coming conspiracy. On 22 January, he was with friends – including Arnold Bennett – at the
Reform Club, when he heard 'many things about L.G. and his set. Gardner
thinks that this Parliament is the most corrupt since the days of George III, and
gave me many instances of honours shamelessly bestowed. He says that this is a
war of a military system against the civil governments of the world, and that L.G.
does not place the case fairly before the public.' Like Billing, Repington saw
Lloyd George as wrong-headed and leading the country to doom; while Lloyd
George's radicalism seemed part of a modern movement against the militarists'
reactionary stance. On 24 January, Gwynne published – without sending to the
censor – Repington's attack on the 'procrastination and cowardice of the
Cabinet'. Lloyd George's reaction to such flagrant mutiny was to ask the War
Cabinet to imprison both Repington and Gwynne – an act made possible by
DORA. That afternoon, Mr Justice Darling, now Acting Lord Chief Justice,
invited Repington to dinner with the Benchers at the Inner Temple.* Repington
accepted: in the circumstances, he thought it 'a sound thing to do to make friends
with the heads of law'. He liked Darling but the judge rebuked him for his
actions.

Repington was not the only one at work behind the scenes: the former Prime

---

* Billing's London address was close by; he lived at 3 Essex Court, The Temple, EC4.

Minister's wife was 'intriguing busily' to return her husband to power. Taking advantage of Repington and Gwynne's anti-Lloyd George campaign, Margot Asquith attempted to manipulate the press. In February, Lord Haldane wrote privately to his sister, 'There is a grand political row now on. Margot is up to her elbows in intrigues and actually (do not mention this) had Gwynne of the *Morning Post* at Cavendish Square today! But the Liberals are too pacifist ... to get a vote of no confidence in Ll.G.' Nevertheless, Margot was said to be 'up and down Bond Street like the Ancient Mariner clutching at mannequins, commissionaires, friends, taxi-drivers, policemen, and whispering to them the good news of their return to Downing Street'.

Events would overtake such hopes. On 21 March the predicted German attack on the British front caused panic in the War Cabinet. As they discussed plans to evacuate British troops back to England, Lloyd George told Parliament that manpower was as great as it had ever been on the Western Front. This lie gave Repington more ammunition for his conspiracy with the disgusted military power base, and as the government told more untruths, it emerged that Lloyd George had been secretly discussing peace with the Germans. The generals were enraged. Ever since the German 'peace offensive' of 1917, international channels had been used to pursue possible peace negotiations (it was even rumoured that Haldane had been sent on a secret mission to Berlin and had brought back peace proposals from the Kaiser. 'I was told this as a fact by a well-known woman,' wrote Marie Belloc Lowndes, 'who added, however, that Mr Asquith wished to accept these peace proposals, but had been stopped from doing so by Lloyd George!') Early in 1918, Kuhlmann, the German Foreign Minister and former Counsellor at the German Embassy who was well connected with British aristocracy, had suggested through his friend Sir William Tyrell that they should meet in Holland, at a castle belonging to Count Bentinck (cousin to the British Dukes of Portland, the Cavendish-Bentincks). Prince Hatzfeldt-Wildenburg was to lead the German deputation. Repington knew the Prince's mother socially in London, often dining with her and Lady Cunard, Elizabeth Asquith, Diana Manners and others. It is therefore likely – especially in light of his work with the British Secret Service – that he knew of these new secret peace moves, of which he wholeheartedly disapproved.

On 23 April, Repington asked Billing, due to appear at the Old Bailey the following day, to join the conspirators against Lloyd George. He proposed that Billing should get his trial postponed, then use the Black Book 'to smear various guilty politicians at the Old Bailey, and work up anti-German feeling in the House of Commons by persistent questions on aliens ...'. This would ruin the peace talks and wreck Lloyd George's authority. He would fall, and the war could be run as the military wished. Billing's reputation for attacking German aliens in British public life was well known, and Repington said it was just those people whom Kuhlmann was using. It was also convenient that Billing was fulminating against Jack Grein, originally a Dutchman, for his misuse of the Red Cross and the YMCA: the peace negotiations were to take place in the Hague, and Kuhlmann had been using both the Red Cross and the YMCA as communication channels.

It was a neat plan. If Billing could delay his trial (thereby causing maximum disruption to the coming negotiations), then Repington could ensure him the overt backing of the *Morning Post*. To Billing, who had recently lost Beaverbrook's support, it was too good an offer to refuse. The conspirators encouraged Billing to conduct his own defence – a ploy to cause yet more trouble. However, as insurance, his backers acquired for their pawn an eminent but anonymous King's Counsel to give expert guidance. It was also proposed that Asquith could be 'worked up' as the offical leader of the plot to get rid of Lloyd George – thereby providing a cover for Repington, presumably.

On 4 May came clear signs that the Germans were suing for peace. A Norwegian source revealed that the Germans admitted to losing 600,000 men up to 18 April, and that public opinion there was not prepared to allow the attrition to continue. There was also a report of 'mysterious persons' arriving in London from Holland, 'promptly denounced by the Foreign Office and in an Admiralty communique as enemy agents'. Two days later, on 6 May, *The Times* published a leader on the German 'peace offensive', claiming it could be a ruse to gain time.

*

The prevailing atmosphere of mutiny and conspiracy was fed by widespread feelings of despair. As the war wore on, hysteria grew. Suspicions became virulent hatred; a nation whose patriotic spirit was eroded by loss and death was susceptible to the ever more xenophobic outbursts of the *John Bull*/Horatio Bottomley brigade, of which Billing represented the extreme edge. The generals would take advantage of this bitter, tabloid-stirred cocktail to bring down Lloyd George's government and sabotage what they regarded as traitorous peace talks. But Lloyd George was a wily opponent, and knew through his own channels what was going on. He and his supporters would use any means necessary to fight their corner, and would, like their opponents, cynically attempt to manipulate public opinion to achieve victory. The Black Book inspired them to think that a smear campaign of sexual perversion was the best way to discredit the conspirators; it would also remove a potential barrier to the secret peace talks, for the government feared that Billing's renegade xenophobia could stir up public opinion against the talks. So the government decided to send an agent to 'kill' Billing politically – an aim with which the likes of F.E. Smith would be in ready agreement.

On 6 May, Billing received a letter from an Eileen Villiers-Stuart:

Dear Mr Pemberton-Billing,
Please forgive the gross impertinence of an entire stranger in writing to you. But altho' I admit until a few weeks ago I'd really never heard your name (I've not long returned to England), you've touched upon a subject very near to my heart – by that I mean you are endeavouring to carry out (and I'm sure you will succeed) a work my Godfather spent his life trying to complete. He tried very hard to save England from becoming a 'glorified Berlin' where its morals are concerned!

Many times he was quite rudely informed he was practically a 'fool' – and of course the War was not on then, had it been so, and had there been so much evidence at hand he would probably have been successful, but unfortunately he died before this present crisis. But you are alive and you can 'carry on', and any help I can give you I'll most willingly offer. It may be a strange subject for a woman to choose, but I just feel I want to carry on the work he commenced.

I am so glad you inserted that paragraph in the *Vigilante*. Of course you were sued for libel, because when you wrote it you apparently 'hit home', and I consider always that a libel action is merely a cloak of pretended innocence for the apparently guilty. Also I will say that I do not consider you were nearly severe enough when you said the 'First 47,000' – I should have written the 'First 470,000'.

Writing from the Grosvenor Court Hotel in Davies Street, Mayfair, Mrs Villiers-Stuart protested:

There are places around here, not a hundred yards from my hotel, where the disgusting devices adopted by the late Oscar Wilde are hourly carried on, and considering the main people concerned in these places, or to put it plainer, the principal habitués, are men high up in naval and military circles. [*sic*]

The tone of Mrs Villiers-Stuart's erratically-written letter was quite obviously one of a dictated, constructed missive; her knowledge of male brothels is unlikely to have been extensive.

Then one wonders how many of our State secrets and army positions are exposed under these conditions. I say most vehemently that if these conditions were to cease, our armies would be in much better positions. One cannot write everything on paper, it would take too long, but if you'd care to take luncheon with me any day this week or next, I may be able to tell you many things that may interest and help you.

May I wish you all success

Yours very sincerely
Eileen Villiers-Stuart.

While others might have dismissed this as no more than the ranting of a paranoid, there was an underlying tone of inside information to the letter which engaged Billing's interest – and might have roused the suspicions of the wary. So they should, for in fact Villiers-Stuart was an agent provocateur sent by the government, a modern female adventuress with a career as colourful as Maud Allan's and a penchant for political intrigue to rival Mata Hari's.

*

Eileen Graves was born at New Brighton, Cheshire in 1892; her father, Emerson Graves, was a traveller for the toothpaste company, Nelson Richards. Petite, plump and attractive in the fashion of the time, she somehow worked her way into London society, and in the summer of 1912, 'at a luncheon party at Princes' Hotel, Jermyn Street', at the age of nineteen, Eileen met the Hon. Neil Primrose, possibly the 'godfather' of her letter. Primrose was the second (and favourite) son of Lord Rosebery, the former Prime Minister (himself implicated in the Wilde affair as putative lover of the Marquess of Queensberry's elder son, Viscount Drumlanrig*). Primrose was then acting as Liberal Chief Whip in Asquith's government. 'She knew he was married, but she had not met his wife.' Eileen became Primrose's mistress for the next five years, during which time she met and married Percival Douglas Bray, a bus driver from Putney (in court, Eileen described him as 'interested in the motor trade') as a cover for the fact that she was pregnant by Primrose. She left Bray after a month, and said that he was 'killed in action in August 1914'.

Formerly MP for Wisbech, Primrose had served in France with the Buckinghamshire Yeomanry Hussars, but was recalled to become Under-Secretary for Foreign Affairs; then Joint Parliamentary Secretary to the Treasury.† However, he argued with Lloyd George, and rejoining his regiment, was posted to Palestine. While her lover was away, Eileen met her second husband-to-be, Captain Percival Villiers-Stuart, scion of Anglo-Irish gentry, then serving in the

---

* Rosebery succeeded Gladstone as Prime Minister in 1894. The Marquess of Queensberry suspected Rosebery of homosexuality, and of corrupting his son, Drumlanrig – Rosebery's private secretary. Queensberry pursued Rosebery in much the same manner as he did Wilde, albeit less successfully. In 1893 he followed Rosebery to Bad Homburg with a dogwhip, but was ordered to leave by the Prince of Wales. Drumlanrig committed suicide the following year, possibly fearing blackmail over his relations with Rosebery, whom Queensberry referred to as one of 'the Snob Queers ... that cur and Jew friend [?fiend] Liar ...'. When Wilde came to trial, Rosebery considered helping him, until he was warned by Balfour that doing so might lose them the coming election. He didn't, and they lost it anyway.

† In March 1915 Marie Belloc Lowndes recorded in her diary having met Primrose and a diplomat, Frank Rattigan (father of Terence Rattigan) at a dinner given by Mrs de Rothschild, at which Primrose 'talked a good deal about British prisoners', who were on 'practically starvation rations'.

Cheshire Regiment. Despite the opposition of Percival's mother – who saw Eileen for what she was – the pair were married in Birkenhead (where Villiers-Stuart was stationed) in July 1917. Captain Villiers-Stuart, like the other two men in his wife's life, was also posted abroad to India, conveniently leaving the ambitious twenty-five-year-old Eileen a single woman, mixing with a 'fast set' and associating with Primrose's friends and others on the fringe of political life. It is probable that she acquired her commission from British Intelligence through her relationship with Primrose; it was as a private detective and sometime agent that she came recommended to the government's attention. Thus had this daughter of a travelling salesman, like Maud Allan, moved up the ranks of society; an amateur, slightly podgy *femme fatale* opportunist who found herself deep in high level political intrigue.

Eileen had been sent by Lloyd George and Conservative Central Office (therefore the coalition government) with instructions to lure Billing to a male brothel at 11a Duke Street, off Manchester Square – the sort of premises to which she referred in her letter to Billing. After the trial Eileen confessed: 'I was instructed on behalf of certain Political Associations in London in my capacity of a private detective, to endeavour to entrap Mr Pemberton-Billing and to compromise him, with the object of damaging his character so as to put an end to his Parliamentary career.' The plan was for him to witness some scene of degradation involving a pathetic elderly military or naval gentleman who might be mistaken for a high-ranking officer, and for Billing himself then to be secretly photographed, 'or otherwise fatally compromised'.

The meeting between Eileen and her target had a rather different resolution, as she would admit in her post-trial statement: 'The outcome of the correspondence was that an interview was arranged between myself and Mr Pemberton-Billing, when he put before me his position, and the objects which the Vigilante Society was fighting for, and I was so impressed with his sincerity, and with the purity of his motives, which were entirely for the benefit of this country, that I decided to throw over my employers, and to give Mr Pemberton-Billing all the information in my possession for use in his defence.' Soon Mr Billing possessed Mrs Villiers-Stuart, too. It was not an unscripted scenario. It appears that Villiers-Stuart was a double agent from the start, having been intercepted by the military conspirators, probably drawing on Repington's acquaintance with the workings of British intelligence. Eileen's affair with Billing was part of the ploy. Meanwhile, her self-proclaimed occupation as private investigator encouraged other rumours. Cynthia Asquith, who probably knew of Villiers-Stuart beforehand, was told after the trial by the writer Charles Whibley that 'Mrs ——, the witness who claimed to have been shown the "Black Book" by Neil Primrose and Evelyn de Rothschild [both of whom Cynthia knew socially], was originally employed by Maud Allan as a detective to find out what Billing knew and he had won her over as a weapon on his side'. If true, this gives credence to the theory that Maud may have had some sort of espionage role (her European connexions would have made her a prime candidate for recruitment by either side). It certainly appears that she was concerned about rumours of her relationship with Margot Asquith. Given her past, and her readiness to resort to law, her actions do appear to be suspicious – understandable, with the number of skeletons she had in her cupboard.

The fact that Villiers-Stuart claimed to have actually seen the Black Book was crucial to the coming trial; no better witness could have fallen into Billing's open arms. Her defection sent the politicians into panic. 'My political employers became aware that I was giving Mr Pemberton-Billing information', she said in her subsequent sworn statement, 'and that I had deserted them, with the result that I received letters, written I believe at the instance of my political employers, in which my life was threatened unless I returned to their employment and do all that I could to secure the downfall of Mr Pemberton-Billing ...' Billing took these threats seriously, and rather tactlessly asked his new mistress to make a sworn statement about the 'The First 47,000' so as to leave behind evidence should her employers' retribution succeed.

The politicians had good reason to fear the emergence of all this in court: His Majesty's Government using agent provocateurs, male brothels and threats of murder to further their aims was not a handsome story. They may well have feared the revelations of the Black Book, too. Neither Asquith nor Lloyd George led blameless moral lives: Asquith had his mistress, Venetia Stanley, to whom he wrote in more detail about political matters than he did to the king; while Lloyd George's sexual adventures were wide-ranging and accomplished, and he was said to have worked his way through most of the Downing Street typing pool.

Lloyd George was busy blustering through Parliamentary and military opposition – to Repington's fury, especially as moves towards peace also continued: 'Will history ever realise the dirty games played by this administration and its Press gang?' It was from the military that the challenge came. On 7 May *The Times* published a letter from Major-General Sir Frederick Maurice, who defied military discipline by accusing the Prime Minster of having 'misrepresented to Parliament the number of British troops deployed in France during the recent German offensive'. This was perilous insurrection for Lloyd George: his generals driven by lack of confidence in the coalition War Cabinet to criticise the PM openly. Lloyd George needed to beat down such talk quickly and effectively. A critical parliamentary debate on the subject followed. It was an opportunity for Asquith to take the lead, but in his 'innocuous contribution', he denied Maurice's allegations. Asquith's performance did not impress the public, who wanted answers. The *Manchester Guardian* noted: 'People do not understand this legalistic attitude to affairs of life and death.' The paper's editor wrote privately that the 'Maurice affair is something of a mystery ... Asquith is discredited.' It was clear to political observers that other motives were at work. The scent of conspiracy hung in the air, emanating from a general sense of frustration, suspicion and anomie, which Billing, and his backers, would exploit.

*

On 21 May, Billing entered his Plea of Justification, his legal statement of defence. 'Noel Pemberton-Billing says he is not guilty,' it stated, 'and for a further plea he says that all the defamatory matters alleged in the Indictment are true.' This was fighting talk. Details were given of *Salome* and its author, 'a moral pervert'; the play was 'an open representation of degenerate sexual lust, sexual crime, and unnatural passions and an evil and mischievous travesty of a biblical story'. Billing reiterated the Black Book story – which some might have considered a travesty itself – and the fact that 'it was for the public benefit' that he had drawn attention to the affair. Previously, Billing had offered to pay £1,000 into Court as a guarantee against damages and costs; now he claimed that all he had published was true. In the meantime, Billing's apparent defence of Christian values and Messianic pose brought him the bizarre support of the Christian Scientists, who had decided that he was 'the Saviour, Christ the King, come to redeem them in this moment of national peril'. Afraid that if he went to prison – for a possible sentence of nine years – he could not carry on his work, they selected a woman – 'a senior lady in the movement – reputedly extremely plain' – who was sent to bear his child. Straightforward heterosexual lust was no problem for this virile son of Empire. He did his duty, and his heir was conceived in the days before the trial proper began.

While their proprietor was thus occupied, the broadsheet pages of the *Vigilante* continued to stoke the debate about insidious foreign decadence in Britain. Harold Spencer noted that Christopher Millard, Wilde's bibliographer and Ross's secretary, had recently received his second prosecution for indecent assault, quoting the London Recorder 'who remarked that it had been his misfortune to try "an astounding number" of similar cases since 1914', cases 'which disclosed a condition of things which was simply appalling'. It was a case which much exercised Millard's friends, not least Robbie Ross, who could see trouble coming. The public conviction and imprisonment of Millard would draw unwelcome attention to Ross's sexuality, already an open secret – Ross having been publicly identified as a close friend of Wilde's since the latter's conviction. The source of this subplot was obvious: the affronted Lord Alfred

Douglas was at work, determined that Robbie Ross and the cult of Wilde should suffer ignominy.

It suited Billing to side with Douglas, not only for the opportunity it gave him to twist the knife in Wilde's reputation and damn 'moral perverts', but also to attack the Liberals; Billing's antipathy to the Asquiths was bound up in the same prejudices. Spencer's article reminded readers of the previous legal battles between Douglas and Ross, quoting from the 1914 trial: ' "If you, the jury, find that the prosecutor (Ross) is a ——, you will probably find that he is also a blackmailer." Ross, it will thus be seen, WAS UNSUCCESSFUL IN BOTH PROSECUTIONS.' He also referred to the money Ross had received on his testimonial and the fact that he had become President of the Imperial War Museum through Asquith's lobbying. Douglas's dislike of 'Squiffy' Asquith was almost as great as Billing's, and the *Vigilante* quoted Douglas's sardonic doggerel, *All's Well With England*:

> Scorn not the 'literary executor'
> He is 'officially condoned,' for he
> Has rescued Oscar Wilde from obloquy
> And planted him in our heart's inmost core ...
>
> Out there in Flanders all the trampled ground
> Is red with English blood, our children pass
> Through fire to Moloch. Who will count the loss
> Since here 'at home' sits merry Margot, bound
> With Lesbian fillets, while in front of her brass
> 'Old Squiffy' hands the purse to Robert Ross?

Having aired this libellous verse, the article concluded with reference to *De Profundis* 'which contains gross, foul and wicked libels upon persons at present living' and which was 'handed to the [British] Museum authorities by Mr Robert Ross, whom Mr Asquith and the others seek to glorify. These portions of the manuscript are not to be published until 1960, by which time the persons libelled in them will have passed away. Why was the manuscript not destroyed?' Such editorials make clear the connexion between Billing, Spencer, and Douglas. In the lead-up to the court case, the *Vigilante* continued to publish Douglas's attacks on Ross and the cult of Wilde. On 20 April, before the trial proper began, it quoted two poems by Douglas: *The Man Named Ross* ('All praise Priapus should engross/ Rise, morbid muse, and sing the man named Ross'); and *The Rossiad*. The effect was to bring the Ross-Douglas battle back into court (Croft-Cooke observes that the list of names supposedly to be found in the Black Book was remarkably similar to the signatories to Ross's testimonial). The embattled Ross, no longer protected by a Prime Minister, attempted to keep a low profile, but he would not be left alone. While waiting for the trial to come to the Old Bailey, Ross faced 'continued harassment and visits from the police',* as he told Charles Ricketts on 6 March 1918:

> I don't know if it is a *post hoc* or a *propter hoc*, but yesterday morning as I was opening my letters, including one from yourself, detectives arrived from Scotland Yard. I concluded of course that it was the usual thing. (I have long become accustomed to the Douglas cum Scotland Yard conspiracy, for it is really nothing else, to drive me either to murder or madness.) However I found that it was a cheerful change. Information has been laid against me that … [I was] an art critic! a pacifist, a consorter of the company of conscientious-objectors, a sympathiser with and visitor of Geman prisoners: a former professed Roman Catholic and now a professed and militant atheist.

Perhaps Ross had been one of the proposed targets for Beverley Nichols's 'raids' on the Café Royal. In the last years of the war, the DORA-empowered establishment had become sensitive to any possible rebellion which might undermine the struggle to maintain Britain at war. But Ross had not been a friend of Wilde for nothing, and used his wit to defuse the situation.

> They were rather flabbergasted when I said it was all perfectly true, and that I could produce documentary evidence to prove it. It is so grotesque that I am not in the least alarmed, and would not have recorded the matter to you at all, except as an explanation of why I cannot, as I intended, do anything further about the person of whom you wrote, at all events for the present. By a brilliant instinct, when the detective arrived, and assuming a search of my rooms, I hurled your letter into the fire. I mention this lest you should anticipate similar enquiries, of which, of course, there is no fear. But everyone must be careful.

Billing was successfully exploiting this climate of fear – and the ancient war between Ross and Douglas – and could have pointed to Ross's letter to Ricketts as positive evidence of the Wilde cult at work; but Ross refused to stop helping his friends (the unnamed person in his letter, evidently in trouble over sexual indiscretions, was Christopher Millard, about to be gaoled again for homosexual offences). The paranoid, philistine strains of this encounter would run through the coming trial: indeed, at times it would appear that modern art and Bohemia were as much on trial as anything else.

*

---

* During the Douglas-Ross libel trial in 1914, a retired police inspector named West had volunteered evidence to the effect that during fifteen years' service in the West End, he had known Ross as an associate of 'sodomites' and 'male prostitutes'.

Billing's campaign seemed to be working; all London society appeared to be dragged into the maelstrom. It was a sense of precipitate doom reflected in events across the Channel. The German push on the Western Front continued, and by 29 May they were approaching Paris; it seemed France might fall. The political crisis deepened. In Parliament, Tory backbenchers turned on Asquith for having lost the Maurice debate against Lloyd George, and for his supposed favouring of peace talks. Billing would have their support. But more crucial to the success or failure of his coming battle at the Old Bailey would be the conduct of the trial, and the character of the man chosen to oversee it. Acting Lord Chief Justice Darling – a Tory MP for ten years, and known to some as 'little Darling' – had been specially selected to hear the case; the usual Old Bailey rota had been ignored to enable him to take it. It was a critical choice, not least because Justice Darling was the most celebrated judge in the country, in whose courts Billing, Douglas and even Grein had all already appeared in libel suits.

Born in Essex in 1849, Charles Darling was described by F.E. Smith as looking like 'a very delicately fashioned cameo'; his biographer Evelyn Graham sensed French blood in his family, for 'there are a daintiness and a finesse in his manner and in his physical "make-up" never associated with the average Britisher born'. Darling was called to the Bar at twenty-four, but spent rather more time on his career in journalism than in court, appearing to prefer the pose to the actuality: 'Certainly in those days, he was the youngest-looking and best-dressed man at the English Bar.' He became a QC in 1885, and three years later won Deptford against the Liberal candidate, Wilfrid Blunt;[*] he held the seat for the Conservatives until 1897. In 1892, Darling became the youngest of the contemporary appointments to the Bench. The appointment outraged the Liberals; Asquith, who regarded it as a 'Tory job', was 'particularly incensed'.

Darling was notable for the celebrated cases he tried: the sensational Steine Morrison case of 1911, when a murdered Jew had been found on Clapham Common with two Ss cut into his cheeks; 'Chicago May' Churchill, 'the worst woman in the world'; and Roger Casement's appeal against the death sentence for treason in 1916 (which he dismissed, as he did Dr Crippen's). In court Darling displayed his erudition and wit, managing, in one case, to quote from Matthew Arnold, Shakespeare, Wordsworth, Disraeli, Dickens, Goldsmith and Tennyson. Such exhibitionism drew adverse press criticism, although, ironically, Darling's love of word-play came from his early experience of journalism, writing the occasional lampoon on modern artists such as Whistler. Darling's marriage, at the age of thirty-five, to Mary Wilberforce, was seen as a renounce-

---

[*] Wilfred Scawen Blunt (1840-1922), Soul, poet, and traveller, was imprisoned that year for his activity in the Irish Land League.

ment of his reputation as a *flaneur*, but in 1913 Mary died suddenly, leaving Darling to assume the role of maudlin widower.

In maturity, Darling seems to have been a frustrated writer, subsuming his literary desires in law, a flamboyant figure revelling in the performance of the courtroom. His favourite tone was one of lofty naïveté, for which his breed are renowned. Once, when a counsel referred to Charlie Chaplin, Darling intervened: 'Who', he said, 'is this Mr Chaplin?' The counsel replied, 'My Lord, he is the Darling of the Halls.' The pun delighted the justice. He was equally pleased when accorded the signal honour – reserved for the truly celebrated – of a Max Beerbohm caricature: the cartoonist portrayed him in a black cap 'tinkling with bells'. Like Beerbohm, Darling was a dandy. While other judges took advantage of their robes to wear old clothes underneath, he was impeccably outfitted '... in the glossiest of silk hats and the most perfect fitting of morning clothes, seemingly transcending Savile Row, black as a Jesuit priest and equally inscrutable'. The judge's vaguely foreign, sartorially elegant air, combined with his lordly wit of privilege, marked him out as other; he represented all that Billing hated. In the context of the forthcoming trial, Darling himself would be portrayed as one of the 'enemy'.

*

With its transferral to the Central Criminal Court, the prosecution of the Billing case had been automatically taken over by the Crown. The young lawyer Travers Humphreys would act for the prosecution, but just as Billing would be instructed by a KC, so it was decided that Travers Humphreys should be led by an elder, apparently complicit in the government conspiracy, who would see to it that Billing lost the case and was imprisoned. Ellis Hume-Williams was fifty-five years old, an experienced barrister and Tory MP (for Bassetlaw, Nottingham); he had served in the Munro Ambulance Corps at Flanders, and on the Red Commission in Russia in 1916 and 1917. According to his friend C.G.L du Cann, who attended the trial, Hume-Williams was 'a fashionable divorce man rather out of his depth'. Subsequent evidence would call such a description into question.

Set-pieces such as the Billing trial seem little different from stage drama; the fact that many of the participants in the theatre of jurisprudence had been or were involved in the world of theatre gave the proceedings an added histrionic edge. To a backdrop of national crisis, the issues that seemed to threaten the future of the country would be played out in a performance that verged on farce. But it would become clear that the movements in the wings were more important than the acting out front. The case opened at the Old Bailey on the morning of 29 May, and took an unprecedented five days (defendants representing themselves were traditionally allowed longer to make their case) to lay out its extraordinary series of allegation, counter-allegation, sensational disclosure and shameful hypocrisy.

The excitement outside the courtroom was evident as queues formed for tickets for the public gallery. Inside, the participants bustled about, readying themselves for the drama about to begin; in the corridor, Billing was seen deep in discussion with Lord Alfred Douglas. Among the merely curious were supporters and observers: the National Party's Lord Beresford; Robbie Ross's friend, Edmund Gosse; and the novelists Sir 'Anthony Hope' Hawkins, Bart Kennedy, and Hugh Walpole. Du Cann recalled the atmosphere: 'As a young officer I had snatched 48 hours from "winning the war" in Flanders and I went to the Pemberton-Billing trial for a little healthy excitement', he wrote. 'Pantomime, circus, farce: that unique Court performance contained elements of all three ... the excited gallery-audience cheered like spectators at a football match.' Billing, 'black-haired, square-browed, clean-shaven and wearing a monocle', was 'a striking figure at the solicitor's table ... His staccato, deep-voiced sentences vibrated with force and fire, like a machine-gun.' Billing's first action was to challenge the make-up of the court itself – an audacious pre-emptive strike. He appears to have realised that Darling was a set-up, and so protested at his taking the case, citing Darling's well-known 'levity', and the fact that they had clashed before (when Billing had been the plantiff in a civil action). 'The fact that you may take an unfavourable view of me can be reason why I should not try your case', remarked Darling '... by the same process you might exhaust every Judge upon the Bench.'

Now Maud Allan made her entrance, dramatic in red-feathered picture hat and black cloak. The *Daily Mirror* noted, 'There was a murmur of excitement when Miss Maud Allan entered the witness-box. At first she was almost inaudible, but, when asked to speak in a louder tone, she faced the jury with a smile – and complied ...' As she did so, no one but she could have expected the surprise attack of Billing's cross-examination. He asked if 'Maud Allan' were her full name. She replied that it was 'Beulah Maud Allan Durrant'. Billing then produced *Celebrated Criminal Cases of America*, a book published by the San Francisco Police Department in 1910. He asked her to turn to a marked page. 'Is that a photograph of your brother?' It was. 'You are the sister of William Henry Theodore Durrant?' 'I am.' 'Was your brother executed in San Francisco for murdering two young girls and outraging them after death?' The sharp intake of breath of those not already privy to this secret must have been audible.

Maud's failure to disclose her family history to the prosecution was a crucial mistake. Forewarned, they would have been forearmed, and ready to counteract. She may have hoped that Billing did not know the details (as her apparent hiring of Villiers-Stuart shows). But Billing's informants had briefed him well, and his revelation had the optimum shock value. Having exhibited this skeleton, Billing went on to question Maud about the offensive paragraph. Did she understand the meaning of the word 'clitoris'? Maud said she did, but only because of her amateur reading in medicine (she could well have cited Marie Stopes's *Married Love*, which had introduced the term to the book-reading public for the first time that March, although not to the readers of *The Times* which refused to review the book on grounds of decency). 'Are you aware, Miss Allan, that out of twenty-four people who were shown that libel, including many professional men, only one of them, who happened to be a barrister, understood what it meant?' The use of this scientific term in open court was the source of much interest, amusement, and uninformed outrage: press reports had to substitute a row of stars or a line for the word.* As the *Married Love* controversy showed, sexual censorship remained the order of the day; the public must be protected.

Billing's third line of attack was on Allan's connexions with Germany. As with her unfortunate medical knowledge, Maud's Teutonic associations would, in this fourth year of war, condemn her out of hand. Billing quoted from her book, *My Life and Dancing* – 'It was decided I should go to Berlin to take up my studies there' – as if the mere fact of Maud's European ambition was enough to imply outright guilt. Billing pointed out that the authorities in Munich had objected to her *Vision of Salome* (the implication being that even decadent Germany was shocked by her performance). Maud's reaction was to look down haughtily on these smears on her life and dancing; she was, after all, an artist: 'The critics who have suggested I was scantily clad were only of opinion that I was so by comparison. I was a pioneer in art. I presume the selfsame critics would say this day I am too much clothed probably.' Billing's tack was unerringly xenophobic: 'This type of dancing is a German art?' he asked. '... You had your instruction or training in Germany, did you not? ... This art was quite foreign to the British public before you presented it?' 'As far as I know,' replied Miss Allan, as the shade of Isadora danced before her.

Billing then turned to Maud's social connexions. He remarked on her 1908 success at the Palace Theatre, and her acclaim by the aristocracy: 'Did you ever go to 10 Downing Street?' Yes, but not to dance, as he suggested; nor had Mrs Asquith subsequently visited her in her dressing room at the Palace Theatre – an obvious piece of innuendo on Billing's part. Darling reprimanded him for bringing the name of a 'third person' into court, and threatened to call Mrs Asquith as a witness to prove the truth of the matter – which rather defeated the

---

* Even in 1951, when reviving the scandal, the *Evening Standard* substituted a dash for the word 'clitoris'.

object of his protest. It was this sort of exchange, and possible production of star witnesses, which made Darling's conduct of the trial notorious. When Billing launched into an amateur textual analysis of Wilde's *Salome*, Darling suddenly began to read a random extract about the moon: 'She is like a dove that has strayed. She is like a narcissus trembling in the wind. She is like a silver flower.' The judge, playing the philistine, turned to the court, shaking his head: 'I do not see where the Art is. Of course, I cannot understand it. (Laughter in Court.)' It was a disingenuous, crowd-pleasing remark.

Billing continued to elucidate – at great length – the text for the benefit of the court, finding 'incestuous lust', necrophilia and sado-masochism in Wilde's words. Miss Allan saw no such references: 'I cannot be responsible for what other persons read into it.' Billing asked if she had read the works of Krafft-Ebing or Bloch. She had not. 'When John the Baptist is referring to the crimes of Sodom and Babylon, did you know what that referred to?' he asked. 'That she is a daughter of Babylon,' replied Allan. 'A daughter of Sodom too, I think,' said Billing, demonstrating the contemporary belief that to be guilty of one form of sexual perversion was to be a practitioner of them all. He declared that 'this play was founded on the scientific works of Krafft-Ebing'; to which Darling replied, 'You must prove that.'

'You do not think there is anything in this play which is calculated to arouse any passion or any emotion either in the actors or the audience?' Billing asked. 'I do not,' replied Maud, 'any more than *Hotch Potch* or *A Little Bit of Fluff* or any of the others that are being played now.' 'Are you aware that there are people in this country who practise unnatural vices,' Billing continued; his search for vice sounded a little desperate. 'There are everywhere,' she returned succinctly, 'but I am not responsible for that.' 'Are you aware that Mr Robert Ross has said that *Salome* has made the author's name a household word wherever the English language is not spoken?' said Billing. 'I know nothing of Mr Robert Ross,' said Maud, and the prosecution protested at the introduction of his name. Billing pointed out that the play's production required Ross's permission. He was to employ that as an excuse to call Ross and use his reputation as a pro-German homosexual to 'blacken' the Asquiths.

Next, Billing handed Maud a copy of the Beardsley edition of *Salome*. He hoped that its indecent illustrations would confirm the obscenity of the play itself, but Darling disallowed such evidence on the grounds that 'there are editions of the Bible with the most objectionable and profane illustrations'. This was less a defence of Wilde than a subversion of Billing's case, and it annoyed him. Billing protested that 'there are a number of people in this country, moral perverts, practising sexual vices and others, and being moral perverts, with their perversions lying dormant in some cases, might be led by seeing pantomimic acts of sadism to practise them themselves'. The question was phrased to constitute another reference to Theo Durrant; as was Billing's description of Salome kissing the severed head of John the Baptist as a sadistic act (had he known its meaning he would have used the term necrophilia). The prosecution sprang to Maud's defence: 'I submit, my Lord, that that is a very indecent question to ask this lady. He puts to her some vice, and asks her to describe it to the Jury. It is ... highly improper.' Darling agreed, but Billing persisted, talking of 'the head of a man ... used as a means of generating sexual excitement in a young girl ... I have suggested that you are playing the principal part in ministering to social perversion.' 'Are you aware of the type of man that Oscar Wilde was?' If Billing had known that Maud had met Wilde in Paris, he would have delighted in confronting her with the fact. 'I know nothing about Oscar Wilde at all,' Maud replied, disingenuously. 'I only know what you took good care to let everybody else know in the Court at Bow Street.'

Billing now presented his next shock revelation. He announced that Miss Allan was being used by politicians, pointing out that she could have brought her action against him in the civil courts, rather than end up with a crown prosecution. He was accusing her of the sort of complicity of which his current lover, Eileen Villiers-Stuart, was more definitely guilty. Maud certainly was being used by the politicians: but how far her complicity went it is difficult to know; she must have had, at least, the support and encouragement of her friends the Asquiths in her libel suit. When Maud was re-examined by the prosecution, it was made clear that the purpose of the trial was to clear her name. And Darling made it clear to Billing – with not a little relish – that Grein's indictment was a separate one, and would be tried separately. This infuriated Billing, who had hoped to face Grein – a more worthy opponent than a lady, no matter how tainted with the sins of Sodom – with his xenophobic questioning and allusions to secret peace talks at The Hague. When, on the following day, Billing implied collusion between prosecution and judge, he was not far wrong. He knew that he had been charged 'solely with defamatory libel by means of a legal ruse', and that the political conspirators were using Maud Allan to keep Grein out of the witness-box. Having expected Grein to take the witness box, Billing had not prepared for the rest of the case; his witnesses would not be ready until the following day. As a result, the case was adjourned.

*

When it opened at 10.30 the next morning, the public gallery was 'filled with a crowd of fashionably dressed people'. It was also packed with wounded soldiers in pyjama-like blue hospital uniforms whom Billing had persuaded to attend. It was a clever theatrical ploy on his part. These men, with their sleeves sewn short where limbs should be, were an emotional sight, a silently remonstrative chorus to the drama. Throughout the duration of the trial, crowds gathered outside the court as well as in, swelling in intensity and fervour with each new revelation in the press. To observers and participants alike, it seemed they were baying for blood. Maud Allan recalled: 'The Court was packed to suffocation and it was said that everybody who was anybody in London had managed, by hook or by crook, to get inside the trial room. Besides the occupation of every seat, a number of persons jammed themselves around the walls of the Court, making the atmosphere unbearable and trying the temper of everyone engaged in the case.' The near-hysterical climate within and without threatened to prejudice the case – were it not already infected. 'Right from the start,' wrote Allan, 'there was an atmosphere of nervous tension that affected the Judge and perhaps the Counsel as well ...'

Before opening his defence, Billing had discussed it with Eileen Villiers-Stuart who, along with Harold Spencer, was to be his main witness. Eileen agreed to appear only on the assurance that she would not have to mention any names. She later claimed that Spencer had told her he had never actually seen the Black Book, but that he would perjure himself by saying he had in order to support her evidence. He maintained he had been told of the book by Neil Primrose, whom he knew to have shown a copy to Eileen. When she asked Billing if he would allow Spencer to tell such lies, he replied, 'Yes, he will have to go in and tell them, in order to corroborate your evidence, because if he does not, they will not believe you.' 'They are all lies,' she replied. 'Yes, I know,' said Billing, 'but it has got to be done.' The phrase suggests Billing was not acting on his own.

Villiers-Stuart took the stand, told the court she had indeed seen the Black Book, and that the article in question was true. The prosecution objected that 'no evidence has been given of the existence of this book. Either it must be produced, or evidence must be given of the fact that it cannot be produced before its contents can be given in this case.' Darling put this to Billing, who could not say whether the book would be produced. Darling ordered Eileen to leave the stand and questioned Billing further. 'It will be impossible to produce this book at this stage of the trial,' argued Billing. Darling replied, 'It is no use to tell me that it will be impossible to produce this book. You must tell me where it is. Perhaps if you cannot get it, I can. I still have some powers left. (Laughter in Court.)'

Eileen was recalled, and announced not only that she had seen the book, but that she had handled it, too: it was a 'big, flat book', 'about that thickness', she said, indicating a book 'about the size of a *Chambers Nineteenth Century Dictionary*'. Billing now broke his promise: he asked his witness to name the person who had shown her the book. Taken aback, Eileen hesitated, but was ordered to answer the question by Darling. She named her former lover, Neil Primrose. 'Were you alone?' asked Billing. Eileen mentioned Major Evelyn de Rothschild; she had been shown the book over tea at a small hotel called The Hut in Ripley, to which she had been specifically summoned by the men for that purpose. Primrose had brought the book, having been told about it 'at a luncheon party in May 1915' by Captain Spencer. Yet Spencer admitted to never having seen the book; somebody must have been lying. Possibly Eileen introduced Spencer in this manner to substantiate the claims he would make in court after her testimony. Primrose and Rothschild had watched her inspect the book: 'They had turned the pages over with her, and explained the whole thing to her; and she had found names in the book.' Afterwards, she had returned with the men to London, where they left her, taking the book with them. She had not seen it since, and thought it was probably now in Germany.

Billing asked her why she had come forward to give evidence, but was overruled by Darling. Billing began, 'Are you acquainted with the fact that there exists in this country – ' but was again cut off in midstream by Darling. Billing resumed for a third time, with comments about the 'First 47,000'. He asked Villiers-Stuart: 'Is the paragraph justified by the contents of the book?' For a third time he was beaten down by the judge: 'No, no, no, you must not ask that.' Billing asked Darling if he could recall Eileen later to state the contents of the book. Only if he could prove its existence, said the judge. Billing pointed out that 'the two holders of the book are both dead. I cannot call them to prove that they destroyed it'; then quickly asked Eileen, 'Has your life ever been threatened in this connection?', to which she replied, 'It has.' The prosecution wondered what this had to do with the case. Darling agreed, saying he had allowed Billing far more latitude than he would any professional counsel. 'If you undertake to conduct your own case, you must conduct it according to the ordinary rules of evidence; and if you do not know how to conduct your case, you really should have employed someone.' Darling seemed unaware that Billing was indeed being advised, behind the scenes.

Proceedings in the staid courtroom began to overheat. Billing, irritated by Darling's constant carping, lost his temper, and waving his right hand in the air, shouted at the judge, 'I know nothing about evidence, and I know nothing about law. I come to this Court in the public interest to prove what I propose to prove.' 'Very well, then you must prove it according to the ordinary rules of evidence.' 'I say this, my Lord – ' Again Darling interrupted him: 'I do not want you to say anything to me. I only ask you to try to put only such questions – ' Billing lost control. He banged the table, and pointed at the Bench. He and Villiers-Stuart began shouting at each other:

119

Mr Billing: 'Is Justice Darling's name in the book?'
Mrs Villiers-Stuart (shouting): 'It is.'
Justice Darling: 'Just a moment.'
Mrs Villiers-Stuart (still shouting): 'It can be produced.'

The court was in uproar, with the ushers calling for 'Order'. Darling demanded, 'It can be produced?' Both Billing and his witness were shouting at the tops of their voices. Pointing at the judge, Villiers-Stuart declared, 'If it can be produced in Germany, it can be produced here. Mr Justice Darling,' she shouted, waving her hand wildly, 'we have got to win this war, and while you sit there, we will never win it.' 'My men are fighting [in Eileen's case, the plural was apposite], other people's men are fighting –' Billing, carried away by the uproar, egged his lover on:

Mr Billing: 'Is Mrs Asquith's name in the book?'
Mrs Villiers-Stuart: 'It is.'
Mr Billing: 'Is Mr Asquith's name in the book?'
Mrs Villiers-Stuart: 'It is.'
Mr Billing: 'Is Lord Haldane's name in the book?'
Mrs Villiers-Stuart: 'It is.'

Having been trapped by Billing, Eileen decided to go all the way, revealing name after name in a McCarthyite litany. This was sensational stuff; the gentlemen of the press, unable to believe their ears, scribbled furiously in their notebooks. Darling was in imminent danger of losing all control over his court and the case; if this witness wasn't stopped, there was no knowing whom she would incriminate. The judge barked 'Leave the box' to Villiers-Stuart. 'You dare not hear me,' she retorted. Billing, 'his face white with anger', paused; Villiers-Stuart remained in the box. 'Have you finished?' asked Darling; 'I have not,' said Billing. Darling ordered him to ask no more such questions. 'I have not the least objection to your having asked the one regarding myself, but I am determined to protect other people who are absent. (Applause in Court.)'

Lord Haldane's Germanophilia was not his only crime in Billing's eyes: Haldane had visited Wilde in prison, and attempted to secure better conditions for the playwright. He was thus a prime suspect for inclusion in the Black Book. Margot Asquith – who considered the whole affair 'the dirty work of Lloyd George and Beaverbrook' – commiserated with Haldane over the introduction of his name into the proceedings: 'Truth used to "prevail sooner or later" but now it never prevails. It is as out of fashion as Christ's teachings.'

In the Old Bailey, Darling continued his eccentric pursuit of the truth. Again he asked Villiers-Stuart if the book could be produced. 'The book is in Germany, and can be produced from Germany, and it will have to be produced.' The courtroom met Eileen's statement with 'startled silence'. After a dramatic pause, Billing went on with his examination: 'On 6 May 1918, you wrote me a letter, Mrs Villiers-Stuart.' 'Yes,' she replied, but before Billing could introduce this new piece of damning evidence, the prosecution protested, instructed by the politicans to prevent the indicting contents of this letter from being made public. Darling asked Billing to show him the letter; Billing said it was 'in a safe close by'. Darling instructed him to proceed with any other questions. Thus frustrated, Billing took another pause, and asked Villiers-Stuart if she knew of any 'houses in London that are being conducted for the purpose of practising criminal and unnatural vices?' She did. 'Do you of your own knowledge know whether these houses are so conducted for a political reason?' Eileen gave the address of 11a Duke Street. 'Who is running that house?' asked Billing. 'The name of the person supposed to run it,' intrigued Eileen, 'or the name of the person who is actually running it? A woman named Highfield is managing that house. She is known as Lally Highfield.'

The jury would have assumed that the 'political reason' referred to the '47,000'; they did not know that it was their own government, rather than the Germans, who were implicated in this sordid attempt at blackmail. Duke Street runs south of Manchester Square – famous as the home of the Wallace Collection – towards Oxford Street. It may not have been coincidence that this particular bordello was chosen, as it is but a short walk down from Cavendish Square, the London home of the Asquiths. The Post Office Directory for 1918 indicates a 'Miss Highfield' was indeed resident at 11a Duke Street, and had been since 1914; No. 11 was occupied by a surveyors' office; nearby was a Victorian 'Ragged' School, and various tradesmen and warehouses. The accommodation still exists, now above a shop specialising in Irish goods: Wilde would have appreciated the irony, although he might have written better dialogue for the characters in this drama. When Billing asked, with a flourish of rhetoric, if Miss Highfield was 'a woman of good or bad reputation', Darling reprimanded him, and tellingly commented in a sub-Wildean phrase, 'what puzzles me is how women of good reputation know women of bad reputation'.

Billing asked Villiers-Stuart if she knew who was really running the house, his implication being that it was 'a prominent figure in the political parties'. She said she could name the person. 'Then you must not say it,' said Darling. 'It will take more than you to protect these people, my Lord,' said Billing. When Darling threatened Billing that he would close the case for the defence if he did not behave, Villiers-Stuart announced, 'Very well, Mr Billing, if you are convicted, I will carry on.' Darling ordered the feisty Eileen: 'You stand down. I will not have you interfering in the proceedings.' She claimed later that she was 'very angry' with Billing for having reneged on his promise not to ask her to give details of the Black Book, and pledged not take the stand again.

*

Captain Spencer was the next witness; his testimony would raise the temperature of these already heated proceedings to boiling point with some of the wildest allegations yet heard in a British courtroom. Spencer unfolded a colourful tale of espionage and conspiracy. Sent to Albania as a member of the international peace-keeping force in 1913, he had become aide-de-camp to the German Prince William of Wied at his palace in the Albanian capital, Durazzo. Albania had been created as a puppet Hapsburg state after the Balkan Wars – denying Serbia access to the sea – with William (described as having 'a kind heart, a soft voice and a broad smile) installed as its ruler. There had been fighting in Albania since April 1914, and Spencer left the country in mid-September. During his time there he claimed to have had access to the Prince's private papers, gathering secret information about the intentions of the Austrian army's contingency plans for war. After various adventures in Italy, Spain and America, Spencer returned to England in 1915, and became a Captain in the Royal Irish Fusiliers. In October he was sent to Admiralty Intelligence to 'continue his work ... on the relief of the Serbian Army'. He returned to the Balkans as a political officer, and went to Scutari to attempt to make peace between warring factions in Albania and allow the retreating Serbs to get across the mountain ranges.

At this point, the prosecution wondered if all this detail was necessary; they might also have wondered if it was true. Darling allowed Spencer to go on. The American was told to return to London and report to the Adjutant General, where he gave information on the Black Book to the Principal Private Secretary to the Secretary of State for Foreign Affairs: 'Among other books of German intelligence which Prince William of Wied had was a report or co-ordinated reports of German agents, appended to which was a list of names of people who might be approached, and the method in which they could be approached, for the purpose of obtaining information.' The book was in dark binding, said Spencer, slightly smaller than *Odgers on Libel*, a copy of which lay on the barristers' table. The Prince had shown him the book 'personally one day, and explained it at some length'. Spencer said he reported the matter 'almost immediately' to the commander-in-chief in the Adriatic, Admiral Troubridge, a man whose wife would become famous as Radclyffe Hall's lesbian lover.* 'I

---

* Ernest Charles Thomas Troubridge, son of the 3rd Baronet, was an accomplished officer with a sweep of silver-blond hair and a penchant for long cigarette holders; he had been called 'the

know that he passed the information to Admiralty Intelligence,' said Spencer. He did not tell the Prince he had done so, as he considered it his duty to get the information back to England in the light of Germany's plans to declare war. This remark was met by loud applause and stamping feet from the wounded soldiers in the gallery. 'If that occurs again,' said Darling, 'the people in the Gallery will leave the Court.'

Emboldened by his audience, Spencer went on to tell the court that the Prince had explained the book to him, reading out sections and showing 'a morbid curiosity in such things' – an obvious imputation as to the German's own perversity. Billing asked Spencer if the book contained a 'precis' of instructions. At this Darling cut in to ask if Spencer could produce his notes. 'They may be found,' stalled Spencer, 'I have a great deal of luggage stored.' He had left 'certain papers bearing on this case', at the American Embassy in Rome and the Italian Embassy in London. 'Did you see the list of public houses and baths, and recognise the nature of any of them in London?' asked Billing. 'Yes, that was gone into with Admiralty Intelligence,' said Spencer. 'Admiralty Intelligence did their best to close the whole matter as far as they could, with reference to these baths and public houses. They conducted a very thorough campaign and I believe stamped out part of the German system here in London.'

There were certainly in London, as in other sophisticated cities, bath houses used by homosexuals (such as the Jermyn Street baths, where Duncan Grant sketched the clientele), and the authorities were well aware of their reputation. In New York, for instance, there were regular raids on such premises in the early years of the century. Although there is no evidence for seditious whispers in clouds of steam, the authorities probably kept these establishments under surveillance. As Beverley Nichols's experience and other evidence shows, British intelligence was populated by men who imagined sexual perverts and German spies going literally hand-in-hand. 'Were there German agents using these public houses, and baths and massage establishments?' asked Billing. Spencer said yes, and stood by his statement in his original article, with its allegations of deep-rooted vice among 'Privy Councillors, youths of the chorus, wives of Cabinet Ministers, dancing girls, even Cabinet Ministers themselves, while diplomats, poets, bankers, editors, newspaper proprietors, and members of His Majesty's household follow each other with no order of precedence'. Billing asked him to name names, and despite the prosecution's objection, Darling allowed the

---

handsomest man in the British Navy'. He married Una, his second wife and twenty years his junior, in 1908. Troubridge was posted as Head of the British Naval Mission to Serbia in 1915. Months later, with her husband miles away, Una met and fell in love with Radclyffe Hall. As Troubridge's son was Billing's political agent, it is likely that Billing knew about Una's lesbian relationships, already common knowledge by 1918 and further evidence of society decadence.

question. Was Mr Asquith's name in the book? Spencer could not remember seeing it there. 'That shows the gross impropriety of putting a leading question,' said Darling, but he had only himself to blame for that.

Spencer seemed to be becoming aware of the perjurous nature of his testimony. When Billing pressed for names, Spencer turned to Darling: 'My Lord, these names in the book are merely people whom [the Germans] can approach … I will only give the names of those whom I think have been approached, and who have succumbed to German agents. Those that have been approached and not succumbed, I see no reason to drag their names into Court.' It was a surprising turn of conscience; Billing's defence team seemed to be cracking up. Darling told Spencer it was up to him if he mentioned these names; 'I shall not commit you to prison if you do not.' But after some vocal bullying from Billing, Spencer announced, 'Mrs Asquith's name was in the book.' 'And?' After hesitating, Spencer mentioned Lord Haldane. 'A man whose spiritual home is in Germany,' said Billing triumphantly. But Spencer appeared concerned, and declared, 'I did not see any others that have any bearing … I would rather not mention any more.' However, the fact that he admitted he had never actually seen the book belies his honour in the matter; he had already mentioned the names of two public figures, with no evidence other than what he had been told by someone else.

Spencer felt safer complaining about the political machinations – conspiracy, as he saw it – which had effectively hushed up the evidence of blackmail he had uncovered. Having gone to the Admiralty, War Office and Foreign Office intelligence departments, 'great political pressure [was] brought to bear, and I was told that if it were published it would undermine the whole fabric of the Government. I then took it to the so-called party machine.' 'Who told you that it would undermine the whole fabric of the Government?' asked Darling. Spencer said he had been at a weekend party at Colonel Aubrey Herbert's house, at which intelligence officers told him as much.

Colonel Aubrey Herbert was the half-brother of the Egyptologist Lord Carnarvon, and had been attached to the Adriatic Mission from December 1915, where he was Spencer's superior officer. A former diplomat, now Unionist MP for Somerset, he and his wife Mary (their daughter Laura would later marry Evelyn Waugh) were also friends of the Asquiths. He was an adventurer, heavily involved in Albanian affairs. Herbert was denounced by Spencer because in late July 1917 he had been an intermediary between Lloyd George and agents acting for the Turkish Grand Vizier, who was attempting to make peace. Spencer said that it was in August 1917 ('at the time of the September crisis, when they were trying to bring Asquith back') when he had been told to keep quiet about the Black Book at the Herbert house party; an ADC, Captain Lane, said it was a 'very complicated subject and had better not be touched.'

6. The Trial

Spencer emerges as a troubled, troublesome man hawking his madcap ideas around the outer fringes of political and military power. He told Billing and the court that while at lunch with Mrs Waldorf Astor in St James's Square, he had mentioned names to Neil Primrose, then the Coalition Whip. 'I thought some political action could be taken.' Primrose's role is also suspect. With his father's shadowy past to dispel, he may have been at pains to prove his opposition to the cult of Oscar Wilde; like many others involved in the affair, he also appears to have been a sympathiser of the radical right. Afterwards the two men went to the Travellers' Club, where Primrose said he would meet Admiral Hall, Director of Naval Intelligence and a powerful figure in Whitehall. 'I have gone into the whole thing with Mr Lloyd George's private secretaries,' Spencer told the court. 'They have everything.' Having mentioned the names he had, they told Spencer, 'They are not here in Downing Street now; let the matter die' – evidently a reference to the Asquiths. The whole affair assumed yet more conspiratorial proportions when Billing put another of his leading questions: 'Have attempts been made to cause your disappearance?' Spencer replied, 'Yes ... At the time I gave the Italian Ambassador certain information, Colonel Aubrey Herbert said: "They will have you shot in a fortnight." ' He added, somewhat unnecessarily, 'They did not.'

With this new intimation of dark forces at work, Billing turned to Darling and asked for police protection both for his two endangered witnesses and for himself. Darling said he would have to apply to the Police Commissioner for such cover, at which point Spencer interjected, 'Sir Cecil Spring-Rice had no protection, my Lord.' Spring-Rice, British Ambassador in Washington, had recently died of a heart attack, but it was rumoured he had been murdered after discovering a German plot – an example of international war hysteria. Spencer felt pessimistic that 'the Germans had such a grip on our affairs that nothing could be done' – until he met Captain Beamish. It was a propitious introduction for these two like-minds, so attuned to conspiracy and xenophobia.

They met through Admiral Troubridge's sister-in-law, Miss Hope, who, like Troubridge's son (who acted as Billing's political agent), was also connected with the radical right-wing National Party.* The party recruited in a series of 'At Homes' at their offices in King Street, and it was to one of these that the Hopes invited Spencer. There he met Beamish, who 'seemed to have a grip on the whole situation'. Beamish introduced Spencer to Billing. A week later, when Billing had proved himself 'fearless enough', unlikely to be 'bought by office' and someone

---

* It is an indication of that tangled internecine society that Laura Hope, née Troubridge, had been a good friend of Wilde's, and had once illustrated one of his poems. She married Adrian Hope, who was a relative of Constance, Wilde's wife. During his imprisonment, the couple had been guardians to Wilde's children.

who 'would carry the thing through to the bitter end, and try and break the grip of these German Bankers and German Secret Service that are murdering our men in France', Spencer decided to let Billing in on his secret.

Together they had written the 'First 47,000' article and made sure that interested parties received copies. They had waited for a libel action, which never came. 'The attack was continued week by week to induce the people concerned to remember our men in France, and many letters were received telling them they were on the right track,' reported the *Morning Post*. And so the 'Cult of the Clitoris' was born. Spencer gave details as to its genesis. He consulted the village doctor, 'as to an anatomical term ... He spelt it to me over the phone.' Evidently Spencer, as a mystified male, had sought a medical definition of lesbian activity. He was not alone in his ignorance: for the tabloid-reading public, the Billing case would be their first introduction to the phenomenon. (Three years later, in 1921, when an extension to the anti-homosexual laws was proposed to encompass lesbianism, it passed the Commons, but not the Lords, where Lord Desart reasoned, 'You are going to tell the whole world that there is such an offence, to bring it to the notice of women who have never heard of it, never thought of it, never dreamed of it. I think that is a very great mischief.')

Billing pointed out to the court that the offending paragraph was not in the copy he had 'passed for the press'; Spencer had added it later. Billing recalled asking Spencer the meaning of the word clitoris: 'I told you that in consulting with a physician I had been informed it was a superficial organ that, when unduly excited or over-developed, possessed the most dreadful influence on any woman, that she would do the most extraordinary things if she was over-developed in a superficial sense.' In a world whose eyes were only just being opened to the intricacies of sexual technique by the campaigning zeal of Marie Stopes, this description must have struck wonder, anxiety and fear into otherwise ignorant men. It certainly seemed to obsess Captain Spencer. Billing asked if it was the 'best title that could have been employed to explain what we wished to explain?' 'Yes,' said Spencer, 'I meant to say that only people that were abnormal – ' 'You were not asked that,' interrupted Darling. Spencer continued, 'Yes, that it was the most decent and technical way in which a disagreeable thing could be expressed.' When Billing asked his witness if he expected Maud Allan to bring an action, Darling again interrupted to say he could not ask such a question. Spencer remarked, 'I thought of Miss Maud Allan merely as – ' 'You must not tell us what you thought of Miss Maud Allan,' declared Darling; although that was precisely the effect of the whole trial.

Turning from the uncomfortable terra incognita of female genitalia, Billing brought up the topic of the secret peace talks. He asked Spencer why he had gone to Herbert about the German 'peace offensive' of 1917. Spencer said there was a 'so-called September plot or September crisis', in which German agents were planning to return former French and Spanish politicians to power in their respective countries, 'and make a German peace'. Herbert had asked Spencer for a copy of his memorandum to the Italian Foreign Ministry as he was about to leave for that country, on a political mission. Having read it, Herbert told Spencer, 'They will have you shot.' Spencer presumed 'they' were Herbert's friends, 'the so-called Camarilla or clique that, under German influence, were trying to restore Mr Asquith'. Billing asked Spencer about the operations of this camarilla: 'Have there been any messengers sent by England to Germany with this information?' 'The principal one has been Mrs George Keppel,' replied Spencer.

Here was a new sensation. The introduction of the late king's mistress in this context caused consternation in court, and in Fleet Street: the next day; the *Morning Post* and the *Manchester Guardian* merely referred to 'a lady'; only *The Times* and the *Daily Mail* printed Mrs Keppel's name. And it was a significant, and glamorous, name to drop: Alice Keppel's reputation as a royal mistress lent weight to Billing's assertions about high society decadence. Such suspicions would have been confirmed had Billing known that a tempestuous lesbian love affair had just begun between her daughter, Violet Trefusis (whom Repington so admired) and Vita Sackville-West. Even as the trial was in progress, Violet and Vita were sequestered in a cottage in Cornwall, lent to them by the sympathetic Hugh Walpole,* who was attending the trial. Vita's husband, Harold Nicolson, elsewhere preoccupied in his new friendship with Oswald Mosley, had given up sexual relations with his wife. 'I wish I were more violent, and less affectionate …' he wrote to her, unready as yet to admit his homosexuality, 'only I suppose I am too cultured and *fin de siècle* to impose my virility.'

Mrs Keppel's friendship with the Asquiths and the Liberals also made her a fitting target for Billing and the radical right – as did the fact that the Jewish financier Sir Ernest Cassel had, because of his position as financial advisor to Edward VII, helped Alice Keppel amass her own fortune. Political, social, and personal attachments combined to make this king's mistress vulnerable to Billing's attack. Darling asked Spencer how he knew of Mrs Keppel's involvement: 'The persons I got it from I have reported to the Intelligence Department,' he replied; Spencer maintained he had seen Mrs Keppel return from Holland.

---

* Prolific novelist, of whose work *The Wooden House* Robbie Ross wrote, 'he is endowed with unusual imaginative gifts, not quite so wholesome as he fancies them to be'. Walpole was supposed – by Truman Capote – to be a lover of both Henry James and Harold Nicolson. For this reason, he could well have been suspected of being one of the '47,000', especially as a friend of Robbie Ross. However, his attendance was probably due more to innate curiosity than anything else.

He was probably confusing her with the Baroness Daisy de Brienen, who leased her eighteenth-century house, Clingedaal, near the Hague, to the Keppels.* Repington noted in his war diary for 4 May: 'Miss Daisy full of the interned prisoners in Holland, whence she has just returned.' Spencer admitted he was in London when he 'saw' Alice Keppel return. 'You can only know she came from Holland by what you heard,' said Darling. 'That may be the law,' said Spencer, 'but there is such a thing as justice.' 'Law is justice,' retorted Darling, riled by this American's denigration of his profession. 'Do not be impertinent ... The laws of England are not to be altered for you to say what you like about a number of persons because you choose to do so' – although such an admonition came a little too late for Mrs Keppel's reputation.

Spencer proceeded to give a garbled account of his efforts to alert the authorities to the menace of the Black Book. He cited foreign interests at work in British embassies in Montenegro, the Vatican and Rome. Having met Neil Primrose and Philip Kerr – Lloyd George's secretary – at lunch at the Astors' in St James's Square, Spencer had sent secret telegrams to Lloyd George to alert him to the facts. He received a reply from Kerr, ordering him to board a warship, where he was instructed to return to General Headquarters at Salonika. His attempt to report on 'the state of affairs in Rome' was dismissed. Spencer was ordered to his battalion in the trenches, but refused to go unless his report was forwarded to London. He then asked to be court-martialled for disobeying orders, a request which must have assured his superiors of the diagnosis they were about to make. He was told he could have a week to write his report, then could go to a rest camp. 'I was put in an ambulance with an escort, a horse-drawn ambulance,' said Spencer. 'What happened to you then?' asked Billing. 'I was then put – ' but Spencer stopped before he could incriminate himself; his next port of call had evidently been a secure place for the mentally-disturbed. 'I arrived at Salonika eventually ... I was taken up on the hills and put into a small hut, locked in.' In the hut was one other man. 'He was sitting on a small bed with his head in his hands ... After a few minutes he got up and held out his hand and said: "Good-bye, old man; they are shooting me at 3 o'clock." ' The man was Lt-Colonel Warren, commanding officer of the Connaught Rangers, who had arrested his own general; rather than being detained for political reasons as Spencer claimed, Warren was confined for 'mental aberration'.

On his arrival, Spencer had been greeted by medical officers. 'I gather they

---

* Violet spent the summer of 1914 at Clingedaal, visited by the Asquiths (Margot was there the day war was declared) and Diana Manners, as well as 'Bim' Tennant, Raymond Asquith, Patrick Shaw-Stewart and Julian Grenfell, 'all the brilliant, doomed young men the war was to annihilate', sons of the Souls. Violet reacted to the war in a different manner: during the air raids of 1917, she was to be found 'lying full length under the dining-room table, tightly buttoned into a sealskin coat, sniffing a gardenia'.

gave you a certificate?' Darling asked the now-evasive witness. 'Yes, it came through the War Office,' said Spencer, '... it was a leave certificate.' The doctors asked if he'd prefer to have a 'pleasanter' room 'under the old Orphan Asylum ... They said they had had a wire that I was suffering from the most unusual hallucinations, and should be locked up.' 'Did they certify you insane?' asked Billing. 'They told me to keep very quiet, and I should get out of it all right; that somebody had their knife in me.' 'So you have never been certified insane by the doctors?' 'No, I was released,' said Spencer. There was nothing new in this apparent charade, he said; 'It is often done in the Army.' At this Darling interposed, 'People with hallucinations often think these things. They said you must keep very quiet and they would get you out of it.' Billing protested that the doctors 'did not say he was suffering from hallucinations'; but it is clear Spencer certainly suffered from schizophrenic or hypomanic delusions. Spencer escaped from the asylum wearing an RAMC orderly's clothes. He got to Salonika, now dressed as a private soldier, and told 'certain people' where he was. Via the American Consul – rather than the British Secret Service – these 'certain people' contacted London. GHQ in Salonika arranged for him to go to Malta; on board ship, he was kept in a locked cabin, and on arrival, the Governor had him examined by a specialist. He was then sent back to England, arriving on 1 July 1917, where he was examined by another medical board, composed of three Scottish doctors: 'They were very honest men', remarked Spencer, to the court's amusement. 'They said I was unusually fit, mentally and physically ... I went to the Air Board to be examined for a pilot, as I had been in the Air Service before.' He wanted to go into an 'honest clean business', and like Billing and other modern-minded men, aeronautics appealed to him. But having taken a pilot's course in Reading, he was suddenly summoned back to London over his Secret Service reports, which were 'put aside in some way', and he was now passed medically unfit. Thus Spencer evaded the fact that he had been discharged on 17 September 1917, suffering from 'delusional insanity'.

Darling's attempts to pin Spencer down proved ineffective. When asked which organisation had passed him medically unfit, Spencer was evasive, citing a Colonel Engleheart. 'Attend to me, without dragging in the names of other people maliciously, out of what were you passed medically unfit, that is the question put to you?' 'Out of the reserve,' said Spencer, again evasively. Billing asked who Engleheart was. 'It is a German name,' replied Spencer; he did not know if he was in the 'British Service' or not. When pressed by Darling, Spencer blurted, 'There are three million men in France being injured – ' which brought a new cheer from the hospital contingent in the public gallery.

Spencer said that when he returned to England, he reported to the War Office and was given a biennial gratuity of fifty pounds for life; wanting 'quieter work', he was now Examiner of Aircraft under the Chief Examiner – 'a more unsuitable position', says Michael Kettle, '… it is difficult to imagine'. He still held the honorary rank of Captain. 'When you left the Service, did you take any steps to try and make plain the condition of affairs which must have been a very heavy burden on your mind?' asked Billing. 'Only with people who I thought would have authority,' said Spencer. 'One man to whom I told my story, and who promised to help me, got a peerage.' At which Darling quipped, 'For what he had done for you? (Laughter in Court.)' 'When Mr Beamish introduced you to me,' asked Billing, 'did you think I was going to get a peerage?' 'I thought you were a very disreputable character.' More 'Laughter in Court'.

'Have you received information as to the kind of vices catered for by the German agents …?' asked Billing. Spencer said he had, and went on to name sodomy and lesbianism, 'both of which he knew to be unnatural vices, and one a criminal offence'; he also maintained that he had read *Salome*. 'Are you aware that it is only perverts who practise these vices?' asked Billing. 'I do not know if the German agents are really perverted,' said Spencer, alleging that they stooped as low as that 'in the interests of their own country', and 'against their own instincts … If a German agent is instructed to practise sodomy by his chief, probably he does.' 'Do they succumb?' asked Billing. 'I know they do,' said Spencer, '… Through the Intelligence; through the Admiralty.' 'And these perverts are people who take an interest in all sorts of sexual inversion,' noted Billing. 'Do you know of your own knowledge that only pantomime perform-ances of unnatural passion appeal to the German people?' 'The [Intelligence] people think so,' said Spencer.

It is ironic that, while no evidence was ever produced of these German methods, the techniques cited by Spencer certainly were being used by British intelligence. Indeed, the British had their own Black Book, albeit with a rather more prosaic index than its putative German counterpart, for it held the names of firms known to be trading with Germany via the Netherlands; British Secret Service agents and diplomats based at the Hague used it as a form of blackmail in order to persuade the relevant companies to provide information, an 'abso-lutely scandalous business', as one agent saw it. As the Hague was the last known resting place of the German Black Book, the actual existence of the British list may have been confused with the more salacious German version.

Although there is no record of a British list of German perverts, such human weaknesses were as well exploited by the Allies as they were by the enemy. The scares over the Kaiser's 'vampires' and spy-courtesans – with their association with sexual perversity – had at least some basis in fact. The British logged rumours that the Kaiser visited Belgium because he was having an affair with a singer in Brussels, just as the Germans filed away such titbits of information as the fact that the Foreign Secretary Sir Edward Grey's first marriage was a sexless *mariage blanc*.* More salacious details were obviously more useful for potential blackmail, propaganda and other secret service activities. One historian, Michael Occleshaw, notes that 'in Germany ... there was ... a considerable demand for morphia and cocaine. Homosexuality was also rife – even the Kaiser was implicated. The Secret Service was to employ this demand for drugs as a form of currency, better than gold, to bribe the narcotics-hungry German soldiery.' (The sensational *Umpire* reported that German troops were supplied with ether 'either to dull their terror under bombardment, or, in the case of *Sturm-Truppen*, to send them into berserk frenzy'.) A civilian, Sigismund Payne Best, had been employed by the Intelligence Corps at the outbreak of war; he was described as a 'shy, sensitive man for whom music was the most important thing in life'. He was also imaginative and persuasive, 'and could turn his hand to most things'. Fluent in German and French, he was able to cross the border from the Netherlands, where he was based, into Germany. 'In those days the Germans were just as keen to get hold of morphia or cocaine as addicts are nowadays with heroin', he recalled. 'I had a great deal of difficulty in getting permission to do this drug-pushing, in fact, I had to go to the Prime Minister, to Lloyd George, and get his authority to buy large quantities of morphia tablets and cocaine. With this I was able to suborn quite a number of people in the German Army.'

It is remarkable that the First World War British Secret Service was involved in widespread drug-trafficking – especially in the light of drug abuse scares in London. It appears such exploitation was on a large scale, and by bribing addicted border guards with morphia, Best was able 'to get as far as the German General Headquarters where, as a result, I got most valuable documents'. Another agent used a Belgian source 'who has a hold on a German officer in Brussels. The latter goes to Holland once a week for unnatural purposes, and our Belgian got to know of this, and threatened to denounce him.' The very sins of which Billing accused the enemy were being adeptly practised by the Allies. The extent to which the British Secret Service used homosexual entrapment and the narcotic addictions of the enemy may never be known. As Michael Occleshaw notes, 'It is one of the most dangerous facets of Secret Service work that its practitioners so frequently employ methods contrary to accepted moral standards. Information gained thereby may be vital, it may save lives, but its acquisition may involve conduct of a nature that can explain the fog of official secrecy that shrouds Secret Service operations, even though ... over seventy years old ...'

---

* Grey was intimate with Pamela Tennant, whom he would marry four years later, on the death of her husband, Lord Glenconner.

*

Back in the Old Bailey, the cult of Wilde had returned to the dock. Billing and Spencer fell to an amateur textual analysis of *Salome*, seeking to prove that it mimicked unnatural practices. When Salome says she will bite the mouth of Jokanaan's decapitated head, Spencer declared, 'That is pure Sadism, which is the lust for dead bodies ... the mutterings of a child suffering from an enlarged and diseased clitoris.' At this the prosecution began to laugh. 'I beg to call your Lordship's attention to the humour that that arouses in Counsel,' said Billing. 'I was writing in my book,' replied Darling, 'and did not see it.' 'You said *what*?' said Billing to Spencer, who repeated his phrase, adding, '... And I got that from a medical treatise by a German ... I think the Germans were clever in advocating this as a means of corrupting people by means of Sadism as they have ... in advertising *Salome* to attract Sadism – I can bring their own books.' He ended his peroration by playing to the gallery with another reference to soldiers dying in France. 'You appreciate the enormous gravity of the evidence you have given?' asked Billing portentously. 'It is no good asking him that,' said Darling.

In his cross-examination, Hume-Williams capitalised on the ludicrous nature of Spencer's testimony. He sought to take him back to his dramatic criticism, hoping to make a fool of him, but Spencer insisted on returning to the Germans. 'You are not asked that,' said Darling. 'You are not being asked whether the Germans were justified, or anything about what the Germans do. Get them out of your head for a moment.' 'I wish more people would get them in,' said Spencer. Hume-Williams continued: 'You give it now as your considered opinion that the kisses on the lips which had been refused to her during his lifetime were Sadism?' 'And produced an orgasm,' replied Spencer. This time it was the prosecution's turn to be fooled. 'What?' said Hume-Williams. 'What is the word you used?' asked Darling. 'I am quoting from Bloch,' said Spencer, authoritatively. 'Repeat the word you used,' Darling instructed. 'Orgasm,' said Spencer. 'Some unnatural vice?' queried Hume-Williams. 'No, it is a function of the body,' said Spencer.

It is extraordinary that among these learned and professional men, only a deluded lunatic appears to have known the meaning of the word, and that from reading – or being told about – the work of a German sexologist. It is, perhaps, indicative of the general ignorance of sex (and, indeed, of the lower status of women), which Marie Stopes was only just beginning to change. But the very fact that sex was being discussed in a public court and, to a certain extent, in the press, was indicative of a modern mentality which the new sciences would shape. Billing and the moralists represented, to a discernible degree, a rearguard action.

132

6. The Trial

Confused and outwitted by these matters of sex, Hume-Willams turned to the question of the 'First 47,000'. He implied that Spencer had been disloyal to the Secret Service by using material 'acquired ... while you were in the Secret Service of this country ...' Spencer denied having been in the Secret Service, saying that the information was 'the property of the country', and that 'the circumstances are such that those rules must be broken to win' – another crowd-pleaser. Hume-Williams then suggested that when ADC to Prince William of Wied – this 'accommodating gentleman' who had shown him the book – Spencer may not have been acting for the British. This was a surprise development. He pointed out that Spencer was American-born – although Spencer tried to say he was born by the 'English Great Lakes ... In Wisconsin. I was technically born on the British border.' The judge established that Spencer had not been naturalised as a British subject. He had come to the country as a midshipman in the US Navy in 1910, and that Christmas, after an accident with his knee, resigned while his ship was in a British port. He said he was 'of independent means', and had friends and relatives in England. He had travelled and studied in Europe. 'Eventually I went to Rome, and it was arranged by the British Embassy there, whom I know, that I should go up to Oxford.' According to other accounts, Spencer's behaviour in Rome, Taormina and Albania resulted in the British Embassy having to bail him out of Italy.

The prosecution questioned Spencer about the Black Book. It contained reports from German agents, names of people to approach for information in England, and, 'after the names ... notes describing their different vices in medical terms'. The book was printed, and he had seen it twice with the Prince; once, finding the key to the cabinet on the bookshelf, he had examined it by himself. When questioned by Hume-Williams, Spencer said that most of the notes he had taken were now with the Admiralty; others he put 'in another book, in an Albanian book of Albanian personalities with their failings and vices ... The whole thing was cabled for and given to Commander Cozens-Hardy, of Naval Intelligence.' If what Spencer had told Villiers-Stuart (that he had never actually seen the book) was true, then most of this convincing detail was at best secondhand information; at worst, pure fantasy. Doubtless Spencer and Billing justified such invention as the necessary means to a righteous end. But Hume-Williams scented deceit, and pressed Spencer for more details. What had he done with his notes and the book? 'I put all the notes in the book, and everything in a trunk,' he replied, but could not be pinned down as to the whereabouts of his luggage, talking about various trunks left in Rome and Wisconsin. But he did not tell Admiral Troubridge at that time, 'I did not consider it a great discovery ...' And yet he wrote an article about it. 'I did not think that so many of the 47,000 of my countrymen would succumb to German blackmail as they have,' reasoned

Spencer. Hume-Williams tried to establish which 'English Government Department' he first approached with the information. 'The Admiralty Intelligence,' answered Spencer. '[In] November 1915, we began to see there was something in it. Commander Cozens-Hardy sent for me, and asked me if I could see anything in it. He said the circle of vicious women is betraying England.'

Now Spencer admitted he had left his notes behind in a box in a flat in Rome in which he had been staying – incriminating evidence to neglect. 'It was merely a list of names in a book of personalities,' he told Hume-Williams, '… they might have been people I had invited to dinner.' When asked why he hadn't given the list – 'if it ever existed' – to the British Ambassador, Spencer said, 'Because the British Ambassador was on the list.' 'Now we have got it,' said Billing with delight. 'Conduct yourself properly,' admonished Darling. The British Ambassador to Rome was Sir Rennell Rodd, later Lord Rennell. While at Oxford he had been a friend of Oscar Wilde's; in 1882 Wilde wrote an 'envoi' to a volume of Rodd's verse, for which he had suggested the title, *Rose Leaf and Apple Leaf*. Wilde arranged for it to be published, and 'brazenly inserted a dedication to himself as "heart's brother" which embarrassed Rennell Rodd at the time, and even more during his diplomatic career', notes Harold Acton in his biography of Nancy Mitford, who married Peter Rodd, the ambassador's son.

With this new introduction of an establishment name, Darling declared Cozens-Hardy should be called to clear up matters. He was in Paris, said Spencer, 'he will come back, I'm sure. He did his best to stop the matter. He was powerless.' Darling suggested he 'communicate' with the Intelligence Department. 'It would be Admiral Hall,' said Spencer. 'I don't know whether he is there now. You can telephone and find out if he is there.' Hume-Williams pointed out that nearly a year elapsed between discovering the book and telling the department about it. Spencer said he was not his fault if Intelligence were not doing their job. Hume-Williams then asked for details of 'one written report about the existence of these 47,000 people in bondage to Germany that you have sent?' 'On the 28th of May [1917], that was the last report …' said Spencer. He said he reported in writing to the Chief of Staff of the 16th Corps, 'that we were being undermined in Italy, because the British Ambassador in Italy was being blackmailed by the Germans, and was afraid to forward information to England … I have kept a copy of the report.' But it was not produced.

Hume-Williams now asked Spencer, 'At what date did anybody first suggest that you were suffering from hallucinations?' 'It was suggested by Mr Gabriel in Rome in May 1917,' said Spencer, 'when I suggested that German agents controlled houses in which they lived, and that plans they have since effected were being carried out.' 'And he suggested that you were the subject of hallucinations, that your mind was not quite right?' 'He suggested it would be the easiest way of shutting me up,' said Spencer. 'It is often done ... in the Secret Services, and they get shut up, and they get marooned on islands.' 'And that is an English system?' asked Hume-Williams. 'No, it is a German system, practised in England,' said Spencer. 'It is Germany working in England.' 'So that the people who are able to get Secret Service agents marooned by the orders of British Government are in the German Service?' 'Yes, I think I told you that privately,' said Spencer.

This was a new shock for the courtroom. Spencer addressed the Counsel: 'Do you never remember meeting me at dinner, and my talking to you?' Hume-Williams had been caught out. 'I? Never!' 'When I came back from Albania, you met me at dinner at a house, and we had a conversation together.' 'I never met you before in my life!' exclaimed Hume-Williams. 'I quite expected you to say that,' said Spencer, to the audible amusement of the court. 'Because it is right!' said Hume Williams indignantly. Spencer alleged that they had been at a dinner party together, given at the house of the Chief Censor with Mrs Clitheroe. 'You were never at the Clitheroes?' asked Spencer; at which point, Darling cut in, 'I expect one or other of you will get marooned,' followed by more loud laughter. It was the sort of destabilising witticism for which Hume-Williams and Travers Humphreys came to resent the judge. Hume-Williams was also a member of the Central Prisoners of War Committee; his involvement with the peace-makers made him suspect to the Billing camp, and Spencer's evidence gave them an important weak point to attack.

Hume-Williams asked if Spencer expected the jury to believe that there were Germans in Britain who held such important positions that they could have British agents marooned. Spencer insisted it was true. Darling asked which islands were used. Spencer replied that certain Greek islands on which British submarines were based, were used, and that Admiral Troubridge had told him of 'five on one island'. Spencer intimated that some might be released, and come to court as witnesses. By this time, the witness's long-winded testimony had sent the presiding justice to sleep, and Darling sat dozing as Spencer went on: 'We have small islands there for submarines, and they are ordered to report for submarine service, which is practically marooning them. In the Boer War it was called "saarbosching".' 'You call that marooning,' said Darling, roused like Lewis Carroll's Dormouse from slumber. 'Do they go down in the submarine and never come up?' 'No, they simply stay there on rations,' averred Spencer, who added that the mysterious Mr Gabriel was there now. This final remark once again met with the 'Laughter in Court' which was becoming the trademark of the whole surreal business.

7

Kicking Oscar's Corpse

For a few days London forgot all about the war, in its excitement over the case. The populace were entirely on the side of Billing and ... quite convinced that all he says must be true. Kicking the corpse of Wilde has also been a pleasure to the English people even if they disapprove of Billing's methods.

Robbie Ross, letter to Cecil Sprigge

On Friday morning, 31 May, the press reported 'Extraordinary Scenes and Suggestions' at the Old Bailey in articles which took up entire pages of newsprint. The same papers also maintained – falsely – that the German advance on Paris had been checked. Yet at the Front, the Billing trial seemed to have boosted morale, and acted as an excellent, if unserious, diversion. Neville Lytton, a British Army press officer, noted that 'the anxiety about Paris ... was relieved by an episode which had a great effect on the spirits of the army ... On one particular day I passed through many units from front to rear and I found everyone, without exception, waiting watch in hand for the arrival of the newspapers. The disruption of the British Empire and the collapse of civilisation was as nothing compared with the odds on being one of the 47,000, or with the satisfaction of seeing the names of the witnesses called before the Court to vindicate the purity of English society.'

Such was the effect of the extraordinary allegations made during the second day of the trial that as the third day of the proceedings began, a whole new set of barristers assembled outside the central court of the Old Bailey, all acting for the high profile names cited in Captain Spencer's testimony. Pre-eminent among this bewigged throng was the renowned Sir Edward Marshall Hall, representing Lord Carnarvon and his brother Colonel Aubrey Herbert. He told Mr Justice Darling that his clients were quite prepared to go into the witness box if necessary to clear their names. Darling replied – to Marshall Hall's annoyance – that in his view, 'people who are mentioned in this way must simply put up with it'. At least one name was not going to 'put up with it': George Herbert Head, representing Alice Keppel, complained of the 'cruel suggestion' that she had been involved in negotiations with Germany. She in turn could appear to deny the suggestion, and testify that she had 'never been in Holland since the outbreak of the War'; she had been working in a field hospital in France. Billing was determined to challenge Head, and through him, Mrs Keppel. He announced, 'The question of Mrs George Keppel's visits to Holland, as submitted to the Court by the witnesses, are relevant, and very relevant, to the case which we are now trying.' 'Oh, no,' said Darling wearily; but he decided to allow Mrs Keppel to be called.

This was a remarkable decision. For a royal intimate to be summoned to the Old Bailey on the evidence of a deranged American soldier was hardly good law procedure on the part of the Acting Lord Chief Justice. Hume-Williams, who had evidently been instructed to attack with greater rigour, cross-examined Spencer on the subject. 'It is my firm belief,' said Spencer, 'that Mrs George Keppel has been to Holland since the War, where she saw a certain Baroness Brienne [*sic*]. I have been told since last night that Mrs George Keppel – ' 'You cannot tell us what you have been told,' interrupted Darling. 'If you really are in possession of your senses, you must have realised that by this time.' Spencer insisted that Mrs Keppel had been to Holland to interview Germans, including Kuhlmann, the Foreign Minister (whom she certainly knew socially). 'Baron Kuhlmann?' queried Darling, somewhat taken aback. 'Yes, my Lord,' said Spencer, 'at the Hague.' It was now clear that the case was really about a struggle between the two power bases, and Maud Allan merely an instrument of the affair. Spencer alleged Mrs Keppel was acting as a go-between 'for the English members of the Camarilla' – by which he meant 'people under German domination'.

The previous evening Spencer had been told – probably by Repington – of Mrs Keppel's links with Baroness Irene de Brienen. Daughter of Baron de Brienen, she was born in The Hague, and in 1904 married Cyril Augustus Ward, son of the Earl of Dudley, who himself had been mentioned by Maud Allan in court on the first day (as having played her in 1909). The Baroness was a close friend of both Mrs Keppel and Repington – she was probably Repington's lover; in his diary, he refers to her as 'Miss Daisy'. All three knew what was going on in Holland; the Baroness had 'a considerable knowledge of both Dutch and European politics', talking of Amsterdam as 'very pro-English, Rotterdam equally pro-German, and all the rest of the country rather pro-French than pro-Ally'. While Spencer appears to have confused the Baroness with Mrs Keppel, the Baroness certainly seems to have been intimately involved with the secret moves towards peace. She became President of the local YMCA and Commandant of Clingendaal Hospital; both the Red Cross and the YMCA were secret conduits of communication between England and Germany. She had indeed returned from Holland in early May – in the company of the former

Dutch War Minister, M. Coleyn, who was Kuhlman's agent – having seen interned British prisoners there, and wanted to get them home. But in Spencer's eyes, she was equated with Maud Allan as another Mata Hari.

*

The next witness due in the box was Admiral Hall, an appearance which threatened to wreck Billing's case. Director of Naval Intelligence and one of the 'military conspiracy', Hall had been backing Billing, but now felt that Spencer's wild allegations against Admiralty Intelligence had gone too far. Billing protested that there was already a witness in the box, and Darling ruled that the admiral could not give evidence at that moment – another questionable decision, as Darling had already allowed Mrs Keppel to be summoned. Hume-Williams cross-examined Spencer in an attempt to erode his testimony. Were there any copies of the Black Book? Spencer said only the one he had seen in Albania. Suspecting that he had never actually seen the book, Hume-Williams asked Spencer, 'What one did you describe? We have not had a copy described. Tell me of one copy?' 'If your memory is failing you, I cannot assist you,' said Spencer. 'I described it yesterday to his Lordship, and you were present. It was the book itself I saw, Mr Hume-Williams.' He said his notes consisted of some names scribbled on half a sheet of paper, which he had then hidden in a German/Dutch book, *Albanian Personalities*, which was similar to the Black Book. Hume-Williams asked how this evidence could possibly produce a dossier of 'the First 47,000'. Spencer told him that before the *Vigilante* article was published, Billing had read it down the telephone to Arnold White, 'a gentleman who has been fighting German influence in England for fifty years'. 'Does he know the 47,000?' asked Hume-Williams. 'He said that he did over the telephone, and that Mr Pemberton-Billing was wrong, that at present it was 53,000 they had collected.' This bartering over the exact figures raised suspicions; it seemed that these numbers had been dreamt up by the Billing-White axis. This evidently occurred to Hume-Williams: 'Did you suggest to Mr Billing that it was rather astounding that somebody else knew the 47,000, and you were not the only one in England who knew?' Spencer replied, 'Our Intelligence has been in possession of that fact for some time.' Hume-Williams pointed out that Arnold White had no access to 'Government Departments. Did you ask him how he came into possession of 53,000 names?' Spencer said he thought no information 'detrimental to Germany' ever came out of government departments – another of his inflammatory statements.

Spencer said he had submitted his information to the Prime Minister. 'But where did you get it from?' asked Hume-Williams. 'From certain French Deputies, from certain Italian Deputies, from certain members of the American Embassy in Rome who were present at a consultation at a house in the Piazza di Spagna on the 17th May [1917]. Their names I cannot remember, but have written somewhere.' Asked in what capacity he attended this impromptu international conference, he replied, '... I was known at the American Embassy as a special officer, who had the politics of the Adriatic in hand; and it was most natural that they should ask me if they trusted me.'

Spencer stated that on 16 November 1915, the Foreign Secretary, Sir Edward Grey, had appointed him as a political officer; he produced the letter of appointment in court, to the prosecution's bewilderment. The text was reported in the press the following day: 'It stated that defendant had been appointed a political officer on the civil side, attached to the Serbian Relief Commission, from Nov. 16, 1915, to February, 1916, owing to his somewhat special knowledge of Albania, and that his duties were those of an Intelligence Officer. It was signed H.H. Lamb, and dated from the 9th Battalion Royal Irish Fusiliers. There was, it was stated, no indication of the person to whom the letter was addressed.' Here was official confirmation of at least part of Spencer's story. Spencer said the letter had recently been sent to him 'by an officer who thought I might have use for it', who had anticipated 'the attitude which the Crown sees fit to take ... in view of the fact that I had not kept silent about certain affairs, it was the opinion in the Army among men I knew that the politicians and political officers of the Crown might try to make things very disagreeable for me.'

Hume-Williams ridiculed the notion that the prosecution was a 'deep laid plot by some Officers of the Crown'. But Spencer's retort that 'most of the Officers of the Crown of the old regime were appointed by politicians who lived on German money' was greeted by applause in court, and had a degree of truth about it: Asquith's connexions with German financiers and other figures were strong, and men like Edgar Speyer helped finance the Liberals. However, Lloyd George had done his best to purge political office of such German-sponsored figures, said Spencer. Asked about his mental health, Spencer again alleged that he was 'passed medically unfit as the easiest way to avoid a Court-Martial'. 'You seem to be a victim of a most unfortunate conspiracy,' said Hume-Williams. 'Not in the least,' replied Spencer, 'I think I am the cause of my own trouble.' With such a rational statement, Spencer appeared to have gained the upper hand. Hume-Williams asked who Spencer thought would sue over the 'First 47,000' article, as no one was specifically named in the piece. 'Perhaps the Crown, as it has done,' said Spencer. Darling intervened to instruct the jury that this was most definitely a 'private prosecution' in which the Crown was prosecuting on behalf of the libelled because the libel was a criminal offence. This nice legal point went over the heads of many, including the jury; to them, as to the press, it seemed Spencer was nearer the truth.

Spencer said that after the article was published, 'a solicitor' (in fact, Hertford's Town Clerk and Vigilante treasurer, Arthur Baker) pointed out 'that the Government could take steps, and ... that any Cabinet Minister or dancing girl could bring a prosecution'. 'Did you really anticipate that some member of the Cabinet would come forward and say "Bless my soul! Here is the secret of my life disclosed at last. I must bring an action and say it means me?" ' 'No,' said Spencer coolly. 'I thought they would bring up some puritan who had nothing in his life against him ... He would certainly be acquitted. They would be clever enough to do that ... and thus clear those who were guilty ...' 'And you want the Jury to believe – do be careful – that reading this article attacking 47,000 corrupt people, the Town Clerk said that somebody who was not touched by it all could bring an action?' The point hinged on the identification of the names on the list; and so it all swung back to the Black Book again. Darling commented that no prospective litigant could prove he was on the list 'without getting hold of the book. It is like trying to get hold of a rainbow.' Darling's poetic flight was countered by Spencer's typically strange retort, 'They both have ends of gold.'

*

As the third day of the trial continued, the prosecution addressed the libel itself. Why was it necessary to print such a heading as 'The Cult of the Clitoris'? 'In order to show that a cult exists in this country who would gather together to witness a lewd performance for amusement during war time on the Sabbath ...' said Spencer. ' "The Cult of the Clitoris" meant a cult that would gather together to see a representation of a diseased mad little girl.' Hume-Williams attempted to show that the term in question was a natural aspect of the human body: 'The clitoris is part of the female organ?' 'A superficial part,' said Spencer. 'In which the sexual sensations are produced?' 'It is what remains of the male organ in the female,' said Spencer – a telling reflection of the perceived role of women in sex, as was this whole exchange. 'Do you mean to tell my Lord and the Jury that when you wrote those words, "The Cult of the Clitoris", you meant anything more than this, the cult of those sensations by improper means?' 'I meant superficial sensation which did nothing to help the race.' 'By improper methods, methods other than ordinary connection between man and woman?' 'Than the usual connection between man and woman,' averred Spencer. 'An exaggerated clitoris might even drive a woman to an elephant.' This remark – unprecedented in the courts of British justice – elicited loud laughter.

Hume-Williams now turned to Spencer's reference to Theo Durrant's crimes.

141

'As a child it was one of the dreadful tales they used to frighten us with in Canada …' said Spencer. 'I knew of the execution of Durrant for what was supposed to have been a Black Mass … I am afraid nurses tell you dreadful things.' Darling asked what he meant by a 'black mass'. 'When I was in Canada I heard of a man who took young girls and put them on the altar instead of the Host, and afterwards ill-treated the bodies. That was known as a black mass.' Spencer was not only recycling an exaggerated account of Durrant's crime, he was echoing atavistic notions of satanism and witchcraft, historically used to besmirch women, updated in modern times to ideas about female hereditary insanity and sexual degeneracy. Spencer had not known of the connexion with Maud Allan when the libel was published; asked how he found out, Spencer declared that there had been 'at least one hundred letters received at Vigilante headquarters with much more than that about Miss Maud Allan, which we have not seen fit to use … signed by very reputable people … I regard Miss Maud Allan as a very unfortunate hereditary degenerate … I am afraid in the circumstances it had to be done.' It is clear that Lord Alfred Douglas pointed out the useful connexion; and that the letters also referred to Maud's sexuality.

Asked if he had ever given the names of the 47,000 to Scotland Yard, Spencer said he had had 'several interviews' there; he had sent the article, along with a list of the subscribers to the performance of *Salome*, to the Assistant Commissioner of Police, Basil Thomson, who had written to thank him for it. Sir Basil Thomson was also chief of Scotland Yard's Special Branch. His politics leant heavily to the right: he was vehemently anti-Communist and anti-Lloyd George, whose ideas seemed dangerously socialist to those who feared the threat of the Bolsheviks. Thomson was 'doing his best to crush the German agents, and to protect unfortunate English men and women from them'. Yet Spencer had not – so Hume-Williams established – sent the names of any of the 47,000 to Scotland Yard. Cross-examination had underlined the tentative nature of the witness's grip on reality, and yet, such was Spencer's conviction – and the atmosphere of the time – that it all seemed quite credible.

Billing rose to re-examine Spencer, and asked him to tell the jury 'what took place when I rang up Mr Arnold White …' Spencer quoted Billing's conversation with White, in which he said he had received certain information confirming things White had told him 'two and a half years ago, and I think now is the time to make it public, and stop this German blackmail of our people, and I am going to do it. I am told the Germans, through agents, have gathered a list of 47,000 people, which looks as though it had been furnished by a firm of solicitors in England, because private family things were given; and can you confirm it?' Spencer went on, 'Then, I believe, Mr Billing said: "What? 53,000?" Of course, I could not hear Mr White, but the idea I got was that Mr White had confirmed, and said yes that the Germans had now 53,000 names of people whom they might blackmail. "It was for the purpose," said Mr Billing, then, "of keeping these people out of German blackmail that I am going to publish the article." '

His honour thus vindicated, Billing asked Spencer to explain what he had meant when he had said that Maud Allan was 'administering to the cult':

> I meant that any performance of a play which has been described by competent critics as an essay in lust, madness and sadism, and is given and attracts people to it at from five guineas to ten guineas a seat, must bring people who have more money than brains; must bring people who are seeking unusual excitement, exotic excitement; and to gather these people together in a room, under the auspices of a naturalised alien, would open these people to possible German blackmail, and that their names, or anything that transpires, might find their way into German hands, and these people would be blackmailed by the Germans; and it was to prevent this that the article was written.

Billing and Spencer claimed that the article had prevented the play by influencing the Lord Chamberlain who had 'stopped it as a public performance'. In fact, the licence for a public performance – as opposed to the private – was withheld because of the trial, as the Lord Chamberlain's papers show. 'Did you know from your own knowledge that he has stopped it going abroad?' Billing asked Spencer. Again, this was not true – nor was it within the Lord Chamberlain's jurisdiction to do so. Billing went over Spencer's story again. Was the time he had spent under restraint unpleasant? 'After my letters reached Downing Street,' said Spencer, 'everything was done to what they say "remove the bitterness".' 'Yet you were never certified insane?' enquired Billing. 'Never,' said Spencer. His medical reports had been lost by the War Office; the Prime Minister 'had thereupon taken the matter up on his behalf ... The result was that they could not find them ...' Keen on appeasing Lloyd George, Spencer told Billing that the pervasive influence of the Germanophiles was now much less. Although he had told the prosecuting counsel that many members of the present administration were involved, Spencer reasoned that such appointments had been made by the old Liberal Party 'whose secret funds originated from persons born in Germany'. Was Spencer 'satisfied that Mr Lloyd George is not mixed up with it?' The prosecution objected to this introduction of the Prime Minister's name, but Spencer replied, 'I think Mr Lloyd George has been most courageous in turning inefficients out of office.' Lastly, Darling asked Spencer if he was employed by the State now: 'Yes, my Lord ... It is something to do with the present air defence of London. I do not know that it is politic to say what it is.' The prosecution requested that Spencer remain in court – they hoped to produce his medical records.

Lieutenant Thomas George Galbraith, a young Scottish officer friend of Spencer's, followed him into the witness box. He had been with Spencer in the Balkans, and testified to having stood next to him when he talked to Admiral Troubridge, 'whose attitude seemed to be very friendly'; considering Troubridge's affiliations with the National Party, this was to be expected. Galbraith had also been in hospital at Salonika when Spencer arrived, escorted by a sergeant, in May 1915. 'Captain Spencer was not allowed to keep his medical papers, and was subsequently placed under restraint in the basement ...' Galbraith said he had helped Spencer to escape 'as far as an ordinary friend could'. Although he had seen Spencer often afterwards, he had been ordered not to speak or write to him. During this interrogation, a juror asked Hume-Williams to raise his voice. The latter said that if he did, 'there is an echo in the Court, and I have to hear it twice over'. Darling, finding this part of the case tedious, took the opportunity to introduce a little wit into the proceedings: 'There is a story in connection with this Court, that a person in the dock who received seven years collapsed because he added the sentence to the echo, and thought he had received fourteen years. (Loud laughter in court.)' Such witticisms – with their rehearsed air – annoyed the professionals; Travers Humphreys later noted, 'his humour was much to the taste of the public, but those engaged in the case ... were apt to resent the efforts, sometimes rather transparent, to drag in the joke'.

*

Billing's next witness was Dr Serell Cooke, a friend of the homeopath anti-semite, Dr J.H. Clarke, who wrote for the *Vigilante*. They had met at Edinburgh University, and were of like mind; although a TB specialist, Cooke had also worked in the psychiatric department of St Mary's, Paddington, and whilst there had read Krafft-Ebing's *Psychopathia Sexualis*. The book was unprecedented in its descriptions of sexual practice and new psychological ideas illustrated in detailed case histories – theories which had been applied to Theo Durrant's case. Cooke had his own thoughts on the subject, and was set on proving his theories on his patients. Having attended the hearings at Bow Street, Cooke had gone off to read *Salome* and consult Harley Street specialists, producing, as a result, a detailed medical analysis of the play. He was, therefore, Billing's key medical witness, presenting a mélange of pseudo-analysis and quack diagnosis assembled by a conspiracy of eccentric doctors apparently willing and able to support Billing's campaign.

Cooke's testimony began badly. Billing asked if he had come to give evidence. 'Of course he has,' said Darling impatiently, 'I understand he has come here to tell us something about immoral sexual acts.' Billing began again: 'Have you had

144

any experience of perverted moral or sexual acts being lighted up by reading immoral literature?' Dr Cooke said he had. Billing now used his witness to attack Jack Grein *in absentia* as he could not attack Grein in person. Cooke bore testimony to Grein's 'psychology', alleging him to have a 'mental aberration' because of his apparent delusion over his appointment to the Ministry of Information (despite Beaverbrook's attempts to distance himself from the affair, Donald's letter confirming his request to the Independent Theatre Company had been published in the newspapers, proving Grein's engagement by the MoI). He also questioned Grein's artistic judgement. 'The language he used was most extraordinary,' claimed Cooke, '... Things which were physical, material, he described as spiritual, poetic, beautiful.' As he had done with Maud Allan, Billing was seeking to portray Grein as mentally unstable; he was also proceeding on a tack disturbingly similar to that to which Wilde had been subjected, in that same court, twenty-three years previously. 'What language would you describe that as in this case?' prompted Billing. Cooke replied, 'The language that is usually employed by homosexuals.'

The exchange between Billing and Cooke rehashed all the old shibboleths of the Wildean era; only now, prejudice masqueraded as pseudo-medical 'evidence'. It was the barely cloaked philistinism of an age whose cultural horizons were foreshortened by war and desperate blind patriotism. In 1918 – nearly two decades into the twentieth century and the modern era – these words were a direct reversion to Victorian values and hypocrisy. 'Is it customary for sex perverts to describe as beautiful and glorious all their perversions ... for them to read into the distinctly physical acts of sex something spiritual?' prompted Billing. 'Spiritual, poetic, beautiful, pure love,' intoned the lunatic Dr Cooke, 'those are their expressions.' 'Is that done with malice, or is it done because they are mental perverts?' asked Billing. 'It is done because they cannot help themselves,' replied Cooke, 'I think it is part of their mental condition.' At which point, Justice Darling asked, 'Have you any opinion where they ought to be?' 'Locked up,' replied Cooke.

Asked by Billing to define 'sadism', Cooke – drawing on his personal reading of Krafft-Ebing – testified that it was 'of course, the most monstrous of all the sexual perversions. Lust and sexual excitement are brought about by cruel acts and violence. It is not necessary to perform these acts; these passions may be brought about by simply thinking of the bare idea of them; imagination may bring them about. Very often sadism takes the form of biting, the biting in intercourse; that is to say, such females cannot get any sexual excitement unless they bite with violence enough to draw blood, even suck it, taste it, and then they have a violent sexual orgasm.' This was lurid, if inaccurate stuff, and conjured up images in impressionable minds of Miss Allan taking part in just such activities – as indeed it was intended to do. 'Has sadism anything to do with the lust for dead bodies or parts of dead bodies?' asked Billing. 'Yes, that is sadism,' said the deluded doctor, who added that it was 'undoubtedly ... a mental disease.' When Billing asked if it was hereditary, his target was obvious. 'It occurs in families which have an hereditary taint either of insanity or some other neuropathic condition,' said Cooke. 'It is congenital; it is born in a person. The person who has this disease or this condition is probably not aware of it until something or other happens to light up the whole thing in them. It is more of an impulse when it does come than an actually thought out thing ... An incontrollable impulse.' 'The play, of course, is ... an open display by physical means of several forms of sexual perversion,' stated Cooke. Billing asked if he thought it would be difficult to get 'a lady to take the part of Salome?' 'Well, if the lady knew what she was about to portray, I should think it would be a very, very difficult thing.' Darling asked, 'How can you tell? There are people perverted enough to do anything, are there not?' He spoke from judicial experience. 'I think so,' said Cooke. 'For money?' enquired Darling. 'I think so,' repeated Cooke. Having grossly abused Maud Allan, Billing and Cooke's insults were joined by Darling's injury. Such testimony portrayed her as little more than a prostitute.

In this gallery of perverse specimens, talk naturally turned to Wilde, 'a well-known monster, who became a monster (from all the records that we have) after reading about and taking an aesthetic interest in sexual perverts,' according to Cooke. 'Unfortunately these sexual perversions seem to occur in people who are very highly gifted and intellectual. One authority puts the figure as high as five per cent.' Cooke thought it impossible for Wilde to have written his play without 'a close and intimate knowledge of sexual perverts'. 'The probability is that he had von Krafft-Ebing's book *Psychopathia Sexualis* in front of him all the time.' (Lord Alfred Douglas would claim that *Salome* had indeed been written after Wilde had read Krafft-Ebing's book.) Cooke suggested that Wilde had written the play motivated by perversion: 'With a man like Oscar Wilde, the mere thinking out of such scenes would cause in him all these sensations ... the writing of them ... and the imagining the thing being acted would cause in him all these forms of sexual lust ... it would give intense pleasure to other perverted individuals to see such a thing enacted.' By associating with Wilde, those with tendencies 'to any of these sexual forms of perversion' would 'generally all become affected and bad'. Poor Oscar – eighteen years dead and buried and still being blamed for the ills of modern society. Meanwhile, Darling, who claimed to find Wilde's works 'tiresome', was pleased to have this confirmed by Dr Cooke as a natural reaction in a 'healthy-minded person'.

A 'person of perverted instincts' 'would take extreme delight in the whole play', claimed Cooke, 'it would appeal to them immensely, they would probably have sexual excitation, and even orgasm, watching the play.' Jack Grein and Maud Allan's artistic venture – admittedly overlaid with a taint of decadence – was now being turned, in the minds of the jurors and the tabloid-reading public, into a theatrical orgy of lust attended by orgiastic perverts; that this audience putatively included the highest strata of British society confirmed Billing's pervasive conspiracy theory. With such shocking scenes in his audience's minds, Billing turned the screw: 'Are you of your own knowledge aware there are such people in England?' he asked Cooke, who was as well primed as his interrogator: 'Unfortunately, there are very, very many,' he confirmed. 'Authorities who have calculated the number put it down as something like a million.' 'Other authorities?' asked Darling, to which Billing replied loudly, 'I am sorry we cannot call von Krafft-Ebing.' The sexologist, who had died in 1902, would have been aghast to hear his scientific theories being bent to fit this conspiracy, conflating as Billing and his witness did, the newly defined state of homosexuality with sado-masochism and necrophilia. 'It does not matter to a thousand or two how many there are in England,' averred Darling. 'As long as they are not holding positions of importance in this country,' added Billing. 'I agree with Dr Cooke,' concluded the sage judge, apparently convinced by Billing and Cooke's concoction of mangled medical theory, 'where they ought to be is, locked up.'

Aided by Darling's bluff assumption of the role of 'healthy-minded' sceptic, Billing and Cooke fell to dissecting *Salome* for sexual perversion. Cooke described the ending with Salome kissing Jokanaan's decapitated head, 'tasting or … sucking that blood, intense sexual excitement … going on until sexual orgasm is produced', and quoted Herod's line, 'Kill that woman,' to which Darling remarked, to the loud amusement of his audience, 'That is the best thing in the play.' Billing took advantage of Darling's complicity to press his point: 'Do you think, Dr Cooke, that a sexual pervert, witnessing that final act of sadism, could really have sufficient imagination and be sufficiently perverted actually to realise an orgasm in themselves?' 'Exactly,' said Cooke. 'As they sit in the audience, it would appeal to them, as I said, immensely. They are lunatics.' He compared Wilde's symbolic use of the moon to its effect on 'female erotomaniacs' – literally, lunatics. Cooke's testimony was overtly misogynistic, from its reference to 'womanish nonsense' in amatory affairs, to its subtextual allusions to menstrual cycles. He and Billing even tried to put forward a theory that 'a very artistic intellectual producer' of the play would schedule it for production 'on certain days in the month, during which the moon is passing through certain phases'. The trial had become a medieval inquisition, with Maud Allan as a modern witch, her company a coven choreographed by Grein in a *danse macabre* for Teutonist perverts.

Cooke and Billing turned their attention to clothes and hair fetishism, 'the sort of thing that is seen daily in the Police Courts …' maintained Cooke. 'You hear of cases which are taken up for cutting off girls' hair. You hear of cases again of the theft of shoes and stockings.' By the time the lunatic doctor and rogue politician got round to masochism – cited in Salome's self-abasement before John the Baptist – Darling's patience had been tried: 'Do you not think we have had almost enough? The Jury can read it all through for themselves, and judge whether it is a proper play.' Undeterred, Cooke concluded with a discussion of Herod's incestuous feelings for Salome with a relish which must seem suspicious to modern eyes. 'I offer this witness for cross-examination,' said Billing dramatically, reverting to one of his former occupations. 'You need not say that,' retorted Darling, vexed by these histrionics. 'That the witness will be cross-examined follows without your introduction. This is not an actor whom you present to the audience.'

But Billing had a further question for this productive witness. He asked Cooke what was meant by the 'Cult of the Clitoris'. 'Of course, clitoris is a Greek word, it is a medical term altogether; it has nothing to do with ordinary language …' 'Did you think that the title referred to Miss Maud Allan?'; Cooke said she had never crossed his mind. Yet Darling prompted the next assertion by remarking to Cooke that the role of Salome would be a 'painful' one. 'It is very, very difficult, my Lord,' said Cooke, 'to imagine any woman acting such a part. If any woman did so, in order to reproduce what Oscar Wilde actually wanted to be produced, she would have to be a sadist herself.' Almost incredibly, Billing's case was being proved. Billing asked Cooke if there was a less offensive term which could have been used to describe the phenomenon. 'Well, I do not see how that is possible. I mean it is such an offensive thing to talk about that you would have to choose the mildest term you could think of … There are many other terms, but they are so filthy and vulgar, and so well known to the general public; that I do not think you could have chosen a better name.' 'You mean if an indecent thing is said in Greek,' asked Darling, 'it is not so offensive – except to the Greeks, of course? (Laughter in Court.)'

Hume-Williams, cross-examining, questioned Dr Cooke's over-zealous testimony on matters perverse. Apparently drawing on private knowledge, he used the same tactic Billing had used on Maud Allan. He referred to Cooke's youth, which was spent in India, as having been subject to 'evil Eastern influences'; that in fact, the topic of 'sadism' was, for him, a 'hobby'. Cooke denied this, but allowed he had 'made a special study of these cases'. Hume-Williams went on to attack Cooke's 'terrible' allegation that Grein had used the language of a 'sodomist'. The doctor denied having made any such claim, but his denial did not go down well with the court. The prosecution had the advantage, and continued on the offensive, ridiculing the notion that Salome was 'such a horrible play that anybody of average intelligence connected with it must have a perverted mind'. By citing Strauss's respected opera, Hume-Williams led Cooke to agree that 'if the words are the words of Oscar Wilde textually produced, and the music of the opera is the music of Strauss,' it would, in his opinion, 'be legitimate to head the programme "The Cult of the Clitoris".' The obvious absurdity of this claim – which would have labelled thousands of respectable opera-goers as perverts – opened both the court's and the judge's eyes to the extent of the doctor's delusion. Darling was now tired of Cooke's testimony, and Hume-Williams used that to his advantage. 'You told me anybody of ordinary intelligence taking part in that part as it is written must be a perverted sexualist ...' Cooke backtracked: 'No, I do not say that at all, but I do say that a person performing the part of Salome must be a sadist.' 'And the effect on the audience must be to incite improper sexual passion?' enquired Hume-Williams. Cooke tried to regain ground: 'If the audience consisted of entirely pure healthy-minded people, it would have no effect upon them except disgust ... but if the audience consisted of persons who were well-known perverts, it would produce in them feelings of intense satisfaction.' It was a desperate reiteration of his claims, and Hume-Williams ridiculed them: 'If the audience consisted of people with your mind, I could understand it, but fortunately all audiences do not.'

*

Billing now announced he would be calling Robert Ross – a known homosexual – to examine him on the preface he had written for *Salome*. But first he called Sir Alfred Fripp, the king's personal surgeon; another royal-connected figure, this time more than willing to take the stand. It was rumoured that Fripp might reveal something about the Royal Family – who had their own skeletons in the cupboard – perhaps something along the lines of the Cleveland Street scandal, when Eddy, Duke of Clarence had been named as a visitor to a male brothel. Billing had little respect for a ruling dynasty of German provenance, and would not hesitate in bringing evidence to discredit the Windsors, as they were now known. However, Darling stated that Fripp's evidence would not be material, a blow for Billing's case. Billing later claimed that Darling had prevented Fripp from giving evidence 'which would have done much to convince many who were still incredulous'.

Fripp testified to having heard about *Salome* since it had been banned by the Lord Chamberlain (he probably referred to the publicised 1910 licence refusal, rather than the original ban of 1892), but had not read it. He had, however, discussed it with 'certain individuals' with regard to 'sexual aberration'. Billing asked if he knew of such perverts in London. He did. 'In the highest grades of society?' asked Billing. 'It is a little difficult to say what you consider the very highest,' said Fripp, 'but certainly in the ruling grades and governing grades of society.' He stopped just short of including the Royal Family: beyond the obvious references to their German background, could he have had some personal knowledge about the predilections of its younger members? After the Cleveland Street affair, any prince could fall under suspicion, even the Prince of Wales. Fripp certainly seemed intent on smearing the Asquiths; as Cynthia Asquith reveals in her diary of the time, Fripp had reason to dislike Margot: 'We agreed that it was monstrous of Fripp to give such evidence. I attribute his attitude largely to reprisals on Margot for her manifold professional libels on him. When he was about to operate on my appendix, Margot telegraphed to Mamma: "For God's sake don't have Fripp – damndest ass in London." '

Billing asked Fripp if he knew, without mentioning them, the names of 'any members of our governing classes who are moral perverts'. Billing would claim that before Fripp went into the witness box, he had told the surgeon, 'When I ask you a certain question, I want you to put your hand in your pocket and take out this piece of paper. Don't answer me. Just stand there.' In Billing's account, he then asked Fripp, 'In the interests of your country, are you prepared to give the court the names of those people in Government positions?', at which Fripp made to put his hand in his pocket. 'Before his hand was withdrawn, the Judge leaned over towards the witness-box and said: "Give me that paper," nearly snatching it from Sir Alfred's hand. "My Lord, if that paper is handed to you," shouted Billing, "it becomes an exhibit, and must also be handed to the jury." The Judge paused. Then he ordered: "Put that paper back in your pocket, Sir Alfred." Sir Alfred put the paper back, not knowing what only Billing knew, that it was perfectly blank and contained no names!' Although extant transcripts do not record any such exchange, there are enough errors and omissions in the official record to allow for the excision, especially considering the political conspiracy behind the affair. The idea that Fripp may have been about to disclose embarrassing names would have been enough for such an incident to be censored. However, it seems clear from later comments that Fripp's remarks about possible corruption in Buckingham Palace had more to do with the royal household of equerries and manservants than the Royal Family itself.

Billing's third medical witness was Dr Leonard Williams, a well-known Harley Street doctor who said that he had read *Salome* in the original French version (why, he did not say), and that from a medical perspective, it had bored him; having recently read Lord Alfred Douglas's translation, 'in view of criticisms which I have heard of it ... I saw it was meant to be a sadistic play.' He agreed with Billing that it was a harmful play for the public to read, and that 'neuropathic tendencies, such as sadism, ran in certain families'. Williams's testimony bore weight because of his reputation, and added to the previous medical evidence – no matter how misguided.

*

The press reports of this third day of the trial were lengthy, but could not, for reasons of decency, print Dr Cooke's evidence. The fourth day promised equal sensation, as Mrs George Keppel was to take the stand, and 'a definite and highly salacious attack' on the Royal Family seemed certain. That evening, 'great political pressure was evidently put on the Judge ... to alter his ruling'. The Germans were bombarding Paris, the British army was threatened; even Lloyd George was panicking. Yet negotiations at The Hague, led by Sir George Cave, the Home Secretary, were set to continue, undeterred by Billing's antics and the machinations of the military.

As the trial resumed, Alice Keppel and her small entourage of ladies sat in the courtroom. Her lawyer told the court that his client was prepared to deny that she had been to Holland or seen Kuhlmann since the war began. Darling understood 'the anxiety of people whose names are mentioned in this very unpleasant case'; since yesterday, he had decided not to allow Mrs Keppel to be called (this was evidence of overnight lobbying by the politicians). Travers Humphreys took the opportunity to attack Spencer for naming Mrs Keppel, and threatened to produce War Office files proving Spencer had been declared insane. But he could not, legally; Billing knew his case was safe.

Mrs Keppel and her ladies left the court, to be replaced by an equally well-known figure. The sensationalism of the last three days was about to be capped by a performance as extraordinary as had ever been seen at the Old Bailey as Lord Alfred Douglas took the witness-box. Billing's announcement that he would call Ross had encouraged Douglas's appearance, 'an unfortunate decision', according to Rupert Croft-Cooke, 'which put him in the position, false to his nature and to his sentiments before and after this period, of doing what Ross called "kicking Oscar's corpse" and ranging himself with the philistines'. However, Ross was ill – at least in part because of the stress of his recent battles with Douglas – and Billing's threat to sub-poena him would come to nothing. Without Ross's sharp wit to reign him back, Douglas therefore had a clear run. His appearance – with all his past history known, in varying detail, to most of the court – was a potent one. From having been Wilde's lover, defender and cause of his downfall, he had become embittered by his feud with Ross, and ready to denounce Wilde, posthumously but publicly, in court. Added to this heady mix was Douglas's feud with Darling, who had judged against him in his case against Arthur Ransome in 1913. Bosie's appearance in court, therefore, was bound to be spectacular.

As he took the stand, Douglas appeared normal enough, almost a City gentleman in his loose-fitting three-piece suit, bow-tie, bowler hat and cane; only his habitual heavy boots gave any hint of eccentricity. He began his testimony calmly, reiterating the history of *Salome*, and his participation in its translation. 'I have a very particular knowledge of what [Wilde] meant by the play,' said Douglas; '... he intended [it] to be an exhibition of perverted sexual passion exicted in a young girl; and there are other things in it ... there is one passage which is sodomitic [presumably the reference to the young Syrian and his page] ... Wilde was a man who cloaked those things in flowery language.' Cooke's evidence about Grein came to mind. 'He never used the word "sodomitic",' claimed Douglas. 'He would express horror at such language. Anything like the "Cult of the Clitoris" would fill him with as much horror as it apparently does Mr Hume-Williams.' Douglas's use of the word 'apparently' was intentional.

Billing asked Douglas if he knew from his 'own knowledge' that Wilde was a 'sexual and moral pervert'. 'Yes, I do,' said Douglas. 'He admitted it; he never attempted to disguise it after his conviction ... whoever was there, he always began by admitting it, glorying in it.' Douglas said he regretted ever having met Wilde. 'I think he had a diabolical influence on everyone he met. I think he is the greatest force for evil that has appeared in Europe during the last 350 years.' From lover to demon in twenty short years; jealousy and self-disgust were powerful forces. With his reference to the Reformation, the Catholic convert's hyperbole rose. 'He was the agent of the devil in every possible way. He was a man whose whole object in life was to attack and to sneer at virtue, and to undermine it in every way by every possible means, sexually and otherwise.' He thought all Wilde's works ought to be destroyed, 'I do not think he ever wrote a thing in his life that had not an evil intention ... except perhaps a stray poem or two.' Would Bosie have included the sonnets written by Wilde to himself among these? Douglas claimed that while writing *Salome*, Wilde (who read German) had showed him Krafft-Ebing's *Psychopathia Sexualis*, 'a study by a doctor of sexual perversions of all kinds'. 'Is it scientific?' asked Billing. 'I believe it is supposed to be, but it is not accepted by the *Lancet* and those people,' claimed Douglas (there had been much medical debate on the subject). 'It is pornographic; that is the view that is taken of it by the medical authorities in England, so I am told.' In stating that *Salome* was 'founded on Krafft-Ebing', Douglas had produced good evidence in Billing's favour.

'Normally healthy-minded people would be disgusted and revolted by it', said Douglas; sexual perverts 'would revel in it. That is just what they like.' Billing asked if he knew of any stage production of *Salome*; Douglas had read of a performance in Germany (Reinhardt's 1904 production, which had inspired Maud Allan). Darling protested at this hearsay evidence. 'It is notorious; everyone knows it,' countered Douglas, 'it would be ridiculous to deny it … As a matter of fact, I know a man who produced it in France [Lugné-Poë's 1896 production], and who told me he produced it.' 'Will you wait until you are asked a question?' said Darling. 'It is ridiculous if I cannot answer a plain question,' said Douglas. 'He asked me if I knew that the play had been produced, and I do know it. I knew the producer; I was personally acquainted with the gentleman who produced it in Paris.' Exacerbated by Darling's rulings, Douglas's hysteria was mounting.

'Have you read the preface?' asked Billing. 'Ross's preface?' said Douglas, doubtless with disgust in his voice, 'I have read it.' Billing, quoting from the preface, noted that the Berlin production of *Salome* had, according to Ross, 'an unprecedented run for the Prussian capital'. At this Douglas addressed Darling, 'I said I knew it had been played in Berlin.' 'Is the idea in this book rather more German kultur than British ideal?' asked Billing; this was true enough. 'Yes, decidedly,' said Douglas. He noted it had never been produced in England: 'Wilde rehearsed it with Sarah Bernhardt at the Palace Theatre, but at the last minute the censor stopped it.'

Wilde was now being paraded before a British public which had already secured his head. 'In your opinion,' asked Billing, 'has Oscar Wilde used the moon as a canvas on which to paint pictures which were almost too revolting to do in any other way?' 'Oh, yes …' said Douglas, 'To him all that sort of thing, whenever he was going to do anything particularly horrible, it was always disguised in the most flowery language, and always referred back to Art. That was his idea of Art.' And Wilde's opinion of those who did not understand his Art? 'He thought them beneath contempt,' said Douglas. 'He was the most conceited man that ever lived.' Likewise, these people thought modern art risible. 'Intellectuals are people who believe in Art for Art's sake, and all that sort of rubbish; but not necessarily wicked people; more or less merely foolish people.' Darling added, 'They may be merely cubists, and so on?' Predictably, this elicited more 'laughter in court'. But with Wilde, Douglas said, there was a more sinister 'Movement … He really meant, well, simply unnatural vice … people were in the Movement for popularising and also largely freeing from legal restraint that particular vice … He succeeded to an enormous extent.' Douglas was discerning an underground group of perverse activists, among whom were numbered Robbie Ross, Reggie Turner, Christopher Millard *et al*. 'A man with a more analytical mind would call it a cult,' remarked Billing. Such notions had been encouraged by Wilde when he told his devotees to wear green carnations as a 'masonic' sign of their cult.

Billing turned to the text of *Salome*; but Douglas's involvement with the original text made him loath to explain it. 'I had nothing to do with it; I merely translated it ... I did not at the time understand the play as I do now.' Yet Billing pressed, 'Would you call that language the language of a sodomite?' When Douglas paused, Darling repeated the question. Bosie had to be careful in answering: his own historical involvement in the affair lacked innocence. 'I think he was referring to the language used by people who described it as spiritual ... those sort of people always refer to revolting things under pretty names. They try to disguise the horribleness of the action by giving it such names; they say beautiful, classic, and so on. They will not speak of it by the outspoken English name; they disguise.' Perhaps unconsciously, Douglas echoed the line from his own poem, 'The Two Loves': 'I am the love that dare not speak its name.' 'Have these people a common patois?' asked Billing. 'Yes, they have a jargon,' said Douglas, adding, 'I have not had anything to do with them for twenty years.' Billing pressed his star witness for some confirmation of what *Salome* was really about, 'the spiritual love of a young girl finding salvation in the spirit of the Prophet, or a young girl seeking lustfully the body of the Prophet'. Was Wilde writing spiritually, or physically? 'The point is that is exactly how he would describe it,' said Douglas. 'He probably did call it spiritual. That was part of the jargon.'

More detailed textual examination of the play followed. 'Was it intended by the writer that [Salome] should work herself up into a state of great sexual excitement?' asked Billing. 'Yes,' said Douglas, '... a sort of orgasm.' 'A state of sexual excitement from which nothing but an orgasm could release her?' 'Yes,' said Douglas, 'it is meant to be the culmination of sexual excitement.' Such informed evidence confirmed what Billing had been trying to establish. He asked if Douglas had visited Wilde in prison. Douglas said that while he had been prevented from visiting Wilde, both Robbie Ross and Lord Haldane had gone to see him. Darling deemed this smear 'absolutely irrelevant', and tried to prevent Billing from asking Douglas if it were in the public interest for the play to be banned; Douglas said everything ought to be done to prevent the play being produced, 'whether by so-called legitimate means or otherwise. I do not hold with everything they call legitimacy in this country; in some things you have to go outside the law sometimes if you want to do things.' Such anarchic remarks were unlikely to endear Douglas to Darling.

Billing's witness had done his work, but unfortunately for the defence, the very qualities and intimate knowledge which made Douglas so useful in condemning Wilde would undermine his testimony in cross-examination. 'I understand you to say that Mr Oscar Wilde had a habit of putting into language of beauty things which were really disgusting?' asked Hume-Williams. 'Yes,' replied Douglas. Hume-Williams said, 'For instance, is this the sort of thing he would write: "My own Boy, Your sonnet is quite lovely –" ' Douglas was enraged. He interrupted this quotation, shouting furiously, 'That is a letter which he wrote to me. It has been kept for twenty-five years. It was stolen by that German blackmailer, George Lewis, who is bringing it out for the fiftieth time. I think there are limits to human endurance. Every time I come here, this bestial drivel is brought out.' Sir George Lewis, the well-known London solicitor, was an old friend of Wilde's. His wife was German; his own ancestry is less certain. In 1892 Wilde had asked him to help Douglas, who was then being blackmailed over some 'indiscreet' letters. Lewis, used to covering for clients, paid the blackmailer £100 for the incriminating document. Now Bosie was again embarrassed by correspondence, this time, ironically, provided by Lewis himself: the letter had featured in Wilde's trial, when Sir Edward Carson, Queensberry's counsel, had used it against the doomed playwright. It was an age when indiscreet words were truly dangerous.

'Why do they want to drag this muck up?' objected Billing. 'It is hardly for you to protest against the past of a witness being called up,' answered Darling, telling him that if he interrupted again, he would have to leave the court. Hume-Williams continued to read from Wilde's letter to Douglas. 'It begins, "My own Boy". Then it says, "Your sonnet is quite lovely, and it is a marvel that those red roseleaf lips of yours should have been made no less for music of song than for madness of kisses. Your slim gilt soul walks between passion and poetry … Always, with undying love, yours, Oscar." Is that a sample?' 'Yes, it is,' said its recipient. 'It is just exactly what I said it was. It is a rotten sodomitically inclined letter written by a diabolical scoundrel to a wretched silly youth. You ought to be ashamed to bring it out here.' 'You are not here to comment on Counsel,' reprimanded Darling. At this, Douglas lost his temper completely, displaying the sort of behaviour which made his relationship with Wilde so problematic, and which seemed a legacy of his equally irascible father (an ironic situation given Billing's suggestions about Maud's genetic perversity). Darling seemed to relish Douglas's reaction: the lord was as easily goaded as a spoilt child. 'I shall answer the questions as I please,' spat Bosie. 'I come here to give my evidence. You bullied me at the last trial [the Ransome case]; I shall not be bullied and brow-beaten by you again. You deliberately lost me my case in the last trial. I shall answer the questions as I choose, and not as you choose. I shall speak the truth.' Darling assumed the air of a long-tried parent: 'You shall not make rude speeches, or you will be removed from the Court.' He might as well have told the witness to go and stand in the corner. 'Let me be removed from the Court,' said Douglas petulantly. 'I did not want to come here to be cross-examined to help this gang of scoundrels they have at the back of them' – a reference to the politicians engineering behind the scenes. 'If you are taking down a note of anything I said, take down all I have said.'

This last outburst was met by more laughter in court, which Darling greeted with, 'Anybody who interferes in this case in a disorderly manner, I do not care who it is, will be at once expelled from the Court.' Billing impertinently remarked, 'May we laugh at your jokes, my Lord?', to which Darling's answer was, 'No, you may not. I was going to tell you, Lord Alfred Douglas, that ... the shorthand writer in the Court takes down every word that is said, whether it is relevant or not.' This was not true: many remarks, and many of Darling's witticisms, were intentionally excluded from the official record.

Somewhat relishing their effect, Hume-Williams read yet another of Wilde's letters to Douglas: 'Bosie, you must not make scenes with me ... They kill me, they wreck the loveliness of life. I cannot see you, so Greek and gracious, distorted with passion. I cannot listen to your curved lips saying hideous things to me. I would sooner be rented than have you bitter, unjust, hating ... I must see you soon. You are the divine thing I want, the thing of grace and beauty.' Douglas replied, 'That is the letter that was produced by my father in his effort to smash up Wilde to save me, and that has been the result. My father comes before the Court to save his son, and you lawyers come here twenty-five years afterwards to spit it up again for money, because you have been paid to do it.' To this, Hume-Williams replied, 'When you did you cease to approve of sodomy?' 'When did I cease to approve of sodomy?', retorted Douglas. 'I do not think that is a fair question. That is like asking: When did you leave off beating your wife?' Now a third letter was produced (it was said that Sir George Lewis kept a fileful of stolen letters, lent to those in litigation with Douglas). 'If you show me letters in my handwriting,' said Douglas, 'I give you fair warning that I shall tear them up. It is a stolen letter, stolen by a blackmailer, and you having it there makes you a partner in that theft and blackmail: you yourself are a thief and a blackmailer if you make use of such letters.' Darling directed that the letter should be held out of Lord Alfred's reach.

But it was the next letter which would completely undermine Douglas's testimony. Dated 9 June 1895, it was a reply to accusations from the editor of *Truth* that Douglas had abandoned Wilde and that the 'acts which resulted in Mr Wilde's incarceration are not practised by others'. On the contrary, Bosie had written, 'I personally know forty or fifty men who practise these acts. Men in the best society, members of the smartest clubs, members of Parliament, Peers, etc., in fact people of my own social standing ...' Many contemporaries of his at Oxford 'had these tastes', and he would produce a translation of a pamphlet written by 'Professor Krafft-Ebing, the celebrated Austrian physician [he was in fact German, but took a chair at Vienna in 1889] ... a special plea written for the express purpose of obtaining a repeal or modification of the law on this subject in Austria, and which has been to a very large extent successful. It is designed to prove what I maintain, viz., that these tastes are perfectly natural congenital tendencies in certain people (a very large minority), and that the law has no right to interfere with these people, provided they do not harm other people; that is to say when there is neither seduction of minors nor brutalisation, and when there is no public outrage on morals ...' He went on to cite favourable conditions under French and German law. 'England alone has refused to take any cognisance of the now known and admitted facts of modern medical science.' In his campaigning zeal, Douglas said he would send the pamphlet to 'every judge and lawyer in England, and ... every legislator. I confess I have not many hopes for the present age, but ultimate liberation from conventional slavery and tyranny is as inevitable as death.'

Douglas had come a long way from calls for 'ultimate liberation' in the twenty-five years since his letter was written. In it, he had not only justified 'the cult of Wilde' and his participation in 'these tastes', he had also acknowledged the intellectual and legal arguments of Krafft-Ebing. This evidence therefore substantially reduced his credibility. 'The period which you hoped for in which sodomy, unchecked by the law, will flourish, has not arrived?' said Hume-Williams. 'Yes, I do think it has,' said Douglas, 'At the time I wrote that letter, sodomy was condemned by all decent people.' 'You were not a decent person?' 'No, I was not,' admitted Douglas, 'and I have said that. Much good may it do you.' Douglas set off accusing 'Prime Ministers, judges, lawyers, and everyone' of conspiring to support the perverts, and said that the reason why he was attacked was because he was no longer one of them.

Douglas's affair with Wilde had placed him outside society; his row with Ross had done the same, and he felt it. 'If I were still on Oscar Wilde's side, I should be getting praise from judges and Prime Ministers, and praise from greasy advocates,' he ranted. 'Like Ross, I should get a testimonial from Asquith and £700 given to me from people in society saying what a fine person I was. Asquith and all these people presented Ross with a testimonial and £700 because he was a sodomite.' Billing stood up to interject, 'Are you a sodomite today?' 'No, of course I am not,' said Douglas (who had married in 1902), as Darling ordered Billing to sit down. Douglas did his best to substantiate the theory of the 47,000. 'I say there are several judges, and many people in the highest positions in this land, who protect sodomites all in their power, and actually give them public testimonials. I have said it. I have written it to the Prime Minister. I will prove it in the dock with the greatest of pleasure in my life. I have been here three times, and I am ready to go there again. I am ready to go to prison for the rest of my life in a good cause. I have said it about Mr Asquith, and I will prove it.' 'It is a good thing, if you want to get on, to be a sodomite,' he averred, '... and everything in this trial goes to prove it. As for that letter, I cannot conceive anything more calculated to corroborate everything Mr Pemberton-Billing is here to prove; it simply shows that what was true then is still truer now.' Douglas's assertions of a homosexual 'mafia' were not entirely ridiculous; indeed, there was a secret organisation in Oxford, the Order of Chaeronaea, dedicated to establishing a subversive homosexual power base.

Hume-Williams then read from a piece Douglas wrote while at Oxford in 1893 ('He was trapped by Oscar Wilde,' cried Billing), which justified all that was said about *Salome*:

> I suppose the play is unhealthy, morbid, unwholesome and un-English, *ça va sans dire*. It is certainly un-English because it is written in French, and therefore unwholesome to the average Englishman, who can't digest French. It is probably morbid and unhealthy, for there is no representation of quiet domestic life, nobody slaps anybody else on the back throughout the play, and there is not a single reference to roast beef from one end of the dialogue to the other, and though it is true that there is a reference to Christianity, there are no muscular Christians ... But the less violently and aggressively healthy, those who are healthy to live, and do not live to be healthy, will find in Mr Oscar Wilde's tragedy the beauty of a perfect work of art, a joy for ever, ambrosia to feed their souls and honey of sweet-bitter thoughts.

It was perfectly true, then, for Douglas to answer Hume-Williams's question, 'That is your opinion of the play?' with, 'It is exactly the same opinion as your witnesses now have about it. The only difference is I have escaped from the influence, and your witnesses are still under it.'

Re-examining Douglas, Billing noted, 'You said in this letter that the best men in the best society, members of the smartest clubs, members of Parliament, Peers, were all sodomites?' 'I believe it and knew it as a fact when I wrote it,' said Douglas, 'and it is a great deal truer now than then, because it has advanced tremendously.' Billing asked, 'Is this all true about being able to pick up male prostitutes in Piccadilly? Have you told Scotland Yard that this thing is going on?' 'I have been there over and over again about it ...' said Douglas. 'I tried to put them on to Ross, but nothing happened; they would not do anything.' Ross, perpetually harassed by the police, might disagree. 'They told me they were not allowed to do anything; they wished to goodness they could, but their hands were tied. That is what Basil Thomson told me.'

Douglas complained, 'I have been blackmailed all my life. I am being blackmailed still. I have been blackmailed to try and prevent me coming to this Court ... "If you come to the Court, you will be abused, and held up to scorn, ridicule and contempt" I have been told.' Far from being blackmail, this seems to be a perfectly reasonable prediction. Billing's grandiloquence had no bounds: 'And in spite of that, in the public interest, you stand there and tell this Court the truth?' 'Yes,' said his interlocutor, and with that self-righteous affirmation, stepped down. Douglas's colourful testimony would provide lurid copy for the next day's papers, even in the august pages of *The Times*, from which his accusations and continuing vendetta against Asquith and Ross – so ably represented by his satiric sonnets – leapt vividly into the readers' imaginations.

*

Billing's next witness was G.E. Morrison, drama critic of the *Morning Post* – the anti-semitic and xenophobic newspaper that was secretly backing Billing; Morrison's appearance was probably the work of Repington, the *Post*'s war correspondent and ringleader of the military conspiracy. The examination began with reference to Morrison's published criticism of *Salome*, in which he had described the play as 'a bizarre melodrama of disease'. Billing asked him to define the disease; Morrison delivered pseudo-medical evidence even less credible than that of the doctors' conspiracy, and which he was even less qualified to give: 'If you take Herod, it is what is usually known as erotomania. If you take Salome, I do not know what it is. It was pretty clear from the book that it was a disease of a certain class,' said the critic, 'but I think some of the symptoms had disappeared by the time it was put on at the Court Theatre.' Had Wilde depicted sexual vices on stage? 'You see an erotomaniac in what I should call eruption,' said Morrison.

After Morrison and Billing had discursed on the nature of tragedy and comedy, appetite and indecency, Hume-Williams cross-examined: 'I think you said it was a play which healthy people could see without much harm?' 'Yes, because healthy people are less liable to get disease,' said Morrison. He conceded that 'if you make vice attractive, it will attract young people as well as anyone else'. 'And there are a great many plays nowadays,' said Hume-Williams, referring to current theatrical trends, '... in which women show a great part of their nudity?' 'Oh, certainly,' said Morrison. 'Those are not very good for young people, are they?' asked the counsel. 'I should think not,' said the critic. Annoyingly for Billing, his evidence seemed to support the case for the prosecution. 'Miss Allan's dance was quite decent?' asked Hume-Williams. 'I think it would be impossible to object to that dance as "indecent" at this time of day.' 'There was nothing in her dance to suggest the Cult of the Clitoris, was there?'

'I do not know whether it would suggest to highly experienced people that sort of thing. It did not suggest it to me.'

Billing re-examined Morrison, paying particular attention to the question of Maud Allan's dress – or rather, her state of undress – as he saw that this interested Darling. 'As far as I remember, she wore a very light costume, according to old ideas; but I do not think she was in as light a costume as she wore in the dance years ago, and it was certainly no lighter than the costumes I have seen worn at fashionable matinees lately by scores of girls and young women of the very highest class.' 'Do you mean in the audience?' asked Darling. 'No, my Lord,' replied Morrison. 'There was an Egyptian Ballet, with a lot of distinguished amateurs.' Darling was much taken with this image: 'That was on the stage?' Morrison alluded to influence of the Russian Ballet, Poiret, Isadora Duncan's flimsy Grecian chiffons and Anna Pavlova's costumes in her 'Syrian Dance' (produced the previous year). To the morally proscriptive, the loose, diaphanous modern dresses symbolised a similar looseness of living.

Billing's next witness was Father Bernard Vaughan, a Farm Street Jesuit used to ministering to the fashionable Catholics of Mayfair. The Church of the Immaculate Conception on Farm Street was a spiritual home for aesthetes and Society alike; here Father Martin D'Arcy would guide Evelyn Waugh and Edith Sitwell towards the Church of Rome. An opinionated and political Christian who was interested in socialism, Fr Vaughan wrote sermons on 'Socialism from the Christian Standpoint', 'The Menace of the Empty Cradle', and 'The Workers' Right to Live', as well as specialising 'in a highly cultivated form of religious sado-masochism ... Society women flocked to Farm Street to hear themselves cursed and abused.' His decidedly secular love of publicity had already earned him a place on Wyndham Lewis's *Blast* list of figures to be despised (along with Marie Corelli and Lord Glenconner). Fr Vaughan lived up to expectations. 'I should not like to trust myself to speak as a priest about this abomination, which I look upon as constructive treason against the majesty and sanctity of God,' declared the priest. 'But I will speak as an Englishman, as a patriot who loves his country, and wants to see –' Darling interrupted, telling him he could save such a speech for the pulpit. 'You are not asked here simply to give your views about patriotism, and everything else.'

Fr Vaughan admitted he had read the play, and thought its performance would have a bad effect on any audience; his reasoning seemed personal. 'Anyone who knows human beings must say so. It takes us all our time to keep normal and straight and pure when we are standing in the rear of our animal passions; but when we give way to them and have them fanned, inflamed, we are ablaze with devouring flames.' It was a taste of what his sinful congregation might expect on Sunday morning. He confirmed Billing's notion of 'moral perverts in all classes';

to Billing's note of self-aggrandisement – 'Is it in the public interest that this play should be produced? I ask you that as a last question. I am trying to stop it' – the priest replied, 'You are trying to do a very good work.' One account maintains that Vaughan then gave Billing a Catholic blessing. Billing said, 'I thank you, Father,' and sat down. The prosecution's cross-examination was brief, and Billing returned to ask Fr Vaughan, 'Would you consider a woman who consented to depict that part, with all its bestial passion, on the stage – ?' Hume-Williams objected, and was told to sit down – by Billing. 'I should say she must be a perverted creature,' said Fr Vaughan. 'Could anyone libel her?' queried Billing. 'I cannot see how any woman could allow herself to go there,' concluded the priest.

The last witness of the day was Dr J.H. Clarke, Billing's colleague, proto-fascist and organiser of the doctors' plot. He could in no way be regarded as a reliable or objective witness. Clarke testified as to the pervasive nature of perversion in a telling (and perhaps personal) reference to *le vice Anglais* and the origin of its supposed prevalence among the upper classes; it was well known, he said, that 'one vicious boy will often corrupt a whole school'. Billing asked him what his impression of the notice advertising *Salome* had been: 'It gave me the impression that it was put forward by the enemies of England; that bringing forward in that prominent way the name of Oscar Wilde ... was the work of no friend of England; and the suggestion of alien blood in the promoters confirmed the impression that it made on my mind.' He agreed with Dr Cooke's analysis of the play. 'It might be produced in a medical theatre,' he said. 'The whole play is a perfect museum of sexual pathology ... but even then it might corrupt the medical students.' He thought all of Wilde's works – saving, perhaps, *The Ballad of Reading Gaol* ('which shows the good that imprisonment does to some') – ought to be suppressed and considered the title, 'The Cult of the Clitoris', entirely justified; only 'Lesbianism' could have been substituted, 'and that word would be equally well known to the initiated, and equally unintelligible to the uninitiated.' Clitoris itself was not a libellous word; it was 'a Greek term ... There is nothing at all obscene about it ... There is no obscenity in an anatomical term.' The mounting medical and moral evidence, as tainted as it was, had its effect, and Hume-Williams's cross-examination could do little to dispel the impression that the case was swinging inexorably towards Billing.

*

The weather on that first weekend of June was exceptionally hot, and as London sweltered, so did the political climate. Both at home and abroad, fervid discussions raged over the latest developments at the Old Bailey. The latest rumours

of the Asquiths' apparent corruption reached the trenches quickly (so geographi-
cally near was the war that newspaper boys sold that day's editions of the *Daily
Mirror* on the front line). Duff Cooper wrote to Diana from France: 'We argued
about Asquith and Lloyd George. One of my brother-officers maintained that
Asquith was "all in with the Huns" and he believed that Mrs Asquith was a
"female b——" that being as near as his limited vocabulary allowed him to get to
Sapphist.'

The idea that Billing might win the case was shocking to many members of
Society; especially to those with a vested interest such as Cynthia Asquith, with
her relationship to the former Prime Minister and his accused wife. At the same
time as Siegfried Sassoon was railing against 'this foul "Billing case" ' at the
Western Front, Cynthia Asquith was attending a garden lunch party with Liberal
wives Adele [Countess of] Essex and Mary Herbert (wife of Aubrey). 'Of course
we waded in the Billing cesspool. What with my name, my acquaintance with
——, and my relationship with Lord Alfred, I expect to find myself in the box at
any moment.' It was still the subject at teatime. 'One can't imagine a more
undignified paragraph in English history: at this juncture, that three-quarters of
The Times should be taken up with such a farrago of nonsense!'

The trial resumed on Monday, 3 June, after a break which gave both sides
time to regroup. With the improvement in war news – the German threat to Paris
had receded, and their advance on the Western Front had been contained – panic
subsided, and the political imperative returned to the forthcoming secret peace
talks. During the weekend there had been behind-the-line manoeuvrings: Repington had been to the Foreign Office to see Lord Robert Cecil who, together
with Balfour, was hostile to the idea of peace talks. At this meeting, discussions
took place 'in the knowledge that Billing's trial had the same purpose as
Maurice's letter, namely the scotching of any peace discussions'. Repington was
the link between the two. He was determined to keep the war going, and on
Sunday, spoke with officials at the American Embassy, who agreed 'that we must
steel our hearts against the German blackmail of trying to squeeze us into a peace
by squeezing France'.

The politicians behind the peace talks knew that Billing proposed to call
Eileen Villiers-Stuart again; Darling would permit her reappearance on condition that she produced the letter from her 'employers' in which she had been
instructed to lure Billing into a compromising situation. But if she did so, the
politicians' plot would be exposed. In a desperate attempt to prevent this
happening, they had even offered to get Mrs Keppel into the witness-box, as long
as Billing kept Villiers-Stuart out of it. Eileen's subsequent sworn statement –
printed in a post-trial edition of the *Vigilante* – went so far as to claim that threats
of assassination had been made against her. But the politicians had a more potent

piece of ammunition: they had discovered that Mrs Villiers-Stuart was bigamously married, and her first husband was alive and well and driving his army transport lorry in France.

*

Darling opened proceedings that Monday morning by remarking that he had received anonymous and abusive letters making various wild allegations. 'Everybody is bombarded with the same thing ...' said the prosecution. 'Miss Maud Allan herself has been inundated with filthy and obscene communications.' 'I have received one in which a person makes a most libellous attack on a witness, and has been incautious enough to sign it,' said Darling. 'I shall send that to the Public Prosecutor [Mathews] ... It is a postcard, and it has therefore been published to all who have seen it.' The card appears to have referred to Eileen's dubious marital state, and to the fact that she had perjured herself in the witness box, as she had discussed the Black Book with others. Apparently aware of this, Billing attempted to defend his mistress: 'The Defence has suffered from the same sort of thing. In one case, a threat has been made on the telephone and otherwise that if Mrs Villiers-Stuart goes into that box again, she will be shot from the Gallery'. To which Darling replied laconically, 'Perhaps we had better have the Gallery cleared' – well aware that Billing would be aghast at the loss of his very vocal audience.

Billing had applied to Darling for Mrs Keppel to be called, and was told he must call her himself. But if he did, Billing could not cross-examine her, so he determined to recall Eileen Villiers-Stuart. Before he did so, he called Jack Grein. This was a mistake, for the same reason that calling Mrs Keppel would have been: as his own witness, Billing could not cross-examine or discredit Grein, and his attempts to question Grein failed miserably, frustrated by Darling's ruling at every turn. It was a gift to the prosecution. When Hume-Williams cross-examined Grein, he established that the producer saw nothing in *Salome* to suggest lesbianism, sodomy or sadism, and noted that the libretto of Strauss's opera was exactly similar to the play's dialogue, and had been often performed before audiences of 'all classes of English society ... Including our Royal Family.' He also pointed out that although Dutch-born, Grein had been naturalised in England for twenty-three years, and he looked like an Englishman: 'I feel an Englishman,' averred Grein.

Grein was followed in the witness box by Eileen Villiers-Stuart. As the politicians had feared, Billing began his examination by producing her letter of 6 May. The prosecution protested, and Darling ruled it inadmissible as evidence. Vexed, Billing asked his lover if she had tried to tell 'any public man' about the

Black Book. Eileen said she had told the counsel himself, Hume-Williams, when they met at tea in May 1916, at the Albany set lent to her husband (although they were not then married) by Bevan Ellis, 'a cousin of Lord Howard de Walden'. Once again the counsel for the prosecution appeared to be intimately bound up in the affair. Eileen, her husband, and a Mrs Wynne (a Red Cross ambulance organiser, and a close friend of Hume-Williams's) were present; when she had brought up the subject of the Black Book, Hume-Williams had told her that there were 'too many people involved for anyone to make a personal sacrifice to expose it'. This sounded like conspiracy, and to the jury would have been confirmation that highly-placed persons were involved; possibly numbering some of the 47,000.

Travers Humphreys cross-examined – Darling ruled that in the circumstances it would not be admissible for his senior, Hume-Williams, to do so – and had Villiers-Stuart admit that Hume-Williams had not gone to the Albany to hear her story; he was there to take tea. 'I never really bothered to find out how he got there ...' said Eileen. She remained steadfast when questioned again about the meeting with Primrose and de Rothschild at 'The Hut' in Ripley in 1915. She had chosen Ripley – a village near Woking in Surrey – as the meeting-place because it was quiet. It was her private detective mentality at work, and Mrs Villiers-Stuart was a clever woman, not quite so easily caught out as the prosecution assumed. She confirmed that Primrose had the Black Book. 'You think he probably got it because he was one of the Whips?' asked Darling. She thought so. 'And there being the name in it of his chief, the Prime Minister, he proceeded to show it to you?' asked Humphreys. 'He did'; although Primrose had not been concerned to show her Asquith's name in the book. 'That merely came out looking through the book. He did not take me out just to show me Mr Asquith's name. He could probably have opened it in the taxi to show me Mr Asquith's name. He took it out to show me several names.' She said Primrose suggested something ought to be done about the matter, and that he was in a 'very awkward position, and he would like to get right out of public life, to get back into the Army again so that he could come out [of public life] and then handle the whole book. Those were his very words to me.' Officially, Primrose left political life and rejoined his regiment because of policy disagreements with Lloyd George in the coalition.

Humphreys asked her if Primrose was mad when he had said this; he appeared to be suggesting that her lover suffered from similar delusions to Captain Spencer's. Darling ruled that inadmissible, and Villiers-Stuart said Primrose was a 'very brave man'. Evelyn de Rothschild had read the book too: like Primrose, he was also an MP; this was the first time she had met him. Yet she had asked Primrose to show her the book. She must therefore have heard of the book beforehand? She had heard rumours, but it had been Primrose who had mentioned the book to her. Her testimony had the ring of truth. Villiers-Stuart said she had not read every name in the book – 'I should be there now if I did' – but that there were 'several hundreds' in the book, the names of 'public men', although she could not, as Humphreys asked, remember the name of the British Ambassador in Rome (Sir Rennell Rodd) among them; they merely looked at the names at random. However, Primrose seemed to know 'pretty nearly every one'.

Humphreys was a more efficient interrogator than his senior, and his exchanges with Villiers-Stuart were crisp and to the point:

'Did he point out to you certain names?'
'He did.'
'Including Mr Asquith's?'
'Including Mr Asquith's.'
'Was anybody else present beside yourself and those two gentlemen?'
'None at all.'
'And they are unfortunately both dead?'
'Yes, unfortunately, because they both knew of the book.'

Darling was shaken by this claim, and repeated Eileen's answer back to her. Humphreys asked if he could repeat his question, but Darling said no, so Humphreys said, 'Do you wish to withdraw what you have just said that these two gentlemen are dead because they knew of this book?' 'I do not,' she said. It was a sensational statement, later denied by members of the men's regiment: officially, Primrose had been killed by a 'stray' bullet. (Primrose and de Rothschild were both serving in the same regiment, fighting the Turks at Gaza: Primrose died in a rearguard skirmish; de Rothschild was killed shortly afterwards.)

Asked the whereabouts of the Black Book, Eileen told the prosecution that she believed it was in Germany, although it may have been moved; she knew it was there in the autumn of 1917. It was in Berlin, '... at the house that was the late British Embassy' – now used for billeting German officers, she claimed – seemingly from personal knowledge. Such remarks raise tantalising questions: was Mrs Villiers-Stuart another Mata Hari? Primrose had told her, just before leaving for Palestine, that the book was in the possession of an officer of the Prussian Guard. This may have been Count William Bentinck, a former Prussian Guardsman and subsequently attaché at the German Embassy in London; it was his castle in Holland which was the proposed venue for the negotiations between Kuhlmann and a senior British statesman.

Humphreys wondered at the sequence of events which allowed such important evidence to pass from a British officer and politician to a German diplomat. But Eileen kept her wits about her, and reasoned that Primrose had merely borrowed it, although she denied that she knew the identity of the lender. 'I did not ask him,' she said. 'That book had travelled such a lot … I was sorry … that such a book should be allowed to go about the world which contained such statements and such names.' Primrose had told her this in the lounge of the Adelphi Hotel in Liverpool; she was living in Birkenhead, where Captain Villiers-Stuart's regiment was stationed, and the hotel was a favoured gathering place (Robert Graves, stationed nearby with Siegfried Sassoon, recalled its cocktail bar being 'generally crowded with very drunk Russian naval officers'). The meeting happened 'quite by accident', she claimed; and Primrose had mentioned that the book 'had got back to Berlin'. The meeting may have been accidental, but the relationship between the two was not, and again raises questions as to Villiers-Stuart's complicity in the affair. Was she being used by British Intelligence? Darling interrupted to ask a question of his own, prompted by the anonymous postcard: had Mrs Villiers-Stuart told her husband whose names were in the book? This was a slip-up in her otherwise successful testimony: by saying she had, she perjured herself, having previously maintained that she had told no one at all about the book.

Resuming his examination, Humphreys asked what else was in the book. A great deal, but Eileen had not been able to read the German text. 'I suppose Mr Neil Primrose explained to you what the meaning of those names was there?' He did. 'It meant that the names of those people were the names of people under German influence?' It did. 'Traitors?' Yes. 'And one of those traitors, the Prime Minster of England?' Mrs Villiers-Stuart repeated the allegation with evident satisfaction, 'It was the then Prime Minister.' She added that the list included members of both houses of Parliament. 'In fact the majority of people in public life in England?' asked Humphreys. 'Oh no, not the majority,' said Eileen, '… I did not read the majority; there may have been among the 47,000; not the names I read.' But all 'traitors to their country during the War?' Villiers-Stuart asserted that she could prove they were traitors, 'they would not be in that book if they were not'. Darling remarked, 'That assumes accuracy in recording the truth on the part of Germany, which I never heard attributed to that country before.'

Humphreys established that Primrose had told her that these were all traitors; thereby also establishing that the rest of her assertions came from the same source. 'And this gentleman, Mr Neil Primrose, I suppose you knew that he bore a very honoured name?' 'I did,' she said – adding that it was not in the book. 'And you understood from him that he was going to take no steps to try and save his country, except by going into the Army, later on getting out of the Army, and then retiring from public life so as to expose it?' 'That was his information,' she said. Travers Humphreys asked again from whom Primrose had borrowed the book, and to whom he had returned it. She could not say. Why hadn't she asked him? 'Because he asked me not to ask the question,' she said. Humphreys began to hint at her relationship with Primrose: how long had she known him? 'Quite a long time.' But the cross-examination ended there, abruptly – possibly due to behind-the-scenes intervention from Primrose's father, the former Prime Minister, Lord Rosebery. Hume-Williams was seen whispering to Humphreys. When Billing got up to re-examine her, he noted, 'Did you hear Mr Hume-Williams tell the Junior Counsel to leave her alone just now? Did you hear that remark?' At this Hume-Williams rose to his feet, and accused Billing of lying, and not for the first time. 'In a court of law, we use legal methods,' said Billing, with not a little of the swaggering braggadocio he had employed with Colonel Archer-Shee. 'Outside we use others. If you call me a liar outside, I will thrash you.' 'Don't be an idiot,' replied Hume-Williams.

Billing asked Eileen if the book Primrose showed her was the same that was returned to Germany. 'There may be many books,' she said, 'there may be many copies of the book.' 'Is it a fact that amongst certain people in Society this book has been fairly freely discussed?' asked Billing. 'I have heard it discussed, yes.' The book seemed to be becoming fact; yet unless it could lie on the judge's bench, a physical presence, it would remain, for the purposes of the court, a work of fiction. Many involved in the case hoped it would stay that way. Darling obstructed Billing's attempts to have Eileen reaffirm her belief that Primrose and de Rothschild had been killed; again, perhaps because of Primrose's eminent father. But Eileen averred, 'I firmly believe that because they knew of that book, they both died on active service within a few days or weeks of each other.' 'Do you mean they were murdered in battle?' asked Darling. 'I do,' she said.

Eileen said that she had discussed the 'eight or ten' names she could remember from the book with Primrose and de Rothschild, and the information against their names. 'Was it only for sex perversion,' asked Billing, 'or were there other reasons why names should be put in this book?' 'There were other reasons,' she said. She described how the book was laid out, with a list of German agents in England; then the names of the 47,000; then paragraphs containing information about them; there were also instructions in German to agents. 'Did it explain the work of the agents in this book,' asked Billing, 'what they were supposed to do?' 'It did,' said Eileen, '... It was to create an atmosphere of indecency in England ... to spread vice ... so that we should practically lose this war. It has been very successful up to now.' When Darling reprimanded Billing for asking leading questions about blackmail, members of the jury could well have come to the conclusion that Darling, himself named as one of the 47,000, was seeking to cover things up.

The detail of Eileen's testimony was convincing. She maintained she could remember names of the agents in the book, 'not put down as German subjects;

possibly of German extraction'. Billing referred to her meeting with Hume-Williams at the Albany, when he asked details about the book. 'Did Mr Hume-Williams take you seriously, and ask you serious questions?' asked Billing. 'Quite seriously,' said Villiers-Stuart. Her following statement appears to have been deleted from the official court record, and printed only in the *Daily Mail*: 'I mentioned the name of Mr Justice Darling as one of those which appeared in the book. Mr Hume-Williams said he knew Mr Justice Darling.' Again, this must have cast doubts in the minds of the jury as to the judge's innocence and impartiality. Eileen claimed a serious discussion ensued about the book, and that she gave Hume-Williams the name of one enemy agent: Jack Grein. 'If this was true, it was no wonder that Counsel had not called Grein as a witness. If it was not true, Counsel would no doubt make haste to deny it.' Like Maud Allan, Grein had enough foreign connections to make him a good candidate for espionage. But Eileen claimed that Hume-Williams had not seemed surprised when Grein's name was mentioned in this traitorous connexion. He may not have been then; but he certainly gave the appearance of it now. Hume-Williams leapt to his feet, saying, 'What?' 'You did not seem surprised, Mr Hume-Williams,' said Eileen. Again, this latter exchange was omitted from the court record, and appeared only in the *Daily Mail* and the *Manchester Guardian*.

Emboldened by these revelations, and untroubled by Darling's harassments, Billing attempted again to have Villiers-Stuart's letter of 6 May produced. Darling forbade it. The political conspiracy seemed complicit when Billing's further questions to Eileen about other names in the book and other houses of vice in London were suppressed. Almost in retaliation (and probably directed by the government camp), Darling turned to the question of Mrs Villers-Stuart's marital state – as insinuated by the anonymous postcard he had received. 'You have told us you were married last July?' he asked. She said she had been, and that her first husband, Percival Douglas Bray – whom she described as being 'in the motoring trade' (he was a bus driver), had been killed in France in August 1914. She had met Primrose before her marriage to Bray – in 1912 or 1913, she thought. He had married Lord Derby's daughter, Lady Victoria Stanley, in 1915, but Eileen had never met his wife. Re-examining, Billing confirmed that she had met Primrose at a luncheon party in 1912 or 1913; and that she had subsequently met him at 'many places' – none of which she could name. 'There are so many …,' she pleaded, adding sarcastically, 'probably somebody will write to his Lordship and tell him.' Eileen's performance had been almost too good – certainly for her own welfare, if the threats from the political camp were to be taken seriously.

Arnold White was to be the next witness. His testimony was liable to be as dramatic as his arrival: he was at that moment driving from Farnham by fast car, having been detained on his way to the Old Bailey. Darling, however, refused to wait for White, although he allowed Travers Humphreys to go off to telephone the Admiralty to ask Admiral Hall to appear (Spencer had said that the Black Book was in Hall's room). When he returned, Humphreys reported that Hall was not expected back at the Admiralty until 3 pm. Darling refused to wait for him, too, despite the prosecution's desperate plea for time: 'If not, it is a misfortune from which we must suffer; but Admiral Hall could not stop here because of his public duties.' It is likely that Hall had in fact refused to come, eager, like many others, for the trial to end as soon as possible.

*

Darling now declared both the case for the prosecution, and that of the defence, closed. He directed the jury on the nature of the libel. The case was confined to the paragraph heading and the first sentence, which implied that the play was a private performance for the 'Cult' only. It was for the jury to decide if *Salome* was an indecent play. 'But as to all this about Scotland Yard and the 47,000 and the German agents, and who may be on the list and who may not, I shall rule that that is absolutely irrelevant and immaterial in these proceedings, and no questions will be left to the Jury about it, and I shall tell them not to consider it.' Having let ample evidence be given on this latter subject, it was remarkable and, to some, suspicious that Darling should now declare that it had nothing to do with the case. But had it been disallowed, an appeal might have quashed a guilty verdict on the grounds that evidence of possible relevance had not been heard. Although Darling's ruling appeared to be in Billing's favour, the defendant protested that he would not be allowed to refer to the Black Book in his closing speech; 'I have said what I have said,' said Darling in suitably biblical paraphrase, '... I do not suppose that I can keep you to the point in any way ...'

Sure enough, Billing's final address to the court was a tour de force of exhortation and rhetoric. He began by accepting responsibility for the libel 'of which I knew nothing until eight or nine hours after it was published and issued; because I deemed it in the public interest to do so'. Once again he railed against the 'mysterious influence' which supported German interests in Britain, and claimed he was attacking this influence through his libel. 'I am a libeller,' he brazenly declared. 'I have libelled public men for the last two and a half years ...' 'Do you think I am going to keep quiet in my position as a public man while nine men die in a minute to make a sodomite's holiday?'

True to form, Billing made detailed reference to the Black Book He alluded to possible conspiracy and political dealing behind the legal processes; he derided judge and counsel, and appealed directly to the jury. 'I expect there are

169

people in this country today who think I am mad. I am mad ...' he confessed, 'I am obsessed with one subject. And that is, bringing our Empire out of this war a little cleaner than it was when it went in. That is my obsession; and I plead guilty to it ... Maud Allan is only an incident'; greater issues were at stake. Billing claimed that certain evidence (regarding Spencer's mental state) was being withheld from the court. The jury now wondered at the behind-the-scenes machinations, and whether Billing might not be right. He appeared to be gaining the upper hand. He cited Villiers-Stuart's and Spencer's evidence: '... it fitted in with the many things which I knew to be going on in the House of Commons ... with the many mistakes, the many tragedies, the regrettable incidents, the apathy, the protection which the Germans (particularly German Jews) in this country get ...' Billing ought to have been careful here, for his own half-German wife was sitting in the public gallery. 'I know why. Because at the head of it all is this mysterious influence which seems to prevent a Britisher getting a square job or a square deal.'

It was the speech of his career, and Billing took advantage of the theatrical setting. With the dust motes floating in the still, stuffy midsummer air of the Old Bailey, he folded his arms and addressed the jury like the Edwardian showman he was. 'I do not want to touch a dramatic note' – a characteristic disclaimer – 'but here we are at just twenty minutes to four, I shall be talking to you for perhaps another half an hour' – hearts fell – 'between now and when I sit down, there will be thousands of men "gone out" because of our "mistakes". Nothing but "mistakes". I want to know why those mistakes have occurred. That is my great crime.' To the newly-bereaved, or to those who had said goodbye to their boys on bleak station platforms, such appeals struck home when they read accounts of the trial in their newspapers. Why had the war demanded so much sacrifice, for so little return?

Billing sympathised with Maud Allan; he had only examined her because Grein would not come to the dock; 'it grieved me very much to have to cross-examine Miss Maud Allan at all ...' Billing's concern was disingenuous; he might have considered the effect on her career and reputation. Forever after, Maud Allan would be defined by this trial, just as Oscar Wilde was condemned in memory by his own appearance at the Old Bailey. The legal process can turn the spotlight of history on the innocent and guilty alike. Before, Maud had been known as the sister of a murderer; now she would be known as a lesbian. Little wonder that from the end of this day until the conclusion of the trial, Miss Allan was observed to be in tears.

Billing declared he was merely fighting for moral values. 'And what have I said in my libel? Have I said that Maud Allan was a lesbian? I have never suggested it.' This was patently untrue: in his Plea of Justification, Billing had admitted to the libel, the Indictment of which claimed that the paragraph alleged Allan to be a lesbian. In a neat and clever move, possibly inspired by the advice of his anonymous KC, Billing turned on the prosecution to make them appear culpable; with Hume-Williams already implicated in the affair, this was not difficult. He accused them of using Maud Allan – 'they know that the sympathy which goes out from every Englishman's heart to a woman may capture a sensational verdict' – again, he was referring to the political machinations. Having denied that he had libelled Allan, he now tried to prove that he had published in the public interest, and that 'the Cult of the Clitoris' referred to the 47,000, not to her. 'Miss Maud Allan may be a pervert, or she may not,' he said, contradicting his previous contention. 'We are not here to decide that; we are here to decide whether the title refers – this is on the question of Not Guilty or Guilty – to the first half or the second half of that paragraph.' This completely contravened Darling's directions as to what the case was about.

If *Salome* was 'such a wonderful piece of English prose or poetry', why had the Lord Chamberlain seen fit to ban it? Yet another misrepresentation, one which much vexed the Lord Chamberlain's office. 'By now *Salome* would have been on its way to Holland and Spain as a work of British art if it had not been for that paragraph ...' he claimed. 'It stopped it. You who have read your papers have read the fact that Lord Beaverbrook owned this.' What appears in the papers is not evidence,' said Darling. 'You ought to know that.' 'And so the paragraph was successful,' continued Billing. 'Are you going to send me to gaol for this?' Billing appealed to the jury – each and everyone an Englishman, he hoped. 'Is there anything in that paragraph one half so indecent, one half so revolting, as any one passage which you have had read to you from that play? ... this social leper, Oscar Wilde, had founded a cult of sodomy in this country, and travelled from end to end of it perverting youth wherever he could. He was not satisfied even that his evil influence should die with him; he left behind his works, so that his crimes may be perpetuated even after he was dead. And I tried to stop that ... Have I convinced you that this is a beastly play? I trust I have ... The Prosecution will follow. I can almost hear what they will tell you. They will say that I not only wrote the libel, but I exaggerated my offence by calling up something with regard to the past of this woman, which no Englishman would have done. Well, they have only themselves to blame [because he had not been able to examine Grein]. When I found they were not going to call him, I had to cross-examine the one witness they called. But it is a fact, and we might as well face it. Her brother was executed for an act of sadism, for murdering two young girls and outraging them after death.' Counsel and judge objected, and with good reasons – among them, the fact that Theo Durrant had not sexually violated his victims.

'Now, Gentlemen, let us dismiss that unfortunate thing from our minds,' declared Billing hypocritically. 'But the evidence showed it was a common thing for perverts (reliable medical evidence was called to support it) to commit these crimes in actuality, and for others to do them in pantomime.' Billing concluded: 'I ask you first and foremost not to say that this is a clean play, not to give a verdict in favour of it. I ask you to send me away from this place with the confidence that a verdict of twelve of my countrymen will give me to carry on the very heavy task which, in the interests of my country, I have seen fit to commence.' Billing's peroration was highly effective. For the jury, it was a complicated case to try; and the names of Wilde and his play, associated with such unheard-of perversions, left a sour taste in their mouths. Billing's plain appeals to patriotism and decency meant more than intricate arguments of legalese or questions of literary aesthetics. As he sat down, Billing received great applause, an ovation which he hoped would be repeated at the end of the trial, on the following day.

8

The Verdict

> The cruel thing is that, to the public mind, the mere suggestion of such things is in effect the same as though they were proved. Adele [Essex] said the shop-women sort of strata were saying, 'We always knew it of the Asquiths, and we're so glad they're being exposed.' Margot, of course, attributes the whole thing to an anti-Asquith ploy – to make it impossible for him ever to return to office – and I should think there is a good deal of truth in this theory.
>
> Cynthia Asquith's diary, 3 June 1918

As it drew to a dramatic close, the trial continued to transfix society at every level, especially the growing middle classes, horrified yet vicariously excited by this exposé of their supposed betters. To that elite, the Billing affair was a subject of concern, not least because it threatened their own integrity and supremacy. On Monday 3 June, Cynthia Asquith noted in her diary a lunch at the Asquiths' house in Cavendish Square, with Margot, Sir Charles Russell (who had acted for Queensberry in the libel suit brought by Wilde), Lord Stamfordham (private secretary to the king), and Sir Edward Henry, London's Commissioner of Police (and Basil Thomson's immediate superior). It was a high-powered assembly of experts in their fields, well-placed to comment on the affair:

> Of course the Billing trial was discussed – poor Margot greatly incensed, but fairly rational I thought. Lord Stamfordham said he understood the whole of the Royal Household were in the 'Book' [hence the scare over Fripp's evidence]. To my horror, Sir Charles said there was no chance of a conviction against Billing. It is monstrous that these maniacs should be vindicated in the eyes of the public. What an Alice in Wonderland cast! Billing, Father Vaughan, Marie Corelli, Lord Alfred Douglas, etc. Sir Charles considered Lord Alfred might well be at the bottom of a great deal of it. Why that lunatic is at large, Heaven only knows! Sir Charles was in the old Oscar Wilde-Lord Queensberry case and says that, ever since, Lord Alfred rings him up on the telephone about once a week and pours a torrent of filthy language into the receiver. He once let his house to a respectable lady who was much upset by this custom.

Given the extreme nature of the allegations made against her, Margot Asquith could have instituted her own criminal proceedings against Billing and the *Vigilante*. Doubtless she was counselled against any such action by her husband; but Margot was also supremely indifferent to others' opinions when it suited her. When E.F. Benson caricatured her in his satire of the Souls, *Dodo*, Margot's only response to the author's letter of apology was to say, 'Dear Mr Benson, have you written a novel? How clever of you.' There were good reasons for Margot not to cross swords with Billing: Cynthia Asquith wrote that 'Sir Charles naturally urged Margot to make no effort to force herself into the box: Billing would, of course, ask if it were true she had a German governess after the war, and if Sir Ernest Cassel stayed with her, and all kinds of irrelevant questions – just as he would ask Mrs Keppel about her relations with King Edward.' In a later discussion, Cynthia noted, 'Asquith, bless him, is so out of touch with the stupidity of humanity, and will not bother about the mud thrown at him. We wondered whether any advice would have made any difference to such indiscretions as having Sir Ernest Cassel at the Wharf [the Asquiths' country house], and so on.'

Marie Belloc Lowndes, whose husband wrote for *The Times*, commented that 'The only time I ever knew Margot "rattled" was as regards the Pemberton Billing case. She thought [rightly] … that he was financed by part of the Press. She declared that that type of man causes a crowd to become a mob, that the mob then acts on the Press, and the end of it is that without knowing it, certain journalists do a frightful amount of harm.' Over lunch, Margot Asquith may have seemed 'fairly rational' at first, but her daughter-in-law went on to observe that the trial had induced a certain level of paranoia in the ex-Prime Minister's wife, which may or may not have been justified. Certainly, Margot portrayed a society looking over its shoulder, a sense of conspiracy abroad with which Billing's allegations had managed to infect innocent and guilty alike.

> Margot screamed out about the whole odious system of espionage under Lloyd George. How far it is true, or whether she has a bee in her bonnet on the subject, I don't know. She says there is always a secretary in the Square to watch her comings and goings [an extraordinary notion, considering her position as the wife of a former Prime Minister] and that when she entertains the blinded soldiers from St Dunstan's and helps them into their taxis, a photograph is taken and published under the heading 'Mrs Asquith says goodbye to her pacifist friends.'

Cynthia Asquith found such protests ingenuous, and Margot a victim of her own innocence:

> Poor Margot, her indiscretions are so naive, so childlike, that they ought in themselves to furnish a certificate of innocence. Where there is so much smoke

there couldn't be fire. She told us what I had never heard, that the woman who swore to having seen her at Fortnum and Mason's sending a parcel to a German prisoner – and then retracted, saying she must have mistaken Dardanelles for Donnington Hall – was the present Lady Curzon, then Mrs Duggan. There has been an article in the *Vigilante* accusing the wives of Cabinet ministers of lesbianism.

It is a tribute to Billing's powerful rhetoric (and evidence of the hysterical atmosphere) that he had whole sections of high society running scared or plainly outraged by claims printed in his tiny circulation newspaper. In that, his campaign had succeeded, and hardly needed the verdict of British justice. At the Old Bailey, the final day of these remarkable proceedings opened with Billing having seated himself in the dock, from where he told Darling, 'My Lord, I wish no further privilege from the Bench.' It was a brash move; by playing the plantiff in the dock, he sought to emphasise his sense of 'injured innocence'.

Hume-Williams's address to the jury reminded them that the trial was 'purely a prosecution undertaken by Miss Maud Allan at her own expense for the purpose ... of clearing her character'. He refuted 'wild suggestions of interference by the Crown, some attempt to prosecute Mr Pemberton-Billing hiding behind the skirts, I think it was said, of Miss Maud Allan ...' But there was evidence of outside interference: Hume-Williams, compromised in court by references to his meetings with Spencer and Villiers-Stuart, also had connexions with Lord Newton, part of the British delegation to the Hague; elsewhere, Bonar Law had written to the Attorney-General, F.E. Smith, to request his intervention. It was hypocritical (if correct), therefore, of Hume-Williams to accuse Billing himself of being subject to extra-court influence. 'All this interminable nonsense about the Black Book and the demoralisation of our country; the prevalance of sodomy; the fact that no high-placed individual can hope for success, according to Lord Alfred Douglas, unless he is a known and pronounced sodomist ... would have been shut out' had not 'some legal mind' assisted Billing 'in the preparation of these particulars'. Hume-Williams and Darling now knew that an eminent KC was advising Billing.

Hume-Williams said Billing had not proved that Maud Allan had 'the slightest tendency' to lesbianism, and rightly directed the jury that it was 'ludicrous' to suggest 'that the issue for you is whether [*Salome*] is a moral or an immoral play'. Hume-Williams said it was not his brief to defend *Salome*, or the works of 'this wretched man who wrote the play, curious perverted genius that he was', who also wrote 'some of the best comedies produced in England, clean and amusing plays ... drawing crowded houses'. Anyone might go determined to find in the play 'some extraordinary moral perversion, some allusion to some of the many "isms" which have been brought forward in this case, sadism, a thing which I suppose none of you ever heard of before you came into Court; I personally never did ...' At this Billing interrupted, accusing the prosecution of being afraid to call Jack Grein. 'If you interrupt the proceedings again,' Darling told him, 'I will have you removed from the dock, as it is a misdemeanour, and your presence is not necessary.' Hume-Williams referred to Dr Cooke's testimony as 'these erotic criticisms of this Indian doctor'; the prosecution was not above making a few racial slurs. 'This Doctor ... finds some horrible suggestion of some practice known as sadism, a vice imagined by a lunatic for lunatics, which ... I should think has never been practised in this country out of the confines of an asylum.' 'We spent a great deal of time listening to Captain Spencer and Mrs Villiers-Stuart', and their extraordinary stories about the Black Book; when Hume-Williams referred to Primrose as 'a gentleman ... who is supposed to have had reposing in him this secret', Billing again interrupted, 'As you had in you, Mr Hume-Williams.' At this Darling severely threatened Billing with removal. Such a threat satisfied the prosecution.

Hume-Williams read out the '47,000' article; and appeared to change his mind about it. 'Considering what we now know of German ways and German thoroughness, it is not at all unlikely that such a list did exist, a list of people in prominent positions in England whom it might be desirable to approach if you could ... that Captain Spencer saw it, and that out of that truth the whole of this imaginative superstructure has grown.' Hume-Williams's suggestion that the book had a factual basis was probably done on 'official "inspiration"'. His remarks on the public imagination are a fascinating self-portrait of the national psyche at war. 'We know the wild stories that run from mouth to mouth every day ... Your nerves and my nerves, nobody's nerves, are in the condition which they were before. Things are readily believed ... which in pre-war times would have been incredible ... Every yarn, however silly, obtains some credence, and it is in my submission very probable that some list of that kind did exist, and does exist for all I know ...'

Hume-Williams appealed to the jury. 'Supposing one of ... your sons had been taking some small part in this play,' he postulated, 'and that fact had been chronicled ... under the heading, "The Cult of the Penis", what would you have done?' Once again, Hume-Williams gave a telling indication of the national mentality: 'In this country at present, the most horrible suggestion that you can make against any man is that he is addicted to sodomite practices. The next most horrible suggestion is that he is a traitor to his country, and is in the pay of the Germans' – an interesting precedence. Counsel's appeal was, like Billing's, to moral values and patriotic fervour. 'What would you do? Do you think that you would not have found out who wrote the article, and taken immediate steps to clear your character, or that of anybody near and dear to you involved under a heading so repulsive as, "The Cult of the Penis"? Yes, but "The Cult of the Clitoris" is worse … It means lesbianism.'

Such contorted logic could only have bemused a jury already faced with an eye-opening barrage of sexual deviancies, but Hume-Williams felt secure in his analogy. He was determined that Billing should not have all the drama to himself; he fired up his address, attacking Billing's moralistic stance. 'An apostle of purity! I stand here, says this man, in the interests of public decency. Public decency! The people who put in that heading would attack a woman … and when ultimately she takes the only steps that are open to her to clear her character, they formally tell the Jury is is true; she is a lesbian … a filthy, abandoned, lewd, unchaste woman.' Billing was discomforted by this, the prosecution's first really effective attack on him and his methods. Interrupting, Billing implied that he had not accused Maud of lesbianism: 'The accusation that I made was that she was pandering to those who practised unnatural vice by this performance.' 'Do I understand then that you withdraw any suggestion that she is a lesbian?' asked Darling. Billing replied that if it was suggested that he had made such an allegation – that she was a lesbian – he would withdraw it.

It was a telling point. The indictment against Billing said that he had claimed Maud Allan was 'a lewd unchaste and immoral woman' about to give a performance which would encourage 'obscene and unnatural practices among women'; that she was guilty by association. Billing's Plea of Justification merely stated that he was not guilty, and that 'all defamatory matters alleged in the Indictment are true'. It would appear that Billing was caught. 'It was perfectly plain from that moment', wrote Travers Humphreys later, 'that the Plea of Justification had failed, publication was admitted, and the only question for the Jury remaining was, "Did the paragraph in the newspaper constitute a libel on Miss Maud Allan?" ' Yet Darling said nothing, and Hume-Williams – whose grasp of the case was less encompassing and clear-headed than Humphreys' (perhaps because of his own implied involvement in it) – merely picked up on Billing's withdrawal of one allegation.

Hume-Williams' final comments were reserved for the way Billing had personally conducted his case. 'Perhaps it is not a bad plan, particularly if you … have been, as Mr Pemberton-Billing is careful to tell you he has been an actor for four years … it is much better to do it yourself; and the first thing to do … is, if possible, to insult the judge …' – a sycophantic appeal to Darling's ego. 'It so happens that the Judge is the senior Judge among the Common Law judges of our country; he has been a Judge for nearly twenty years.' 'For over twenty years', corrected Darling, preening like some Lewis Carroll character. 'For over twenty years, his Lordship has been a Judge in our land. It has recently pleased the King to make him a member of the Privy Council, and to add the title of

177

Right Honourable to his other distinctions as a mark of appreciation.' 'I wish you not allude to that, because Privy Councillors are particularly mentioned among the 47,000. (Laughter in Court.)' Darling's case had become *Alice in Wonderland*, with Billing as the knave who stole the tarts; observers such as Cynthia Asquith may have wished they were Alice, seeking to sweep them all away, 'You're nothing but a pack of cards!'

Hume-Williams deprecated Billing's predilection for bringing celebrated names into court: 'Lord Carnarvon, Colonel Aubrey Herbert, Sir Rennell Rodd, Mr Asquith, Mrs Asquith ... Mr Pemberton-Billing even condescended, or his witnesses did, to bring in such a very humble individual as myself.' Despite protests from Billing that he was now giving evidence, Hume-Williams made his own attempt at a Darlingesque quip: 'I have been expecting to be told that I was on the list. I rather wonder that that is not given. His Lordship is on it apparently; at any rate, I should have been in good Company. (Laughter in Court.)' He spoke of Billing's intimidation of 'everybody in connection with this case. He has created a sort of atmosphere by his friends in the gallery, and his followers outside, calculated to intimidate the Jury if he can do it ...' Again Billing objected, telling Darling pointedly, 'I can't help the gallery applauding any more than you can help them laughing at your jokes.' This enraged the judge, whose self-esteem and self-righteousness had been puffed up by Hume-Williams: 'You have tried, as Mr Hume-Williams has pointed out, to insult everybody in this case. You have told me that you have insulted me in your paper and in Parliament, although I have not known it. You have now insulted me to my face.'

Lastly, Hume-Williams turned to Billing's comments on Maud Allan's family tragedy: 'He justified it by the statement that he was going to prove that this murder had got some sadistic tendencies which would run in the family, and which therefore be attributed to Miss Maud Allan herself ... Absolutely shameless and unjustifiable was that question.' Yet, bizarrely, there is indeed some justification for Billing's citation of Theo Durrant's crimes and the bearing they had on Maud Allan's creative persona. Hume-Williams pointed up what Cynthia Asquith had privately noted: that the interference of Lord Alfred Douglas had much to do with this aspect of the affair. 'Of all the shocking attacks that this case has witnessed, that is the most unmanly, the most un-English, and the worst,' concluded Hume-Williams. It was a peroration which must have in turn wounded Billing. Above all else, said the prosecution, it was the business of this trial, and the jury to clear Maud Allan's name. On this emotive note, Hume-Williams sat down.

*

Darling summed up the case. The fact that Billing had asked for Scotland Yard to protect him proved that the libel had provoked a breach of the peace. Billing protested that these threats were to do with the 47,000, nothing to do with Maud Allan; Darling instructed him, 'Do not interrupt me again.' Yet Billing was right, and Darling's comments appear to betray his ignorance about the political machinations behind the case.

'A matter I regretted more than anything was to have the name of Viscount Grey introduced into such a case as this ...' said Darling. 'I should have thought if there was a man in England whose character ... could not be mentioned in such a case ... it would have been Viscount Grey.' Billing objected, 'I never mentioned the name of Sir Edward Grey.' 'Your witness did,' said Darling (Spencer had named Grey as the man who appointed him as 'political officer' in November 1915). 'No, my Lord.' 'Your witness said so in the box,' stressed Darling; at which point, someone in the gallery spoke out, 'Never, my Lord.' 'Turn that man out of Court at once,' demanded Darling. An unnamed person on the barristers' bench told the court that it had been Spencer who named Grey.

Darling recalled Billing's remark that he, Darling, was merely the referee in this affair; the judge commented that he pitied any football referee who had to deal with a player like Billing. It was an earthy analogy intended to show his own healthy morality, a contrast to the decadence of *Salome*, 'a play written with the vilest possible intention; it was written to advocate – to excuse – to glorify – unclean love'; Darling commented naively on Douglas's testimony, '... he can have no motive in saying this because it is the deepest disgrace to himself'. Wilde's ghost was again in the dock. 'It is an awful thing, of course, to think that anybody could sit down and write such a play,' said Darling, 'and heaps of abuse have been poured upon Oscar Wilde for it. Oscar Wilde wrote filthy works, as you know; he was guilty of filthy practices; he was convicted in this Court, and suffered imprisonment, and social extinction, and death in due course.' The judge found all this talk of sadism and fetishism '... a little dangerous ... you may push theories too far; people may be too clever by half'. He got rather carried away on this point; as a widower, the subject rather depressed him, and he descended into Victorian sentimentality. 'This fetishism is dangerous when you remember how many a person has desired to have a flower from the bouquet of a lady – a glove that belonged to her – a bit of ribbon that she wore – a lock of her hair: that was mentioned. It is a mournful thing to know that all those who have preserved a lock of hair of the lady they loved, and perhaps put it at the back of her miniature, were victims of fetishism.'

Salome may have been an unsavoury play; but Miss Allan hadn't written it, or produced it; she merely appeared in it. Darling pointed out that the drama critic of *Morning Post* had not seen Maud bite the lips of the severed head of

Jokanaan. 'If she were representing a sadist, if she is a sadist herself, what would be the natural thing? Would you not expect she would bite the lips? Of course you would. That is the conduct of the sadist.' Darling read out the relevant lines, 'and it is what Lord Alfred Douglas wrote; that is the sadist; that is the sadist writing ...' The translator of *Salome* could bear it no longer. Douglas leapt to his feet, waving his arms. 'You have no right to say that I wrote it. You lie. You are a liar, a damned liar. If you say it outside Court, I will prosecute you.' This met with cheering and applause and cries of 'Bravo!' from the gallery. The rumpus lasted for a minute, and swamped Darling's order for Douglas to be removed from the court. Bosie was bustled out, followed by an elderly lady in a bonnet, brandishing a parasol, also ejected by Darling for shouting at him. 'There must not be that,' declared Darling, but he was losing control of the court. Douglas could be seen through the glass doors, to the loud amusement of the crowd, demanding that a constable fetch his stick and hat, which he had left behind.

Darling continued to mislead the jury by stating that Douglas had written the play. He said again that Miss Allan had not bitten the head, at which Billing interrupted, 'My Lord, she spoke the words.' 'Of course she did,' he retorted. 'Do not interrupt me, or you will go where your witness has gone.' This was met with loud hissing, aimed at Darling, which he pretended not to hear. He returned to the *Morning Post* critic's evidence, which had evidently stuck in his mind, with its descriptions of high society ladies in scanty dress. 'Gentlemen, that is a most remarkable thing. I have no doubt Mr Morrison was speaking the absolute truth. He mentioned a play he had seen played by people who should be, as I understand they were, ladies and gentlemen ... I think he said it was an Egyptian ballet in which these amateurs were. And mind you, Gentlemen, you are asked to say that Miss Maud Allan is a sadist, a lewd woman, and so on and so on; among other things because she wore a too indecent costume, too light for the stage.' How much more shocked would Darling have been, had he heard Magnus Hirschfeld's stories of Soho clubs where not only the cloaks were left in the cloakroom. The jury retired at 3.15 pm. Billing, the accused, waited in the corridor beneath the dock, pacing the floor nervously and smoking cigarettes passed to him by friends in the courtroom. The jury returned at 4.40 pm. Their foreman, 'a dour-looking Scot, with a beard and side-whiskers', gave their verdict: 'Not Guilty.'

*

The verdict was greeted with uproar in the courtroom. The entire gallery stood cheering, applauding and stamping their feet as though at a boisterous first night.

8. The Verdict

They were joined by the defence witnesses and Billing's friends seated behind the dock. 'There has never been such an excited throng in the new Central Criminal Court,' observed the *Daily Mail*, 'or one which gave vent to its feelings more noisily. In vain did the judge try to give an order to suppress the demonstration. His lips were seen moving, but his words stood no chance of being heard.' Having failed to make himself heard, Darling 'motioned fiercely towards the gallery with his arm'. The court ushers attempted to quieten the row. 'When the noise had died down the judge, with set lips and pale face, said: "Clear the court. Turn everyone out of the gallery." A woman's voice was heard above the few cheers which were still coming from various corners: "You tried to – ." A man broke in with a loud shout of "Hip, hip, hooray!" ... "Turn all those people out at the back," said the judge, pointing to the back of the dock. There were more cheers, and the police began to turn people out of the court. For several minutes, the shuffling of feet and "Pass out quickly, please" filled the court. Outside a distant murmur of voices and a faint cheer; inside a last hysterical giggle as a woman went and a parting "Hooray" deep-toned, from a soldier in hospital blue. "See all those noisy people leave the precincts of the Court altogether," enjoined the judge. During this demonstration of delight the defendant remained quiet, watching the Bench and waiting for the next move. Counsel for the prosecution intimated he would not proceed with the other counts. Directed by the clerk to the court to return a verdict on these, the foreman again rose and said, "The verdict is Not Guilty." '

After a parting polemic on the undesirability of scantily-dressed dancers on the public stage (thereby sealing Maud Allan's misery), Darling rose. So did Billing. 'My Lord – ' 'You have nothing to say, sir,' said Darling with evident contempt. 'You are discharged.' 'My Lord, I beg formally to apply for the costs of these proceedings.' This was the last straw. White in face, having lost the case his political superiors had counted on him winning, and perhaps facing his own disgrace, Darling repeated, 'You are discharged,' and left the court.

In the wide street outside the Old Bailey, the crowds had been gathering for some time. They cheered as they heard the verdict; and their cheers grew louder as Billing, his rather plain wife and his more glamorous lover, Eileen Villiers-Stuart, came out of the main entrance and into the bright sunlight. 'Mr Billing, who paused, in the midst of many congratulations, within the hall to light a cigarette, stood for a moment on the steps, his wife clinging to his arm. The crowd cheered.' To a man and woman, they wanted to shake hands with the hero of the hour: 'Good old Billing'; 'Good luck'. Billing grinned widely and saluted his admirers. They surrounded his car, summer straw boaters and cloth caps raised in the air to cheer him. 'Hands were thrust through the window to shake his. A vigorous but fruitless effort was made by the police to pull the hood down, and the car drove off amid a parting cheer.' The surging throng likewise greeted Lord Alfred Douglas enthusiastically; he waved his bowler to them, saying, 'It is splendid, splendid.' Captain Spencer told one of the waiting reporters that he was rushing back to his work of aeroplane inspection. A sizeable squad of constables was required to clear the crowd. Meanwhile, beyond this clamour, 'Miss Maud Allan left unobserved by a side door.' But the affair was not yet over; the politicians remained determined to discredit Billing and his witnesses, and as they left, an unnamed person handed Eileen Villiers-Stuart a slip of paper and asked her, 'Do you know that your first husband is still alive?'

*

The Assistant Commissioner of Police and head of Special Branch, Basil Thomson, was apparently unaware of the political conspiracy still working itself out. Thomson wrote in his diary on 4 June that everyone involved appeared to be insane: 'One might treat the case with contempt, were it not for its pernicious influence throughout this and neutral countries. The German wireless has already been commenting upon it in the tone one would expect.' That evening, Repington met the Asquiths at a dinner party, and the former Prime Minister, together with his once Chancellor, McKenna, gave Repington 'the most severe reflections on all concerned'; McKenna 'thought it made public life almost impossible. Asquith much interested to know how the Press will comment on it.'

That depended on their circulation and political outlook. The *Daily Mirror* ran three photographs on its front page: Billing, his triumphant reception from the crowd outside the Old Bailey, and Lord Alfred Douglas looking particularly pleased with himself. The next day, 6 June, the *Morning Post* published its opinion of the trial, fully supporting Billing, while agreeing with Darling that *Salome* should not be produced. Its editorial bore all the hallmarks of Arnold White's particular obsessions:

> The old English instinct is right in these matters; the play is not merely immoral; it is morbid and leads to the black and hopeless portals of criminal insanity ... These perversions of sexual passion have no home in the healthy mind of England. They have, like scum on water, a floating root in the international population which drifts between capital and capital. It is like a pestilence of which sporadic cases and even epidemics are sometimes brought to our shores; but it is abhorrent to the nature of this nation – so abhorrent is it, indeed, that the mere suspicion of it is enough to destroy a career and blast a reputation.

In its evocation of metaphors of disease, the piece was an echo of the 'Condy's

Fluid' references to English decadence which hung about the earlier years of the war.

If the tabloids saw it all as a victory for the common man, morality and patriotism, then the broadsheets determined to analyse the affair more closely. The *Manchester Guardian* and *The Times* concurred in castigating Darling for his performance in the trial; others intimated that he had something to hide. 'He lost control of it almost from the start,' observed the *Daily Mail*, 'was petulant where he should have been firm, and conveyed the fatal impression that there was something he was trying to hide. A weak judge, a feeble counsel, and a bewildered jury combined to score for the defendant a striking and undeserved success.' 'There was no attempt at guidance,' said the *Guardian* in one of the most sensible commentaries on the case. 'Indeed, the Judge was just as much a Philistine as the Jury, for in his observations after the trial, he had nothing to say about anything but the indecency, real or supposed, of certain performances; and the test of indecency, it would appear, is the amount of clothes worn.' 'There was much more in Wilde than was revealed at the trial, and there is much more in Miss Allan's dancing than would be gathered from the discussions on the precise sexual pathology of Salome after John the Baptist's head had been cut off.' The left-wing *Herald* berated Billing for his attacks on Maud Allan: 'No one outside Bedlam would hang a dog on the evidence given at the Old Bailey ...'; while the *Daily Chronicle* blamed the tabloids for encouraging Billing and making the whole thing possible.

The Times accepted that a German list of 'men and women in English public life' probably did exist, but that 'It would be no discredit to figure in it.' Other papers, appeasing their middle-class readership, warned of 'the follies and moral laxity of the ruling classes'. Privately, the *Daily Mail* had a list drawn up of the figures involved in the trial, together with their addresses and the allegations made against them or by them: perhaps its own attempt to test the existence and substance of the Black Book. Although the paper does not appear to have acted on the information, the threat was there, as seems clear from its editorial in which the *Mail* hoped Billing's grotesque allegations would serve as a warning to 'people of every class, and especially those in high places, against a careless-ness of behaviour and a too-easy tolerance of evil which may be fashionable in some circles but are detestable to the mass of our countrymen and women of all ranks'. The fact that the paper had a comprehensive list of those involved – and besmirched – in the trial indicates that the witch-hunt atmosphere continued, yet more so with Billing's acquittal and the apparent acceptance of the existence of the Black Book; not a few members of the establishment with secret lives to hide feared reprisals in this new punitive state. The Northcliffe press, as rivals to Beaverbrook's papers, supported Billing; the *Mail* took his line on the internment of all enemy aliens: 'Who prevents the Naval and Military men from acting firmly and justly with these dangerous people? The Home Office.' It was also an attack on the Home Secretary, Sir George Cave, about to lead the country's delegation to the Hague; suspicions were raised about what might be going on in the Hague negotiations. *The Times* knew the real issues behind the coming prisoner-of-war negotiations (it had, after all, shared its employee, Repington, with the British Secret Service), and cast Billing-like aspersions on the 'fitness of the British delegations to meet the Germans, who are certain to exploit any weakness of the kind to their own advantage'.

Such was the publicity surrounding the trial that it made the headlines overseas; foreign commentary said much of how Britain was regarded from without. The *Daily Mail* regretted that 'so reputable and influential a newspaper as the "Corriere della Sera" ' was prepared to accept the 'unsavoury "revelations" ' of the trial without appreciating 'the light in which they are regarded by responsible people in this country'. In Germany, in the Berlin evening papers of 29 June, *The Times* reported, a 'well informed source' contended 'that Captain Spencer had never been Adjutant to Prince William of Wied, as was asserted; neither has he been in the service of the Prince's Albanian Government in any capacity. The ex-Mbret of Albania, the message adds, first heard of the alleged existence of the mysterious Black Book through newspaper reports of the Billing trial.'

*

The reaction to the trial verdict in the salons of Society ranged from amusement to outrage. Cynthia Asquith was taking tea with Violet Bonham Carter* when Cynthia's father came in with the news 'that the monster maniac Billing had won his case'. The Liberal and the rational in Cynthia came to the same forthright reaction: 'Damn him! It is such an awful triumph for the "unreasonable", such a tonic to the microbe of suspicion which is spreading through the country, and such a stab in the back to people unprotected from such attacks owing to their best and not their worst points.' She was thinking specifically of H.H., 'bless him'. Billing, the middle-class upstart, had succeeded in disturbing his betters. 'The fantastic foulness of the insinuations that Neil Primrose and Evelyn de Rothschild were murdered from the rear makes one sick.' Cynthia's barrister friends had evidently given her inside information, although she was not privy to the deeper conspiracy: 'How miserably conducted a case, both by that

---

* H.H. Asquith's daughter by his first marriage; later Baroness Asquith of Yarnbury. Cynthia remarked, 'I think Billing and [Antoine] Bibesco between them have at last completed her education and extinguished her as an *enfant terrible*.'

contemptible Darling and Hume Williams! Darling insisted on having the case out of rotation.'

The authorities, fearing for the effect on public opinion, sought to bring it back into line. The plot to discredit Asquith had gone too far, and the people must be encouraged to reinvest trust in their superiors. The events of the past few years of war had crucially introduced a note of distrust in the 'lower orders'. The inept management of the war, combined with distaste for the draconian powers of DORA and the government (even the king referred to Lloyd George as a 'dictator'), had produced a dangerous atmosphere of dissent. If the class system was not to break down entirely, then such allegations as Billing's must be counteracted, and swiftly. His connexion with the Die-Hards and the coalescing groups of the radical right was all the more worrying: the state had only to look to the precedent of Russia, which had just undergone tumultuous revolution, to take such concerns seriously. Hugh Walpole, then working in the Ministry of Information, had been in Russia in 1917. Having attended the trial, he was scandalised by the Not Guilty verdict: 'I mark it down in my diary as the opening of the Great English Revolution.'

These were the fears of the highest level of government. On 4 June, the Lord President of the Council, Lord Curzon, drew the War Cabinet's attention to the press reporting of the trial, which 'was doing more harm than anything that had appeared in this connection for many years. Opportunity was being taken to attack every section of society, and the social effect must inevitably be bad. Insinuations and accusations were being made against public men without a shred of foundation.' Curzon wanted censorship of such events, if they occurred again. But the Home Secretary, Sir George Cave, said that the press must be trusted not to publish obscene evidence from such trials (as indeed they had not), and that there was no penalty for disobeying the censor (F.E. Smith) unless they contravened the Defence of the Realm Act in publishing material prejudicial to the war effort. Cave said he had told Darling to ask the press not to publish some of the evidence, and the judge had warned the newspapers that they could be prosecuted if they used obscene material. Cave added, 'The Judge could not direct such cases to be held in camera; and, even if this could have been done, the suspicion and talk which would have arisen outside the Court, relative to what had been suppressed, would have been endless.' Although there was little they could do, Bonar Law, the Chancellor of the Exchequer, wrote on behalf of the Cabinet to F.E. Smith in his capacity as Attorney-General to ask if he had any suggestions; Smith, as Billing's sworn enemy, would surely apply himself to the matter.

Curzon had been prompted to his questions by Lord Rosebery, the former Liberal Prime Minister. After Eileen's allegations about Primrose's death, his father made 'immediate representations' to the War Office. Rosebery never recovered from his son's death, having had an unusually close relationship with Primrose, an 'easy and affectionate intimacy' said to be more like that between brothers than father and son. Bitterly mourning his 'charming, gifted' son (as Churchill had described Primrose), he asked Curzon to do something about the allegations. Rosebery may well have suspected his own name to be in the Black Book, given the rumours about his private life.

Those who had been unfortunate enough to be named in the trial would find its effects far-reaching. Mary Herbert told Cynthia Asquith that she had been 'railed at across the Ritz dining room', and later that 'she and Aubrey are having fearful difficulties with their constituents. In addition to thinking him a pervert and a pacifist' – the general smear of the Liberals, post-Billing and post-Maurice debate (during which Aubrey Herbert voted on Asquith's side, and incurred the wrath of his constituency as a result) – 'they now say, "How is it that once a prisoner [of war] he contrived to escape?" The answer being "The Hidden Hand". They consider an election in November a certainty now.' Arnold White's involvement in the Billing trial had evidently been efficacious.

On the night the Billing verdict was announced, the two artists Charles Ricketts and Henry Lamb met at a concert, and in the interval discussed its significance. Ricketts, aesthete and partner of Charles Shannon, reported the conversation in a letter to Robbie Ross. Lamb, who had been serving in the war, said 'Nothing will be altered, the brute philistine is the big gut of the nation, it is disturbed and we are all mad and suspicious just now.' Ricketts said he thought it could be the first act of the Revolution. 'No,' said Lamb, 'the country will always be the same.' Ross replied to Ricketts:

> I foresaw the result of the Billing case, and warned Grein not to bring the action. When the trial began, everyone thought I was mad because I said Billing would be acquitted ... The English, intoxicated into failure, enjoyed tearing poor Maud Allan to pieces, simply because she had given them pleasure, and kicking Oscar's corpse to make up for the failure of the 5th Army ...
>
> However, I have not lost all sense of proportion, and these things are small compared to the fate of Paris, which will be lost and destroyed owing to the vanity and incompetence of the English generals ...

Ross's biographer observes that 'the jury might have been persuaded differently if the Defence had called one serving soldier to give his view on the war. They might have decided it was not the German influence on the Government which was at fault but the ineptitude of the military machine.'

Ross wrote about the trial to a number of close friends. To Cecil Sprigge, on active service in India, he complained of having been 'used as a piece of mud ...

or rather to make a more suitable image; once a lion in the zoo of Alfred Douglas, I am now a minnow in the Pemberton Billing Aquarium!' After the trial, Beaverbrook, alarmed by Ross's pacifist and pro-German sympathies, attempted to have him removed from all committees connected with the Imperial War Museum; post-Billing, Ross was seen as a danger to the war effort. Arnold Bennett, who was also sitting on these committees, was disgusted: 'There can only be one reason for getting rid of Ross ... his friendly relations with Oscar Wilde are well known; and Alfred Douglas is his declared enemy', he wrote on 12 June 1918. Bennett had a rather rose-tinted view of Robbie:

Ross is an entirely honest man ... He is not a sodomist, never was, and never defends sodomist doctrines.* He merely has a weakness for looking after people in adversity ... It is inconceivable to me that such a man should be got rid of merely because Alfred Douglas has hooked himself on to Billing and there is a fear of Ross being attacked in the House or elsewhere. To get rid of him would be a very dangerous thing. It would be equivalent to stopping Billing in the Strand, putting up one's hands, and crying 'Kamerad' ... My opinion is that if any question is asked in the House [presumably about Ross as a threat to the war effort] ... a straightforward answer would dispose of it at once. It would assuredly arouse such a protest in the press as would surprise the questioner. Ross's friends, and he has many powerful friends, would see to that. I should certainly see to it.

In correspondence with his friends, Ross appeared entirely phlegmatic about the trial and its outcome; but one letter indicates he was not quite master of his emotions. In a rare fit of pique and bitter sarcasm, he wrote to Sir Charles Mathews, the Director of Public Prosecutions:

I write to congratulate you on the complete rehabilitation of your protege, Lord Alfred Douglas. Your connivance at his campaign against myself and subsequently against others of much greater importance in the world [their involvement in the case gave Ross the muscle to be able to write such a letter] than I can pretend to be, has been crowned with a success which must have been unforeseen even by yourself ... You have shown your unreadiness and unwillingness to investigate or interrupt his campaign of calumny, which has now been brought to such a triumphant issue. For some time I was a little puzzled, but now I understand what Shakespeare intended in presenting so vividly the venom and snobbery of a bastard, particularly the bastard of a mummer.

*

---

* Bennett's defence recalls Frank Harris's professed astonishment when told by Wilde that he was guilty as charged; Harris had always believed in Oscar's innocence, he maintained. Later, at the time of the *Well of Loneliness* trial, Hugh Walpole noted that Bennett 'ardently defended the liberty of the abnormal'.

Billing's campaign had distinct class overtones: he was against the upper classes, and sought to exploit the distrust of the middle classes (whom, ironically, Douglas hated) which the war had exacerbated. Cynthia Asquith's report of shop women gossiping – 'We always knew it of the Asquiths, and we're so glad they're being exposed' – was underlined by Arnold Bennett's observation that 'there can be no doubt that Mr. Pemberton Billing had a very great deal of support from plain people throughout the country. These people said: "He is not attacking; he is defending himself. And what has he to gain from his attempt to expose an alleged huge conspiracy of vice and pro-Germanism? Nothing. Hence he must be a patriot." ' Set against this, and underlining the class overtones of the affair, is the attitude of many members of Society towards the case. A degree of *hauteur* pervades the reaction of those whose privileged station and behaviour set them beyond the petty morality of the bourgeoisie. They were guilty, or playfully assumed guilt, of the practices and values against which Billing railed. With ironic Wildean wit, they treated the trial as a joke, as is evident from a letter from the trenches written by Duff Cooper to Diana, his wife: 'No one here speaks or thinks of anything but the Billing case. Even my Commanding Officer – the most regular of regular soliders – greeted me when I met him for the first time today not 200 yards from the front line trenches with – "What did you think of Fripp's evidence. I should have thought he knew more about clap." ' Diana told Duff that Lord Albemarle had walked into the Turf Club and asked who was 'this Greek chap Clitoris' they were all talking about?

Yet in the wake of the trial, the sexual threat to society from a supposed decadent cult continued to be taken seriously, not least by the 'decadents' themselves. Just as enemy aliens feared the radical right's xenophobic campaigns and had in many cases to go into hiding, so the flight of homosexuals overseas, initiated by Wilde's conviction (when Ross bought a one-way ticket to Calais), continued at a greater rate than ever in the post-trial atmosphere of prejudice and retribution. The likes of Beverley Nichols, already under suspicion from the authorities, had much to fear, especially if, like Nichols, they were enlisted and subject to harsh military discipline. On leave in London, Nichols plunged back into society life 'in the setting of the Savile or the Bachelors' Club, the Ritz, the Carlton or the Café Royal'. He partied with the Sitwells and Sickert, and made 'trips to the Turkish Baths for casual encounters', where rather than sedition being whispered in the steam, the predominant topic of conversation must have been the Billing case. Indeed, many who had had brushes with the law, like Nichols, would have had cause to fear its outcome, and as in the aftermath of the Wilde trials, there was a general air of apprehension and attempts to cover traces.

They appear to have been successful, for there is little extant evidence of the effect of the trial on such characters. For that reason, Nichols's diary for May 1918 is intriguing. From the entry for 24 May – five days before the trial opened – a cutting from *The Times*, with the date 24 May written below it, and stuck in with postage stamp selvage – has been removed. On 27 May, Nichols records visiting London, seeing a boyfriend called Barclay at Hyde Park Mansions, meeting his make-up wearing friend Egie Egerton at the Regent Palace Hotel, and going to Lyons Popular Restaurant in Piccadilly, something of a pick-up joint. They then went to the Café Royal, which shocked Beverley's friend Percy. The following day was taken up with much the same thing, and on the 29th – the day the trial began – Nichols met an army friend called Barber at the Piccadilly Hotel, and they went to see Maud Allan at the Pavilion. The next three lines have been carefully excised from Nichols's text. On 30 and 31 May, another large chunk has been cut out; as has text from the 2 June entry. Nichols may have been protecting famous names or friends; or he may have taken fright – after his police raid earlier that year – and feared that in the homophobic atmosphere of the Billing trial, the authorities might come after him. His position in army intelligence underlines this possibility, as does his experience of entrapment used by the authorities to snare those of his kind.

The heightened anti-homosexual atmosphere after the trial was evident that October, when A.T. Fitzroy [Rose Allatini]'s book, *Despised and Rejected*, was charged under DORA in October 1918; the books were destroyed (burned by the public hangman, said Virginia Woolf) and the publisher fined. The story of a young man, Dennis Blackwood, a homosexual artist and pacifist who is imprisoned for his beliefs, is reticent in its descriptions, but frankly acknowledges homosexuality in both sexes, and proposes that homosexuals are 'the advance-guard of a more enlightened civilisation'. Some may have hoped for a better world after the war; others were more cynical. The most important consequence of the Billing trial, and the issues of xenophobia and homophobia – these 'home-front wars' – was their effect on post-war English culture. By intensifying the repression of English society, they 'helped create a post-war sub-culture of outsiders, composed of an odd mixture of persons – opponents of the war, artists, homosexuals – whom the war spirit had identified as subversive ...' 'Disobedience, in the eyes of anyone who has read history, is man's original virtue,' wrote Oscar Wilde in *The Soul of Man Under Socialism*. 'It is through disobedience that progress has been made, through disobedience and rebellion.' Ironically, Billing's efforts helped unify a whole culture of confrontation, and set a course for the frenetic, disquieted decades to come. The spirit of Wilde lived on.

This Generation of Vipers

Society before the war showed signs of becoming what French sociey before the
Revolution had been – curious, gay, tolerant, reckless and reasonably cynical. After
the war I suppose it will be none of these things ... The war has ruined our little
patch of civility as thoroughly as a revolution could have done.

Clive Bell, *Cambridge Magazine*, 12 May 1917

Emboldened by his acquittal, membership of Billing's Society of Vigilantes rose
dramatically in the summer of 1918. Their leader continued to fight 'for a
Cleaner England' in the press, proposing 'a sort of semi-corporate State within
the Commonwealth', racially pure and publicly incorrupt. A mass rally was held
at the Royal Albert Hall on 15 June, at which Billing called for alien internment
and proposed that the government should 'take powers under the Defence of
the Realm Act to provide that all aliens shall for the duration of the war exhibit
on the lapel of their coats an emblem of their nationality'. Less than twenty years
later, Mosley would hold his own British Union of Fascists rallies in the same
venue.

Ever the lover of new technology, Billing decided to make a propaganda film
to promote the work of the Vigilantes. He had already appeared before the
camera during his Mile End campaign, declaiming from his monoplane, enjoy-
ing the attention of the lens. Now he used the medium to propagate his message.
Although never completed, parts of this, perhaps the first party political film
ever made, still exist, a fascinating glimpse of Billing in action. An unedited
sequence, shot in Hertford with Vigilante actors, illustrates the sort of moral
problems Britain was facing. Two long-haired young women are seen embracing
by a riverside; a shifty-looking man in a cap is seen leading one off up some
wooden steps. The young woman is later seen walking in a town square, object
of the townspeople's stares – presumably because she has been lured into
prostitution; a later scene of a distraught young woman seems to depict the
horrors of the white slave trade. In another sequence a man in minstrel
'blackface' and check suit accosts a young man reading on a bridge. Then three
men are seen – among them Billing himself – all wearing distinctive round

badges in their lapels, with an emblem that looks like a Boy Scout fleur-de-lys –
possibly indicating Billing's latest campaign, the Silver Badge party for ex-
servicemen. They stand outside a building – evidently the Vigilante office – with
posters in its windows proclaiming 'petition the King'. The next sequence is set
in Billing's Hertford House: 'Mr Pemberton Billing at work in his study'. Billing
is seated at his desk, writing and smoking, the picture of an urbane politician; he
takes a book from a shelf behind him, then picks up the telephone, a master of
technology. In close-up, Billing appears handsome, ascetic, and vaguely cruel in
manner, with his slick black hair and a cigarette always held in his long fingers which
gesticulate flamboyantly. He radiates nervous energy; his image is undeniably
dynamic. He is futuristically dressed in high-cut double-breasted suit, dandified
bowler hat, and an exceptionally long-collared shirt with a metal decoration –
something like a Western bootlace brooch – instead of a tie. Altogether, he looks so
much more modern and alive than the grey shadows around him.

A caption reads, 'The Society was formed in May 1917 for the purpose of
promoting purity in public life', and a long leatherbound tube is held up to the
camera with the words 'The Constitution of the "Vigilantes" formed 1917'.
' – And at play Mr P.B. is a lover of dogs'; our heroic MP is shown in informal
mode. In the extensive grounds of the rather bleak Victorian, apparently
concrete-rendered (self-built?) Hertford House – complete with sun-scorched
tennis court – Mrs Billing sits on a garden seat, playing with a peke; a plain-
looking woman, when she stands up we see she is much shorter than her tall,
elegant husband. Billing comes out of the summer-house, and together with a
decidedly more glamorous, fashionably-dressed woman whose presence is not
explained, the group inspect some beehives and stroll through the gardens. A
poster depicting 'Flying machines designed by Mr P.B. from 1904 to 1916' is
unfurled before the camera, then Billing's gleaming 'Torpedo Motor Car', a
cigar-shaped roadster, is seen speeding up the Hertford lane as duty calls for the
Futurist. 'After the famous trial huge crowds flocked to hear him speak at the Albert
Hall, London, over 8,000 people being present.' A final clip shows the Albert Hall
itself, with a notice outside: 'The Vigilantes. Saturday Next at 3. Mass Meeting.
Pemberton Billing MP. Subject, – "A Cleaner Britain" (The Ideal We Are Fighting
For). Admission free by ticket. Apply 5, St James's Place, SW1.' The film ends with
enthusiastic supporters arriving by cab and on foot, going into the meeting.

The Vigilantes were following up the Billing trial success with a push for
power. In Clapham, Beamish stood as a Vigilante candidate in the by-election.
Billing, playing his usual games, claimed to have handed a telegram to the
Clapham Post Office, addressed to Lloyd George and stating, 'If you are
prepared to give a written undertaking this day to intern all enemy born subjects
in this country within 30 days from this date, and to close all German and

Austrian Banks forthwith, we are prepared to concede this seat to the Government nominee.' Mysteriously, instead of the telegram being sent, it appeared on a pamphlet published by the coalition government office at Clapham, discrediting Billing, Beamish and the Vigilantes. They lost the election, although by a narrow margin.

Billing continued to pursue the alien question in Parliament, putting questions to virtually every government department, asking each minister for 'a list of all members in and employees of his Department who are of enemy origin or birth; and, in cases where their names have been changed, will he state their names at birth and also, if naturalised, the date upon which they were naturalised?' Bonar Law said the alien question was being considered by the government, 'and all necessary information will be obtained ... whether this information should be published or not will receive consideration'. Billing countered with a further question which surprised Bonar Law. 'May I ask the Right Hon. Gentleman whether the President of the Board of Trade [Sir Albert Stanley] is a German of the name of Nuttmeyer, whether the name of Stanley has not been adopted since, and whether he holds his position owing to the influence of a German Jew called Edgar Speyer, who is now working out the damnation of this country in America?' Bonar Law denied that Stanley had any German blood, or connexions; Speyer, the dedicatee of Strauss's *Salome*, had had to leave British public life in the anti-semitic aftermath of the Marconi scandal. Billing persisted in his questioning, and such was the post-trial atmosphere that Stanley was obliged to come before the House and explain that his father had changed the family name from Knattries, 'an old English name' with 'no possible connection with any German name'. Billing's questions had raised the subject of enemy aliens to the point where the government would have to do something; other MPs placed similar questions, in the knowledge that the Home Secretary himself was, even as they spoke, 'fraternising' with the enemy in peace talks at The Hague.

But the authorities would have their revenge. Although neither of her husbands requested it, Eileen Villiers-Stuart was arrested on a charge of bigamy on 18 June, and appeared at Marylebone Police Court the next day, dressed in the uniform of a Red Cross nurse with a brown mackintosh over her shoulders. She was pressurised to produce a confession which could then be used to prosecute Spencer for perjury; he had, after all, lied about having seen the Black Book. Off the record, she spoke about 'living ... in illicit relations' with Billing, but would provide no more information unless the bigamy charge was dropped. The case was referred to the Director of Public Prosecutions, Mathews, and Eileen was committed for trial at the Old Bailey – she had evidently not satisfied the authorities' desire for information. A Vigilante associate stood her bail, and the following day she made a sworn statement before a Commissioner of Oaths, stating her 'exact position' as regards Billing and the Vigilante Society. Giving her address as the Grosvenor Court Hotel, Davies Street, she outlined the political conspiracy and her part in the attempt to bring down Billing:

> I am now being prosecuted for bigamy ... by the public prosecutor. The Prosecution is in my opinion a vindictive one, launched solely because of the assistance I gave at the Old Bailey ... the Political Associations ... have entered upon a crusade against Mr Pemberton-Billing and every one who assisted him at the trial, and the Vigilante Society also. It has even been suggested that divorce proceedings will be taken against me, with Mr Pemberton-Billing as co-respondent. This is a wicked suggestion for anyone to make. All my relations with Mr Pemberton-Billing have been most honourable and both he and every other member of the Vigilante Society with whom I have come into contact have always treated me with respect, and it is infamous for any person to suggest that there has been any immoral relations between Mr Pemberton-Billing and myself or between any other officer or member of the Vigilante Society and myself.

Evidently, Billing made her write this. Eileen gave the statement to Billing for safe keeping, until such a time as it was necessary to produce it.

Meanwhile, Billing's campaign seemed to be picking up strength, working in informal alliance with the National Party and such politicians as William Joynson-Hicks, who implicitly backed Billing's Parliamentary questions. On 25 June he asked the Chancellor of the Exchequer: 'Is the right hon. gentleman prepared to place on the table a list of the real names of all the members of his Majesty's Government?', a piece of rhetoric which met with laughter in the house. It was, like the humour of the court, the laughter of fools. On 29 June, Billing announced in the *Vigilante* a petition to the king, calling for alien denaturalisation and lapel emblems. Billing was well aware that technically, the king himself was an alien who had recently changed his name; the *Vigilante* piece virtually suggested that the monarch should sport a cloth badge on his coat announcing his unEnglish status. When Bonar Law saw the piece, he decided Billing had gone too far. The tide now began to turn against Billing. The military conspirators who had been backing him had new ammunition for their anti-peace campaign: the sinking of the British hospital ship, the *Llandovery Castle*, by a German submarine. With this potent new anti-German bombshell to deploy, they had no further use for Billing.

In the light of the hospital ship episode, Bonar Law made a pact with the military conspirators: withdraw their support for Billing, and he would call off the peace talks. Bonar Law now made ready to destroy Billing publicly in Parliament. Surreptitious detective work ascertained that Billing's wife was the daughter of Theodore Schweitzer, a Prussian, confirmed by a letter from the

Home Secretary's Private Secretary to Bonar Law's secretary, his 'contact man' with the British Secret Service. 'His wife is the daughter of a German who died in 1901. Mrs B's mother was the daughter of a Scot, who married a German lady, so that there is a double German strain. Mrs Schweitzer was in a convent in Germany until she was 18.' Bonar Law had this information spread abroad in the Commons, and 'with the connivance of a Coalition Liberal backbencher ... laid a careful Parliamentary trap for Billing ...'.

On 1 July 1918, the radical right were much in evidence in the House of Commons. Business began with a question from Brigadier-General Page Croft, National Party MP for Christchurch, who was outraged by a raid made the previous week on the party's headquarters in King Street. Page Croft had been making allegations about Commander Leverton Harris, Parliamentary Secretary to the Ministry of Blockade, accusing him of using his parliamentary position to benefit his commercial interests, and of being friendly with a German metal trust. His accusations were followed by the raid, and other raids on National Party offices in Glasgow, Birmingham, Bristol, Leeds and the Home Counties. The authorities were cracking down on political dissent: that January, the British Socialist Party offices had also been raided, and leaflets confiscated which 'breached the regulations of the Defence of the Realm Acts', along with commu-nications from M. Litvinoff, 'representative of the Russian Government'. Page Croft protested that 'a member ... acting, as he believed, in the interests of the nation (Mr Billing: "Hear! Hear!") and using his information with the view of exposing a public scandal' should not be 'liable to have his offices, and the offices of his associates or his private dwelling-house, ransacked by soldiers and other Government agents ...'.

Billing followed this with embarrassing Parliamentary questions about appar-ent German names in various commercial and bureaucratic organisations. Having been chided by the Speaker for his interventions, he turned his attention to his other hobbyhorse, air power: 'Is it necessary for the independent Air Force to make application to the War Office before they can initiate any raids on Germany?' This sarcastic volley indicated that he knew he had lost the support of his military backers. Then came two announcements to the House: Sir George Cave had been recalled from the Hague; and the *Llandovery Castle* had been sunk. The two events were not unconnected, Billing realised, and he saw that his own campaign was in danger. He asked for, and was refused, an Adjournment of the House. The Speaker informed him that a 'blocking notice had been put down that topic ...' (evidently by Bonar Law). Billing asked if 'whether it is in the interest of the enemy or of this country that such a notice should have been put down? The Speaker refused to discuss such insinuations, and when Billing once again got up to speak, members cried, 'Sit down.' 'I am not going to sit down all the time Germans are running about this country,' said Billing. The Speaker's request for Billing to leave the House was was met by cheers. 'On a point of Order –' said Billing. 'I cannot listen to any further points of Order,' said the Speaker. 'This is not a Court of Law.' This reference to the rumbustious member's recent Old Bailey performance drew loud cheers and laughter. Billing tried to interject, 'It is not a place of free speech either.' The Speaker threatened to suspend the rebel MP for disorderly conduct, at which Billing began to shout, 'I am here to do my duty, and I have no intention of leaving the House ... until the question of the internment of enemy aliens in this country is allowed to be discussed.'

The *Daily Mail* reported these scenes with relish; their columns had seemed dull since the end of the trial. 'Mr Pemberton Billing ... had exhausted the patience of the House by his insistent "supplementaries" to the questions of other members, had been shouted down, and had taken every opportunity, relevant or otherwise, of bobbing up again.' As he contined to shout down the Speaker, Bonar Law declared, 'I beg to move, "That Mr Billing be suspended from the service of the House".' The Serjeant-at-Arms, Sir Colin Keppel (as a cousin of the George Keppels, he may have relished the task) was asked to remove Billing. Billing refused to move: 'I'll not leave. I'm doing what I conceive to be my duty.' The Speaker suspended the Sitting of the House, 'until such time as the hon. Member has left' and he called 'upon the officers to remove him while the House is suspended'. Sitting was suspended at 4.10.

The rest of the scene was dramatically described by the *Mail*'s reporter. 'The Speaker left the House, several members following him. The mace was removed from the table. Four messengers in evening dress, and wearing their gold chains of office, came in from the Lobby and closed round Mr Billing, the Serjeant-at-Arms directing operations from behind. (He did not draw his sword.) Mr Billing struggled hard, but the odds were against him. Two attendants seized a leg each, and two an arm each, and with a desperate wrench they got the member out of his corner and carried him feet first through the door, while other members laughed and cheered.' Another newspaper reported that a few hissed, 'and there was a cry of "Silence", as if in deprecation of any expression of feeling'. 'The last the House saw of Mr Billing, through the swinging doors, was a scene of kicking legs and a flop on the floor of the Lobby. Fortunately the flop was on thick coco-nut mat and not on the hard tiles. In his struggles Mr Billing had grasped the shirt-front of one of his bearers and disarranged his Court dress. He also kicked another on the wrist. Thereupon they dropped him. After being assisted to his feet he was conducted by the four messengers across the Lobby to the members' entrance and there handed over to the police. Inspector Rogers accompanied him across Palace Yard to the iron gates.' The sitting was resumed at 4.12.

This colourful episode had been carefully stage-managed, as the report of the Prime Minister's Chief Whip, Freddy Guest, to Lloyd George intimated: 'On Monday, Billing was carried out shouting "intern the Aliens", but little notice was taken of this incident in the press.' Except in the *Vigilante*, which reported in high dudgeon its heroic leader's ignominious expulsion from the Palace of Westminster, 'a procedure in which he sustained some rather painful injuries, including a sprained wrist ...'. The same issue also announced that Captain Spencer had sent a telegram to Balfour and the Prime Minister, on 2 July 1918:

> The crass stupidity of the Government in suspending Pemberton Billing has brought us nearer revolution than all previous acts combined of our subsidised marionettes. You would do well to sound public opinion, not the opinion of the camouflaged German Jew, of the monocled, eunuch-voiced inefficients who mince or waddle from Whitehall to the Clubs, but the opinion of working men and women ... There may not have been Angels at Mons [the fantasy of the ghosts of Agincourt coming to the assistance of the Allied troops was in fact an Arthur Machen short story], but there is a spirit of Mons that will not be betrayed by Frankfort-born legislators and their money-grasping minions. That the traitors know what to expect is seen by the fact that the Statue of King Charles in Whitehall is now a machine gun emplacement.

*

In the last summer of war, revolution was in the air: accomplished in Russia, fermenting in Germany. Europe seemed more unstable than ever, and in Britain, fear of insurrection from within and attack from without ensured that the issues Billing raised continued to be aired in the press. By 2 July *The Times* was questioning the continued existence of German banks in London 'which grows more and more mysterious ... A very large body of the more suspicious public have come to the conclusion that there is some secret German interest at work.' The paper was devoting much column space to the alien issue, printing letters from concerned citizens and such reports as one about a man found living wild in a Kentish wood who had not registered as an alien. He was imprisoned for six months, damned by the fact that he possessed 'a map of Kent with various places marked on it ...'. Anti-alien fever was at its height. There were continuing rumours of German plots with Sinn Fein in Ireland. Bonar Law made an anti-German speech; it seemed that the Hague peace talks had been firmly extinguished. In Germany, the Kaiser acceded to political pressure and dismissed Kuhlmann, his peace-making, Anglophile Foreign Minister from office. The

Kaiser instructed the ministry to counter the new aggressive attitude of the British with their own 'anti-Entente atmosphere'. On the fourth anniversary of the war, peace seemed further away than ever. The military conspirators, and Billing, their pawn, had achieved their aims.

But Billing's brief reign as king of confusion was coming to an end. On 3 July, he proposed Spencer as 'Independent Vigilante' candidate for the East Finsbury by-election – the east London constituency's MP having died that morning. In response, Eileen Villiers-Stuart wrote to Lloyd George denouncing Spencer, whom she hated, accusing him of perjury during the trial. It was the denouncement which the politicians had been waiting for. The *Daily Chronicle* launched the attack, having been furnished with the fact that although Billing campaigned against enemy aliens, his wife was of German origin. The solidarity of the Society of Vigilantes began to crack. The finance committee resigned, ostensibly because Billing had been using funds without their consent, but more probably because of pressure on members from Lloyd George's supporters. Billing argued with Dr Clarke – accusing him of trying to turn the Vigilantes into an anti-Catholic crusade – and with Beamish, who was accused (with some justification) of trying to turn it into a purely anti-semitic movement. Both men left the society.

More or less alone in their Vigilante laager, Billing and Spencer fought on. Spencer declared to the electorate of East Finsbury: 'I, Harold Sherwood Spencer, of pure British blood and parentage, great-grandson of Robert Spencer of the Napoleonic Wars, offer you my faithful service as your direct representative in the House of Commons. On 15 October 1917, I was invalided from the Army with the honorary rank of Captain after having seen service on three fronts.' He did not give the reason for his invalidity; nor did he mention that he had been born in America. In support of the campaign, the *Vigilante* printed a letter from 'the tenants of Peabody buildings, St Luke's EC1', signed 'women of Finsbury' (impoverished east London, with its high immigrant population, was ever fertile ground for rabble-rousing politics) expressing sympathy for Spencer's 'non-success' in the Clapham by-election, and 'our firm support when we get our vote'. On 10 July, as the War Cabinet addressed the alien issue, Billing and Spencer, having collected one and a half million signatures on their petition (including that of the Lord Mayor of London), proposed another deal with Lloyd George. They offered to withdraw from the East Finsbury contest and suspend their petition to the king if the Prime Minister promised to put into effect the recommendations of his Special Committee on the alien question. Lloyd George did not answer, but the following day declared that there must be a 'comb-out' of aliens, and German banks closed. On 12 July, the Enemy Alien Bill, proposed by Sir George Cave and legislating, among other matters, for the liquidation of German and Austrian banks, passed its first reading in the Commons. The next day there was a mass rally in Trafalgar Square. Nelson's Column was flanked by two giant placards, demanding 'A Clean Sweep' and 'Intern Them All', and among the letters of support read to the crowd was one from Rudyard Kipling.

Billing and Spencer toured East Finsbury, driving down Old Street in a open-top, poster-festooned yellow racing car: Billing in a bowler pulled low down over his eyes, all chiselled features and determination; Spencer in a homburg and sporting a rather neurotic moustache, his deep-set, hooded eyes making him look quite as mad as he evidently was. The *Vigilante* insisted on its candidate's heroic qualities, declaring that Spencer had commanded the troops guarding the Bank of Ireland during the Dublin Easter Rising, and that he was fighting the campaign on the following slogan, sung to a familiar refrain:

> Vote, vote, vote for Captain Spencer,
> Work, work, work to help P.B.
> He's the man who stopped the Huns
> Dropping bombs on little ones,
> He's the man who put the wind up Germanee!

The *Daily Chronicle* countered this eulogistic ditty by revealing that Spencer was an American citizen, despite his British passport, and listed a selection of the lies he had told during the trial. It was not a clean contest. There was another independent candidate called Belsher, who described himself as the 'patriotic get-on-with-the-war candidate', but whom the Vigilantes presumed to have been set up to split their vote; once again Billing offered a reward of £500 for information leading to the conviction of any candidate under the Bribery and Corruption Act. He was sure that both the government and independent candidates had been furnished with harmful material by Bonar Law. It was a reasonable suspicion, but the irony was that it was Eileen Villiers-Stuart, his former mistress, who had supplied the information.

In an attempt to evade the bigamy charge, on 15 July Eileen made a new statement, witnessed by two police officers, in which she stated that she had gone into the witness box at the Old Bailey on the condition that Billing would not ask her to mention any names. When he did so, she was very angry, but was told by Billing that if she didn't continue to give her evidence, none of the rest would be believed 'and all those concerned would probably get into trouble'. Eileen said Mrs Billing also knew of this false evidence. 'I then said that if Mr Pemberton-Billing tried to put Captain Spencer for Parliament, I would go and tell the Government about the whole matter.' To this, Billing had replied, 'If you do, I shall stop at nothing as you know.' When she heard that Spencer was standing at East Finsbury, she went to Lloyd George. 'Mr Pemberton-Billing told me he has been round to various Munitions Factories and has got persons employed there to sign an undertaking to strike if called upon to do so by him, Mr Pemberton-Billing. Mr Pemberton-Billing told me this himself and I have seen long lists of these people who have signed the undertaking.' If true, this meant Billing was guilty, if not of treason, then certainly insurrection. In a world worried by revolution and the rise of the radical right, he was a dangerous man.

*

On 15 July 1918, in an area of London well used to dark stirrings of political dissent, the vague air of revolution erupted in violent fact. On the eve of polling in the East Finsbury by-election, Belsher held a meeting at St Paul's Hall in Banner Street. Billing and Spencer arrived with a thousand Vigilantes. They saw off the police guard, broke up Belsher's car and laid siege to the hall, brandishing sticks and smashing every window. Belsher's men were barricaded in, and the police sent for reinforcements. Meanwhile Billing got up in the back of his racing car to deliver a soap-box polemic. 'Whether or not the people were excited by his references to aliens and to military shirkers is impossible to say,' reported *The Times*'s man on the spot, 'but they set on every person who was apparently of alien nationality and who was of military age. The police had to rescue a number of persons who were rather badly treated.' Rioting ensued in Whitecross Street, and only when Billing was persuaded to stand down were the streets cleared and the ringleaders arrested; it is surprising that Billing himself wasn't apprehended. It is evident that there were 'hired thugs' on both sides, and the skirmish was a foretaste of East End political street violence in years to come.

The poll was declared the following evening: 1,156 votes for the government, 576 for the Vigilantes, and 199 for Belsher. The *Daily Chronicle* declared Spencer unfit to have solicited that many votes, and continued its anti-Billing campaign. Its 18 July edition was headlined, 'Will Mrs Billing be interned? – Mr Billing's Prussian Association.' Mrs Billing had written to the Home Secretary repudiating their statement that she was of German origin, 'saying that her father was Swiss and her mother Irish', and that 'if it found that there is a drop of enemy blood in my veins I demand to be interned at once'. The paper remarked, 'We fear this estimable lady will have to get ready for her self-internment. According to the Billing party, any one of German origin or association, or anyone who is married to a German, is suspect, and so that there may be no mistake, all should be interned. It is therefore rather amusing to find that the leader of the campaign himself has enemy associations.'

Billing was cornered, trapped by his own methods. However, he declared (in the third person) in the *Vigilante* of 20 July that they had been able to 'expose, and ... stultify' the 'political plot against the liberty of our President, Mr Pemberton-Billing'; Mrs Villiers-Stuart had told them that her trial for bigamy had been 'indefinitely postponed', 'undoubtedly with the dual idea of victimising this courageous lady, by keeping her in a state of uncertainty, and of holding the trial at some critical and psychological moment, most probably when a General Election becomes imminent, in order if possible to involve and discredit the Vigilantes'. Also published was Eileen's sworn statement of 27 June, explaining how the politicians had set her up with Billing. By so doing, Billing stopped the politicians from pursuing Spencer for perjury; he also wrecked Eileen's chances of any other deals over her trial; Billing further antagonised the authorities by printing Eileen's letter of 6 May. On 29 July, he wrote to Buckingham Palace informing them that he was about to hand in his petition to the king; but received a frosty reply instructing him to send it to the Home Secretary.

The *Vigilante* of 3 August instructed its readers that their President had been advised by his doctor to have a complete rest. It was a forlorn instruction; Billing would not be beaten down, and the government's plot had merely made him more combative. By the end of the month, Billing was at Tower Hill, addressing the 12,000 police who had called a general strike ('Traffic Managing Itself' headlined *The Times*, noting that at least the reprehensible strikers had agreed to work in the event of an air raid). It seemed he was carrying out his threat of stirring industrial unrest. Billing 'declaimed violently against the Government and urged the strikers to insist on seeing Mr Lloyd George. He advised them to require a settlement in black and white because they were dealing with "some of the biggest political crooks in history", and invited the police when they had got their way to join in the demand for the internment of every German in the country.'

In mid-September, as victory over the Germans loomed and the public lost interest in Billing's antics, Mrs Villiers-Stuart was tried for bigamy at the Old Bailey, defended (expensively) by Marshall Hall, whom Billing had engaged for her. Eileen said she had tried to trace her first husband, but when in spring 1917, she and Captain Villiers-Stuart had been on the parade ground in Birkenhead, a wounded soldier had shown her a group photograph which included Percival Bray. She was told, 'He was blown up in France in 1914.' But no one could corroborate this evidence, and the prosecution caught her out on a number of points. Subsequent research shows that Eileen had not married Bray in 1912, as she claimed in the Old Bailey, but in early 1913, in Fulham. Records also clearly show that in the summer of 1917, she married Percival Villiers-Stuart in Birkenhead, using the surname, Fox-Bray. 'When Mrs Eileen Villiers-Stuart, who was charged with having bigamously married Captain Villiers-Stuart, re-entered the dock at the Old Bailey to-day she withdrew her plea of not guilty and admitted the offence,' the *Globe* reported on 16 September. 'She was sentenced to nine months imprisonment without hard labour.' The politicians were avenged.

*

Rather than expunge a tendency towards unBritish perversions, for one young officer at least, the Billing affair served to rouse interest in the very subjects it sought to proscribe. Charles Carrington, later an eminent man of letters and biographer of Kipling, wrote that 'a reaction against the philistinism around me turned my attention to the decadents of the nineties by way of Oscar Wilde ...'. Until the Billing trial, he had been 'so innocent as not to know that sexual aberrations existed in Society and can describe my experience only as being corrupted by what I read in the newspapers. Some morbid streak in me was strangely stimulated by these new suggestions ...'

Carrington's wartime sexual experiences had been exclusively heterosexual, from a sexual initiation with a prostitute picked up near Leicester Square with whom he had had sex in a taxi going round the Houses of Parliament, to the brothels reserved for serving officers in Paris, complete with Louis XV furniture, ceiling mirrors, pornographic films and girls dressed in baby clothes. But such experiences turned Carrington against mercenary heterosexual sex. One night, after a particularly unsuccessful evening with two street walkers in Amiens, he and a fellow officer fell into bed together. In the morning, they regarded each other guiltily, and did not speak of the incident. Although Carrington found himself attracted to fresh-faced recruits, he had no further homosexual experience in the army until the end of 1918, when he was posted to Valdagno in Italy.

There he became close friends with a wealthy, handsome young officer, Owen Butler, who modelled himself on Byron and had been expelled from Harrow for sexual misconduct. Butler, the only son of the first baronet Sir William Butler, was promiscuous and, although younger than Carrington, much more sophisticated. They would remain close friends until Butler's suicide in 1935. Together they founded the Valdagni Binge Club, devoted to strict military discipline by day and debauchery by night. They drank heavily with two like-minded young sergeants – another instance of the cross-class experience which war – and sex – induced, calling each other by their Christian names and even exchanging clothes to make matters equal. Butler's behaviour was particularly flagrant, and he wanted to invite 'Jimmy' James, the best-looking boy in the regiment, with whom he had already slept. Carrington vetoed this, feeling obliged to protect 'Jimmy's' honour, even though he himself was attracted to boys in the regiment, and had once surprised a handsome corporal by kissing him goodbye.

Carrington had been turned to contemplate illicit vices by the Billing trial; to fellow officers who shared those 'vices', the whole affair seemed both insane and bizarre. As the trial ended, Siegfried Sassoon was back at the Western Front, awaiting publication of his poems, *Counter-Attack*, and struggling with his sexual attraction to at least one private, Jim Linthwaite. He had advised Linthwaite on not getting drunk: 'I suppose I'd have done the same for any man in the Company who had a good character. But there was a great deal of sex floating about in this particular effort. No doubt he dreams about "saving my life". I wish I could save his.' For all his personal involvement in the case through his friendship with Ross, Sassoon could still look objectively at the affair, though not without exasperation. In a diary entry dated 2 June, he wrote: 'The papers are full of this foul "Billing Case". Makes one glad to be away from "normal conditions". And the Germans are on the Marne and claim 4,500 more prisoners. The world is stark staring mad and I don't regret the prospect of leaving it, as long as my friends are with me.' A month later, Sassoon would receive a wound in the head, escaping death by an inch.

With Billing publicly vindicated, any possible display of homosexual feeling was now more proscribed than ever, and the guarded tone of Sassoon's diaries and Owen's letters, and Owen's reaction to the increasingly pressing advances of Scott Moncrieff (who was wilfully disregarding the new moral climate) appear to confirm the point. The fact that Graves's hitherto enthusiastic correspondence with Scott Moncrieff ended abruptly in May 1918 due to his disapproval of Scott Moncrieff's behaviour (about which he had heard from Ross) was also, perhaps, a symptom of the post-Billing taint of association.

As the trial was taking place, Owen was readying himself for his final return to the front. Stationed in Ripon, he met a drummer boy called George whom he'd known before the war, 'an emotional experience'. Owen was evidently well aware of the punitive atmosphere around the Billing affair, and when he was declared fit for General Service on 4 June – just as the trial was ending – he wrote to his cousin, 'Drummer George of Dunsden wept when I said goodbye. (I had seen him 3 times!) This you must not tell anybody. Such things are not for this generation of vipers.' Owen also had a close relationship with his manservant, Private Jones, 'happily wounded: & so away from me', he told Sassoon. 'He had lived in London, a Londoner.' Dominic Hibberd suggests that 'the term had some special meaning in Ross's circle'. Emotionally, socially and creatively, Owen was irrevocably caught up in the 'cult of Wilde'. Jon Stallworthy likens Owen's description of Jones's blood lying 'yet crimson on my shoulder' to a fragment of verse, 'I saw his round mouth's crimson deepen as it fell', itself related to an earlier piece, Uranian in tone, written by Owen in the Regent Palace Hotel, Piccadilly, in 1915:

> Your plum mouth, your rose mouth,
> Give me with this the fullness of the sun
> Of my summers that are yet to come.

The similarity to Wilde's evocation of Bosie's 'rose-leaf lips' as read out in court is telling, as is the resemblance to dialogue in *Salome*; the rose was a favourite sexual metaphor for Wilde. Stallworthy notes that in writing the opening lines of his 1917 (or possibly 1918) poem, 'Greater Love': 'Red lips are not so red/ As the stained stones kissed by the English dead', '[Owen] may ... have been aware of Salome's words to Jokanaan in Wilde's *Salome*: "The roses in the garden of the Queen of Arabia are not so white as thy body." '

As the war shambled to a close, Owen and Sassoon's lives swung somewhat surreally between the battleground of the Western Front and the 'decadent', modern London world of art and letters. Scott Moncrieff showed the Sitwells Owen's 'Mental Cases', and they asked for some of Owen's poems for *Wheels*, the first magazine to feature British modernist verse, edited by Osbert and Edith with Nancy Cunard. Owen's subject matter and technique allied him to the Modernists; like Firbank, he was a link between them and the Decadents. Reviewers saw the Sitwells' magazine as a decadent evocation of the spirit of the *Yellow Book*.

Sassoon was also back in London, recuperating at the American Red Cross Hospital in Lancaster Gate, and keen to reclaim Owen as his own protégé. Their last meeting came one Saturday afternoon in August when they were both guests of Osbert's at Swan Walk; sitting out in the Chelsea Physic Garden opposite, they 'tired the sun with talking and sent him down the sky'. Soon after, Owen was pronounced fit for duty, and on the eve of his departure for France, Scott Moncrieff appears to have made a pass at him on this, Owen's last night in London. The next day, Owen found himself wandering on Folkestone beach, where he met 'a Harrow boy, of superb intellect & refinement' who hated the war more than he hated the Germans. 'It was a strange meeting, almost like finding one's ideal self.'

Owen consciously took Sassoon's place as war poet at the front. He and Siegfried would never meet again. In late October, the furore over the Billing affair having died down, Sassoon made a visit to London, to catch up on old friends. He had a surprise meeting with Winston Churchill on the 3rd; the politician pleased Siegfried by saying he admired his new collection of poems, *Counter-Attack*. Afterwards, Sassoon dined with Maynard Keynes, saw the Sitwells, and called on Ross at Half Moon Street. As they talked intimately, Scott Moncrieff arrived; despite Billing's Old Bailey victory, Robbie still kept open house for those who were 'so'. The Scot brought a new prodigy with him, a gushing pimply young actor called Noel Coward. The boy had an irritating manner, fluttering around Siegfried and telling him he had read *Counter-Attack* while sitting on the rocks of Cornwall with his novelist friend, G.B. Stern. The mere appearance of Noel Coward's name in the golden rooms of Robbie Ross was a presentiment of the decade to come; the new heirs of Wilde taking over from the old; it was pertinent that Sassoon should find this representative of the future effusive and distracting. Vexed by this interruption to what he had hoped would be a quiet tête-à-tête with Robbie, Sassoon left them to their gossip. In his diary, he noted that he had found Ross looking weary and ill. Two days later, Ross was dead.

*

Ross had never really recovered after losing the libel charge against Douglas in 1914; in subsequent years he had become increasingly sickly and withdrawn. Christopher Millard's second imprisonment for homosexual offences preyed on him, but it was undoubtedly the events of the Billing trial which hastened his decline. On 5 October, Robbie's devoted housekeeper Nellie Burton found his body in his rooms. He had had a coronary. On learning of his friend's death, Sassoon remarked that it must have been the only occasion when Robbie's heart had failed him. He was just forty-nine.

Marie Belloc Lowndes attended Ross's funeral, 'a pathetic ... unreal, little gathering, partly owing to the fact that for some reason ... his family, though knowing he was a Catholic, had the Church of England service read at the Crematorium, a thing which would have distressed him very much ... The reasonable thing would have been to have had a discourse by one of his many friends, eulogising his remarkable character, and paying tribute to his marvellous kindness of heart ... I was secretly shocked at the absence of a good many people who ought to have made the effort to come and pay him this very small last tribute of affection, to say nothing of gratitude.' The lamentable attendance may well have been yet another effect of the allegations of the Billing affair.

Given his opposition to it, it is ironic that Ross's demise coincided with the stagnant, stuttering last days of war, and a fervid tremor of London life. It was, as Virginia Woolf wrote to Lytton Strachey, 'the climax of dissipation. What with the approach of peace and the Russian dancers, the gallant Sitwells and the poetical Edith, Ottoline [Morrell] utterly abandoned and nefarious, Duncan [Grant] covered with paint from head to foot ... Robbie Ross found dead in his shirtsleeves, Roger [Fry] going to lay him out, [M.'s] widow bursting in dead drunk – and so forth – all the things that invariably happen in London in October – it's a pleasant change. We went to hear Lord Grey's speech ... and I had the pleasure of sitting exactly behind Mrs Asquith and Elizabeth ... Then there was the Sitwells' party ...'

A week later, at the front, Wilfred Owen heard the news of Ross's death from Scott Moncrieff. In the trenches there was open talk of peace, necessitating a Special Order from General Rawlinson forbidding it and warning against the enemies' 'peace offensive' sapping the Allied will to fight the war to the bitter end. The end for Owen was as bitter as it could be. He died in action near the Sambre Canal, Northern France on 4 November, six days before peace was announced. His poems, with their sacrificial overtones, seemed vindicated: Owen the innocent, dying for his masters' sins. The popular press greeted the war's end with the same necessary patriotic fervour with which it had 'fought' the home front and championed Billing. On 11 November the Armistice was declared. That morning, as the bells of the town church of Wilfred Owen's home town, Shrewsbury, rang out to announce the fact, his mother received the telegram announcing her son's death.

Repington recorded in his diary that day the abdication of the Kaiser and his flight to Holland, 'deserting his armies of over 3,000,000 men. A more or less bloodless revolution is in full swing throughout Germany, and all the kings and princes of the German Empire are toppling down one after another.' At midday, he lunched with Mrs Greville and Mrs Keppel, 'All in great spirits and very happy.' Meanwhile, Margot Asquith was reported to have gone down on her knees in a crowded omnibus to say a prayer. That evening, London greeted the peace. The cheering drunken revellers in Trafalgar Square were observed by Osbert Sitwell and his companions, Serge Diaghilev, bear-like in his fur coat, and Leonide Massine, making mental choreographic notes on 'the shifting general pattern of the mass of people'. Making slow progress through that crowd in their dark red Rolls-Royce, were Antonio Gandarillas – Chilean diplomat, bisexual and opium addict – and the young Noel Coward. 'We screamed with them, and shook hands with as many as we could,' recalled Coward, 'and I felt ignobly delighted, in this moment of national rejoicing, to be in a tail coat, a Rolls-Royce, and obviously aristocratic company.' They arrived at the Savoy, where Alice Delysia, in a glittering pink dress, stood on a table to sing the Marseillaise. A few days later, Billie Carleton overdosed on cocaine in her rooms next door. Beatrice Lillie, 'still in gala mood' on arriving at the Savoy to see her friend, told the desk clerk, 'Lead me to the body!' and made her way to the lift.

The Russian Ballet had returned to London that September, a triumph of the avant-garde and the decadent: an indication that Billing hadn't won, after all; to Osbert Sitwell, it was a 'private and sole omen of peace'. Within months, the jazz-modern shock of *Parade*, created by Cocteau, Satie and Picasso, would be playing at the Alhambra in the Charing Cross Road, thrilling the 'balletomaniac' cruisers of its galleries. Just as the lights were turned up for the first time in four years, the skies free of threat, so London society was opening up; no longer was it necessary to feel ashamed about enjoyment; the end of DORA seemed in sight. It was the beginning of a new era. Repington caught sight of 'the new Jazz dancing' at the 'first big function since the Armistice, a dinner of 100 at 10 tables at Lord Furness's house and a dance afterwards ...'. He didn't quite approve of the frenetic activity on the dance floor, but admired 'a rare lot of pretty women ... Nearly everyone in London seemed to be there. All the new dances, if they can be called dances, and jolly dresses, but very little of them. Many ladies told me that they felt quite dazed in a throng strange to us all for nearly five years. How soon the world forgets!'

10

Aftermath

It's women, women everywhere; and, as Mr George Robey would say, believe me – berlieve me not, but it's mighty few of them are really looking very war-worn. On the contrary ... They say the night clubs are opening up in rows, and dressmakers say they're dizzy with the orders for dance frocks that keep on pourin' in. And they just can't have enough niggers to play jazz music, and I hear they are thinkin' of hiring out squads of 'loonies' to make the mad jazz noises till there are more ships 'vailable to bring the best New York black jazz 'musicians' over.

Tatler, 15 January 1919

The absence of war did not mean that the vacuum would necessarily be replaced by peace. In the no man's land between Armistice and the Treaty of Versailles, Europe revolted and Britain faced chaos as the civil unrest of wartime spread. The khaki riots of 1919 erupted in flashpoints everywhere, even in genteel Surrey, where in Epsom, hundreds of Canadian soldiers set fire to a police station and killed one of its occupants; in Sutton, three regiments mutinied. Demobbed soldiers, physically and mentally traumatised by war, now faced uncertainty and unemployment: the 1919 race riots in London, Cardiff, Glasgow and other ports with substantial foreign populations were fired by xenophobia and fear of foreigners taking potential jobs from soldiers. In Liverpool, a black man was stoned to death in Queen's Dock, and in South Wales, black dockers were stabbed and Chinese laundries attacked.

There were other threats to the nation, too. Coming six months after the Billing case, the Billie Carleton affair had sparked off a new public debate about drugs, sex and the new society. People realised that everything had changed, that the world was not the same place it had been just four years ago. With new scandals of drug-taking chorus girls and lesbian writers most people forgot about the trial. Only a vague remembrance of rumours about Society remained; and anyway, they'd known all about such goings-on for years. The fact that some of the great and good might be addicted to perverted practices merely confirmed suspicions raised by the Wilde trials. 'How completely forgotten is the Pemberton Billing case,' Marie Belloc Lowndes would write, 'and yet in the early summer of 1918 little else was talked of in the world in which I lived. What was the truth about ... "The Black Book"? No one will ever know ... If it ever really existed, it is indeed surprising that no part of it was ever published or quoted.' Belloc Lowndes believed in the book, a belief which drew on notions of a perverted club mentality, echoed in Ford Madox Ford's 1924 trilogy, *Parade's End*, which looked back to 1916: 'There is said to be a book, kept in a holy of holies, in which bad marks are set down against men of family and position in England.' The irony that the British probably did possess a Black Book on the Germans would be paralleled by the fact that in the Second World War, Third Reich efficiency assembled its own black book containing names and addresses of candidates for extermination when the Nazi invasion of Britain was accomplished. Among them was Rebecca West, who wrote to another nominee, Noel Coward, 'My dear, the people we should have been seen dead with.' Coward, the Wilde of his era, was an obvious candidate for inclusion in such a list. In the Thirties, when the memory of the Billing trial seemed to survive in playground folklore, the writer Tony Warren, then a schoolboy, was told: 'They've got a big black book at Scotland Yard. It's full of the names of every homo in Britain – and the first one on the list is Noel Coward.'

*

Prejudice thrived as a virulent legacy of the war: anti-semitism, homophobia, anti-communist hysteria. To a world threatened by the new, the old bugbears of Billing and his supporters still endured, and the post-war period would throw up its own demagogues, succeeding where Billing had failed. But what if Billing's own push for power had worked? Such was their groundswell of public support that Billing and his friends – Beamish, Clarke and Spencer – might have come to power had Britain, not Germany, been the vanquished nation. 'There would have been a similar hunt for the "November criminals", as there was in Germany, and the racialism would have been stepped up to cover everything else,' notes Michael Kettle. 'Billing perhaps was the Goering that we just missed.' It was a close shave: at least one of Billing's wartime allies succeeded to state office. William Joynson-Hicks, xenophobe, anti-semite and admirer of Mussolini, became Home Secretary in 1926, nicknamed Jix for his hated moral prescriptions, closing nightclubs and censoring 1920s life in general. When a visitor to his 'Whitehall citadel' asked, 'But what do you do here?', Jix replied, 'It is I who am the ruler of England.') Even in a victorious Britain, conditions were ripe for fascism, as they were in Germany and Italy. The war was fascism's catalyst, and the activities of Billing and his circle indicate that the British variety, with its roots in prewar anti-semitism and imperialism, developed independently of the German and Italian strain in a myriad of extremist societies.

Having come within 1,181 votes of winning the June 1918 by-election in Clapham, Beamish came second in the Coupon election in the same constituency in December that year. Up until his split with Billing and the Vigilantes, Beamish had been associated with Billing's latest organisation, the Silver Badge Party of ex-Servicemen, formed to exploit the discontent of returning soldiers who found no welcome at home, nor any prospect of the future for which they had fought. As elsewhere in Europe, such men provided important support for the radical right, who appealed to base instincts of envy and prejudice. In the wake of his quarrel with Billing – who disliked the idea of the Vigilantes being turned into a purely anti-semitic organisation – Beamish set up the Britons Society, devoted to the eradiction of 'alien influences in British life' and the expulsion of Jews from England. They held to White's 'hidden hand' theory, fleshed out to a fully-fledged international conspiracy. They published such literature as the *Protocols of the Elders of Zion* and Beamish's *The Jew's Who's Who* (1920). A regular journal, *Jewry Ueber Alles*, appeared in February 1920, changing its name to *The Hidden Hand* in September; it was still being published in the 1970s, becoming an influence on the British National Front. Blind hatred did not have a wide appeal, however: *The Hidden Hand* had a circulation of just 150, while the Imperial Fascist League's magazine, *The Fascist*, produced 3,000 copies, 1,000 of which were bought by a Mr Pope of Porthcawl and most of the rest sent to South Africa.

Other groups with links to the prewar Die-Hards also used the *Protocols of the Elders of Zion* to stir up anti-semitism. Even such respectable newspapers as *The Times* and the *Morning Post* seriously debated the *Protocols* and anti-semitic 'Causes of World Unrest' at the end of the war. In 1924, the Die-Hard Duke of Northumberland bought the *Morning Post* and set up *The Patriot* to spearhead a new campaign, with *Post* editor H.A.Gwynne as its publicist. *The Times* proved the *Protocols* to be a forgery in 1921, but the *Morning Post* (which had published its 'Cause of World Unrest' conspiracy theory in July 1920, and whose correspondent, Briton member V.E. Marsden, had translated the *Protocols**), continued to propagate such ideas. The emergent post-war fascist groups all believed in the *Protocols*: British intelligence reports noted that their meetings heard audience remarks such as 'Kill the Jews', 'Perish Judea', 'We hate them', and 'Bastards'. They were inspired by individual idealists whose theories drew on the 'underground of rejected knowledge' in which the Black Book and the

---

* In 1920, Marsden would accompany the Prince of Wales on his tour of the Empire.

conspiracies of the Billing affair had their roots. Pre-eminent among these was Nesta Webster, a product of the nineteenth-century occult revival, who saw the history of revolution caused by 'secret societies, who used their knowledge of occult forces to undermine authority and the stability of governments'. Webster considered that freemasons were behind the French Revolution, while their role in the Russian Revolution had been taken over by the Jews. Her fears were reinforced by social collapse of the war, blamed on 'the Jewish cabbala ... the force which originally inspired the freemasons'. ('Although her views are still regarded as highly eccentric outside reactionary conservative and fascist circles,' notes Richard Thurlow, 'it is interesting to note that some historians now argue that secret societies like the IRA and the Mafia have indeed played a significant role in world events ...')

The splintering of the radical right, forming pockets of protofascist cadres after the Billing trial, led Beamish to pursue tactics similiar to Billing's. In 1920 Beamish joined with H. McCleod Frazer of the Silver Badge Party to display a public notice at Charing Cross: 'Sir Alfred Mond is a TRAITOR, he alloted shares to HUNS during the war.' Inevitably, Beamish was sued by Mond, and in the libel trial damages of £5,000 were awarded against him. Beamish fled the country to avoid paying, and ever after remained a fugitive from England, eventually settling on a farm in southern Rhodesia. He carried on the work of the Britons, however: in January 1923 he went to Munich, where he met Hitler and gave a speech to the National Socialists, extolling confraternity and admiring 'the magnificent way in which you Bavarians have tackled this Jewish problem ...'.

The infamous Dr J.H. Clarke took over the Britons in Beamish's absence. He was their vice-president from 1918 to 1931, and supposed to have influence with the Conservative Die-Hards in the 1920s. However, the organisation foundered after 1925, despite its well-connected and distinguished supporters, imperialists all, including Lord Sydenham of Combe, ex-Governor of Bombay and Victoria, George Mudge, Professor of Zoology at the University of London, Bessie Pullen Burry, the explorer, Lady Moore, and a number of high-ranking military men. The high female representation in the Britons suggests 'a peculiar side-effect of the suffragette movement; political commitment and involvement could develop in very different directions from the dedicated socialism of Sylvia Pankhurst ...' – as Eileen Villiers-Stuart demonstrates. 'Indeed, the suffragette movement and its link to fascism represented one kind of genteel revolt by spirited upper-middle-class woman against the stultifying effects of the Victorian ethic of limiting the role of respectable ladies to ornaments in the social round.'

Beamish's campaign of hatred did not abate with his exile. He became vice-president of the Imperial Fascist League, and a roving spokesman for anti-semitism. In 1937, he gave a lecture to the IFL entitled 'National Socialism

(Racial Fascism) in Practice in Germany', in which he told members that Germany was great because Hitler had 'named the enemy'. There were three methods which could be used to deal with the Jewish problem: 'kill them, sterilize them, or segregate them'. He hoped that Hitler would march into Russia 'and place one half of the population in the lethal chamber and the other half in the zoo'. Rumours that Germany was supposed to run 'nudist camps of indecent practices' were untrue, said Beamish, who reported that the IFL had sent its photographers to British nudist camps 'which were perfectly foul and run by Jews'. The meeting ended with the entire audience saluting 'Heil Hitler'. The IFL adopted black shirts and Union Jacks superimposed with swastikas, and like the British Union of Fascists led by Mosley, held open-air meetings in the East End; one supporter, A.K.Chesterton, second cousin of the novelist, proposed using lamp-posts to string up Jews (Chesterton went on to join the BUF and later helped found the National Front). IFL literature alleged that Jews were responsible for wartime crime, the white slave traffic, and war casualties. Such societies reached their extreme with the White Knights of Britain or the Hooded Men, a British version of the Ku Klux Klan who at their offices in Lamb's Conduit Street held occult rituals and swore allegiance to Edward I, who had expelled the Jews from England; and with the running street battles of Mosleyites and Communists in the East End.

Perhaps to his credit, Billing's association with extreme right-wing activists tailed off abruptly soon after 1918, although this may have owed more to the vicissitudes of political fate than to rationality. (Again it is interesting to speculate that, had Fate treated him more kindly, Billing's better grasp of popular opinion and public appeal might have led to a more coherent British movement of the radical right.) Like his ejection from the House of Commons, Billing's fall from power was swift and decisive. In 1918 the authorities clamped down on the inflammatory rhetoric of the *Vigilante*, and the newspaper was heavily censored; after the war, Billing closed it down altogether. He was then living in his Temple chambers, where, soon after the trial, his Christian Science woman arrived with his son in her arms. It was an embarrassing development: Billing found her tiresome, and encouraged her departure soon after. Sometime later, another ex-lover came calling at his door: Eileen Villiers-Stuart, released from prison in midsummer 1919. She too became a nuisance, and was dismissed. Billing warned her that the authorities were likely to persecute her further, and she left the country, possibly for the United States. Her subsequent fate remains unknown.

*

The Billing trial passed into history, but for its participants, its memory could not be lived down. Billing, Douglas, Darling, Villiers-Stuart, Maud Allan and Jack Grein all suffered as a result, and for each the affair proved a disastrous breakpoint in their careers.

After the trial, and Robbie Ross's death, Douglas claimed victory and reissued *The Rossiad* in celebration. He raged about 'Government by newspaper!' 'My satire, *The Rossiad*, boycotted by practically every newspaper, bookseller and library in the kingdom, did not quite reach a circulation of a thousand copies, but the effect it produced on certain persons and a certain "movement" was and is incalculable ... it is not too much to say that it has altered the course of history' – a characteristically inflated and uncorroborated claim. Douglas attributed Asquith's downfall to his having signed Ross's Testimonial. 'Many things have happened to change the aspect of affairs since ... 1) Mr Asquith was thrown out of his seat at East Fife and has retired, politically speaking, into obscurity and impotence from which it seems exceedingly unlikely that he will ever emerge; 2) Mr Robert Ross is dead.'

In July 1920 Douglas secured the editorship of *Plain English*, a weekly magazine designed to expose scandal and corruption. He appointed Harold Spencer – who had recently married the daughter of Sir James Beattie, a prominent Dundee citizen – as his assistant editor. It was obvious that the *Vigilante* tricks were about to be repeated. *Plain English* proceeded to make libellous attacks on Churchill, whom Douglas accused of having circulated a false account of the Battle of Jutland to allow Sir Ernest Cassel, the Jewish financier, to buy Government shares cheaply, subsequently profiting by selling them on Wall Street; Churchill was supposed to be in on the syndicate. When Churchill declined to react to Douglas's published libel (on the grounds that the magazine was too insignificant to merit legal action), Douglas persisted, seeking a similar *cause célèbre* to the Billing trial. Unfortunately, Captain Spencer would prove to be his undoing as Douglas discovered the fragile nature of Spencer's mental state. On 16 October 1921, Douglas resigned as editor, and Spencer took over: the pair had quarrelled violently when Douglas found out that much of the information Spencer was supplying was false.

Like Beamish with the Britons' publishing ventures, Spencer used *Plain English* as a vehicle for his anti-semitism and that November published a piece, 'Our Foreign Frescoes', in which he scorned the choice of Sigismund Goetze as the artist responsible for a series of paintings recently installed in the Foreign Office: 'Our Foreign Office is quite foreign enough in our opinion, without the spacious decorations of a foreign Jew at the expense of the British tax payer.' Spencer was sued for libel, and at the trial it emerged that Goetze – a British-born Christian – had financed the paintings himself. Spencer was sentenced to six months in prison for libel, and was stripped of his army rank. Just a few months after his release, he was convicted of unspecified 'disgusting behaviour' and fined forty shillings. Spencer later reported that he had consulted Sir Richard Muir who had 'charged him six guineas for telling him that it was no use appealing as the police had been corrupt since the strike'.

Douglas's latest campaign was also riven with anti-semitism. He was busy laying unsubstantiated claims against Churchill, and personally distributed (with his mother's help) 6,000 copies of a pamphlet breathlessly entitled *The Murder of Lord Kitchener and the Truth about the Battle of Jutland and the Jews*. In it, Douglas referred to a theory that Jews had engineered Kitchener's death. (He drowned when the *Hampshire* sank on its way to Russia in 1916. It was rumoured that a bomb had been placed in the hold. Marie Belloc Lowndes recalled, 'Many weeks later a woman told me, quite seriously, that the person who had arranged for the bomb to be put there was Mrs Asquith. So violent was the prejudice felt against her at that time.') Churchill had had enough. On 6 November 1923 Douglas was arrested on a charge of criminal libel. Inevitably, the Billing case came up in court: for a man as prone to litigation as Douglas, his previous performances would always be brought before him, the ghosts of the past come to judge the cases of the present. Douglas had alleged, in *Plain English*, that Darling had been out to get Billing. Mr Justice Avory asked, 'You wrote that he had been put up by the Government to secure a conviction?' 'These things are done,' said Douglas. Talk of such conspiracy required the evidence of one man: Spencer was called as the only witness for the defence. He claimed to have spoken with Churchill at a civic lunch for Earl Haig, when he had told Churchill that he was going to 'turn him out of Dundee' (the constituency which he represented from 1908-22, and where Spencer was to stand for Parliament; hence his marriage to Sir James Beattie's daughter). Spencer added, 'Your Jutland report was a bit thick, wasn't it?' to which Churchill is supposed to have replied, 'What do you care? We did it to get the money out of the Yanks.'

In court it became clear that Spencer was the source of Douglas's disastrous misinformation. Spencer said he had been under constant surveillance, and accused the Attorney-General of looking at the jury and 'leering', saying he had 'the manner of an old actor'. Spencer claimed the friendship of the Duke of Northumberland (not unlikely, given the Die-Hard duke's affiliation with nascent fascism) and that he had met Churchill at Lady Randolph's flat in St James's Place (much less likely: she had not lived there since 1883). He finished on a familiar note of paranoid conspiracy: 'They murdered Lord Kitchener but they have been very gentle with me.'

It took the jury just eight minutes to find Lord Alfred Douglas guilty. Sentencing him to six months' imprisonment, Mr Justice Avory said, 'It is to be regretted that your undoubted literary abilities have been degraded to such puposes as this.' Douglas was taken to Wormwood Scrubs, where Christopher Millard had been held. He could not eat the food, and survived on milkless cocoa and bread and butter until he lost so much weight that he was admitted to the prison hospital. The experience – so much harsher than Wilde's in Reading – seemed to purge his obsession with Wilde, at least for a while. Like Oscar, he wrote a sonnet sequence while in prison – *In Excelsis* – but unlike Wilde, his manuscript was confiscated, and he had to commit the work to memory.

Douglas's later life was characterised by petty squabbles and brief flashes of literary talent. He retired to Hove, from where he made his eccentric forays into literature and politics. Christabel Aberconway recalled him as 'a considerable poet' but also as 'the man ... whom I have most disliked in my life' who sent her 'threatening, unsigned letters from Brighton ...'. Hugh Walpole met him at Marie Stopes's house in Norbury: 'something of a shock. How astonished was I when this rather bent, crooked-bodied, hideous old man came into the room. How could he ever have been beautiful, for he has a nose as ugly as Cyrano's with a dead-white bulbous end?' Douglas talked nonstop, in a shrill voice. 'When someone he hates like Wells is mentioned, he gets so angry that all his crooked features light up and his nose achieves a sort of sombre glow. In the afternoon he had before all of us a first-class row with young Briant of the *Sunday Chronicle* about the Russians, listening to no argument, screaming like a parrot, repeating phrases again and again. At last he shrieked, "Oh go to Hell!" Upon which the young man went.'

Douglas continued to live off the memory of his past. Loelia, Duchess of Westminster, invited Douglas to a weekend houseparty in 1941, when the guests – who included Diana Cooper – were told that the subject of Oscar Wilde was taboo. 'But hardly was Alfred Douglas in the hall before he began talking about Oscar and we heard nothing else the entire weekend. Unfortunately the old scamp lied like a trooper and said that he was not Oscar's boyfriend. Then, a few months later when he needed the money, he sold his whole story. But he was not unattractive. You could see the ravages of good looks.' Douglas, Wilde's Dorian Gray, died in 1945, and with him, the end of the vendetta.

*

The rest of the cast of the Billing drama met an equally mixed fate. Colonel Repington died in 1921, having destroyed his own social standing by publishing his two-volume diary of the war in which he revealed how Society had maintained its high living during wartime. Repington's remark to one hostess in 1917, about how 'callous' posterity might regard their ability to enjoy themselves during the war, was all too prescient.

10. Aftermath

Travers Humphreys went on to prosecute, in 1922, another political demagogue, the infamous Horatio Bottomley, proprietor of *John Bull*. Humphreys sat
on the King's Bench Division from 1928-51, and published two books, *Criminal
Days* (1946) and *A Book of Trials* (1953). He was knighted in 1925. In his
memoirs, written twenty-five years after the Billing trial, Travers Humphreys
was still annoyed enough (or, perhaps, circumspect enough) to refuse to discuss
details of the 'scandalous proceedings of that trial, or the unfortunate levity with
which the learned Judge treated the abominable insinuations about himself
uttered by the half-mad witnesses put into the witness-box by Billing for the
express purpose of insulting the Judge'. He also attacked Darling for 'misdirect-
ing the Jury. All the evidence produced by the Defendant ... was totally
irrelevant to the Plea of Justification he had entered ...' Humphreys lobbied
vigorously for the repeal of the anti-homosexual Labouchere Amendment of
1885, widely seen as a 'Blackmailer's Charter'. His efforts were noted by the
1956 Wolfenden Committee, whose recommendations would eventually lead to
the decriminalising of homosexual activity in Britain.

Ellis Hume-Williams was knighted in 1918, partly a sweetener after his
humiliating experience at the trial, but also a reward for his work with prisoner-
of-war organisations. At the same time his senior, Justice Darling, was attacked
by legal journals for being 'incapable of grappling with the exceedingly difficult
case he had to try ...'. The *Law Times* seemed to know there was a subtext to
the whole affair: 'It is a matter for deep regret that the rota of Judges for
attendance at the Central Criminal Court was not adhered to.' Had the Lord
Chief Justice himself not been still acting as British Ambassador in Washington,
it is likely that Darling would have been removed from his post as Acting Lord
Chief Justice.

Publicly if unseriously accused of being a pervert and criticised by the press
and his peers, Darling's reputation would suffer in perpetuity; the *Dictionary of
National Biography* recorded with disapproval that his conduct during the
Billing trial 'went far to lower the status of the bench'. He was created Baron
Darling in 1924, following his retirement from the Bench, and spent most of his
time in Europe with his daughter, Miss Diana Darling, writing 'delightful verses'
and 'gossamer-like stories', noted his sycophantic biographer. 'All too infre-
quently there appears in a London newspaper some trifle by Lord Darling, but
what an exquisite trifle it invariably is! A fairy tale with the breath of Provence
hiding its structure in a scented mist; wistful, far-away little stories.' In his book,
Evelyn Graham makes only passing mention of Darling's legal tussles with
Douglas and Billing. Darling died in Lymington on 29 May 1936, leaving £2,228
7s 8d to his surviving daughters, the Hon. Lucia Pulteney, and Diana, who
remained unmarried. Darling's will was most specific on the fate of his art

collection, with detailed instructions as to the maintenance and eventual resting-place of his portrait in oils. In death as in life, he was a vain man.

*

Maud Allan never again reached the heights of her former glory. She spoke of Billing as 'the worst man that ever was', and the ignominious memory of the trial hung next to the other skeleton in her cupboard, Theo's murderous crimes, both to haunt the rest of her days. She was shunned by theatre managements after the trial, and advised not to appear on stage. Although the artistic and theatrical circles in which she moved saw the affair for what it was, an example of prejudice and perverted justice which could well have been applied to them (as her friendship with Courtney indicates, Maud Allan appealed to a certain homo-sexual sensibility, eager to acclaim flamboyant and iconic female performers), 'important acquaintances' fell away. But she maintained the friendship of Busoni, and such figures as George Bernard Shaw visited her at West Wing – the rent for which continued to be paid by Margot Asquith.

Work was difficult. There was a plan to perform Shakespeare for the Inde-pendent Theatre, but Maud's attempt to go 'legit' fell through, like so many of her subsequent attempts to recapture departed fame. In the spring of 1920, she toured somewhat obscurely in South America; in 1921 she appeared at the London Coliseum. *The Times* found her tiresome. Doris Langley Moore, then aged twenty-one, became her assistant and observed the idiosyncrasies of her employer, who would not tolerate the subject of crime and punishment to be discussed in her presence, yet dwelt with morbid fascination on the details and nature of death. 'An atmosphere of extreme decorum surrounded her,' wrote Moore, 'the watchful decorum of one who is conscious of things to be lived down.' After a tour of the Near East, Maud returned to the London Alhambra and another clutch of cool reviews. She never danced in London again. There followed European concerts and a return to the USA in 1925, where she danced at the Metropolitan Opera, from which she had been banned in 1910 at the instigation of J. Pierpont Morgan's daughter. Anne Morgan was now one-third of the socialite lesbian trio of Elizabeth Marbury and Elsie de Wolfe; by 1936, it appears that Maud was a good friend of her former opponent: the two women entered a Rockefeller reception arm-in-arm.

In 1932, Maud took a minor part in in C.B. Cochran's revival of *The Miracle* at the Lyceum Theatre in London and on tour, in which Diana Cooper reprised her role as the statue of the Madonna which miraculously comes to life. Maud played the Abbess. Her final British appearance came in *The Barker*, a play about an American circus troupe. Maud established a school of dance in the West Wing, but this faltered when Margot Asquith stopped paying the rent. In the meantime, Maud took the besotted Verna Aldrich, her secretary-companion, as her lover. It was an uneven relationship: when Verna planned to marry in 1930, Maud threatened suicide, and Verna's wealthy family attempted to dissuade Verna from the association, without success. Her money subsidised Maud's London lifestyle, and when the affair began to break up, Maud's tenancy of the West Wing was threatened – yet more so when a pyromaniac Welsh maid twice set fire to the place. (The court heard that as the house burned, 'the girl did not seem to realise the seriousness of what had happened. She was the coolest person while the fire raged and walked out humming.') Maud left her affairs in confusion and returned to America, where she moved in with Alice Millard, a rich widow who had commissioned Frank Lloyd Wright to build her a house in Pasenda. The affair ended tragically in a car crash in 1938. Millard died two weeks later, and Maud suffered extensive injuries.

She returned to the West Wing, physically and financially crippled. Newspapers reported that she and Verna were living alone in a 'wrecked home of 360 rooms', now largely derelict. In November 1938 the *Daily Mail* interviewed Maud at the West Wing: 'MAUD ALLAN HAS – Broken Spine, But – "I'll Dance Again".' The disabled dancer lay on a couch in the corner of her great white drawing room, her famous legs draped with an old rose-coloured coverlet. 'Just because I happened to be well-known in 1908,' Maud told the fawning reporter, 'lots of people seem to think I'm either dead or an old, old woman.' 'She chuckled when I mentioned the famous Salome dance,' said the *Mail*'s reporter. 'How one little thing like that sticks in the public mind,' replied Maud. 'Do you know, that costume to-day would take me to the North Pole and back and keep me cosy and warm!' When asked if her house was haunted, she told the reporter, 'There are no ghosts here – but there are fairies! Often in the past I have heard them running down the wide staircase after midnight and heard them dancing round and round in the hall to faint tinkling music. I'm tired now – and fall asleep before midnight – but I'll hear them again.'

This picturesque scene was belied by the facts of Maud's decline. Her relationship with Verna had deteriorated to the extent that Maud accused her lover of theft; Maud's life in the West Wing was increasingly impoverished. In July 1939, two months before the outbreak of war, it was revealed that three units of the Territorial Army had moved in next door; Maud told the *Daily Express* that she was driven mad by the clump of army boots on marble floors. 'Miss Allan prefers her side of the house to remain unchanged by the year. Spikes of barley tower in the lawn. Paint peels on the walls, plaster has fallen, leaving great scars. Shutters, half unhinged, flap in the breeze to show beyond palace-sized rooms richly furnished with gold hangings, antique French chairs with spindly gold legs, and a battered trunk in one corner. Seldom has one house held greater contrasts – the deserted peace of Miss Allan's territory and the efficient bustle of the other side. Recruits were parading in gas-masks last night on the Army side of the lawn ... "We need more space," the officers say, eyeing the tall brown fence of Miss Allan's territory.'

Maud's quarters escaped requisitioning, but not the Blitz of 1940, when the West Wing was bombed. Maud carried on living in the shell of the building. In February 1941, the *Sunday Chronicle* reported: 'When the ATS received an application from a would-be car driver named "Miss Maud Allan, dancer", they wondered if it possibly be the Maud Allan ...' Another intrepid journalist was sent to investigate. 'To-day she lives in three tiny apartments among 150 empty, echoing rooms of her bomb-shattered Regent's Park mansion, her sole companion her dog Perky. Picking my way past bomb craters and debris that pitted the short carriage drive, I called on her. The side door was so warped by bomb blast that, at Miss Allan's request, I had to burst it in.' 'When the raids are on I just go down in the wine vault and enjoy a perfect illusion of safety,' she told him. Only when life in the dilapidated ruin proved impossible did Maud leave, miraculously procuring a flight to Lisbon, and from there to the USA. Did she use old contacts? Margot Asquith could have helped, while documents show that in 1936, Maud had applied to Lloyd George for his assistance in staving off the bailiffs, indicating a certain connexion between the dancer and the former Prime Minister. If true, it raises questions about her complicity in the Billing trial. Was she knowingly part of the politicians' conspiracy to bring Billing down? Had Lloyd George's government encouraged her to sue for libel? Such questions may never be answered.

Returning to Los Angeles, Maud applied her artistic skills to draftsmanship and went to work for the Douglas Aircraft Company, an ironic occupation for one whose enemy had been obsessed with aircraft. By strange coincidence, Ruth St Denis worked as a riveter in the same factory. But Maud lost her job. She applied for an academic post at UCLA, but was told she hadn't the qualifications. 'From whom could I get a degree in the form of art I created myself ...?' Maud protested. Her celebrated past hung about her redundantly, and with the second half of the century, memory of Maud Allan the dancer faded away. After the war a film was made, loosely based on Maud's life, called *Salome, Where She Danced*, but was as unsuccessful as the rest of the attempts to revive her name. Maud's last years were dogged by poverty, with brief, bizarre flashbacks to her past: at one California party, she was introduced to the man who had hanged her brother. In old age, she would ramble incoherently about death by hanging, evidently haunted by the ghosts of the past. A friend recalled telling her, 'Maud, you have a lovely smile, but when you smile your eyes don't smile.' The grounded dancer looked reflective and replied, 'Yes, that's what they tell me.' Maud Allan, Edwardian superstar, died in obscurity in a Los Angeles convalescent home in 1956. After her death, the Cherniavksys burnt many of her papers, including the letters written by her mother which appeared to indicate that, despite maintaining his innocence, Maud had always known of Theo's guilt.

*

Between the wars Margot Asquith enjoyed a continued position in high society, becoming a countess with the ennoblement of her husband as the Earl of Oxford and Asquith in 1925. But she too was haunted by the Billing case. Marie Belloc Lowndes was inspired by Lord Oxford's death in February 1928 to recall her last visit to the Wharf, when the events of the war were discussed: 'At one moment, Margot said bitterly to me, "It didn't matter what I did during the War, because everybody believed I was a spy." ' Margot lived to experience the Second World War, most of which she spent at the supposedly bomb-proof Savoy Hotel. She died in 1945.

The ill-effects of the Billing trial were perhaps felt most acutely by J.T. Grein. Labelled homosexual and crippled by legal costs, he had a nervous breakdown and was dropped by the *Sunday Times*. His resignation from the paper 'was instantly accepted'. Such was his post-trial reputation that when a group of society women collecting books for military hospitals called on the Greins and found J.T.'s name in one of the volumes donated by his wife, they dropped their booty in horror and fled. It was a period of 'acute mental and physical suffering' for Grein. Although his enthusiasm for the theatre remained, he was drawn back to business and diplomacy, becoming Commercial Attaché and Consul-General of Liberia in London. When Billing staged his own play, *High Treason*, at the Strand Theatre, Grein sent him a telegram wishing him good luck. 'And that in no spirit of heaping coals of fire, but simply in response to the generous impulse of a nature that could not harbour ill-feeling.' Grein died on 22 June 1935. In 1987, a literary prize was established in his name by journalists in London.

One figure did thrive, however. While her name may have meant tragedy and disaster for those involved in her depiction in 1918, Salome's legend remained potent as ever. The myth continued to obsess artists, writers, performers and film-makers both in Europe and America, and like Maud Allan, many women were drawn to this strong female image. Djuna Barnes, bisexual author of *Nightwood* and herself the product of a deeply unconventional family, wrote a number of short stories influenced by Wilde's play and probably Maud's performance, among them 'What Do You See, Madam?' (1915) in which Mamie Saloam has the ambition to dance like Salome and kiss the head of John the

Baptist, and 'The Head of Babylon' (1917), about a sort of female John the Baptist who is paralysed from the neck down but who proclaims biblical prophecies. Maud's successful interpretation of the myth encouraged the commercialisation of Salome. In 1918, the Hollywood vamp Theda Bara, visibly influenced by Maud in her costume and decadent imagery, appeared in a film of *Salome* shown in London the year after the Billing trial, doubtless to capitalise on the publicity. In 1924, Alla Nazimova starred in an opulent Beardsleyan film version of Wilde's story, confirmation that Salome's temptress charms continued long into the inter-war era.

But in a proscriptive Britain, where, despite the war's end, many of the enactments of DORA were still in force and the moral movement against decadence remained as strong as ever, Wilde's dramatic incarnation of Salome fared little better than her detractors and champions had done at the Old Bailey. It is evident from recently released papers that as the events unfolded during the trial, the office of the Lord Chamberlain had kept a wary eye on proceedings. Among other notes from the members of the Advisory Board, written from their clubs or country addresses, is a cutting from *The Times*: 'Mr Billing: – I am glad to say I don't think the jury would understand it. The witness said that he considered the play of *Salome* one of great danger to public morality. Questioned with reference to the article, the witness said the title meant to him a society of people who went in for various forms of sexual perversion.' Written on this is the name of the sender, 'Dr Arthur Serrell Cooke, Cavendish Place, Cavendish Square' – evidently one of the 'doctor's conspiracy' was attempting to manipulate behind the scenes. But the Lord Chamberlain, Lord Sandhurst, appended a note to it: 'I shall not consider the question of this licence until the litigation now in progress is concluded. S. April 1918.' A subsequent note from Sandhurst observes: 'The litigation is now concluded – I shall not license this play should the licence be pressed for & the application made by a manager. And should the occasion arise the Advisory Board can be so informed. S. June 1918.'

The Lord Chamberlain's office was annoyed at the way it had been used to further Billing's case. When the play was submitted for licence in 1927, the now veteran reader George Street noted: 'This play was refused a licence after the notoriety and fuss of the Billing libel action in 1918. I do not find that opinion, as expressed at the time, is altered by anything I read of the opinions about the play held by witnesses in that case. [signed] G.S. Street.' It is clear from this that the refusal of a licence – the banning of *Salome* – was entirely due to Billing's antics, and not to any serious objection by the Lord Chamberlain; as was made clear by this post-trial assessment by Lord Buckmaster:

The licence was accordingly refused but the refusal was not due to an adverse judgement of the play. It may be hoped that the trial of the criminal proceedings is now forgotten and the only question is on what grounds found in the play itself can it be regarded as unfit for performance.

He saw no such grounds, but the application – from Terence Gray for performance at the Cambridge Festival Theatre – was refused in 1927, a decision which appeased the moral crusader Jix – Joynson-Hicks, Billing's old ally.[*] That year, *Salome*'s nemesis submitted his own play to the scrutiny of the officers of St James's Palace. It was a last riposte to the whole affair, albeit cloaked, characteristically, in conspiratorial fantasy.

*

Billing had ceased to be an MP in 1921, resigning his seat on 27 May due to ill health, and despite fighting a number of by-elections, was never again elected. He spent his time sailing his Southampton-based yacht – provocatively named 'Freedom' (equally provocatively, he named his residence in Mortlake 'Cromwell House') – and writing his play, *High Treason*, first performed in Cardiff in 1927. A licence application was sent to the Lord Chamberlain's office, where the redoubtable George Street summarised Billing's creative efforts as 'a mixture of political, religious and ethical talk until the end of Act II, when melodrama sets in …'. The play was set sometime in the near future, when, with war impending, a League of Peace opposes 'to death any command of the Government opposed to the teaching of Christ'. It is lead by a KC and a bishop, and opposed by the Prime Minister, Archbishop, and a 'Press Peer' who seek to discredit the KC and have the bishop certified insane. The melodrama emerges when the Prime Minister is about to broadcast to the nation, recommending war, and is attacked and shot by the bishop. The last act, set in the Old Bailey, is an emotive trial scene, full of exhortative speeches. 'We are not told the verdict,' noted Street. 'As before, I do not think it would be wise to interfere with the expression of opinion, however prejudiced, about the effect of capitalistic interests on war, or the identification of peace at whatever cost with the teaching of Christ as opposed to that of the Church. (The better argument that war will destroy civilisation does not occur to the author).' The play was a muddled charade drawing on elements of Billing's greatest moment. It was licensed, although there were objections from Geoffrey Harmsworth at *The Queen* ('The Lady's Newspaper') that the Rawleigh character was made up to look like his

---

[*] In 1931, twenty-three years after J.T. Grein's disastrous attempt, the People's National Theatre, which Grein had founded in 1923, produced *Salome* at the Savoy Theatre. Gray produced it in Cambridge later that same year, as did the Gate Theatre club.

uncle, Lord Northcliffe, who had recently died. The Lord Chamberlain's office also demanded the deletion of the phrase 'how the Government destroyed the political significance of the ex-service men's organisations after the last great war'. *High Treason* opened, fittingly, on 5 November 1928, at the Strand Theatre. It closed two weeks later.

But Billing saw more potential in his creation. So, apparently, did the experienced film director Maurice Elvey, for he persuaded Gaumont to fund a high-budget science fiction adaptation of *High Treason*, which was released, with a soundtrack, in 1929. Set in 1950, the film opens on a frontier post between the Federated States of Europe and the Atlantic States, manned by guards in uniforms evidently inspired by Mussolini: high-necked rubberised jackets and streamlined helmets seemingly made of plastic. An equally futurist-looking aerodynamic car with porthole-shaped windows draws up at the border. The references are to totalitarianism; at any moment one expects Hitler – or Billing, a much more handsome version of a dictator – to step out of the car, clad in a shiny uniform. Stylistically caught between *Metropolis* and *Things To Come*, this Wellsian vision of the future is full of Billing-like inventions: video-phones (complete with apologies for interference from onscreen operators); art deco TVs broadcasting 'Daily Television News'; and wall displays spelling out messages in electric lights. The star, Benita Hume, showers in a chrome and glass cubicle, then steps into a hot-air douche to dry off, before donning a close-fitting silver satin cap and a silver lamé coat-dress daringly split into broad ribbons. Hume plays Evelyn, daughter of Dr Seymour, Vicar General and leader of the World League of Peace, based in London and desperately trying to stop war between Britain and the Atlantic States. In New York, its Manhattan skyline buzzing with all manner of aeronautic technology, the enemy leaders watch live film of aerial dogfights and bombing of civilian cities – all seven years before the Spanish Civil War.

London too is a modern city, with helicopters and skyscrapers. Here Evelyn is torn between her fiancé, Michael Dane (played by Jameson Thomas), a dashing aeronaut (a Billing role) and her father. 'Will there be war?' asks Evelyn. 'Frankly no,' says Michael. 'Today people are too sensible.' 'That's what they said in 1914,' says Dr Seymour. But Evelyn fights for peace with the League, whose headquarters are staffed by white-clad women sporting enamel badges declaring 'Pax'. They are the heroines of the piece, and their role is evidence of Billing's surprisingly feminist outlook. He believed in the empowerment of women, and had done so since *Imperialist* times – possibly because he saw valuable support in a newly-enfranchised section of the population. The film of *High Treason* has a similar ending to Billing's play, with Dr Seymour killing the President of Europe to prevent him from declaring war. The world is saved – but

Seymour is still tried at the Old Bailey for high treason. This time, we are told the verdict: he is found guilty and receives the death sentence with heroic equanimity: 'I am content.' Despite its lavish production values, the film did not fare well at the box office; perhaps its message was too fantastic for film-goers in 1929.

Billing turned to other ventures. In the early Thirties he went to America, to revive his idea for a casino in Mexico, in partnership with Jack Dempsey. It did not fare well, and Billing returned to England, where he took over the Royal Court Theatre and managed it as a cinema. It was an ironic gesture, for the theatre was the site of the 1918 *Salome* and venue for the Cult of the Clitoris. Billing's two great loves of his youth held his interest throughout the Thirties. By 1935 he estimated his inventions to number five hundred, among them a two-sided stove and a miniature camera; while he applied these talents to his other obsession, renewing his crusade for air power with increasing seriousness as war with Germany crept closer. In 1934 he invented the Durotofin, a full-scale version of the helicopter which appeared in *High Treason*, a single-wing craft with two sets of paddle-wheel blades which, its inventor and the popular press proclaimed, would enable it to fly backwards. This claim went untested, as the aircraft never got beyond model stage. By 1939, Billing was writing long pieces for the press on British air power. But he was also in the papers that year for a different reason. In an attempt to re-enter politics, Billing contested the Hornsey by-election. He alleged that his opponent, Captain L.D. Gammans, while campaigning from a broadcasting van outside the Green Man pub in Muswell Hill, had said: 'A vote for me is a vote for Churchill, but a vote for Pemberton-Billing is a vote for Hitler.' Ever ready to have recourse to the courts, Billing sued for libel. Gammans told the court that on the day in question he was nowhere within 20 miles of the Green Man. Mr Justice Birkett found for Captain Gammans, with costs.

Billing remained resolutely high profile in the early years of the war – in 1940 he produced plans for a pilotless flying-bomb, which foreshadowed the German 'doodle-bugs' – and his gospel of air power was vindicated by the triumph of the Battle of Britain. That victory may have been one reason why the *Sunday Dispatch* allotted him two full pages in January and February 1941 to air his views on 'We Need Bombs – Not Bayonets' and 'How to Get 100,000 Bombers by Noel Pemberton-Billing, Pioneer Airman and, as an ex-MP, one of the most Outstanding Figures of the Last War'. This perhaps ambiguous accolade was printed alongside a photograph of the author in his favourite pose: monocle firmly in place, a pensive but commanding index finger to his forehead, his image as manicured as ever. But Billing's most valuable contribution to the war effort dated back, like his infamy, to the previous war, as the Supermarine factory he had founded in 1914 went on to develop and manufacture the Spitfire. At sixty years of age, Billing could claim some degree of aeronautical prescience: in 1941 he published *The Aeroplane of Tomorrow*, an authoritative technical study, arguing for the future use of jet propulsion. He died on 11 November 1948 in Burnham-on-Crouch in Essex, where he had been a keen sailor. He left his second wife, Elsie Veronica (Lilian died in 1923), a son, Robin, a daughter, Ursula, and £13,813.13s. His will divided his estate between his family and his chauffeur, Edward Reed, with a percentage to the 'very poor and needy' of London. Even in death, Billing was determined to strike a dramatic note: 'I order that after my death my body be cremated after a doctor has opened a vein in my body and that my ashes be cast to the winds.'

Billing's obituaries focused on his notorious Parliamentary career; tributes preferred to dwell on his colourful life of invention. Alan Tompkins, who had worked with him, noted that the obituaries to his friend did not 'do justice to his true mechanical genius. This genius was often dissipated as his darting mind turned restlessly to new ideas. He would toil like a maniac on a promising idea, and then drop it cold for no reason other than it bored him ... Early in the war he made large models of six different slip-wing warplanes, to take off with great loads and then fly fast. "For heaven's sake, you confuse everybody," I said. "Why don't you take the best and stick with it?" ... In 1942 he told me that his patents exceeded 2,000 ... His old friend C.G. Grey agrees with me that it is a national disaster that nobody could manage "P.B." If only we could have selected his inventions, and exercised a little control over that brave, flashing mind, he would have ranked in the eyes of the world with Edison, Parsons and Fleming.'

But the fact is that no one could manage Billing, nor did he wish to be managed. Maverick to the last, he remained fiercely, perhaps pathologically independent, determined to carve out a niche for himself. His campaign was ridiculous, prejudiced, laughable even; yet Billing believed it, believed that society was threatened by perversion and that it was his duty to fight it. In that he was an honourable man, for all his dishonourable ways. He left behind an extraordinary story and not entirely desirable legacy; but there is something in his character which, despite his appalling prejudices, conceits and delusions, makes him almost endearing, a true English eccentric.

11

Ain't We Got Fun

Nicole glanced again at the woman across the deck – she was fragile, tubercular – it was incredible that such narrow shoulders, such puny arms could bear aloft the pennon of decadence, last ensign of the fading empire. Her resemblance was rather to one of John Held's flat-chested flappers than to the hierarchy of tall languid blondes who had posed for painters and novelists since before the war ... They moved into the dining salon and Dick was placed next to Lady Caroline. Nicole saw that his usually ruddy face was drained of blood; he talked in a dogmatic voice, of which only snatches reached Nicole:

'... It's all right for you English, you're doing a dance of death ... Sepoys in the ruined fort, I mean Sepoys at the gate and gaiety in the fort and all that. The green hat, the crushed hat, no future.'

F. Scott Fitzgerald, *Tender Is The Night*

A choice of inheritance faced the new post-war generation: the political problems and psychological horrors of what they saw as a mismanaged war; or the decadent spirit that its puritans had sought to eliminate. For a certain elite – and those who followed them – there was no contest. In the cultural aftermath of the war, the aesthetes won their battle with the hearties. In the 1920s, the rarefied hothouses of Oxford and Cambridge would breed a new society determined to take the blessed Oscar as a martyr, and subvert the values which had allowed the war to happen. Brian Howard and Harold Acton led this new movement of decadence at Oxford; elsewhere, Wilde lived on in the literary antics of the Sitwells, the neo-baroque stylism of Cecil Beaton and Rex Whistler, and in the truly Firbankian figure of the androgynous Stephen Tennant, youngest and most narcissistic son of the Glenconners, lover to Siegfried Sassoon. The death knell of pre-war values was sounded when Sassoon, the decorated war hero, was sent back to their hotel room by the decorative aesthete to fetch his pearls.

It was one of the 'dark flowers' of Bloomsbury who heralded this new post-war era in 1919, and provided a connexion with the old. Lytton Strachey's 'satirically post-war' *Eminent Victorians* was, with its 'mannered prose style, its studied paradoxes, and its arch rhetorical questions ... more *fin de siècle* than *fin de guerre*, the languidly ironical work of a latter-day Oscar Wilde,' writes Samuel Hynes. 'Strachey certainly belonged to that "decadent" opposition that had persisted through the war in spite of the outcries of patriots.' It was Strachey who, when asked why he was not fighting for civilisation, replied, 'I am the civilisation for which you are fighting,' a remark worthy of Wilde in its arrogant wit; and who echoed Firbank in his effete, subversive *double entendre* when asked what would he do if a Hun were attempting to rape his sister: 'I should try to insert my person between them.' Strachey's caricature biographies satirised the Victorian values that had led to war. Strachey's stance was followed by Harold Acton and the Sitwells' championing of Victoriana – a precisely perverse gesture.

It was as if Oscar had never died; as if he had survived to cast a world-weary, cynical eye over the war, and beyond. To a generation who had grown up during the war, the Billing trial was a tantalising introduction to Wilde's unnamed crimes, another focus for their generational discontent. Indeed, critical members of the Twenties tendency had direct links with the Billing affair: Nancy Mitford's father-in-law had been accused as one of the 47,000, as had Evelyn Waugh's; Stephen Tennant was Margot Asquith's nephew. The aesthetes of the Twenties re-ran the Nineties, adding their own ironic overlay: Acton and Howard, Waugh and Mitford, Tennant and Beaton recreated themselves out of Wilde and Firbank, products of Decadence meeting the Modern Era. Far from purging the country of such tendencies, the war had provided the catalyst for this recreation. Just as the disturbed soil of the scarred and bloodied battlefields of the Western Front threw up exquisite red poppies (cousins of *papaver somniferum*, the opium poppy), so its aftermath proved a fertile ground for a new inflorescence of decadent behaviour. Their ironical, knowing version was informed by the true death and decay with which the old Decadents – much attracted to fantasy notions of that sensibility – had come face to face. The rebellion of their modern incarnations was empowered by the wrongs done to Wilde, and the wrongs done to the generation in between: the golden youth who had perished on the fields of France. Now they had the upper hand. Just as Billing's Vigilantes became Mosley's Blackshirts, so the Corrupt Coterie became the Bright Young People.

In London, the cult of youth thrived. Dance clubs sprang up everywhere, both legal and illegal. Mrs Meyrick's frequent brushes with the law over her series of more or less illicit nightclubs embodied the confrontations of the period, yet more so when Joynson-Hicks installed himself as moralistic Home Secretary. The moral panics of wartime mushroomed; sex, race and subculture were the new concerns. Drug scares heightened with the cocaine suicide of the flapper Freda Kempson in 1922, linked to a shady Chinese supplier and impresario, Brilliant Chang, the emblematic Dope King and white slaver, corrupter of British maidenhood. The tabloids ran stories on 'Cocaine Girls in the West End' and dark dancing dens in industrial warehouses, 'decorated on the incoherent Futurist lines usual in such places'. Here 'carefully admitted' crowds experienced feverish excitement, provided by bands which 'crashed out a really good foxtrot' and blue glass bottles or paper wraps full of cocaine. The sexual prejudices and fantasies of the Billing trial were flagrantly affronted, as if the new generation sought perversely to prove its 'perversion'. In certain circles, it was not only fashionable but almost *de rigueur* to be homosexual, or at least look it. 'So long as one acted consistently in accordance with one's personal hypothesis, and was not ashamed of what one did, all was all ...' wrote Robert Graves and Alan Hodge in *The Long Weekend*. 'When anti-French feeling in 1922 caused a revulsion in favour of the poor downtrodden Germans, the more openly practised homosexuality of Berlin seemed brave and honest: in certain Berlin dancing-halls, it was pointed out, women danced only with women and men with men. Germany land of the free! The Lesbians took heart and followed suit, first in Chelsea and St John's Wood and then in the less exotic suburbs of London.' Later, Isherwood, Auden and Spender would decamp to Berlin in search of sex, decadence, and liberation.

The decadent image was passed from the aristocratic Bright Young People to the new middle class via the adeptly propagated image of Noel Coward, photographed in bed in his Ebury Street attic, surrounded by satin cushions and sheets, chatting blithely on the telephone, looking like 'an advanced Chinese decadent in the last phases of dope'. Coward succeeded where Wilde had failed; the times were more propitious, and he and his generation gained from Oscar's martyrdom. While flappers took their cue from female liberation and the German *backfisch*, 'a compromise between pederasty and normal sex', men wore wasp-waisted suits, suede shoes and even the most masculine affected a languid Cowardian pose. 'I am never out of opium dens, cocaine dens, and other evil places,' Coward told the press. 'My mind is a mass of corruption.' His public profile capitalised on the private image already set by Wilde's heirs.

Yet the sexually inverted were still legally proscribed, and in ordinary homes, to speak the name of the man who spoke the name of the love that would not speak its name remained a mortal sin. John Lehmann, an Eton contemporary of Acton, Connolly and Powell, recalled the day that the headmaster, Cyril Al-ington, 'a man who delighted in intellectual surprises and paradox', took as the text for his Chapel sermon Wilde's 'The Happy Prince'. 'When the name of the prisoner of Reading Gaol boomed forth in those hallowed surroundings one could immediately sense the change in the atmosphere. Scarcely any boy dared to look at the opposite pews except in a glazed, rigid way; jaws were clenched, and blushes mounted involuntarily to innumerable cheeks. It was a moment of horror and panic: no one knew what was coming next, and everyone was thinking exactly the same thing. Luxmoore cleared his throat like a thunder-clap, and the ancient Dames in their traditional pews bowed their heads – as if about to be executed. Only Sir Galahad continued to look soulfully out of Watts's picture up near the altar, with a gentle feminine innocence.'

The legacy of prejudice produced more tangible danger, as fascism – a result of sexual repression, if Jung's theories were to be believed (and in an age obsessed with psychology, they frequently were) – took hold; even, ironically, among the very representatives of decadence who had been threatened by the Billing affair. The modern artists who had been regarded by the right as morally corrupt now mixed dangerously with politics, and while Constructivism celebrated Russian communism, Marinetti's Futurism virtually deified Mussolini. In Britain as elsewhere, absolute idealism had its appeal to aesthetes. In 1931, Osbert Sitwell supported Oswald Mosley's New Party – the right-wing precursor of his British Union of Fascists – throwing open Renishaw, the Sitwells' house, for its launch party.

Sitwell only brushed against fascism; other British aristocrats were more tangibly involved. The Duke of Windsor and others of the elite continued the cross-Continental tradition between Britain and Germany that saw more in common in right-wing fundamental nationalism than in international liberalism. The mixture of aristocracy and politics provided yet another irony: that the fascism for which the Billing affair had played the role of midwife should result in an ultimately deadly decadence. Rather than creating a pure Reich out of a Weimar Germany almost glorifying in its hedonistic allure, the Nazi hierarchy would exhibit every symptom of decadence. When the drug-addicted Goering was arrested in 1945, his fingernails were varnished red; on being strip-searched, it was discovered his toenails were painted, too. To the puritans of 1914, it was a logical progression of Teutonic perversion. The image of the languid, drugged aesthete merged with that of the blond beast in fascism's most egregious manifestation. In ironic ways he could never have predicted, history seemed to vindicate Billing's campaign at every turn. His personal cult and preoccupations had evoked those of the age.

The fear of decadence is the fear – and fascination – of the other. It is a fantasy fear of letting go, of the abandonment of principle. In that it is an essentially middle-class fear, for the upper classes with their privilege – literally, private law – were answerable to no one, while the working class were both expendable and by tradition prone to vice. Billing represented the voice of the outraged British middle class, the defining voice of our era, the voice that calls for punitive measures against anything that threatens its own status quo. In the history of the Billing affair is reflected the sway of middle-class sensibility, and all the safety, reason, and stability that it represents. On the other side is chaos, libertinism, vice, danger and the unknown. And the unknown will always remain so to those who do not choose to explore it.

Source Notes

The *Verbatim Report* of the Billing trial, drawing on the official court record and published by the Vigilante Society, is the most complete source for the courtroom dialogue, although not necessarily the most reliable. Contemporary newspaper reports supply more detail, as Mr Billing himself noted:

> It may perhaps be worth remarking that in a Verbatim Report thus officially furnished there are not provided those keys to individual and public temper which in the familiar press reports are usually supplied by parenthetical adjectives and nouns, and therefore that such helps to the imagination as '(sarcastically)' '(warmly)' '(great sensation)' and so forth, must be supplied by the reader's own imagination. [*Verbatim Report*, p. ix]

In order to give a rounded account of the trial, I have used the *Verbatim Report*, Michael Kettle's authoritative narrative, press reports, and the colourful commentary published in the pages of the *Vigilante* – a commentary which, like the rest of that journal's editorial, leaves little to its reader's imagination.

1 'There exists ...' *Imperialist*, 26 January 1918

1 'driving at excessive speed ...' Michael Kettle, *Salome's Last Veil*, Hart-Davis/Granada, London 1977, p. 3

1 'the laughter of fools' ibid.

5 '... was a matter ...' Samuel Hynes, *A War Imagined*, Bodley Head, London 1990, pp. 250-1

6 'Night by night ...' Osbert Sitwell, *Great Morning*, Macmillan, London 1948, p. 230

7 'The great galas ...' Harold Acton, *Memoirs of An Aesthete*, Methuen, London 1948, p. 37

8 'anticipated in the ...' Richard Cork, *Art Beyond the Gallery*, Yale University Press, New Haven & London, 1985, p. 209

8 'Kill John Bull ...' *The Outlook*, 18 July 1914

8 'third generation type ...' Miriam Benkowitz, *Ronald Firbank*, Weidenfeld & Nicolson, London 1970, jacket copy

8 'There was amongst ...' Diana Cooper, *The Rainbow Comes and Goes*, Rupert Hart-Davis, London 1958, p. 82

9 'Our generation becomes ...' Artemis Cooper, *The Diana Cooper Scrapbooks*, Hamish Hamilton, London 1987, p. 49

9 'charmingly bored ...' Martin Green, *Children of the Sun*, Basic Books, New York 1976, p. 40

9 'handsome young men ...' ibid.

9 '... I really think ...' ibid.

9 'I would fly ...' Cooper, *Rainbow*, p. 129

9 'The young were ...' ibid., pp. 142-3

10 'low-ceilinged nightclub ...' Sitwell, *Great Morning*, p. 208

10 'a place given ...' Cork, *Art Beyond*, p. 61

10 'super-heated Vorticist ...' Sitwell, *Great Morning*, p. 208

10 'Exotic gentlemen sang ...' Cork, *Art Beyond*, p. 105

10 'London is in ...' ibid., p. 113

10 'A very bad fellow ...' Marek Kohn, *Dope Girls: The Birth of the British Drug Underground*, Lawrence & Wishart, London 1992, p. 32

11 'Lady Cunard dead ...' Anne Chisholm, *Nancy Cunard*, Sidgwick & Jackson, London 1979, p. 31

11 'calculated to jeopardise ...' Defence of the Realm Act, 1914, Chapter 29 1.a

12 'Duke's daughters ...' Caroline E. Playne, *Society at War*, Allen & Unwin, London 1931, p. 239

12 'Irene's ... "dash ..." ' Lady Cynthia Asquith, *Diaries 1915-18*, Hutchinson, London 1968, p. 421

12 'And after the Grafton ...' Caroline E. Playne, *Britain Holds On*, Allen & Unwin, London 1933, pp. 236-7

13 'War is the great scavenger ...' Hynes, *War Imagined*, p. 12

13 'from the gloomy ...' ibid., p. 35

13 'It was high time ...' ibid., p. 58

14 'Modernist Berlin ....' Paul Delaney, *The Neo-Pagans: Friendship and Love in the Rupert Brooke Circle*, Macmillan, London 1981, p. 184

14 'Ornament of the ...' Dominic Hibberd, *Wilfred Owen: The Last Year*, Constable, London 1992, p. 8

14 'perhaps the most ...' ibid.

14 'perceptibly provincial' Jon Stallworthy,

Wilfred Owen: A Biography, Oxford University Press and Chatto & Windus, London 1974, p. 205

15 'very tall ...' Hibberd, *Owen*, p. 40

15 'Why shouldn't you ...' ibid., p. 56

15 'I was a man ...' *De Profundis*, Oscar Wilde, *Selected Works*, ed. Richard Aldington, William Heinemann, London 1946, p. 441

15 'What must have astonished ...' Richard Ellman, *Oscar Wilde*, Hamish Hamilton, London 1989, p. 259

16 'an amusing little queen ...' Rupert Croft-Cooke, *Bosie: The Story of Lord Alfred Douglas, his friends and enemies*, W.H. Allen, London 1963, p. 49

16 'all young queers ...' ibid., p. 50

16 'I am dying ...' Ellman, *Wilde*, p. 545

16 'flush rosily like ...' Croft-Cooke, *Bosie*, pp. 300-1

17 'a new sense of liberation ...' John R. Bradley, *Independent on Sunday*, 22 September 1996

17 'One of the greatest ...' Maureen Borland, *Wilde's Devoted Friend: The Life of Robert Ross*, Lennard, Oxford 1990, p. 115

17 'English criticism ...' ibid., p. 119

17 'an unsavoury person' Croft-Cooke, *Bosie*, p. 224

17 'conceived a distaste ...' ibid.

18 'I no longer care ...' ibid., p. 225

18 'bogus telegram ...' Max Beerbohm, *Letters to Reggie Turner*, ed. Rupert Hart-Davis, London 1964, 3 June 1913

18 'frequent and crushing' Croft-Cooke, *Bosie*, p. 242

18 'With regard to ...' ibid., p. 243

19 'the High Priest ...' ibid., p. 247

19 'My name being ...' Robert Ross to Lady Phillips, 18 July 1913, Johannesburg Art Gallery

19 'villany ...' Croft-Cooke, *Bosie*, pp. 253-5

20 'to have it out' Borland, *Wilde's Devoted Friend*, p. 200

20 'while he could ...' ibid., pp. 199-200

20 'having committed ...' Croft-Cooke, *Bosie*, p. 257

21 'various terms ...' Marie Belloc Lowndes, *A Passing World*, Macmillan, London 1948, pp. 178-9

21 'the case could ...' Croft-Cooke, *Bosie*, p. 271

21 'at which twenty ...' ibid., p. 272

21 'man of letters ...' ibid., p. 276

22 'Blackness descends ...' Lord Alfred Douglas, 'To A Certain Judge', pamphlet, Robert Dawson & Sons, Galashiels, Scotland 1915 (British Library)

22 'But times have changed ...' Lord Alfred Douglas, *The Rossiad*, Robert Dawson &

Sons, Galashiels, Scotland 1916 (British Library)

22 *n* 'a pillar of ...' Ruth Hall, *Marie Stopes*, Andre Deutsch, London 1977, p. 125

24 'intense love ...' Belloc Lowndes, *Passing World*, p. 210

24 'I and my work ...' Hibberd, *Owen*, p. 61

24 'bravely obscene ...' Paul Fussell, *The Great War and Modern Memory*, OUP, Oxford & London 1975, p. 297

24 'the whole of civilisation ...' Stallworthy, *Owen*, p. 258

25 'hurried, harried city ...' Benkovitz, *Firbank*, p. 144

25 'in the best sense ...' Osbert Sitwell, Introduction to Ronald Firbank, *Five Novels*, Duckworth, London 1949, p. xiii

25 'You pretty little bastard ...' Bryan Connon, *Beverley Nichols*, Constable, London 1991, p. 40

26 'to act as a sort of ...' ibid., pp. 54-5

26 'prodigious drinking ...' ibid., p. 56

26 'presumably because ...' ibid., p. 57

26 'People were saying ...' ibid., pp. 61-2

26 'to make urban life ...' Patrick Higgins, *Heterosexual Dictatorship*, Fourth Estate, London 1996, p. 90

26 'home-front war ...' Hynes, *War Imagined*, p. 223

27 'When we hear ...' ibid., p. 223

27 'huge, brutal ...' ibid., p. 224

28 'It is a misdemeanour ...' ibid., pp. 224-5

28 'homosexualism ...' ibid., p. 225

28 'Two ideas ...' ibid., pp. 225-6

29 'smoothness of shoulders ...' Sitwell, *Great Morning*, p. 11

29 'My dear ...' Michael Davidson, *The World, the Flesh and Myself*, Gay Men's Press, London 1983, p. 134

29 'the nation's pleasure ground' Higgins, *Heterosexual Dictatorship*, p. 91

29 'it was ridiculously ...' L.E.O. Charlton, *Charlton*, Faber & Faber, London 1931, p. 241

29 'young officers ...' ibid., pp. 244-5

30 'musical parties' Noel Coward, *Present Indicative*, Heinemann, London 1937, p. 116

31 'urning' Christina Wolff, *Magnus Hirschfeld: A Portrait of a Pioneer in Sexology*, Quartet, London 1986, p. 33

31 'leading newspapers ...' Magnus Hirschfeld (ed.) *The Sexual History of the World War*, Panurge Press, New York 1934, p. vii

31 'even unattractive men ...' ibid., p. 195

31 'We may assume ...' ibid., p. 49

31 'camp-follower ...' Kohn, *Dope Girls*, p. 30

31 'Men and women ...' *Weekly Dispatch*, 3 June 1917, quoted Kohn, p. 51

31 'orgiastic outgrowths ...' Hirschfeld, *Sexual History*, p. 195

32 'Certain clubs ...' ibid., p. 203

32 'Decadence ...' *Chambers Twentieth Century Dictionary*, W & R Chambers, Edinburgh, nd, p. 238
32 'extremely common ...' Hirschfeld, *Sexual History*, p. 126
33 'homosexual soldiers ...' ibid., p. 130
33 'that a bullet ...' ibid., pp. 127-8
33 'the native population ...' ibid., pp. 132-3
33 'Despite my respectable size ...' ibid., pp. 133-4
34 'very masculine ...' ibid., p. 139
34 'to find death ...' ibid., p. 139
34 'nigger-dancing' Kohn, *Dope Girls*, p. 107
34 'Until World War I ...' George Chauncey, *Gay New York*, Basic Books, New York 1994, p. 140
35 'As the war progressed ...' ibid., p. 143
36 'Morphia dulled the agony ...' Philip Ziegler, *Diana Cooper*, Hamish Hamilton, London 1981, p. 55
36 'I see that other people ...' Kohn, *Dope Girls*, p. 31
36 'The Cocaine Curse ...' ibid., p. 40
37 'Vicious Drug Powder ...' ibid., p. 41
37 'retailers of ...' ibid., p. 43
37 'barbitone, benzamine ...' *The Times*, 8 June 1918
38 'disgusting orgies ...' *The Times*, 14 December 1918
39 'The clergy could help ...' ibid.
39 'sensual-coloured carpets ...' Kohn, *Dope Girls*, p. 106
39 'London's greatest thrill ...' Cynthia Asquith, *Diaries*, p. 459
39 'Doping is quite a hobby ...' Philip Hoare, *Noel Coward*, Sinclair-Stevenson, London 1995, p. 75
42 '... that huge thunderstorm ...' Siegfried Sassoon, 'News From the Front', quoted Hibberd, *Owen*, p. 39
42 'not so much ...' George Painter, *Marcel Proust*, Volume II, Chatto & Windus, London 1965, p. 106
42 'my soulmate ...' Neil Miller, *Out of the Past*, Vintage, London 1995, p. 120
42 'leader of ...' ibid., p. 119
42 'The wretched Eulenburg ...' Painter, *Proust*, p. 106
43 'prided himself ...' ibid.
43 'Yet I must place ...' Higgins, *Heterosexual Dictatorship*, p. 84
44 'my fighting principles ...' Noel Pemberton Billing, *'P.B.'– The Story of His Life*, Imperialist Press, Hertford 1917, p. 1
44 'a peculiarly offensive ...' ibid., p. 14
44 'There was a good deal ...' ibid., p. 19
44 'obsessed with the ...' ibid., p. 24
45 'little brick dairies ...' ibid., p. 39
45 'man-lifting glider' C.F. Andrews & E.B. Morgan, *Supermarine Aircraft Since 1914*, Putnam, London, 1981, p. 1

46 'which, remembering ...' Billing, *'P.B.'*, p. 69
46 'Oh, those buccaneer days!' ibid., p. 75
46 'There was only one ...' *Reader's World*, 24 September 1959
47 'a boat that will fly ...' Gordon Mitchell (ed.) *R.G. Mitchell*, Nelson & Saunders, London 1986, p. 114
47 'a bewildering series ...' *Supermarine Aircraft*, p. 17
47 'alert Germans' Billing, *'P.B.'*, p. 82
47 'It's a dangerous thing ...' ibid., p. 85
48 'It had now become ...' *Supermarine Aircraft*, p. 16
48 'had long considered ...' Billing, *'P.B.'*, p. 98
48 'in support of strong ....' *Supermarine Aircraft*, p. 16
48 'What a political education ...' Billing, *'P.B.'*, p. 104
48 'went off in a huff ...' *Supermarine Aircraft*, p. 17
48 'a certain London daily ...' Billing, *'P.B.'*, p. 107
48 'in accordance with ...' ibid., p. 75
49 'My first sensation ...' ibid., p. 114
49 'in fulfilment of ...' ibid., p. 146
49 'I don't wish to touch ...' *Hansard*, 22 March 1916
50 'Mr Billing as Inventor ...' unsourced newspaper cutting, 19 April 1916
50 'Mr Pemberton Billing's air policy ...' *Daily Mail*, 1 May 1916
51 'This man is dangerous ...' Kettle, p. 3
51 'fascinated by fast aircraft ....' ibid.
51 'unusual clothes' Croft-Cooke, *Bosie*, p. 285
51 'without the usual ...' *Evening Standard*, 27 August 1951
51 'If the gallant member ...' *Reader's World*, 24 September 1959
52 'social tensions ...' Richard Thurlow, *Fascism in Britain, A History 1918-1985*, Basil Blackwell, London 1987, p. 1
53 'farrago of nonsense' Kenneth Lunn & Richard C. Thurlow (ed.) *British Fascism*, Croom Hill, London 1980, p. 37
53 'it was suggested ...' *The Times*, 26 October 1917
53 'the promotion of purity ...' *Vigilante*, 2 March 1918
54 'In South Africa ...' Thurlow, *Fascism in Britain*, p. 68
54 'the "flapper" scandal ...' *Imperialist*, 25 November 1916
55 'Hinder the Huns ...' ibid.
55 'On Friday night ...' ibid.
55 'international expert ...' Kettle, p. 4
56 'Of the vices ...'ibid., p. 4
56 'Weininger's theory ....' ibid., pp. 5-6

57 'There exists ...' *Imperialist*, 26 January 1918

57 'Paphian – *adj* ....' *Chambers Twentieth Century Dictionary*, Edinburgh 1983, p. 918

58 'thrilled' Cynthia Asquith, *Diaries*, p. 150

59 'repeatedly urged ...' *Verbatim Report of the Trial of Noel Pemberton Billing MP on a Charge of the Criminal Libel before Mr Justice Darling at the Central Criminal Court, Old Bailey* (With a report of the preliminary proceedings at Bow Street Police Court, an Appendix of Documents referred to in the Case, Reference Index, etc), published by subscription only, London 'Vigilante' Office, 5 St James' Place SW1 1918, p. vii

59 'Isaacs, Aitken ...' *Vigilante*, 9 February 1918

59 'The Ibsen movement ...' Croft-Cooke, *Bosie*, p. 283

60 'a wretched deplorable ...' *The Concise Oxford Companion to the Theatre*, Oxford University Press, Oxford & London 1972, p. 486

60 'modern ...' Croft-Cooke, *Bosie*, p. 284

60 'cherished dreams ...' Michael Orme, *J.T. The Story of a Pioneer 1862-1935*, John Murray, London 1936, pp. 167-8

60 'as familiar ....' ibid., p. 320

61 'Permission to do ...' ibid., p. 258

61 'immensely impressed ...' ibid., p. 197

61 'finest dramatic work ...' Borland, *Wilde's Devoted Friend*, p. 103

61 'saw no reason ...' ibid., p. 278

61 'a burlesque dance ...' ibid., p. 149

61 'Wilde was in eclipse ...' Croft-Cooke, *Bosie*, p. 285

61 'that George Street ...' Wilde, *De Profundis, Collected Works*, p. 440

61 'It is hardly necessary ...' George S. Street, reader's report to the Lord Chamberlain, April 1918, Lord Chamberlain's Papers, British Library

63 'In reporting ...' Lord Sandhurst, 6 April 1918, ibid.

66 'As his mother ...' Felix Cherniavsky, *The Salome Dancer*, McClelland & Stewart, Toronto 1991, p. 35

66 'found under ...' ibid., p. 32

66 'the muscles ...' ibid., p. 36

66 'mad family ...' ibid., p. 35

66 'the hotbed of ....' ibid., p. 52

67 '*psycho mania* ...' ibid., p. 54

68 'Ha! Ha! ...' ibid., p. 85

68 'instead of ....' ibid., p. 87

68 'a few tunes ...' ibid., p. 106

68 'alleged expressions ...' ibid., p. 107

68 'in which he ...' ibid., p. 108

69 'for fear of ...' ibid., p. 112

69 'You have ...' ibid., p. 118

70 'albeit untrained ...' ibid., p. 124

71 'an exponent ...' ibid., p. 231

71 Many people think ...' ibid., p. 133

71 'I wonder how ...' ibid., p. 135

71 'those who would ...' ibid., p. 134

71 'greater musical talent ...' ibid., p. 137

73 'never considered ...' Hesketh Pearson, *The Life of Oscar Wilde*, Penguin, London 1960, p. 229

73 'bound in "Tyrian purple" ....' Ellman, *Wilde*, p. 353

73 'a dish of gravy' Cooper, *Rainbow*, p. 88

73 'by the end ...' Cherniavsky, p. 142

74 'sent the city ...' Alessandra Comini, *Gustav Klimt*, Thames & Hudson, London 1975, p. 9

74 'It is as if ...' Cherniavsky, pp. 160-1

74 'scion of one ...' ibid.' p. 145

75 'To Maud Allan ...' ibid., pp. 146-7

75 'most intense ...' ibid., p. 147

75 'and, more forcefully ...' ibid., p. 142

76 'I had been told ...' ibid., p. 153

76 '... Miss Allan ...' ibid., p. 163

77 'reincarnation of ...' ibid., p. 164

77 'absolutely free ...' ibid.

77 'One moment she is ...' ibid., p. 165

77 'only her intensely ...' ibid., pp. 165-6

77 'muscular Christianity' ibid., p. 168

78 'She dances like ...' ibid., p. 171

78 'But your brother ...' ibid., p. 20

78 'with a rechauffé ...' ibid., p. 173

79 'really exquisite ...' Benkovitz, *Firbank*, p. 110

79 'So many interesting ...' ibid., p. 111

79 'white and very well ...' ibid., p. 112

79 'massacre of flowers ...' ibid., p. 111

79 'Have you anything ...' Brigid Brophy, *Prancing Novelist: In Praise of Ronald Firbank*, Macmillan, London 1973, p. 382

79 'moralised and *sans* ...' ibid., p. 305

79 'It was about ...' Benkovitz, *Firbank*, p. 115

79 'in the band of ...' *Leader*, 24 February 1945

80 'She can now sign ...' Cherniavsky, p. 173

80 'to watch and learn ...' Cooper, *Rainbow*, pp. 87-8

80 'a refreshingly deviant ...' Cherniavsky, p. 174

80 *n* 'a journal for saints ...' Kohn, *Dope Girls*, p. 132

80 *n* 'it is interesting ...' Peter Burton, introduction, E.F. Benson, *The Inheritors*, Millivres, London 1993

80 'taken very good care ...' Charles A'Court Repington, *The First World War*, Constable, London 1920, Volume I, p. 399

81 'Each of the ladies ...' *New York Times*, 8 August 1908, quoted Cherniavsky, p. 176

81 'is not only ...' *New York Times* 16 August 1908, quoted Julie Wheelwright, *The Fatal Lover*, Collins & Brown, London 1992, p. 22

83 'throughout the history ...' Tim O'Neill,

'The Erotic Freemasonry of Count Nicholas von Zinzendorf, *Secret and Suppressed: Banned Ideas & Hidden History*, ed. Jim Keith, Feral House, Portland 1993, p. 103

83 & *n* 'underground of rejected ...' Richard Thurlow, 'The Return of Jeremiah', Lunn & Thurlow, *British Fascism*, p. 101

84 'the current evil ...' Cherniavsky, p. 185

84 'If people want ...' ibid., p. 186

84 'should be followed ...' ibid., p. 185

84 'a red-letter day ...' *Daily Telegraph*, 22 May 1909

85 'only a shade ...' Cherniavsky, p. 179

86 'famous for his ...' Cynthia Asquith, *Diaries*, p. 486

86 'because she mistook ...' Cherniavsky, p. 183

87 'monotonous ...' ibid., p. 193

87 'a picturesque quality ...' ibid.

87 'New York has ...' ibid., p. 229

87 'Take me to ...' ibid., p. 197

87 '*des raisons* ...' ibid., p. 202

87 'rich native ...' *Daily Mail*, 6 September 1918

88 'ranged from ...' Cherniavsky, p. 239

88 'little symphony ...' ibid., p. 240

89 'the Spanish dances ...' *Sunday Times*, 30 June 1912, quoted Cork, *Art Beyond*, p. 105

89 'The papers announced ...' Orme, *J.T.*, p. 258

89 'Grein ... seems ...' Croft-Cooke, *Bosie*, p. 285

90 'Dear Mr Billing ...' *Verbatim Report*, appendix

90 'Excuse me, Sir ...' William Rothstein, *Men and Memories*, Volume I, Faber & Faber, London 1931, quoted *Selected Works of Wilde*, p. 529

90 'incautious humour ...' Borland, *Wilde's Devoted Friend*, p. 277

90 'the outline of ...' Kettle, p. 18

91 'To be a member ...' *Vigilante*, 16 February 1918

91 'manifestly obscene' Kettle, p. 19

91 'the mysterious influence ...' Hansard, 1918, 78-79 [103]

91 'until all British ...' ibid. 918 [103]

92 'there is a kind ...' Croft-Cooke, *Bosie*, p. 301

92 'There are always ...' ibid., p. 304

92 'boldly takes up ...' *Vigilante*, 23 February 1918

92 'The German through ...' ibid., 23 March 1918

92 'slave labour ...' Hansard, 1918, 1549 [103]

93 'What is the matter ...' ibid., 1643 [104]

93 'No doubt ...' Borland, *Wilde's Devoted Friend*, p. 278

93 'When the paragraph ...' Orme, *J.T.*, p. 260

93 'initiated ...' Kettle, p. 20

94 'typical English ...' ibid., p. 21

94 'The Minister of Information ...' *Daily Mail*, 15 April 1918

94 'I expected this ...' Kettle, pp. 21-2

94 'Two Private Performances ...' *Verbatim Report*, appendix

95 'in a downpour ...' *World*, quoted Cherniavsky, p. 243

95 'a combination of ...' Ellman, *Wilde*, p. 413

95 'Is it a fact ...' *Daily Mail*, 8 April 1918

96 'later used as ...' Wheelwright, *Fatal Lover*, p. 18

96 'the Kaiser's ...' ibid., p. 113

96 'mass of heavy ...' ibid.

97 'The matinee ...' Orme, *J.T.*, pp. 262-3

97 '... a bizarre melodrama ...' *Morning Post*, 13 April 1918, quoted *Verbatim Report*, appendix

97 'This view ...' *The Stage*, 18 April 1918

98 'Are you of ...' *Daily Mail*, 15 April 1918

98 'the presentation of ...' *Vigilante*, 13 April 1918

98 'his own recognisance ...' *Daily Mail*, 15 April 1918

99 'The House of Windsor' *The Times*, 25 April 1918, quoted Kettle, p. 33

99 'spiritual home', ibid. p. 93 *n*

100 'undoubtedly Asquith's ...' ed. Susan Lownes-Marques, *Diaries & Letters of Marie Belloc Lowndes*, pp. 113-14

100 'cunning and serpentine ...' Kettle, p. 35

100 'distinct asset' ibid., p. 36

100 'our one and only ...' Repington, Vol. I, p. 462

100 'powerful-looking ...' Cynthia Asquith, *Diaries*, p. 171

101 'Wrote all day ...' Repington, *First World War*, Vol. I, pp. 467-8

101 'Lady Curzon ...' ibid., Vol. II, p. 299

101 'a sort of ...' Osbert Sitwell, *Laughter in the Next Room*, Macmillan, London 1950, pp. 104-5

101 'gay party ...' Repington, *First World War*, Vol. II, p. 314

101 'such a clever girl ...' ibid., p. 108

101 'another young fellow ...' ibid., p. 314

101 'Miss Daisy' ibid., p. 315

101 'no airs and graces ...' Borland, *Wilde's Devoted Friend*, p. 260

101 'Instead of discussing ...' Repington, *First World War*, Vol. II, p. 316

102 'more than mere ...' John Pearson, *Facades*, Macmillan, London 1978, pp. 105-6

102 'coddling the ...' Repington, *First World War*, Vol. II, p. 187

102 'I should deserve ...' ibid.

102 'many things ...' ibid., p. 196

102 'procrastination and ...' ibid., p. 197

102 'a sound thing ...' ibid.

103 'intriguing busily ...' Stephen Koss,

Asquith, Hamish Hamilton, London 1976, p. 232

103 'up and down Bond Street ...' Cynthia Asquith, *Diaries*, p. 438

103 'I was told this ...' Belloc Lowndes, *Passing World*, p. 81

103 'to smear various ...' Kettle, p. 46

104 'mysterious persons ...' ibid., p. 49

105 'kill' ibid., p. 50

105 'Dear Mr Pemberton-Billing ...' ibid.

106 'at a luncheon ...' *Daily Mail*, 4 June 1918

106 n 'the Snob Queers ...' Ellman, *Wilde*, p. 402

106 n 'talked a good deal ...' Susan Lowndes (ed.) *Diaries and Letters of Marie Belloc Lowndes, 1911-1947*, Chatto & Windus, London 1971, pp. 55-6

107 'I was instructed ...' *Verbatim Report*, pp. 479-80

107 'Mrs -- ...' Cynthia Asquith, *Diaries*, p. 448

108 'My political employers ...' *Verbatim Report*, p. 480

108 'Will history ever ...' Repington, *First World War*, Vol. II, p. 61

108 'misrepresented ...' Koss, *Asquith*, p. 233

109 'People do not ...' ibid.

109 'Noel Pemberton-Billing says ...' Kettle, p. 59

109 'the Saviour ...' ibid., p. 156

109 'who remarked ...' *Vigilante*, 6 April 1918

110 'All praise Priapus ...' ibid., 20 April 1918

111 'continued harassment ...' Borland, *Wilde's Devoted Friend*, pp. 278-9

111 n 'sodomites ...' Croft-Cooke, *Bosie*, p. 273

112 'a very delicately ...' information supplied by Mr Kenneth Rose

112 'there are a ...' Evelyn Graham, *Lord Darling's Famous Trials*, Hutchinson, London nd, p. 25

112 'Certainly in those ...' ibid., p. 36

112 'Tory job' ibid., p. 83

112 'particularly incensed' ibid., p. 81

112 'the worst woman ...' ibid., plate caption

113 'Who ...' Pearson, *Facades*, p. 92 n

113 'tinkling with bells' Graham, *Lord Darling*, p. 89

113 '... in the glossiest ...' ibid., p. 22

113 'a fashionable divorce ...' *Star*, 12 February 1959

114 'As a young officer ...' ibid.

114 'The fact that you ...' Kettle, p. 64

114 'There was a murmur ...' *Daily Mirror*, 30 May 1918

114 'Is that a photograph ...' Kettle, p. 66

115 'It was decided ...' ibid., p. 68

115 'The critics who ...' ibid., p. 69

115 'Did you ever ...' ibid., p. 70

115 n 'clitoris' *Evening Standard*, 27 August 1951

116 'I cannot be ...' ibid., pp. 76-7

116 'there are editions ...' ibid., p. 80

117 'I submit ...' ibid., pp. 81-2

117 'solely with ...' ibid., p. 86

117 'filled with ...' ibid., p. 85

118 'The Court was ...' Cherniavsky, p. 246

118 'Yes, he will ...' Kettle, p. 88

118 'no evidence ...' ibid., p. 89

118 'It will be ...' ibid., p. 90

118 'big, flat book' *Daily Mail*, 31 May 1918

118 'about that thickness ...' *Morning Post*, 31 May 1918

119 'Were you alone?' ibid.

119 'at a luncheon ...' Kettle, p. 91

119 'Are you acquainted ...' ibid., p. 92

119 'Is the paragraph ...' *Morning Post*, 31 May 1918

119 'the two holders ...' Kettle, p. 92

119 'I know nothing ...' ibid., pp. 92-3

120 'Mr Billing: "Is Justice Darling's ..." ' *Daily Mail*, 31 May 1918

120 'It can be produced?' Kettle, p. 93

120 'If it can be ...' *Daily Mail*, 31 May 1918

120 'My men ...' Kettle, p. 93

120 'Have you finished? ...' *Morning Post*, 31 May 1918

120 'I have not ...' Kettle, p. 94

120 'the dirty work ...' Koss, *Asquith*, p. 234

121 'The book is ...' Kettle, p. 95-6

121 'You stand down ...' *Morning Post*, 31 May 1918

122 'continue his work ...' Kettle, pp. 97-8

123 'If that occurs ... ibid., pp. 99-100

124 '... That shows ...' ibid., p. 101

124 'I shall not ...' *Morning Post*, 31 May 1918

124 'at the time ...' *Morning Post*, 31 May 1918

124 'very complicated ...' Kettle, pp. 103-4

126 'The attack was continued ...' *Morning Post*, 31 May 1918

126 'as to an anatomical ...' Kettle, p. 104

126 'You are going to ...' Miller, *Out of the Past*, p. 185

126 'passed for press ...' Kettle, pp. 105-6

127 'a lady' ibid.

127 I wish I were ...' Victoria Glendinning, *Vita*, Weidenfeld & Nicolson, London 1983, p. 92

127 'The persons ...' Kettle, *Salome's Last Veil*, p. 106

127 n 'he is endowed ...' Rupert Hart-Davis, *Hugh Walpole*, Macmillan, London 1952, p. 77

128 'Miss Daisy ...' Repington, *First World War*, Vol. II, p. 295

128 'You can only ...' Kettle, *Salome's Last Veil*, p. 107

128 'the state of affairs ...' ibid. pp. 110-11

128 *n* 'all the brilliant ...' Violet Trefusis, *Don't Look Round*, Hamish Hamilton, London 1952, p. 72

129 'Yes, it came ...' Kettle, p. 112

129 'They were very ...' *Morning Post*, 31 May 1918

129 'They said I was ...' Kettle, p. 112-14

130 'quieter work ...' ibid., pp. 114-16

130 'absolutely scandalous ...' Michael Occleshaw, *Armoured Against Fate*, Columbus Books, London 1989, p. 205

131 'either to dull ...' *Umpire*, 23 July 1916, quoted Kohn, *Dope Girls*, p. 41

131 'shy, sensitive ...' Occleshaw, *Armoured*, p. 205

132 'That is pure ...' Kettle, pp. 116-17

132 'You appreciate ...' ibid., pp. 118-19

133 'acquired ...' ibid., pp. 119-21

133 'another book ...' ibid., p. 122

133 'I put all ...' ibid., pp. 124-9

135 'Laughter in Court' *Morning Post*, 31 May 1918

137 'the anxiety about ...' Neville Lytton, *The Press and the General Staff*, Collins, London 1920, p. 175

137 'people who are ...' Kettle, pp. 131-4

138 'a considerable knowledge ...' ibid., p. 134

139 'What one did ...' ibid., pp. 136-7

139 'From certain ...' ibid., p. 138

140 'It stated that ...' *Daily Telegraph*, 1 June 1918

140 'by an officer ...' Kettle, pp. 139-40

140 'deep-laid plot ...' ibid., pp. 141-3

141 'In order to show ...' ibid., pp. 143-4

142 'When I was ...' *Daily Telegraph*, 1 June 1918

142 'at least one hundred ...' Kettle, pp. 144-5

142 'what took place ...' ibid., pp. 145-8

144 'whose attitude ...' *Daily Telegraph*, 1 June 1918

144 'there is an echo ...' Kettle, pp. 148

144 'Of course he has ...' *Daily Telegraph*, 1 June 1918

144 'Have you any ...' Kettle, pp. 149-64

149 'which could have ...' ibid., p. 166

150 'We agreed ...' Cynthia Asquith, *Diaries*, p. 447

150 'any members of ...' Kettle, p. 167

150 'When I ask ...' *The People*, 21 November 1948

150 'in view of ...' Kettle, p. 168

151 'a definite and ...' ibid., p. 169

151 'the anxiety of people ...' ibid.

151 'an unfortunate ...' Croft-Cooke, *Bosie*, p. 286

152 'I have a very particular ...' Kettle, pp. 172-80

155 'indiscreet' Ellman, *Wilde*, p. 428

155 'Why do they ...' Kettle, pp. 180-7

159 'If you take Herod ...' ibid., pp. 187-95

162 'We argued about ...' Hynes, *War Imagined*, pp. 174-5

162 'this foul "Billing ..." ' Rupert Hart-Davis (ed.), *Siegfried Sassoon's Diaries 1915-18*, Faber & Faber, London 1983, pp. 259-60

162 'Of course we ...' Cynthia Asquith, *Diaries*, p. 445

162 'in the knowledge ...' Kettle, pp. 196-7

162 'that we must ...' ibid., p. 197

163 'Everybody is ...' ibid., p. 198

163 'I have received ...' ibid., p. 197

163 'all classes ...' ibid., pp. 201-9

166 'generally crowded ...' Robert Graves, *Goodbye To All That*, Cassell, London 1957, p. 207

166 'quite by ...' Kettle, pp. 209-22

169 'I expect there are ...' ibid., p. 224

170 '... it fitted in ...' ibid., pp. 227-33

173 'Of course the ...' Cynthia Asquith, *Diaries*, p. 445

174 'Dear Mr Benson ...' Brian Masters, *E.F. Benson*, Chatto & Windus, London 1991, p. 104

174 'Sir Charles ...' Cynthia Asquith, *Diaries*, p. 445

174 'The only time ...' Belloc Lowndes, *Passing World*, p. 223

174 'fairly rational ...' Cynthia Asquith, *Diaries*, pp. 446-7

175 'My Lord, I wish ...' Kettle, pp. 236-47

177 'Perhaps it is not ...' ibid., pp. 250-9

179 'a play written with ...' ibid., pp. 261-6

181 'There has never been ...' *Daily Mail*, 5 June 1918

181 'My Lord – ...' Kettle, p. 268

181 'Mr Billing ...' *Daily Mail*, 5 June 1918

182 'It is splendid ...' Kettle, p. 268

182 'Miss Maud Allan ...' *Daily Mail*, 5 June 1918

182 'One might treat ...' Kettle, p. 269

182 'the most severe ...' ibid.

182 'The old English instinct ...' *Morning Post*, 6 June 1918, quoted Kettle, pp. 276-7

183 'He lost control ...' *Daily Mail*, 5 June 1918

183 'There was no attempt ...' Kettle, pp. 270-1

183 'No one outside ...' ibid., p. 278

183 'men and women ...' ibid., p. 278

183 'the follies ...' ibid., p. 274

183 'people of every ...' *Daily Mail*, 5 June 1918

184 'Who prevents ...' Kettle, p. 274

184 'fitness of the ...' ibid., p. 273

184 'so reputable ...' *Daily Mail*, 15 June 1918

184 'well-informed source ...' *The Times*, 1 July 1918

184 & *n* 'that the monster ...' Cynthia Asquith, *Diaries*, pp. 447-8

185 'dictator' Occleshaw, *Armoured*, p. 255

185 'I mark it down ...' Hart-Davis, *Hugh Walpole*, p. 171
185 'was doing more ...' Kettle, pp. 235-6
186 'immediate representations' ibid., p. 235
186 'easy and affectionate ...' Kenneth Young, *Harry, Lord Rosebery*, Hodder & Stoughton, London 1974, pp. 72-3
186 'charming, gifted' Kettle, p. 235
186 'There can be ...' ibid., pp. 282-3
186 'railed at across ...' Cynthia Asquith, *Diaries*, p. 438
186 'she and Aubrey ...' ibid., p. 473
186 'Nothing can be ...' Hynes, *War Imagined*, p. 231
186 'I foresaw ...' Borland, *Wilde's Devoted Friend*, p. 281
186 'the jury might ...' ibid., p. 280
186 'used as a piece ...' ibid., p. 282
187 'There can be ...' ibid., pp. 282-3
187 'I write to congratulate ...' ibid., p. 283
187 *n* 'ardently defended ...' Hart-Davis, *Hugh Walpole*, p. 301
188 'We always knew it ...' Cynthia Asquith, *Diaries*, p. 445
188 'there can be ...' Hynes, *War Imagined*, p. 231
188 'No one here ...' ibid., p. 231-2
188 'in the setting ...' Connon, *Nichols*, p. 61
189 'the advance-guard ...' Hynes, *War Imagined*, p. 234
189 'Disobedience ...' Oscar Wilde, *The Soul of Man Under Socialism*, Everyman, London 1930, p. 260
191 'for a cleaner Britain ...' Kettle, p. 281
191 'take powers ...' ibid., 283
192 'Mr Pemberton Billing ...' film fragment, British Film Institute
192 'If you are ...' Kettle, p. 285
193 'a list of all ...' ibid., p. 286-7
194 'I am now ...' *Verbatim Report*, pp. 479-80
194 'Is the right hon ...' *The Times*, 26 June 1918
195 'His wife is ...' Kettle, p. 292
195 'with the connivance ...' ibid.
195 'breached the regulations ...' *The Times*, 2 July 1918
195 'Is it necessary ...' Kettle, p. 294
195 'Sit down ...' Hansard, 1918, 1411 [107]
196 'On a point of ...' Kettle, p. 294
196 'Mr Pemberton Billing ...' *Daily Mail*, 2 July 1918
196 'I beg to move ...' Kettle, p. 295
196 'until such time ...' Hansard, 1918, 1412 [107]
196 'The Speaker left ...' *Daily Mail*, 2 July 1918
197 'On Monday ...' Kettle, p. 296
197 'a procedure ...' *Vigilante*, July 1918
197 'which grows more ...' *The Times*, 2 July 1918

197 'a map of Kent ...' *The Times*, 26 June 1918
198 'anti-Entente ...' Kettle, p. 297
198 'I, Harold Sherwood Spencer ...' *Vigilante*, 13 July 1918
198 'A Clean Sweep ...' *The Times*, 15 July 1918
199 'patriotic get-on-with ...' *The Times*, 15 July 1918
199 'all those concerned ...' Kettle, pp. 300-1
200 'Whether or not ...' *The Times*, 16 July 1918
200 'hired thugs ...' Kettle, p. 303
200 'Will Mrs Billing ...' *Daily Chronicle*, 18 July 1918
200 'expose ...' The *Vigilante*, 20 July 1918
201 'Traffic Managing Itself ...' *The Times*, 31 August 1918
201 'He was blown up ...' Kettle, p. 305
201 'When Mrs ...' *Verbatim Report*, p. 480
202 'a reaction against ...' Charles Carrington, *Soldiers From The War Returning*, Hutchinson, London 1965, p. 201
203 'I suppose I'd have ...' Hart-Davis (ed.), *Siegfried Sassoon's Diaries 1915-18*, p. 262
203 'The papers are ...' ibid., pp. 259-60
203 'an emotional experience ...' Hibberd, *Owen*, p. 125
203 'happily wounded ...' ibid., p. 173
203 'I saw his round ...' Jon Stallworthy (ed.) *The Poems of Wilfred Owen*, Chatto & Windus, London 1990, p. 100
204 Red lips ...' ibid., p. 143
204 '[Owen] may have ...' ibid., p. 144 *n*
204 'tired the sun ...' Stallworthy, *Owen*, p. 267
204 'a Harrow boy ...' Hibberd, *Owen*, p. 151
205 'the climax of ...' Leonard Woolf & James Strachey (ed.) *Letters: Virginia Woolf and Lytton Strachey*, Hogarth Press/Chatto & Windus, London 1956, p. 76
206 'deserting his armies ...' Repington, *First World War*, Vol. II, pp. 481-2
206 'the shifting general ...' Osbert Sitwell, *Laughter in the Next Room*, Macmillan, London 1950, p. 1
206 'We screamed ...' Coward, *Present Indicative*, pp. 116-17
206 'still in gala ...' Cole Lesley, *The Life of Noel Coward*, Jonathan Cape, London 1976, p. 52
206 'private and sole ...' Sitwell, *Laughter*, p. 11
207 'the new Jazz ...' Repington, *First World War*, Vol. II, p. 495
209 'How completely forgotten ...' Belloc Lowndes, *Passing World*, p. 224
210 'There is said to be ...' Ford Madox Ford, *Some As Not, Parade's End*, Penguin, London 1982, p. 206

210 'My dear, the people ...' Hoare, *Coward*, p. 362

210 'They're got ...' Tony Warren, *Independent Magazine*, 11 July 1992

210 'There would have ...' Kettle, p. 311

210 'Whitehall citadel ...' Ronald Blythe, *The Age of Illusion*, quoted Kohn, *Dope Girls*, p. 140

211 'Kill the Jews ...' Thurlow, *Fascism in Britain*, p. 62

211 'underground of rejected ...' Thurlow, 'The Return of Jeremiah', Lunn & Thurlow, *British Fascism*, p. 101

212 'secret societies ...' Thurlow, *Fascism in Britain*, pp. 58-9

212 'it is interesting ...' ibid., p. 60

212 'Sir Alfred Mond ...' Gisela C. Lebzelter, 'Henry Hamilton Beamish and the Britons', Lunn & Thurlow, *British Fascism*, p. 43

212 'the magnificent way ...' ibid., p. 44

212 'a peculiar side-effect ...' Thurlow, *British Fascism*, p. 70

213 'named the enemy ...' ibid., p. 74

214 'Government by ...' Preface, *A Fourth Edition of The Rossiad*, R. Dawson & Sons, Galashiels, 1921, p. 2

214 'Our Foreign ...' Kettle, p. 309

215 'disgusting behaviour' ibid.

215 'charged him ...' Croft-Cooke, *Bosie*, p. 308

215 'Many weeks ...' Belloc Lowndes, *Passing World*, p. 74

215 'You wrote ...' Kettle, p. 309

215 'Your Jutland ...' Croft-Cooke, *Bosie*, pp. 308-9

215 'It is to be regretted ...' Andrew Barrow, *Gossip: A History of High Society from 1920-1970*, Hamish Hamilton, London 1978, p. 18

216 'a considerable poet ...' Christabel Aberconway, *A Wiser Woman?: A Book of Memories*, Hutchinson, London 1966, p. 105

216 'something of a ...' Hart-Davis, *Hugh Walpole*, p. 412

216 'But hardly was ...' Hugo Vickers (ed.), *Cocktails & Laughter: The Albums of Loelia Lindsay*, Hamish Hamilton, London 1983, p. 95

217 'scandalous proceedings ...' Kettle, p. 312

217 'incapable of grappling ...' ibid., p. 280

217 'went far to ...' *DNB*, quoted Cherniavsky, p. 244

217 'delightful verses ...' Graham, *Lord Darling*, pp. 20-1

218 'the worst man ... Cherniavsky, p. 244

218 'An atmosphere of ....' ibid., p. 251

219 'the girl did not ...' *Daily Mail*, 17 June 1930

219 'MAUD ALLAN HAS ...' *Daily Mail*, 29 November 1938

219 Miss Allan ...' *Daily Express*, 29 July 1939

220 'When the ATS ...' *Sunday Chronicle*, 2 February 1941

220 'From whom ...' Cherniavsky, p. 283

220 'Maud, you have ...' ibid., p. 296

221 'At one moment ...' Belloc Lowndes, *Diaries & Letters*, pp. 113-14

221 'was instantly ...' Orme, *J.T.*, pp. 264-5

222 'Mr Billing ...' Lord Chamberlain's Papers, British Library, October, 1927

223 'a mixture of political ...' ibid., October, 1928

224 'Will there be ...' *High Treason*, British Film Institute

225 'A vote for me ...' *Daily Herald*, 18 July 1942

225 'We Need Bombs ...' *Sunday Dispatch*, 5 January 1941

226 'very poor and ...' Noel Pemberton Billing, *Will*, 26 September 1946, Somerset House

226 'do justice ...' *Sunday Dispatch*, 14 November 1948

227 'dark flowers' Sitwell, *Laughter*, p. 17

227 'satirically post-war ...' Hynes, *War Imagined*, pp. 244-5

229 'decorated on ...' Kohn, *Dope Girls*, p. 129

229 'So long ...' Robert Graves & Alan Hodge, *The Long Weekend*, Cardinal, London 1991, pp. 101-2

229 'an advanced Chinese ...' Charles Castle, *Noel*, W.H. Allen, London 1972, p. 66

229 'a compromise ...' Graves & Hodge, *Long Weekend*, p. 43

229 'I am never ...' Hoare, *Coward*, p. 139

229 'a man who ...' John Lehmann, *The Whispering Gallery*, Longmans, London 1955, pp. 117-18

Index

Index

Beattie, Sir James, 214, 215
Beaverbrook, 1st Lord (William Maxwell
   Aitken) (1879-1964), 183; supports Billing,
   51; withdraws support, 57; Billing attacks,
   59; disowns Grein, 94, 99, 145, 171; behind
   Billing affair, 120; moves against Ross, 187
Beerbohm, Sir (Henry) Max(imilian)
   (1872-1956), 8, 59, 113
Belcher, Lionel, 38
Bell, Clive, 191
Bellew, Kyrlie, 39
Belloc, Hilaire, 21, 53, 99-100
Belloc Lowndes, Marie Adelaide (1868-1947),
   on Ross-Douglas feud, 20-1; on Asquiths,
   99-100, 103, 174; on Primrose, 106 n; on
   Ross's funeral, 205; on the Black Book,
   209-19
Belsher (Parliamentary candidate), 199-200
Bendall, Ernest A., 63
Bennett, (Enoch) Arnold (1867-1931), 15,
   102, 187 & n
Benson, Edward Frederic (1867-1940), 78 n,
   80 n, 81, 174; *The Inheritors*, 80 n; *Dodo*,
   81, 174
Bentinck, Count William, 103, 165
Beresford, Lord, 53, 114
Berliner Tageblatt, 71
Berners, Lord, 7
Bernhardt, Sarah, 65, 73, 153
Best, Sigismund Payne, 131
Bibesco, Prince Antoine, 184 n
Bibesco, Princess Elizabeth (née Asquith)
   (1897-1945), 100, 103, 206
Billing, Annie Amelia Claridge, 44
Billing, Charles Eardley, 44
Billing, Elsie Veronica, 226
Billing, Lilian Maud (née Schweitzer), 45,
   181, 192, 194-5, 198, 226
Billing, Noel Pemberton (1881-1948), 3, 4, 6,
   15, 60, 63, 72, 83, 84, 88, 97, 99, 101, 102,
   110, 112, 183, 187, 189, 203, 205, 206,
   209, 214, 215, 216, 217, 218, 221, 222,
   228, 230-1; character, 1, 43, 192; early life
   & career, 43-9; political career, 1, 43, 46,
   48-51, 52-5, 57, 61, 83, 91-3, 104, 111,
   185, 191, 198-202, 210-11, 213, 225;
   writes '47,000' article, 1, 57-9; publishes
   'Cult of the Clitoris' article, 90-1; sued for
   libel, 93-6, 98, 109, 113-80; political
   conspiracy, 98, 103-4, 105-6, 107-8 et seq,
   192-5; wins case, 180-3, 186, 188, 189;
   ejected from Commons, 196-7; later life,
   223-6; death & obituaries, 226. Works:
   'P.B.' The Story of His Life, 44-9; *British
   South Africa Auto-car*, 44; *Memory* (play),
   45; *Hampstead Social Review* (magazine) 45;
   An Empire in Embryo (book), 46; *High
   Treason* (play), 221, 223-4; *High Treason*
   (film) 224-5. See also *Imperialist*; Vigilante
   Society
Billing, Robin, 226

Billing, Ursula, 226
Birkett, Mr Justice, 225
Birmingham, Bishop of (Russell Wakefield), 22
   & n
The Black Book, 1, 26, 35, 55, 57-9, 82, 104,
   107-9, 120, 122, 124, 128, 130, 133, 139,
   141-2, 163-9, 175-6, 183, 186, 210-11
Blackshirts, 228
Blast, 8, 160
Blavatsky, Madame, 84
Bloch, Gabrielle, 75-6
Bloch, Iwan, 56, 57, 116, 132
Blunt, Wilfred Scawen, 12 & n
Bock, Artur, 69, 70, 85
Bonham Carter, Violet, Baroness Asquith of
   Yarnbury, 184 & n
Borland, Maureen, 186
Bottomley, Horatio William (1860-1933), 43,
   44, 54, 92, 104, 217
Bow Street Magistrates Court, 95, 96, 98,
   117, 144
Bray, Percival Douglas, 106, 163, 168, 201
Bright Young People, 228, 229
British Library, 18
British Museum, 110
British Secret Service, 100, 103, 131, 166,
   184, 195
British Socialist Party, 195
British Union of Fascists, 191, 213, 230
Britons Society, 211-12
Broken Blossoms (film), 39
Brophy, Brigid, 79
Brooke, Rupert, 9, 33
Buchan, John, 27, 60; *Greenmantle*, 27
Buckmaster, Lord, 222
Burgess, Guy, 43
Burry, Bessie Pullen, 212
Burton, Nellie, 205
Burton, Peter, 80 n
Busoni, Ferruccio, 69-70, 218
Butler, Owen, 202
Butler, Sir William, 202

Café Dorian Gray, 30
Café Royal, 5, 10, 17, 26, 37, 111, 188
Caine, Sir Thomas Henry Hall, 67 n
Cambridge Festival Theatre, 223 n
Cambridge Magazine, 191
Campbell, Mrs Patrick, 45
Capote, Truman, 127 n
Carleton, Billie (Florence Leonora Stewart) (d.
   1918), 37-9, 206, 209
Carlton Club, 188
Carlton Hotel, Johannesburg, 87
Carnarvon, Lord, 124, 137, 178
Carpenter, Edward, 80
Carrington, Charles, 202-3
Carroll, Lewis, 177, 178; *Alice in Wonderland*,
   177, 178
Carson, Sir Edward, 155
Casati, Marchesa, 7

Index